The Theology of the Christian Life in J.I. Packer's Thought

Theological Anthropology, Theological Method, and the Doctrine of Sanctification

T0385272

A full listing of titles in this series appears at the end of this book.

STUDIES IN EVANGELICAL HISTORY AND THOUGHT

The Theology of the Christian Life in J.I. Packer's Thought

Theological Anthropology, Theological Method, and the Doctrine of Sanctification

Don J. Payne

Foreword by Thomas A. Noble

PATERNOSTER

First published 2006 by Paternoster
Paternoster is an imprint of Authentic Media
9 Holdom Avenue, Bletchley, Milton Keynes, MK1 1QR, UK
and
PO Box 1047, Waynesboro, GA 30830–2047, USA

12 11 10 09 08 07 06   7 6 5 4 3 2 1

British Library Cataloguing in Publication Data
A catalogue record for this book is available from the British Library.

ISBN 1–84227–397–3

Typeset by Author
Published by Paternoster
Printed and bound in Great Britain

Series Preface

The Evangelical movement has been marked by its union of four emphases: on the Bible, on the cross of Christ, on conversion as the entry to the Christian life and on the responsibility of the believer to be active. The present series is designed to publish scholarly studies of any aspect of this movement in Britain or overseas. Its volumes include social analysis as well as exploration of Evangelical ideas. The books in the series consider aspects of the movement shaped by the Evangelical Revival of the eighteenth century, when the impetus to mission began to turn the popular Protestantism of the British Isles and North America into a global phenomenon. The series aims to reap some of the rich harvest of academic research about those who, over the centuries, have believed that they had a gospel to tell to the nations.

Series Editors

David Bebbington, Professor of History, University of Stirling, Stirling, Scotland, UK

John H.Y. Briggs, Senior Research Fellow in Ecclesiastical History and Director of the Centre for Baptist History and Heritage, Regent's Park College, Oxford, UK

Timothy Larsen, Associate Professor of Theology, Wheaton College, Illinois, USA

Mark A. Noll, McManis Professor of Christian Thought, Wheaton College, Wheaton, Illinois, USA

Ian M. Randall, Deputy Principal and Lecturer in Church History and Spirituality, Spurgeon's College, London, UK, and a Senior Research Fellow, International Baptist Theological Seminary, Prague, Czech Republic

To my wife Sharon, with love and gratitude

Contents

FOREWORD

James Packer had a significant influence on my early theological thinking. While I was still a student of Modern History, involved in the Glasgow University Christian Union, and before ever graduating to the study of divinity as a second degree, I read *'Fundamentalism' and the Word of God*. I had been brought up in the Wesleyan–Arminian tradition, and I knew that James Packer belonged to that dreaded breed called Calvinists. But in that book, Dr Packer alleged that Evangelical Arminians and Calvinists shared a common position that the Bible was the final authority for Christian doctrine, so that the division between them was not as deep as that between all Evangelicals on the one hand and 'liberals' or 'catholics' on the other. For theological liberals, the reason or experience of the individual was the final authority: for catholics of all kinds (Roman, Anglo, and the Orthodox), tradition was accorded an equal authority to Scripture thus becoming *de facto* the final authority. But for Evangelicals, both Calvinist and Arminian, the final authority was the Bible.

My later discovery of what Albert Outler called the 'Wesleyan Quadrilateral' did not change the conviction that Dr Packer was fundamentally correct in his analysis. The idea of the Quadrilateral (properly understood!) allowed me to see that there is a positive role for tradition, reason and experience in the *interpretation* of Holy Scripture. But essentially Wesley was in accord with Calvin, and all true Evangelicals are in accord with the Reformers as a whole, in the adhering to the *sola scriptura*.

Of course, there is more than one way of understanding the theological epistemology which that implies. And there is more than one hermeneutic for moving from Scripture to doctrine. Indeed, the final authority of Scripture over doctrine relativizes all systematic theologies. That is why there is more than one theological system which may call itself 'Evangelical', and that in turn is why Evangelicals may disagree on many secondary matters (such as predestination!), and that in turn is why they may learn from each other!

I am therefore very happy to recommend this thorough study by Dr Payne of theological anthropology, theological method, and the doctrine of sanctification in the thought of James Packer. It is sympathetic to Dr Packer's theology, as all true Evangelicals should be. For James Packer, like the Puritans he so much admires and takes for his models, unites a concern with theology and a concern for true Christian piety. 'Spirituality' may be the more fashionable term today, and that may have somewhat different nuances and connotation (even a somewhat different meaning), but whatever terminology we use, all true Christian theology must unite theology and *godliness*. Truly Christian theology can never be an abstract intellectual pursuit. It is never enough to know *about* God. True Christian theology is (in the title of what to me is one of Dr Packer's best books) *Knowing God.*

Since however our attempts at systematic theology are relativized by the authority of the Bible, and since even we who accept the Bible's authority learn from each other through our *disagreements*, it is essential for our deeper understanding that a study like this be not only sympathetic, but also critical. This study is precisely that. It not only provides an exposition of this aspect of James Packer's thought based on the most thorough and careful reading. It also pays Dr Packer the compliment of entering into discussion with his thought through critical evaluation. But it does so with the greatest respect for its subject and indeed with gratitude to him for all he has contributed through his writings to Evangelical theology and godliness.

The reader therefore cannot but benefit theologically and personally by joining Dr Payne in engaging with the thought of one of the most influential Christian writers of our day who has done so much to shape today's flourishing Evangelical Christianity.

Thomas A. Noble,
Nazarene Theological College, Didsbury, Manchester
and Nazarene Theological Seminary, Kansas City

ACKNOWLEDGEMENTS

Any significant undertaking seems to depend upon the efforts and support of individuals whose influence is, unfortunately, disproportionate to the meagre recognition that they receive. Though words can never fully capture the scope or character of their contribution, I wish to express my deepest gratitude to the following individuals for their imprint on my life and this work.

Prof J.I. Packer was most gracious and helpful through a personal interview as well as written correspondence. Dr Gerald L. Nelson, Senior Pastor of Southern Gables Evangelical Free Church, first prompted me to engage PhD studies. His belief in me and his personal modelling of a scholarly pastoral ministry have inspired me for many years. Dr Randy MacFarland, Vice President/Dean of Denver Seminary, has provided consistent support for this work by allowing me the necessary time and flexibility in my role to research and write. Heather Clark and Randy Kemp of the Denver Seminary library staff provided valuable research assistance. The computer expertise of David Lute and Chris Sandifer saved me immense amounts of time in formatting the text. I offer a particular note of gratitude to Dr T.A. Noble and Dr Murray A. Rae for their research supervision. Not only have I benefited from their insight and guidance, but also from their examples of what it means to be both a scholar and a Christian. Additionally, I extend my appreciation to the faculty and staff of the Nazarene Theological College, Manchester. They have provided continual encouragement and delightful friendship.

I consider it evidence of divine grace to enjoy the close and enduring friendship of exceptional individuals. The list is too long to mention, but the Loomis, Melton, Morgan, Rupp, Swanson, and Wilson families are among those who have been my greatest allies. May their 'children rise up and call them blessed,' for such they are to me.

Since childhood my parents, Danny and Frances Payne, have modelled a thoughtful, serious, yet good–humoured Christian faith. For longer than anyone else, they have provided an environment of intellectual hunger and a priority on education without which this work would have been neither engaged nor completed. My children, Dani, Jim, and Rob, delight my heart more than they will know until they have their own children. I regret that in my preoccupation with this project I have sometimes failed to adequately convey that delight to them. Yet, they have each encouraged their dad in unique and valuable ways.

Finally, I wish to express my greatest thanks to my wife Sharon. Her patient endurance of my work has only been exceeded by her enthusiastic support along the way. After almost twenty–five years of marriage, her virtues never cease to astonish me. No person could dream of a more faithful companion or a more enjoyable friend. It is to her most of all that I lovingly and gratefully dedicate this work. She is the greatest person I have ever known.

Soli Deo Gloria

PREFACE

For at least five decades J.I. Packer has sought to be a theologian who serves the Church; and not merely the Church in its broader, ecclesiastical, and institutional needs, but the spiritual needs of the Christians who populate the churches. Some have suggested that he should have produced more of the type of theology that makes its way into the footnotes of other theologians or that deals more exhaustively with the full range of classical theological concerns. A careful reading of his writings and even an extended conversation with him are sufficient to convince one that driving his more widely–known writings are unusual intellectual abilities and theological acumen. For many years he has felt a calling to write, teach, and speak about issues with pressing implications for the integrity and vitality of the Church. In whatever measure one agrees or disagrees with his perspectives, there is little argument about his passion for offering substantial theological rigour as a resource for the Body of Christ.

All theologians, it seems, have their favourite and recurring themes or chords. The nature of the Christian life, particularly the doctrine of sanctification, is one of those signature themes in J.I. Packer's repertoire. His thought on this subject has been forged on the battleground of evangelicalism as it has struggled to define a genuine and living Christian experience of salvation.

This book, as a revision of my PhD thesis, seeks to get inside Professor Packer's considerable thought on this subject by examining two key aspects of the theological substructure involved. I hope that the process will clarify why he believes and teaches what he does about the doctrine of sanctification and several directly related soteriological issues. Furthermore, I wish to show how assumptions about the Christian life are directly and profoundly shaped by other areas of theology. Perhaps that second goal needs little defence among theologians but several years of pastoral experience were adequate to convince me that this is not generally taken for granted in the evangelical Church. Third, and most specifically, I propose to demonstrate how the areas known as 'theological anthropology' and 'theological method' have shaped Professor Packer's thought on the doctrine of sanctification and, by implication, how influential those subjects are for the way in which all Christians approach their faith.

Special consideration is given to Packer's understanding of the *imago Dei* and how that concept figures into the notion of sanctification as the image of God restored in holiness. His theological method will be seen as not merely an additional and isolated factor, but intrinsic to both his anthropology and his understanding of sanctification. The three exist in dynamic, triadic (even if not always ostensible) relationship.

The breadth and depth of J.I. Packer's imprint on the English–speaking twentieth–century (and lingering into the twenty–first century) evangelical Church warrants an extended and patient examination of his thought. Such an exercise affords the Church the opportunity to cultivate an informed humility as convictions continue to be forged and debated on existentially loaded theological issues such as sanctification. Hopefully, this endeavour will suggest some lines of inquiry and resources that will encourage Christian piety in its vibrancy, realism, and capacity for encompassing all dimensions of human life. May it also be that Christian traditions long divided by their approaches to sanctification will recognise the value of examining the theological underpinnings that sustain their convictions.

ABBREVIATIONS

CT	*Christianity Today*
EDT	*Evangelical Dictionary of Theology*
EvQ	*Evangelical Quarterly*
Institutes	*Institutes of the Christian Religion*
NBD	*New Bible Dictionary*
NDCEPT	*New Dictionary of Christian Ethics and Pastoral Theology*
NICNT	*New International Commentary on the New Testament*
NDT	*New Dictionary of Theology*
Shorter Writings	*The Collected Shorter Writings of J.I. Packer*
SJT	*Scottish Journal of Theology*

Chapter 1

Introduction

Plato's claim that 'the unexamined life is not worth living'[1] appears to have been a compelling motivation for scrutinising the evangelical Christian experience. This particular historical, theological, and cultural expression of Christianity has been studied from a variety of perspectives. There is yet much to be understood.

Understanding of a complex religious phenomenon can be pursued from multiple directions. Certainly, the nature of religious experience demands investigation into the theological assumptions that sustain a movement and the theological forces that propel it. It is also true, however, that a complex phenomenon will defy reductionism. The theological dimension alone is likely to be multi–faceted, marked by paradox and nuance.

However partial, insight may and must continue to be sought if mistakes are to be corrected and improvements made for the sake of future adherents. Insight into the theological character of a movement may be pursued fruitfully by examining the theology of those who have made a discernable contribution to the movement. This study aims at enhancing the understanding of twentieth–century, evangelical Christian piety by exploring the thought of a theologian who has found a place within and made a noteworthy contribution to its ethos – J.I. Packer.

A comprehensive analysis of Packer's thought is beyond the scope of one book. This study will examine aspects of his thought that have made a significant contribution to evangelical piety. Obviously, this involves a description and analysis of Packer's theology of sanctification. The logic and ethos of his theology of sanctification will be explored by examining the theological anthropology and theological method that support it. This relationship between sanctification, anthropology, and methodology will be viewed against the backdrop of twentieth–century evangelicalism, primarily in the U.K. and U.S., in order to gain understanding into Packer's influence.

---

[1] Plato, *The Dialogues of Plato: The Apology*, in M.J. Adler (ed.), B. Jowett (tr.), The Great Books of the Western World series, vol. 6 (Chicago: Encyclopaedia Britannica, 1993), 210.

Though he is British in origin and education, Packer's greatest influence has been in the context of North American evangelicalism. His particular brand of Reformed theology[2] has found common ground with theological values that have been significant in shaping the ethos of twentieth–century evangelicalism in the United States. Likewise, his writings, both theological and popular, have had and continue to exhibit intense concern with Christian piety, especially as it is sustained by the doctrine of sanctification.

It will be argued that Packer's understanding of sanctification is sustained by a predominately individualistic and rationalistic theological anthropology and method. Significant qualifying factors are found in his anthropology and piety, reflecting an attempt on his part to ameliorate the risks of individualistic and rationalistic extremes. Thus, the inherent rationalism and individualism tend to be obscured from view. However, the influence of these tendencies can be seen in the practical expectations and disciplines he enjoins for Christians.

This chapter establishes a general backdrop, parameters, and rationale for the theological analysis just described. Chapter two offers definitions and genealogies of the British evangelicalism from which Packer emerged and the American evangelicalism in which he has exercised influence, pointing up salient factors that help account for that influence. Chapter three traces Packer's personal theological development in order to relate his views to the context of his overall life and theology. Chapters four through eight consider piety, theological anthropology (with specific attention to the *imago Dei* and the Incarnation), and theological method, respectively. This organisational schema intentionally moves from the phenomena of piety to the theology and then to methodology so as to best illuminate causal and systemic relationships. Chapter eight summarises the trialogue between Packer's piety, anthropology and method in order to identify patterns and implications, then suggest directions for further research.

---

[2] See G.M. Marsden, 'Introduction: Reformed and American', in M.A. Noll (ed.), *The Princeton Theology, 1812–1921: Scripture, Science, and Theological Method from Archibald Alexander to Benjamin Breckinridge Warfield* (Grand Rapids: Baker, 2001), 2–3. Marsden offers further clarification of what it means to be 'Reformed' in America by dividing American, Reformed theology into three categories of emphasis: first, that which places priority on a particular doctrinal structure, second, that which prioritises the relationship between Christianity and culture, and third, that which finds 'in Reformed theology the most biblical and healthiest expression of evangelical piety.' All three strains can be easily detected in Packer's thought, though the first and third may be the most prominent in his writings. In contrast he has not championed Reformed theology through allegiance to a particular denomination.

1.1 J.I. Packer and American Evangelicalism

Any comprehensive examination of twentieth–century, English–speaking evangelicalism must take into account the influence of J.I. Packer. The context and character of evangelicalism in the United States (to be discussed in chapter two) have provided a fertile opportunity for his Reformed theological perspectives to wield influence across a spectrum of denominations. Though Packer has no official relationship to any denomination that has been prominent in the ethos of American evangelicalism, he embodies many of the theological perspectives at the core of its culture. He has played a significant role in American evangelicalism by providing theological resources for the pietistic concerns that mark its past and present character.

The scope and nature of Packer's influence are partially reflected in commendations he has received from within both the United Kingdom and the United States. In a *Festschrift* to Packer, David F. Wright commends him as 'one of the most powerful theologians of the twentieth century.'[3] John R.W. Stott compares his own contribution to the same volume as 'a shrimp paying homage to a whale!'[4] Alister McGrath records, 'On 28 May 1978, Gordon–Conwell Theological Seminary awarded him an honorary Doctor of Divinity, in recognition of his major contribution to the Christian public in North America, especially through his writings.'[5] Roger Steer describes Packer as 'one of the most influential Anglican Evangelicals of the twentieth century,' noting that 'by 1997 Packer's books had sold almost three million copies worldwide.'[6]

Packer's most identifiable influence comes through his writings. His first publication was in 1952.[7] Since that time he has authored or edited nearly three hundred separate pieces. The subject matter of his writings is wide–ranging, including Anglican ecclesiastical concerns,[8] preparation for

---

[3] D.F. Wright, 'Recovering Baptism for a New Age of Mission', in D. Lewis and A. McGrath (eds.), *Doing Theology for the People of God: Studies in Honor of J.I. Packer* (Downers Grove: InterVarsity, 1996), 52.

[4] Ibid., 3.

[5] A. McGrath, *To Know and Serve God: A Biography of James I. Packer* (London: Hodder and Stoughton, 1997), 217.

[6] R. Steer, *Guarding the Holy Fire: The Evangelicalism of John R. W. Stott, J.I. Packer, and Alister McGrath* (Grand Rapids: Baker, 1999), 216

[7] See J.I. Packer, 'The Puritan Treatment of Justification by Faith', *EvQ* 24, no. 3 (1952), 131–143.

[8] See J.I. Packer, *A Kind of Noah's Ark: the Anglican Commitment to Comprehensiveness*, Latimer Studies, no. 10 (Oxford: Latimer House, 1981), 10–11.

ministry,[9] women in ministry,[10] and numerous biographical sketches.[11] However, topics related to soteriology, revelation, and piety surface repeatedly and under a variety of headings.[12]

Response to Packer's work has not, of course, been uniformly complimentary. A considerable number of his writings are aimed at readers outside the scholarly arena. Gerald Bray expresses frustration that Packer never produced a more comprehensive and definitive systematic theology for evangelicalism.[13] Nor have his theological perspectives been consistently embraced, even by others who consider themselves to be evangelical.[14]

In 1979 Packer departed England to teach at Regent College in Vancouver, British Columbia. From this North American venue his popularity and influence rose to new heights. Wendy Murray Zoba observes, 'Regent placed Packer in a position to assert a voice in just about every theological discussion that has emerged in contemporary North American evangelicalism – from the role of women, to the function of the Holy Spirit, to the destiny of those who die without Christ.'[15] In addition to his writings, his thought has made an imprint through regular lecturing and preaching.

As far back as 1958 Packer's publication of *'Fundamentalism' and the Word of God*, won credibility for him with American proponents of biblical inerrancy. Mark Noll states his belief that in this book 'Evangelicals had not possessed as clear or as balanced a theology of Scripture since the passing of Warfield.'[16] In the wake of the intense controversy over the

---

[9] J.I. Packer, 'Training for the Ministry', in C. Porthouse (ed.), *Ministry in the Seventies* (London: Falcon, 1970), 156–167.

[10] J.I. Packer, 'Representative Priesthood and the Ordination of Women', in G.E. Duffield and M. Bruce (eds.), *Why Not?* (Abingdon: Marcham, 1972), 1972.

[11] J.I. Packer, 'George Whitefield: Man Alive', *Crux* 16 (December 1980), 23–26. See also *A Grief Sanctified: Passing through Grief to Peace and Joy* (Ann Arbor: Servant, 1997).

[12] For example, Packer frequently addresses each of these topics in writings on the English Puritans.

[13] G. Bray, review of *To Know and Serve God: A Biography of J.I. Packer*, by A. McGrath, *Churchman* 112, no. 4 (1997), 362–363.

[14] See S. Neill, review of *Knowing God*, by J.I. Packer, *Churchman* 88, no. 1 (1974), 77–78. Though Neill expresses 'massive agreement' with Packer's book, he charges Packer with being 'slightly scholastic' and 'not sufficiently Christo–centric' in his approach.

[15] W.M. Zoba, 'Knowing Packer', *CT*, (6 April 1998), 39.

[16] M.A. Noll, 'J.I. Packer and the Shaping of American Evangelicalism', in *Doing Theology for the People of God,* 119.

authority of scripture, Packer found an eager hearing across the Atlantic.[17] Christopher Catherwood comments that *'Fundamentalism' and the Word of God* was 'the book that established his reputation, and which, as his old oxford contemporary Raymond Johnston once told me, has been the key to his standing in evangelical circles.'[18] This publication may be viewed as a significant starting point for Packer's influence within North American evangelicalism.

The 1973 publication of *Knowing God* has been by far his best seller. According to McGrath, 'It was in North America that *Knowing God* would have its greatest impact. Although Packer was a known writer in the region, the book would propel him to levels of fame within the evangelical community that exceeded anything he had hitherto known.'[19] One indicator of the scope of Packer's impact in the United States is that eighteen of his titles had sold over one and three–quarters of a million copies in the United States by mid–1995.[20]

Statistics and accolades do not fully account for Packer's popularity and influence in the United States. A more complete explanation will be offered in chapters two and three, as Packer's own version of evangelicalism is placed in the context of the American evangelicalism in which he has found such a hearing.

1.2 The Writings of J.I. Packer

Piety, anthropology, and method are frequent themes in Packer's writings. This study relies heavily on the following works in which those subjects are most fully developed.

'Fundamentalism' and the Word of God constitutes his first notable treatment of the doctrine of Scripture. He defends Scriptural authority by resting it on the notion of infallibility. Through the years he has developed this assertion and its implications for theology in general and Christian

---

[17] C. Catherwood, *Five Evangelical Leaders* (Wheaton, Harold Shaw, 1985), 186.

[18] Ibid., 173.

[19] McGrath, *To Know and Serve God*, 190.

[20] Noll, 'J.I. Packer and the Shaping of American Evangelicalism', 195. Noll obtained these figures from five of Packer's American publishers: Crossway, Eerdmans, Harold Shaw, InterVarsity, and Tyndale House. He states, '*Knowing God* from IVP accounts for over half that total; over 200,000 copies of *Evangelism and the Sovereignty of God* (IVP) have been distributed since that book was first released in 1961; two IVP pamphlets, *Meeting God* and *Finding God's Will*, had both topped the 100,000 figure; and *'Fundamentalism' and the Word of God* (Eerdmans) along with *I Want to Be a Christian* (Tyndale) had gone over the 50,000 mark.'

piety in particular through numerous journal articles and in books such as *Beyond the Battle for the Bible* and *Truth and Power*.

Knowing God offers a Reformed perspective on the nature of God from the epistemological starting point of Scripture as interpreted by the Holy Spirit. Packer seeks therein to articulate the implications of the knowledge of God for Christian piety.

Packer's earliest, comprehensive exposition of his theology of piety is *Keep in Step with the Spirit* where he employs Reformed perspectives on pneumatology and progressive sanctification to combat Keswick and other forms of piety that he views as passive or perfectionistic. In *Among God's Giants* he surveys the theology and piety of the seventeenth–century English Puritans, offering their thought as models to be emulated. He presents another comprehensive theology and model of piety in *A Passion for Holiness*. *Growing in Christ* distils his theology of piety into a series of practical essays on the Christian life by developing themes found in the Apostle's Creed, the Lord's Prayer, and the Ten Commandments, with an additional section on baptism and conversion.

Theological anthropology is developed primarily in journal articles and indirectly in the context of writings on piety. It receives direct book length treatment in *Christianity: The True Humanism* which he co–authored with Thomas Howard and *For Man's Sake*. In *Concise Theology* he provides a brief exposition of all the major themes in evangelical Protestant theology. *Knowing Christianity* provides a more general survey of the main topics in Western theology with specific application to the Christian life.

Ninety–one of his journal articles have been collected in a four–volume set entitled *The Collected Shorter Writings of J.I. Packer* focusing, respectively, on soteriology (volume 1); ecclesiology, mission, and the Christian life (volume 2); Scripture (volume 3); and influential Christians (volume 4). Alister McGrath penned a biography of Packer, *To Know and Serve God*, then assembled and introduced sixteen of his journal articles that deal with specifically theological concerns in *The J.I. Packer Collection*.

A total of three doctoral theses have been written on Packer, addressing his epistemology,[21] his understanding of the Holy Spirit's role in biblical interpretation,[22] and his general pneumatology against the backdrop of pneumatology in British Protestant theology and the World Council of

---

[21] K.N. Jones, *Revelation and Reason in the Theology of Carl F.H. Henry, James I.Packer, and Ronald H. Nash* (Ann Arbor: University Microfilms International, 1994).

[22] S. Koranteng–Pipim, 'The Role of the Holy Spirit in Biblical Interpretation: A Study in the Writings of James I. Packer.' PhD thesis (Seventh–day Adventist Theological Seminary/Andrews University, 1998).

Churches.[23] Aspects of this research relate to the present thesis topic, but no thesis deals directly with the particular relationship between sanctification, theological anthropology, and theological method in his thought.

Packer's corpus contains works that have been published in both the U.K. and the U.S., some published only in the U.K., and some only in the U.S. Wherever possible, the U.K. editions of his works are cited. It should be noted that some of the U.K. editions (e.g. *A Passion for Holiness*) utilise U.S. spellings.

1.3 Definitions

1.3.1 Theological Anthropology

'Theological anthropology' will refer to the Christian understanding of humanity's basic nature in light of the biblical literature that alludes to its ontological, structural and teleological dimensions. The biblical portrait of human nature will be framed primarily within the related themes of the *imago Dei* and the Incarnation of the Son of God. Philip E. Hughes recognizes the significance of these themes in claiming that 'the doctrine of the Image of God is the key to the factuality of the incarnation no less than to the understanding of the true nature of man.'[24] Within this framework other related themes will be treated, such as the nature of sin and its effect on the *imago Dei*,[25] and the relationship of the doctrine of the Incarnation to the restoration of the *imago Dei* in salvation.

This study proceeds from the premise that the anthropological assumptions within a theological system make an imprint on the understanding and consequent practice of Christian piety. This causal relationship is observed in the Apostle Paul's depiction of salvation as the restoration of fallen humanity into the image of Christ.[26] In Romans 5:14ff

---

[23] B.G. Cho, 'A Critical Comparative Study of Pneumatology in U.K. (particularly England) Protestant Theology and the World Council of Churches Between 1965 and 1993.' PhD thesis (The University of Wales, Lampeter, 1995).

[24] P.E. Hughes, *The True Image: The Origin and Destiny of Man in Christ* (Grand Rapids: Eerdmans, 1989), 214.

[25] There has been intense debate over whether the *imago Dei* is altogether lost or merely damaged due to sin, and whether it was ever humanity's to lose or was always located only in Christ. See, for example, E. Brunner's 'Nature and Grace' and K. Barth's 'No!' in *Natural Theology*, P. Fraenkel (tr.), (London: G. Bles, Centenary, 1946).

[26] Rom. 8:29 and 2 Cor. 3:18 portray the goal of salvation as restoration into the likeness (*eikonos* and *eikona* respectively) of Jesus Christ. 2 Cor. 4:4 and Col. 1:15 speak of Jesus Christ as the image of God; an interesting parallel to Gen. 1:26–27,

Paul argues for a theological relationship between Adam and Jesus Christ in which the remedy for sin provided by Jesus is thereby relevant to all humanity. To Paul these relationships were of such a nature that both Adam's sin and Jesus' provision of justification from sin had relevance to all humanity because Jesus assumed Adam's role in relationship to humanity. In 1 Corinthians 15:49 he portrays the Christian's hope of future likeness to Christ by drawing a comparison to the likeness shared with Adam. Humanity, as defined by creation in the image of God, is restored through the redemptive work of Jesus Christ because he fully shared that humanity and was himself the perfect image of God.

Paul elaborates on this connection in Colossians 3:10 by placing a series of ethical imperatives in the context of the believer's standing in Jesus Christ, presenting them as the results of having put on the new humanity ('which is being renewed in knowledge in the image of its Creator.')[27] Therefore, to Paul, the themes of the image of God and the image of Christ appear to be connected through Christ's complete sharing of both humanity and God's image. The nature of restoration in the image of Christ, then, is related to humanity's original creation in the image of God. Anthony A. Hoekema clarifies this link by stating, 'What we see and hear in Christ is what God intended for man.'[28] Charles Sherlock expands on this point, claiming, 'It is striking ... that the term 'image' (*eikon*) is not used for humankind in the New Testament apart from reference to Christ.' Further, Sherlock argues that, 'in Christ, the perfect *eikon* of God, the divine image is being renewed through the Spirit, until humanity is re–created into Christ's full dignity, according to the purpose of the Creator.'[29] Here we begin to see the relationship between human nature (theological anthropology) and the nature of the Christian experience (piety).

The human experience of this restoration is portrayed in the New Testament as progressive in nature (Philippians 3:12–14, 2 Peter 1:3–9),

---

5:1, and 9:6. While the New Testament terms translated 'sanctify' (*hagiazo*) and 'holy' (*hagios*) are not used in direct connection with the texts regarding restoration into the likeness of Christ, this restorative process has been associated with the process of sanctification, e.g. R.E.O. White, 'Sanctification', in W.A. Elwell (ed.), *EDT* (Grand Rapids: Baker, 1984), 971. Col. 3:8–10 clearly uses the concept of the image of God as the point of reference for exhorting Christians to a type of moral purification similar to other New Testament portrayals of godliness or holiness, e.g. in 2 Pet. 1:3–9.

[27] The NIV, NRSV, and NASB insert the word 'self' in verse 10, though the original, Greek text simply refers to 'the new,' in contrast to 'the old humanity' (*ton palaion anthropon*) referenced in verse 9.

[28] A.A. Hoekema, *Created in God's Image* (Grand Rapids: Eerdmans, 1986), 22.

[29] C. Sherlock, *The Doctrine of Humanity* (Downers Grove: InterVarsity, 1996), 50.

related to holiness and sanctification (1 Corinthians 1:2), related to humanity's original purpose of reflecting God's character (Ephesians 4:24), oriented toward and preserved at the eschaton (1 Thessalonians 5:23), and dependent on the agency of the Holy Spirit (Romans 15:16, 1 Corinthians 6:11). These connections help establish the relationship of anthropology to piety. Piety is the practical expression and experience of the restoration of human nature as it is understood in the light of creation, the Incarnation and salvation. According to Hoekema, 'The image of God … must … be understood as that likeness to God which was perverted when man fell into sin, and is being restored in the process of sanctification.'[30] One central premise of this book is that the way in which humanity's basic nature is understood, in the light of the image of God and the Incarnation, has direct ramifications for the way in which both the process and product of sanctification are conceived and pursued through the practice of piety.

1.3.2 Theological Method

The phrase 'theological method' refers to the entire range of assumptions that control the way in which theological conclusions are reached. The term 'hermeneutics' may be technically synonymous with theological method. However, it is not uncommon in certain evangelical circles for hermeneutics to be defined primarily in terms of exegetical method, e.g. utilising principles of literal (not necessarily 'literalistic') interpretation, considering literary genre, referencing grammatical structure and historical context. It is likewise not unusual for some evangelical 'hermeneutics' to begin with the assumption that a high view of the biblical text and proper exegetical technique, consistently applied, are all that is needed in order to gain adequate understanding of the text.

Though important to the overall work of biblical interpretation for those with a high view of scriptural authority, these exegetical procedures do not take into account the interpretive influence of assumptions such as the nature of theology, the relationship of theology to textual study and other disciplines, and the organising principles of a theological system. Theological method is the way in which one 'does' theology in a broader sense, which inevitably shapes the content of one's theology.

1.3.3 Piety

The Christian life, for J.I. Packer, can adequately (though not exclusively) be denoted by the word 'piety.' *Piety* is but one term among several that are generally used to denote religious practise and experience. Terms such as *spirituality, holiness,* and *godliness* also appear frequently. Packer uses all

---

[30] Hoekema, 32.

four terms, though sometimes rather loosely and with overlapping connotations. The term *piety* is chosen as thematic in this study for two reasons. First, he tends to use it in a manner that encompasses what he means by *holiness* and *godliness*. He claims that, '*eusebeia*, usually translated "godliness" in EVV, appears ... as a comprehensive term for the practice of Christian personal religion, the worship and service of God and the rendering of reverent obedience to His laws. In the plural the word denotes specific acts of piety (2 Pet. iii.11).'[31] Second, he uses it with more precision and without the need for the qualifications that he sometimes attaches to the term *spirituality* in order to give it the same meaning as piety.

In broader usage the term *piety* is sometimes equated to *godliness* or *holiness* and is cross–referenced to articles on those topics in theological dictionaries. Piety can be defined as 'devotion and commitment to God expressed in the Christian life through a variety of actions.'[32] Some theological and ecclesiastical dictionaries do not offer definitions of piety at all, but do define *spirituality*.[33]

The term *spirituality* is occasionally cross–referenced to piety in theological dictionaries, but is often a broader term, denoting the practices of devotion within any religious faith, whether or not it claims an evangelical or Christian orientation.[34] *Spirituality* originally had more distinctively Christian connotations, evolving from the fifth century when *spiritualitas* was used for 'the quality of life which should result from the spiritual gifts imparted to all who believe in Christ,'[35] to the Middle Ages when it focused on the interior life, through the seventeenth century when it became the distinct branch of theology known as ascetical theology.[36] In Christian usage a slight difference of emphasis between *spirituality* and *piety* can be observed inasmuch as *piety* may refer to practices and experiences of spirituality that are anchored in the theological priorities of

---

[31] J.I. Packer, 'Piety', in J.D. Douglas (ed.), *NBD* (London: Inter–Varsity, 1961), 996.

[32] D.K. McKim, (ed.), *Westminster Dictionary of Theological Terms* (Louisville: Westminster/John Knox, 1996), 210.

[33] Among those sources that define 'spirituality' but do not list 'piety' are E.A. Livingstone (ed.), *The Oxford Dictionary of the Christian Church* (Oxford: Oxford University Press, 1997³) and S.B. Ferguson, D.F. Wright, and J.I. Packer (eds.), *NDT* (Downers Grove: InterVarsity, 1988).

[34] Livingstone, *The Oxford Dictionary of the Christian Church*, 1533. 'In modern times the term 'spirituality' is often extended to apply to believers in religions other than Christianity.'

[35] Ibid., 1532.

[36] Ibid., 1532–1533.

historic Christianity.[37] The *New Dictionary of Theology* states, 'The test of Christian spirituality is conformity of heart and life to the confession and character of Jesus as Lord (1 Cor. 12:3).'[38] In this manner the emphases of both words are integrated by using a Christian theological framework to evaluate *spirituality*.

As in their broader usage, Packer uses the words *piety* and *spirituality* in somewhat interchangeable ways. He uses the term *spirituality* in both general and specific manners. Generally, he takes it to include religious experience that may or may not be regulated by biblical criteria.[39] Specifically, he relates *spirituality* to *godliness* (holiness) by arguing that spirituality should be godliness that is brought under biblical controls. With this qualification he defines spirituality as 'the study of godliness in its root and in its fruit.'[40] This type of spirituality or piety, for Packer, should result in *godliness* or *holiness*. He also calls this 'authentic spirituality.'[41]

The terms *holiness* and *godliness*, then, constitute the essence of piety or biblical spirituality for Packer, apart from which there is no true communion with God. The following description offers several key descriptors that will be seen to comprise the ethos of piety in Packer's thought.

> The Bible views the piety that it inculcates from several complementary standpoints. The Old Testament calls it 'fear of God', or 'the Lord' ... thus showing that true piety is rooted in an attitude of reverence, submission, and obedience towards God. The New Testament calls it 'obeying the gospel' or 'the truth' ... thus characterizing piety as a response to revelation. From another standpoint, as the maintaining of a state of separation from the world and consecratedness to God, the New Testament calls it simply 'holiness' (*hagiasmos, hagiosyne*: see 1 Thes. iv. 3; Heb. xii. 14; 2 Cor. vii. 1; 1 Thes. iii. 13; *etc.*). A full analysis of New Testament piety would include the practical expression of faith in a life of repentance, resisting temptation, and mortifying sin; in habits of prayer, thanksgiving, and reverent observance of the Lord's Supper; in the cultivation of hope, love, generosity, joy, self–control, patient

---

[37] J.A. Komonchak, M. Collins, and D.A. Lane (eds.), *The NDT* (Wilmington, Del.: Michael Glazier, 1987), 982. 'Christian spirituality ... is trinitarian, christological, ecclesial religious experience.' It is in this specifically Christian sense that the term *piety* is used in this study.

[38] S.B. Ferguson, D.F. Wright, and J.I. Packer, eds., 'Spirituality', *NDT*, 657.

[39] J.I. Packer, 'An Introduction to Systematic Spirituality', *Crux* 26 (March 1990), 7.

[40] Ibid., 2.

[41] J.I. Packer, 'Evangelical Foundations for Spirituality', in *Shorter Writings* (Carlisle, Paternoster, 1998), 2.262.

endurance, and contentment; in the quest for honesty, uprightness, and the good of others in all human relations; in respect for divinely constituted authority in Church, State, family, and household.[42]

Piety is reverent obedience. This obedience depends upon revelation for its structure and direction. Consecration results in specific personal character traits, social ethical commitments,[43] and ecclesiological activities. Piety, for Packer, is never authentic or biblical apart from the criteria that emerge from God's character and self–revelation.

Holiness, as the essence of both God's character and Christian obedience,[44] offers a connection between piety and theological anthropology. Christians reflect God's holy character as they are restored into the image of God that is reflected in the character of Jesus Christ. This takes place through obedient response to God's revelation.

In its application to people, God's 'holy ones' or 'saints,' the work [of sanctifying or making holy] implies both devotion and assimilation: devotion, in the sense of living a life of service to God; assimilation, in the sense of imitating, conforming to, and becoming like the God one serves. For Christians, this means taking God's moral law as our rule and God's incarnate Son as our model; this is where our analysis of holiness must begin.[45]

Thus, he uses the terms *holiness* and *godliness* to denote the Godlikeness at the heart of piety. *Piety*, then shall be the term of reference for Packer's use of *godliness*, *holiness*, and Christian or biblical *spirituality*.

Summary

In the middle of the twentieth–century Emil Brunner recognised the importance of theological anthropology for human experience. He drew attention to the fact that throughout history various cultures have been

---

[42] Packer, 'Piety', 996.

[43] Packer, 'Evangelical Foundations for Spirituality', 255. For Packer, '*ethics* means determining what types of action and qualities of character please God.' Spirituality deals somewhat more broadly with the practices or means by which godliness and communion with God are cultivated.

[44] Packer, 'Obedience', in *NBD*, 904. 'Christian obedience means imitating God in holiness.' He also connects piety to godliness, though the word 'holiness' seems to be more descriptive for him of what godliness involves. See J.I. Packer, 'Godliness', in *NDCEPT*, 411.

[45] J.I. Packer, *A Passion for Holiness* (Nottingham: Crossway, 1992), 19.

shaped by their views of the nature of humanity.[46] James Houston, former president of Regent College in Vancouver, British Columbia, points out the poignant existential implications of theological anthropology for piety by expressing concern that theological traditions holding to historic, Western orthodoxy frequently devastate their own adherents by offering sterile, rationalistic answers to painful, existential questions. Houston suggests that in response to this crisis, 'anthropology must be taken far more seriously in theological thought today.'[47]

Only in more recent years has evangelical scholarship begun to realise that the interpretation of Scripture involves more than a high view of scriptural authority and exegetical technique appropriate to the literary genre. Theology is more than the mere collection and organisation of conclusions reached on the basis of appropriate exegesis. The theological methodology utilised, including the assumptions that direct the organisation of conclusions, has profound ramifications for the structure and conclusions of one's theology. Theology method is often the more silent or tacit set of factors that control one's conclusions.

This study will examine the relationship between theological anthropology, theological method, and the doctrine of sanctification in the thought of J.I. Packer, whose integration of theological and pastoral concerns has wielded considerable influence over the ethos of late twentieth–century evangelicalism. It is hoped that this exploration of the anthropological and methodological structure of piety in Packer's thought will lead to greater understanding of how theological anthropology and method can help account for the diversity of perspectives on the Christian life.

---

[46] E. Brunner, *Man in Revolt: A Christian Anthropology*, O. Wyon (tr.), (Philadelphia: Westminster, 1947).

[47] J. Houston, *Spiritual Direction in an Age of Confusion*, audio cassette (Vancouver: Regent College, n.d.).

Chapter 2

J.I. Packer's Theological Context

J.I. Packer's theology is decidedly evangelical in character. Throughout his career he has sought to preserve and advance the cause of evangelicalism. This descriptor is essential to understanding Packer. The term *evangelical* can function as both a noun and an adjective. It carries sociological, denominational, and even political connotations. Theologically, the definition of *evangelical* has differed from one time and place to another, making precise definition and description difficult. Karl Barth calls the word a 'happy generality, covering so much and yet so little!'[1] In the United States particularly and to a lesser extent in Britain, the term crosses denominational lines.[2] In light of various shifts in emphasis the historical development of *evangelical* or *evangelicalism* must be briefly reviewed in order to establish a definition as well as a meaningful context for the theological questions that drive this study.

For two reasons this review will consider the development and meaning of the term *evangelical* in both British and American settings. First, Packer is from Great Britain, yet has demonstrated considerable influence on the evangelicalism of the United States. Second, the mutual influence between British and American evangelicalism has set the stage for Packer to play the role he has played in American evangelicalism.

---

[1] K. Barth, *The Word of God and the Word of Man*, D. Horton (tr.), (London: Hodder and Stoughton, 1928), 225.

[2] R.V. Pierard, 'Evangelicalism', in *EDT*, 379. Pierard characterises evangelicalism as 'transcending denominational and confessional boundaries.' It will be seen later that in Britain, particularly England, the type of evangelicalism in view has tended to be localised within the Church of England.

2.1 Evangelicalism

2.1.1 Definition

Modern evangelicalism emerges from the theological developments of the Protestant Reformation, though its taproot extends to the New Testament.[3] The most basic features of modern evangelical theology, even in all its variations, can be traced to the seismic shifts that took place in this movement. Gabriel Fackre identifies 'belief in justification by grace through faith and the supreme authority of scripture' as the primary principles of the Reformation and as roots of modern evangelicalism.[4] Douglas Johnson points out that, stemming from the Greek, *euangelion*,

> [I]n England its Latin form may be traced back as far as John Wycliffe, who was known as 'Doctor Evangelicus'. ... Its first known use in English was by Sir Thomas More, who in 1532 referred – disapprovingly – to the advocates of the Reformation as 'those Evaungelicalles'. On the continent of Europe, soon after the Reformation, the name was employed to describe Protestantism in general, and more particularly the churches which followed the Lutheran branch of the Reformation.[5]

Henry H. Knight III summarises the Reformation theology of the sixteenth century as a commitment to 'four "alones": grace alone, faith alone, scripture alone, Christ alone. These constitute something like a platform for the reformation of the church ...'[6] In addition to these priorities evangelicalism has also been marked by the intellectual assumptions and methods of Roman Catholic Scholasticism.[7] These

---

[3]   R.S. Anderson, 'Evangelical Theology', in D.F. Ford (ed.), *The Modern Theologians: An Introduction to Christian Theology in the Twentieth Century* (Oxford: Blackwell, 1997[2]), 480. Anderson says, 'As it pertains to the gospel of God's act of saving grace through Jesus Christ, the word "evangelical" is rooted in the earliest traditions of the church's theology including, most certainly, the Pauline and Johannine theology of the New Testament itself. A theology which is not 'evangelical' in this fundamental sense may have betrayed both the formal and material reality of its claim to be a "Christian" theology.'

[4]   G. Fackre, 'Evangelical, Evangelicalism', in A. Richardson and J. Bowden (eds.), *TheWestminister Dictionary of Christian Theology* (Philadelphia: Westminster, 1983[3]), 191.

[5]   D. Johnson, *Contending for the Faith: A History of the Evangelical Movement in the Universities and Colleges* (Leicester: Inter–Varsity, 1979), 22.

[6]   H.H. Knight III, *A Future for Truth: Evangelical Theology in a Postmodern World* (Nashville: Abingdon, 1997), 22.

[7]   See R.J. VanderMolen, 'Scholasticism, Protestant', in *EDT*, 984–985

assumptions and methods reflect the fact that the theology of the Reformation was forged in a context of conflict with the Roman Catholic Church and that Roman Catholicism established the terms of engagement. Thus, the theological method that evangelicalism inherited from the Reformation was not as distinct from Roman Catholicism as were the four 'alones.' This will be seen to have profound implications for the ethos and practice of the American evangelicalism in which J.I. Packer has found a wide audience. Knight concludes that the term *evangelical* evolved from Reformational roots, involves an identifiable scope of doctrinal commitments, is shaped by revivalism and pietism, and now denotes a particular sociological expression, especially in post–World War II America.[8] R.V. Pierard adds to this profile the influence of Puritanism 'with its strong emphasis on biblical authority, divine sovereignty, human responsibility, and personal piety and discipline.'[9]

Pierard's mention of Puritanism points to the significant British contribution to the development of evangelicalism. D.W. Bebbington offers a British perspective in his oft–cited description of evangelicalism.

There are four qualities that have been the special marks of Evangelical religion: *conversionism*, the belief that lives need to be changed; *activism*, the expression of the gospel in effort; *biblicism*, a particular regard for the Bible; and what may be called *crucicentrism*, a stress on the sacrifice of Christ on the cross. Together they form a quadrilateral of priorities that is the basis of Evangelicalism.[10]

Oliver Barclay, past General Secretary of the Inter–Varsity Fellowship, suggests that the order of Bebbington's list be rearranged to reflect more clearly evangelicalism's true priorities. Barclay stresses, in sequence, biblicism, crucicentrism, conversionism, and activism; then adds to Bebbington's description the '*Christ–centred* nature of the evangelical position.'[11] Barclay's placement of biblicism at the forefront of evangelical distinctives will be seen to reflect the characteristic method and ethos of evangelical theology and its piety as expounded by Packer.

Martin E. Marty add nuance to the picture by comparing evangelicalism to non–evangelical Protestantism. 'Mainline Protestants' share the heritage of a theological legacy that was 're–formed in the sixteenth century,' but

---

[8] Knight, 20.

[9] Pierard, 380.

[10] D.W. Bebbington, *Evangelicalism in Modern Britain: A History from the 1730s to the 1980s* (London: Unwin Hyman, 1989), 2–3.

[11] O. Barclay, *Evangelicalism in Britain, 1935–1995: A Personal Sketch* (Leicester: Inter–Varsity, 1997), 10–11.

'have chosen to give more attention to nurture than to conversion. Their theology incorporates a vision of public order alongside that of personal conversion.'[12]

Packer himself understands evangelicalism as 'rooted in Reformational theology, Puritan–type pietism, and eighteenth– and nineteenth–century ideals of evangelistic outreach.'[13] Early in his career (1961) he identified two features of evangelicalism and their implications for evangelicalism's relationship to the rest of Christianity. He states, 'In a word, evangelicalism is Bible Christianity, gospel Christianity, apostolic, Christianity, mainstream Christianity. It is an understanding of the Christian revelation based upon two principles: the final authority of Holy Scripture in all matters of faith and life, and the centrality of justification by faith in the Lord Jesus Christ.'[14]

His Reformed orientation shows through in his view that 'the Reformed Christianity to which John Calvin gave definitive shape is, I judge, evangelicalism in its purest form.'[15] His clearest and strongest description has a decidedly doctrinal tone with the doctrine of infallible Scripture at the forefront. He states,

> By evangelicalism I mean that multidenominational Protestant constit–uency within the world–wide church that combines acknowledgment of the trustworthiness, sufficiency, and divine authority of the Bible with adherence to the New Testament account of the gospel of Christ and the way of faith in Him. Characteristic of evangelicalism is its claim that the conceptual categories, arguments, and analyses in terms of which biblical authors present to us God, man, Christ, the Holy Spirit, Satan, sin, salvation, the church, and all else on which they give teaching are in truth God–taught and so have abiding validity.[16]

Elsewhere he offers a similar definition of evangelicalism that distinguishes between its *substantial* character, i.e. 'the salvation of sinners by grace alone in Christ alone through faith alone, as against any thought of

---

[12] M.E. Marty, *The Church: Mainline–Evangelical–Catholic* (New York: Crossroad, 1981), 13.

[13] J.I. Packer, 'Maintaining Evangelical Theology', in J.G. Stackhouse, Jr. (ed.), *Evangelical Futures: A Conversation on Theological Method* (Grand Rapids: Baker, 2000), 183.

[14] J.I. Packer, 'The Theological Challenge to Evangelicalism Today', in *Shorter Writings*, 4.330–331.

[15] J.I. Packer, *Beyond the Battle for the Bible* (Westchester, Ill.: Cornerstone, 1980), 38.

[16] J.I. Packer, 'Infallible Scripture and the Role of Hermeneutics', in J.D. Woodbridge and D.A. Carson (eds.), *Scripture and Truth* (Grand Rapids: Zondervan, 1983), 327.

salvation by effort and merit on the one hand or by the working of ecclesiastical mechanisms, institutional and sacramental, on the other,' and its *methodological* character, i.e. that it 'determines its teaching, attitudes, worship style, and practical priorities by expounding and applying Holy Scripture, which it receives as authoritative instruction from God the Creator, the God who speaks.'[17] This methodological commitment to the Bible, particularly its place and role in his theological system, will later be seen to have vast implications for his theological anthropology and theology of piety, as well as for other aspects of his theological method.

For the purpose of this study, the term *evangelicalism* or *evangelical*, in both British and American contexts, will be understood as involving a particular combination of theological and historical distinctives, each of which by itself may not be unique to evangelicalism. Theologically, it denotes a personal commitment of faith that operates within the boundaries of the historic, orthodox Christian creeds. While evangelicalism is not merely a restatement of historic orthodoxy, it assumes adherence to the creeds of orthodoxy as a foundation.[18] This broad commitment to historic, Christian orthodoxy takes the specific form of belief in the crippling effects of sin on human nature, the inability of humanity to provide its own salvation from sin (either individually or corporately), the necessity of Jesus Christ's atonement for sin as humanity's only hope of salvation, the need for personal conversion through faith in Jesus Christ and the regeneration of the Holy Spirit, the necessity of godly living, and the future judgment of all humanity by God. It emphasises, though in differing ways, the divine inspiration and authority of the sixty–six books of the Old and New Testaments.[19]

---

[17] Packer, *Beyond the Battle for the Bible*, 37–38.

[18] Pierard, 'Evangelicalism', 380.

[19] The statement of faith of the National Association of Evangelicals, drafted in 1942, reflects these commitments. It has been a mooring point for many in the United States who desire to be known as 'evangelical' regardless of their denominational affiliation. The statement of faith reads: '(1) We believe the Bible to be the inspired, the only infallible, authoritative Word of God. (2) We believe that there is one God, eternally existent in three persons, Father, Son, and Holy Ghost. (3) We believe in the deity of our Lord Jesus Christ, in His virgin birth, in His sinless life, in His miracles, in His vicarious and atoning death through His shed blood, in His bodily resurrection, in His ascension to the right hand of the Father, and in His personal return in power and glory. (4) We believe that for the salvation of lost and sinful man, regeneration by the Holy Spirit is absolutely essential. (5) We believe in the present ministry of the Holy Spirit by whose indwelling the Christian is enabled to live a godly life. (6) We believe in the resurrection of both the saved and the lost; they that are saved unto the resurrection of life and they that are lost unto the

From a historical perspective, *evangelicalism* in the United States is often closely identified with the tradition that came to be known in the United States as *neo–evangelicalism* since the Second World War.[20] This is a 'movement,' loosely defined, that emerged from an aggressively separatist and anti–intellectual fundamentalism. George M. Marsden reviews the genesis of neo–evangelicalism.

> Most simply understood, the 'new evangelical' reformers repudiated both the doctrinal and the cultural implications of a thoroughgoing dispensationalism while they remained loyal to the fundamentals of fundamentalism. Put another way, their version of fundamentalism was defined primarily by the culturally centrist tradition of nineteenth–century American evangelicalism. Theologically, they stood for a moderate form of classic Calvinist Protestantism as opposed to some of the innovations of dispensationalist Bible teachers. Though they were influenced heavily by the conservative Princeton Theological Seminary, they were neither rigid 'Old School' Calvinists nor champions of strict confessional and denominational orthodoxy. Rather, they were much more like the broadly Calvinist interdenominational evangelicalism that had wide influence in nineteenth–century American culture.[21]

The personality of this evangelicalism distinctly reflects the influence of the holiness and revival movements of both Britain and the United States, as well as the heritage of the Puritans. Richard Quebedeaux points out that 'the term *neo–evangelical* has generally been replaced by the more historic and inclusive designation, evangelical' and that this is but a subculture within broader evangelicalism.[22]

The theological and historical profile of evangelicalism, so defined, describes the general context in which J.I. Packer has been influential. In order to more fully understand his influence, however, the development and key influences of evangelicalism must be examined.

---

resurrection of damnation. (7) We believe in the spiritual unity of believers in our Lord Jesus Christ.'

[20] G.M. Marsden, *Reforming Fundamentalism: Fuller Seminary and the New Evangelicalism* (Grand Rapids: Eerdmans, 1987), 172. Marsden attributes the descriptor 'new evangelicalism' to Harold Ockenga.

[21] Ibid., 6.

[22] R. Quebedeaux, *The Worldly Evangelicals* (San Francisco: Harper and Row, 1978), 9.

2.1.2 Development

From the Protestant Reformation onward, numerous historical factors have contributed to J.I. Packer's evangelical context in Great Britain and the United States. The following narrative traces the development of this context through its primary historical streams.

2.1.2.1 ENGLISH PURITANISM AND THE WESTMINSTER ASSEMBLY

As Calvinistic theology was crystallised in the Westminster Confession its influence was extended into the theology and piety of evangelicalism. The English Puritans helped provide a bridge between Calvinistic theology and pietism. Knight attributes the influence of the Puritans to their combination of 'intellectual rigor with spiritual depth.'[23] Despite their attempts at integration, evangelicalism has experienced a perpetual conflict between the intellectual and the affective dimensions of Christian experience.[24]

As pastoral theologians the English Puritans directed the bulk of their theological work at the needs and challenges found within the daily Christian experience of their parishioners. Their repeated emphasis on 'experimental' Christianity found expression in their rigorous moral casuistry and their fascination with cases of conscience. They were intensely interested in the inner life of faith, i.e. the moment–by–moment state of the soul. Packer reflects that, 'To bring what they knew about God down to the level of ordinary people in sermons and in print seemed to Puritan clergy a supreme privilege and a prime duty, and they saw their practical writing – sermon material, mostly – as no less important than anything else that they wrote.'[25] This combination of emphases on introspective piety, precise moral reasoning, and popular orientation prepared the way for a codification of theology that would give the Bible and the Christian experience a reliable, enduring structure. Many prominent Puritans of the seventeenth century were, to varying degrees, Calvinistic in their theology. Yet, the Calvinism to which they adhered bore marked differences from the original work of John Calvin.[26] The Westminster Confession codified these developments.

---

[23] Knight, 24.

[24] Ibid.

[25] J.I. Packer, *Among God's Giants:The Puritan Vision of the Christian Life* (Eastbourne: Kingsway, 1991), 83.

[26] See R.T. Kendall, *Calvin and English Calvinism to 1649* (Oxford: Oxford University Press, 1979). Kendall argues that it was through the influence of Theodore Beza and William Perkins that the doctrine of predestination was moved from being a subordinate theme in the Christology of Calvin's Institutes to the dominant place at the forefront of the Calvinistic theological system. According to Kendall, this shift

Against a backdrop of political conflict surrounding Charles I[27] the Grand Remonstrance of 1641 called for a synod to address 'theological and ecclesiastical grievances.'[28] Despite the King's rejection of a 1642 Parliamentary bill calling for the Assembly, both houses proceeded in 1643 to call the Assembly. The commission of the Westminster Assembly was to provide Parliament with theological advisement, particularly vis-à-vis issues such as Arminianism and Romanism, which had direct political ramifications.[29] This politico–religious context provided a reactionary character that differentiated the resulting Confession from other creeds that were less politically charged.

The philosophical and theological background of the Westminster Assembly also shaped its work. John H. Leith points out that the prevailing cultural worldview focused on an orderly universe in which events were oriented to the will of God rather than to natural causes. Yet, the Assembly took place at a period when the broader intellectual world was shifting its interests from metaphysics to experimentation.[30] He observes, 'By the time of Westminster, orthodox theology was already being carried on in isolation from the intellectual currents of the day. After Westminster, as society became increasingly secular, orthodoxy would finally become very defensive in its intellectual isolation.'[31]

Benjamin B. Warfield surveys the factors that account for the influence of the Westminster Confession. First, federal theology figures as the most important theological focus of the work done by the Westminster Assembly. He states, 'The architectonic principle of the Westminster Confession is supplied by the schematization of the Federal theology which had obtained by this time in Britain, as on the Continent, a dominant

---

gave rise to the doctrine of limited atonement and, consequently, to the Puritans' preoccupation with determining one's status as elect or non–elect through introspective examination of one's faith.

[27] The political events that spawned the Assembly are summarised by J.H. Leith, *Assembly at Westminster: Reformed Theology in the Making* (Richmond, Va.: John Knox, 1973), 23–30. Specifically, Leith highlights the importance of the attempted enforcement of the prayer book on the Church of Scotland by Charles I, the National Covenant in Edinburgh, the General Assembly of the Church of Scotland, the First Bishops' War, and the King's calling of Parliament to raise funds.

[28] Ibid., 24.

[29] Ibid., 26. Leith mentions that Arminianism was 'associated with episcopacy and the divine right of kings' and that 'Romanism specifically referred to those elements in the liturgy and government of the church that the Puritans did not feel had been sufficiently reformed.'

[30] Ibid., 31–33.

[31] Ibid., 34–35.

position as the most commodious mode of presenting the *corpus* of Reformed doctrine ...'[32] Warfield goes on to credit the Westminster divines with developing a statement that held preeminence in Reformed theology even until his own time.[33] This took place through the immediate and broad spread of the Confession. He chronicles the late seventeenth–century adoption of the Confession, with minor adaptations, by groups outside the Church of England, e.g. Independents and Baptists, as it made its way to America.[34] Eventually, the Westminster Confession became the Puritan formulation of the Reformed tradition on which evangelicalism drew.

2.1.2.2 EIGHTEENTH– AND NINETEENTH–CENTURY EVANGELICALISM

Despite the intent of the Westminster divines to strengthen and perpetuate Calvinism, the Reformed tradition diversified in Britain, eventually falling into camps that were more or less stringent about faithfulness to a Calvinistic theology. It is noteworthy, according to Leith, that 'much of the Assembly's work was not acceptable to the Episcopalians on the one hand or the Independents on the other,' making more impact on the English dissenting churches and the Church of Scotland, than it did within the Church of England.[35]

Richard Baxter (1615–1691) exercised considerable influence in seventeenth–century England, yet held only partially to the Calvinism expressed in the Westminster Confession. Baxter held that Christ's atonement was sufficient for all but efficient only for those who believe. The diversity emerging within British evangelicalism was reflected in Baxter's ministry. Alan C. Clifford also places the well–known Isaac Watts in the line of Baxter's soteriological descendants known as 'modified Calvinists.'[36] The multiformity within British evangelicalism was perhaps most acutely evident in the ministries of John Wesley and George

---

[32] B.B. Warfield, *The Westminster Assembly and Its Work*, in *The Works of Benjamin B. Warfield*, vol. VI (Grand Rapids: Baker, 1981), 56–57.

[33] Ibid., 58–59.

[34] Ibid., 60–61. Warfield states, 'By both of the bodies it was transmitted to their affiliated co–religionists in America, where it worked out for itself an important history. It was of course also transmitted, in its original form, by the Scotch Church to the Churches, on both sides of the sea, deriving their tradition from it, and thus it has become the Confession of Faith of the Presbyterian Church of the British dependencies and of America. ... It has thus come about that the Westminster confession has occupied a position of very widespread influence.'

[35] Leith, 63.

[36] A.C. Clifford, *Atonement and Justification: English Evangelical Theology 1640–1790: An Evaluation* (Oxford: Clarendon, 1990), 76.

Whitefield. As Wesley and Whitefield contended for their various understandings of soteriology, theological party lines were drawn.

A key, though understated influence on British evangelicalism was the Scot, Henry Scougal (1650–1678), whose book *The Life of God in the Soul of Man* exercised 'crucial influence in the 18th century revival of religion,' according to Douglas Johnson.[37] Johnson records that the book was one of Susannah Wesley's favourites. She recommended it to her sons, John and Charles, when they went to Oxford. When Charles Wesley founded the 'Holy Club' at Oxford and the young George Whitefield visited during a time of acute spiritual struggle, Wesley gave him Scougal's book. It transformed Whitefield's spiritual experience. Scougal's book was also influential as the pattern for John Wesley's class meetings that grew from the revival.[38]

George Whitefield (1714–1770) contributed to the transmission of Calvinism through his preaching. In England Whitefield helped shape the tenor of Calvinistic thought within the Anglican Church. John T. McNeill claims,

> The real force of Calvinism in England is seen in the Evangelical revival and its influence in Anglicanism. … The word 'Methodist' was applied in his [Wesley's] time to manifestations of evangelical piety whether Wesleyan or not. George Whitefield, who was firmly Calvinist, carried that label. … Many Evangelicals of Calvinist persuasion became prominent within Anglicanism[39]

Whitefield's influence extended to the United States, where his participation in the First Great Awakening (1739–1742) helped cultivate a priority on regenerated church membership in Presbyterian churches that had previously accepted members merely on the basis of baptism at birth or letters of recommendation from previous pastors.[40] Whitefield's influence was part of an overall shift in the socio–political context of Calvinism in America, where it had become less associated with the Church of England and more supportive of the socio–political ethos emerging in the New World.

Jonathan Edwards was another central, Calvinistic figure in the Awakening. R.S. Anderson attributes the beginning of the Awakening to

---

[37] Johnson, 26.

[38] Ibid., 27–28.

[39] J.T. McNeill, *The History and Character of Calvinism* (New York: Oxford University Press, 1954), 371.

[40] See J. Tracy, *The Great Awakening: A History of the Revival of Religion in the Time of Edwards and Whitefield* (Carlisle, Pa.: Banner of Truth, 1976), 22–23, 391.

Edwards's preaching wherein he 'emphasized the saving grace of God received by faith which was itself a gift of God.'[41] The face of this evangelicalism was to change, however. Anderson records a monumental shift that took place.

> In the 1820s, under the influence of Nathaniel Taylor at Yale Divinity School, a 'New Haven Theology' emerged which emphasized the positive side of human nature and a God more friendly than the 'angry God' of Edwards's day. Taylor considered himself to be orthodox, Calvinistic, and evangelical. The Princeton theologians, however, recognized as the nineteenth–century standard–bearers of evangelical orthodoxy, held a different view of him. His positive view of human nature placed him on the side of Pelagius and not Augustine, in their opinion. …
>
> The popular American evangelist, Charles Finney, an ordained Presbyterian minister, broke with the 'Old School Calvinism' in favor of a gospel which appealed to the free moral agency of sinners. Finney's pragmatic approach became popular among the evangelical churches which wanted results and found them in applying his methods. … The revivalism which characterized the 'New School' Presbyterians carried a powerful evangelical theology of redemption, liberation, and tranformation.[42]

Due to the revivals, American Calvinism took on a more varied complexion with the 'New School' interest in conversion, evidence of regeneration, and pietism and the 'Old School' emphasis on doctrinal purity. George Whitefield appears to have provided a bridge to the modified Calvinism of 'New School' Presbyterianism. George M. Marsden comments,

> By the time of the Great Awakening, the New England party [Puritans] was closely linked with the more pietistic revivalist group of the Presbyterians. In 1741 this revivalist 'New Side' group split from the antirevivalist Scotch–Irish or Scottish 'Old Side.' Remarkably, these two Presbyterian 'sides' reunited in 1758, thus suggesting that pietist revivalism and doctrinalist confessionalism were compatible. But the tension between these two emphases repeatedly reemerged. The classic instance was in the Old School/New School schism of 1837–38, in many ways a repetition of the Old Side/New Side conflict. The Old School was clearly the stronghold of confessionalism. The New School, on the other

---

[41] Anderson, 'Evangelical Theology', 481.
[42] Ibid., 481–482.

hand, represented an alliance of more strongly pietistic or prorevivalist Presbyterians with New England Congregationalists.[43]

Marsden also states, 'In the eighteenth century, such revivalist Calvinism had been called "New Light" and was central to America's first Great Awakening.'[44] The modified form of Calvinism in New England Congregationalism tended not to adhere to the doctrine of limited atonement. It eventually worked its way into the theological ethos of dispensationalism,[45] which has had a significant impact on American fundamentalism.

Though Whitefield may not have intended his revivalism to have a modifying effect on Calvinistic thought, the outcome was the same. A more self–consciously modified Calvinist who was likewise highly influential in nurturing the ethos of British evangelicalism was Charles Simeon (1759–1836), who ministered at Holy Trinity Church, Cambridge. Hugh Evan Hopkins declares that Simeon 'was far from being a true Calvinist,'[46] though Simeon admitted to having been called a Calvinist at times and once questioned John Wesley pointedly, taking a broadly Calvinistic stance on soteriology.[47] Hopkins describes Simeon as one who characteristically resisted taking sides in the debate between Wesley and Whitefield, stating, 'With a succinctness which really over–simplified the controversy Simeon maintained that both parties "are right in all they affirm and wrong in all they deny."'[48] Simeon seemed to be a master at taking a middle ground or balanced approach to contentious issues, insisting that he was only

---

[43] G.M. Marsden, 'Introduction: Reformed and American', 4–5.

[44] Marsden, *Reforming Fundamentalism*, 6.

[45] L.S. Chafer, *Systematic Theology*, vol. 3 (Dallas: Dallas Seminary, 1947–1948), 193–199. Based on the dispensational schema of C.I. Scofield, Chafer provided the first comprehensive systematic theology from within a dispensational frame of reference. His personal 'Doctrinal Statement' shows that as early as the turn of the century he clearly held to a covenantal, Calvinistic theological framework, but questioned the doctrine of limited atonement. He states, 'That every man may enter this divine life in Christ is the teaching of Scriptures, and none are precluded from this great redemption' (p. 4). Chafer's work institutionalised and perpetuated dispensationalism through his founding, teaching, and presidential leadership at Dallas Theological Seminary. Dispensationalism has been prominent in the ethos of American neo–evangelicalism that derived from earlier fundamentalism.

[46] H.E. Hopkins, *Charles Simeon of Cambridge* (London: Hodder and Stoughton, 1977), 141.

[47] Ibid., 174.

[48] Ibid., 175.

interested in what the Scriptures taught. For this reason he rarely utilised Patristic or Reformation resources.[49]

As one whole–heartedly committed to the Church of England, Simeon wielded a multi–faceted influence on religious life. Hopkins observes, '[A]s one of the recognised leaders of the evangelical wing of the national church, Simeon had a formative part to play in the rise of that vital Christianity.'[50] Faithfulness to the authority of Scripture, the primacy of the Gospel, and the need for personal conversion were hallmarks of his ministry. The particular evangelical mark he made, however, was considerably more tolerant than that of the Puritan tradition.

Evangelical students at Oxford experienced opposition due to their involvement with Methodism in the late eighteenth century. Evangelicalism became an underground movement there until Alred Christopher became rector of St. Aldate's Church in 1859.[51] The situation was not quite as repressive at Cambridge, but took a decided turn in a congenial direction with the conversion of Simeon and his appointment as Vicar of Holy Trinity in 1782. He established a long legacy of evangelicalism with students at Cambridge.[52] This influence was to bear fruit much later through the Cambridge Inter–Collegiate Christian Union (CICCU), which became the seedbed for Inter–Varsity Fellowship, a primary carrier of evangelicalism in Britain during the late nineteenth and early twentieth centuries. Simeon's moderating approach to theology, however, stands in the legacy of the 'liberal evangelicalism' that much later became suspect to the IVF.[53]

An evangelical counterpart to Simeon, though somewhat later in history, was John Charles Ryle (1816–1900), who eventually became Bishop of Liverpool. Like Simeon, Ryle was highly committed to the Church of England and, according to Peter Toon and Michael Smout, 'did not shirk the responsibility of sitting alongside men of different persuasions in the debating forums of the Church, the Church Congresses and Diocesan Conferences.'[54] Toon and Smout claim that 'Ryle was a leader of Victorian Evangelicalism and to begin to understand him is to begin to understand the ethos of that Evangelicalism and its continuing influence today.'[55]

---

[49] Ibid., 173.

[50] Ibid., 220.

[51] Johnson, 29–30.

[52] Ibid., 32–33.

[53] O.R. Barclay, *Whatever Happened to the Jesus Lane Lot?* (Leicester: Inter–Varsity, 1977), 79f.

[54] P. Toon and M. Smout, *John Charles Ryle: Evangelical Bishop* (Cambridge: James Clarke, 1976), 5.

[55] Ibid.

A key distinctive of Ryle, for the purpose of establishing J.I. Packer's theological context, is his commitment to the Reformed theological tradition of the Puritans. Ian Farley comments, '[H]is evangelical sermons, based on a personal study of Reformation and Puritan 'saints', remained the heart of his ministry.'[56] Ryle's Calvinism was qualified, however. Alan C. Clifford notes that he was adverse to the notion of particular atonement, feeling that it had damaging effects.[57] With regard to revivalistic developments within British evangelicalism, Toon and Smout record that Ryle had mixed feelings about Moody and Sankey. 'Though he became a personal friend of Moody and believed his basic theology to be acceptable, he was never entirely happy with the techniques of mass evangelism.'[58] Ryle stands, then as a noteworthy figure in the lineage of Puritan Reformed evangelicalism in Great Britain. He made extensive use of this theological tradition while maintaining connections with an evangelical ethos that was moving in a significantly different direction in the latter half of the nineteenth century.

The general intellectual tendency of British evangelical theologians in the 1800s, according to D.W. Bebbington, was defensive.[59] He notes a slow decline of Evangelical prominence and influence in the second half of the nineteenth century. 'Despite the innovations of [Edward] Irving's circle, the bulk of Evangelicals at mid–century retained their confidence in the Enlightenment appeal to evidences, scientific method and an orderly universe governed by cause and effect.'[60] Bebbington points out a softening of interest in doctrine, 'sub–Romantic influences,' and a general loss of 'the incisiveness of Evangelical theology'[61] The stage was apparently set for the revival and holiness movements.

Douglas Johnson identifies three late nineteenth–century developments in North America that influenced the British Isles: 'the impact of the evangelists Moody and Sankey; the arrival from North America of representatives of the Holiness Movements ... and a great increase of zeal in the cause of overseas Christian missions.'[62] These streams increasingly integrated the evangelical cultures of Britain and the United States. Johnson records the beginning of the Keswick movement and its influence on the British student movement.

---

[56] I.D. Farley, 'Ryle, J(ohn) C(harles)', in D.M. Lewis (ed.), *The Blackwell Dictionary of Evangelical Biography: 1730–1860*, vol. II (Oxford: Blackwell, 1995), 967.

[57] Clifford, 81.

[58] Toon and Smout, 55.

[59] Bebbington, *Evangelicalism in Modern Britain*, 141.

[60] Ibid., 143.

[61] Ibid., 144, 145.

[62] Johnson, 49.

In the Spring of 1874, two Americans, Pearsall Smith and his wife Hannah Smith, who were leaders of what in North America was known as 'The Higher Life Movement', came to Cambridge. Their visit to Britain had resulted in the beginning of a number of conventions in various parts of the country to promote higher standards in practical Christian life. ... The Bishop of Liverpool, J.C. Ryle, had already outspokenly and publicly opposed the new views. Some of the undergraduates, however, who had expressed favourable interest in what the speakers were teaching, were subsequently invited, with a small party from Oxford, to take part in a summer conference at Broadlands, the home of William Cowper–Tempel, M.P. ... For several years this became a centre for such conferences and the Cowper–Temples annually invited parties of undergraduates from Cambridge and Oxford.[63]

This set of events comprised part of the beginnings of the Keswick movement and its subsequent impact on the British evangelical student movement.

A revivalist strain was encouraged when in 1882 the president of CICCU invited D.L. Moody to speak.[64] In the early 1890s plans were made for a national student Christian movement. In 1893 the first conference was held at Keswick and for several years thereafter. The Inter–Varsity Christian Union was the product.[65] The interplay between revivalism, the Keswick movement, and British evangelical students continued into the twentieth century as various American speakers were invited to address the student unions (e.g. R.A. Torrey's crusade at CICCU in 1911[66]) and the annual Keswick conference became a place of nurture for students.

Evangelicalism in Great Britain was taking on a predominantly middle–class ethos. Bebbington contends that the social and cultural character of British evangelicalism shaped the pietistic ethos of the movement.

Attendance at the conventions, which necessarily implied the possession of a good deal of leisure, provided a congenial answer for the conscientious Christian. ... The explanation of its social appeal is to be found in the nature of its message. The greater educational opportunities of the upper middle classes meant that they had commonly acquired a taste for Wordsworth, the poetic temper and elevating spiritual influences. The call to holiness, with all its Romantic affinities, was bound to have far more impact on them than on lower social groups. Although Keswick

---

[63] Ibid., 50.
[64] Ibid., 54–55.
[65] Ibid., 66–67.
[66] Ibid., 78.

teaching was later to spread to a wider public, its initial constituency was drawn very largely from the well–to–do.[67]

Along with the temperamental and sociological traits of these movements, came a shifting theological mood.

Bebbington contends that the revivalist movement in Britain contributed to the softening of relations between Calvinists and Arminians. He states, 'There was less of a doctrinal barrier to co–operation. Consequently, too, Calvinists of the revivalist stamp had fewer inhibitions about embracing teaching that rejected traditional Reformed convictions on sanctification. The lower version of Calvinism in vogue among them was a more elastic worldview.'[68] However, even in this more relaxed theological climate issues such as eschatology, social responsibility, and the nature of Christian piety provided ample material for controversy as evangelicalism approached the twentieth century. In the United States controversy and division would reach new levels of intensity.

2.1.2.3 TWENTIETH–CENTURY EVANGELICALISM

Late nineteenth–century evangelicalism in both Britain and America was marked by a growing preoccupation with the prophetic interpretation of the Bible and a particular brand of pietistic individualism nurtured by the Keswick conferences. Keswick encouraged a piety of passive rest on God; a piety that offered relief from the wearying struggle with sin that seemed prominent in the Reformed view of piety.[69] Sanctification, in this view, was to be experienced in the same manner as justification; received by faith as God's gift.

The Keswick conferences offered a tight and formative relationship between British and American evangelicalism. Into the early twentieth century this relationship would grow even stronger. Ian S. Rennie notes, 'The close links between British conservative evangelicalism and American fundamentalism were particularly shown by the presence of Americans on the Keswick Convention platform from year to year.'[70] Rennie claims,

---

[67] Bebbington, *Evangelicalism in Modern Britain*, 177.
[68] Ibid., 162.
[69] Ibid., 170.
[70] I.S. Rennie, 'Fundamentalism and North Atlantic Evangelicalism', in M.A. Noll, D.W. Bebbington, and G.A. Rawlyk (eds.), *Evangelicalism: Comparative Studies of Popular Protestantism in North America, the British Isles, and Beyond, 1700–1990* (New York: Oxford University Press, 1994), 339. Rennie's use of the word 'fundamentalism' here may seem somewhat anachronistic since he is referring to the late nineteenth century before the most recognizable form of American fundamentalism had yet emerged from the early twentieth century controversy with

'Verbal inspiration, premillennialism, and holiness were particularly woven together in Keswick.'[71] These British conferences were a platform for the integration and popularisation of these theological emphases that were simultaneously gaining momentum in the United States.

Despite the growing mutual influence between British and American versions of evangelicalism in the late nineteenth and early twentieth centuries, they were also quite distinct. D.W. Bebbington notes that, 'Withdrawal from Christian bodies apparently tainted with error has been much more common in the United States.'[72] British evangelicalism was enabled by an established denominational structure because of its presence in the Church of England. J.I. Packer contends that the primary locus of British evangelicalism shifted from outside to inside the Church of England over the issue of biblical criticism. He claims,

> While the word 'evangelical' may be variously applied, its meaning in Britain was quite definite at the beginning of the twentieth century. It denoted the position of those in all the churches who, in opposition to rationalism on the one hand and sacramentalism (Roman and Anglo–Catholic) on the other, maintained the theology of the Reformation, the piety of the Puritans, and the evangelistic ideals of the eighteenth–century Revival, basing these tenets on a robust belief in the plenary inspiration, entire truth, final authority, and vitalizing power of Holy Scripture as 'God's ord [sic] written' (Thirty–nine Articles, XX). In the mid–nineteenth century, evangelicalism was the norm in all British churches except the Church of England, where latitudinarians ruled and Tractarian 'catholics' crusaded. But before the century ended most non–Anglican evangelicals had accepted higher criticism. … Within a generation, classic evangelical theology, at least at the ministerial level, had almost vanished. The strongest resistance occurred in the Church of England, where many evangelicals rejected higher criticism and preserved their historic position intact.[73]

---

modernism. Rennie's reference is to the seedbed from which that fundamentalism later grew.

[71] Ibid., 338.

[72] D.W. Bebbington, 'Evangelicalism in Its Settings: The British and American Movements since 1940', in M.A. Noll, D.W. Bebbington, and G.A. Rawlyk (eds.), *Evangelicalism: Comparative Studies of Popular Protestantism in North America, the British Isles, and Beyond, 1700–1990*, 370.

[73] J.I. Packer, 'British Theology in the First Half of the Twentieth Century', in *Shorter Writings*, 4.319.

This relationship to the Church of England was facilitated largely by the presence (though marginal) of what became the Inter–Varsity Fellowship in the British universities. The most prominent expression of this presence was the Cambridge Inter–Collegiate Christian Union (CICCU), but noteworthy influence also took place through the Oxford Inter–Collegiate Christian Union (OICCU) and other chapters. In contrast, the tendency in the United States was for evangelicals to separate from denominations.

As Bebbington and others point out, evangelicalism is propelled by a number of positive theological commitments. Those commitments, however, were perpetually forged in a crucible of conflict. In the twentieth century the battles became fierce as evangelicals contended that higher criticism undermined the divine inspiration and authority of the Bible and, in consequence, the major tenets of historic, Western orthodoxy. The controversy in the United States also broke into intense debates over creation and evolution. Evangelicals knew this panorama of conflict as the battle with 'modernism.'

Among the general characteristics of 'modernism,' from the perspective of the fundamentalists, were acceptance of higher critical theories of the Bible's origins, the questioning of accepted doctrinal formulations such as the necessity of Christ's atonement for personal salvation, acceptance of Charles Darwin's evolutionary theory,[74] and emphasis on humanity's temporal, social ills as the primary focus of the gospel.[75] To fundamentalist evangelicals each of these ideas radically threatened the foundations of the Christian faith. American fundamentalists, therefore, gave enormous attention and energy to defending their commitments to the verbal inspiration of the Bible, to a hermeneutic that understood the book of Genesis to describe a creation process of six literal, twenty–four hour days, to a soteriology that prioritised salvation for the afterlife over penultimate remedies, and to a piety that valued inner, personal transformation over social change. Since these theological traits were seen as sustaining the veracity of the Christian faith, they bore great emotional weight for adherents. Thus, evangelicalism in the United States took on a militantly defensive posture to protect the 'fundamentals' of the Christian faith. Adherents proudly called themselves 'fundamentalists.'

---

[74] D.W. Bebbington notes that in Britain the issue of evolution was generally not considered to be as central to the theological integrity of evangelicalism as it was in the United States. 'Many evangelicals [in the UK] had no qualms about evolution.' *Evangelicalism in Modern Britain*, 207.

[75] *The Fundamentals: A Testimony to the Truth*, 4 vols. (Los Angeles: The Bible Institute of Los Angeles, 1917). These four volumes contain a diverse collection of essays and articles attempting to defend evangelical theology against the attacks of modernist scholarship and its perceived effects on Christianity and culture.

The battle with what evangelicals called 'modernism' moved evangelicalism through a clear developmental cycle. George M. Marsden highlights the irony of this cycle. In the United States evangelicalism gave rise to a fundamentalism that later spawned another version of evangelicalism.[76] This later version, as previously mentioned, emerged in the 1940s and was called 'neo–evangelicalism,' a posture intent on being less combative and more willing to dialogue with those of differing theological commitments.

American evangelicalism (as it was becoming fundamentalism) and its piety were further shaped by the popularisation of premillennial eschatology after the American Civil War.[77] The postmillennial eschatology that had been popular prior to that time emphasised that Christ would return to earth as the culmination of the progressive restoration of righteousness on the earth. This eschatology appears to have cultivated widespread expectations that the Kingdom of God was imminent through world evangelisation and efforts to remedy societal ills. World War I helped undermine that optimism[78] and redirect the hopes of evangelical Christians toward a future Kingdom of God that was unrelated to life in the fallen world and immune to the vicissitudes of world politics.

R.V. Pierard comments, 'Emerging from the struggle against theological liberalism and the social gospel in Britain and North America was a narrow fundamentalism that internalized the Christian message and withdrew from involvement in the world.'[79] The disillusionment experienced with postmillennialism's social orientation after World War I merged with the rejection of modernism's social orientation to intensify evangelicals' openness to an alternative eschatology. Thus, a millenarian theology that held to a future, historical, one thousand year reign of Jesus Christ on earth can often be seen in the fundamentalism of the late nineteenth and early twentieth centuries.

Dispensational premillennialism is an interdenominational movement[80] that took millenarian theology in an even more specialized and radical direction. R.S. Anderson contends, 'The theology of the fundamentalist movement was largely developed out of dispensational theology, leading to a blending of revivalism, evangelicalism, and orthodoxy in a movement

---

[76] G.M. Marsden, *Fundamentalism and American Culture: The Shaping of Twentieth–Century American Evangelicalism: 1870–1925* (New York: Oxford University Press, 1980), 3.

[77] T.L. Smith, *Revivalism and Social Reform in Mid–Nineteenth–Century America* (New York: Abingdon, 1957), 228.

[78] Marsden, *Fundamentalism and American Culture*, 146.

[79] Pierard, 381.

[80] Marsden, *Fundamentalism and American Culture*, 119.

which lacked connection to the mainline denominational churches.'[81] Dispensationalism utilised a highly literalistic hermeneutic to identify multiple, distinct economies in which God has related to people throughout human history. This affinity for distinct economies is evident in the insistence on an absolute distinction between the nation of Israel in the Old Testament and the Church in the New Testament and beyond.[82]

Dispensationalism was initially popularised at annual prophecy conferences in Niagara Falls, New York and Northfield, Massachusetts.[83] The most notable early proponent of dispensationalism was John Nelson Darby,[84] who was trained as a lawyer at Trinity College, Dublin, then became a vicar in the Church of Ireland[85] before joining the Plymouth Brethren movement. American dispensationalists did not slavishly follow Darby's schema, however. Cyrus I. Scofield offered the most influential version in his 1909 publication of Bible study notes in an edition of the

---

[81]   Anderson, 'Evangelical Theology', 482.

[82]   The rationale for this distinction is articulated at length by C.C. Ryrie in *Dispensationalism Today* (Chicago: Moody, 1965). Dispensationalism's hermeneutic produces this distinction by interpreting all Old Testament prophecies regarding the nation of Israel as applying to a literal, restored political entity. In this view, interpreting these prophecies as (even partially) fulfilled in any other manner would be to abrogate the integrity and trustworthiness of Scripture. The earliest documented development of this approach to Scripture is in the writings of Pierre (Peter) Poiret (1646–1719), who purported, by means of this approach, to unify divisions within the church and secure Christians against the threats of scepticism. See P. Poiret, *The Divine Economy: or, An Universal System of the Works and Purposes of God Towards Men Demonstrated*, vol. I (London: 'Printed for R. Bonwicke in St. Paul's Church–Yard, M. Wooton in Fleet–Street, S. Manship and R. Parker in Cornhill', 1713), no page. Poiret's dispensations are (1) 'The Economy of the Creation,' (2) 'The Economy of Sin,' (3) 'The Economy of the Restoration before the Incarnation of Jesus Christ,' (4) 'The Economy of the Restoration after the Incarnation of Jesus Christ,' (5) 'The Economy of the Co–operation of Man, with the Operation of God,' and (6) 'The Economy of Universal Providence.'

[83]   See E.R. Sandeen, *The Roots of Fundamentalism: British and American Millenarianism 1800–1930* (Chicago: University of Chicago Press, 1970), 175. Sandeen notes that although D.L. Moody, sponsor of the popular Northfield conference, did not wholeheartedly adopt a dispensationalist eschatology, he had met J.N. Darby and was influenced by dispensationalists Harry Morehouse and C.H. Mackintosh. In 1886 the Northfield conference was entirely given over to dispensationalist teaching. G.M. Marsden records that the Niagara conference, which ended in 1901, drew its ethos from dispensationalist teaching. R.A. Torrey, a disciple of C.I. Scofield, was a prominent and influential speaker at the Niagara conference. See Marsden, *Fundamentalism and American Culture*, 51.

[84]   Marsden, *Fundamentalism and American Culture*, 46.

[85]   Sandeen, 31.

Authorized Version of the Bible.[86] This was of landmark significance in helping his version of dispensationalism gain a firm footing. George Marsden claims that this publication was probably the most important factor in the promotion of dispensationalist views.[87]

Darby and the Plymouth Brethren denigrated institutionalism and clerical roles while emphasizing the accessibility of ministry to the laity. Only a minority of American evangelicals embraced these themes to the same extent as did Darby and the Plymouth Brethren. Nevertheless, the ideals fit well with the individualistic and entrepreneurial temperament of the United States. Against the backdrop of anticlericalism, anti–institutionalism, and a widespread assumption of Baconian epistemology in emphasising the perspicuity of Scripture, dispensationalism's appeal was heightened by the threat of biblical higher–criticism. It offered the assurance that the Bible reflected a unified, coherent, even systematic divine plan that would yield itself to diligent study.[88] Thus, little value was placed on formal education as a prerequisite for understanding the Bible.[89]

Dispensationalism was representative of the American evangelical fundamentalism that was swept into the intellectual defence of conservativism during the early twentieth century. It offered American fundamentalists the security of a highly rational system for interpreting the Bible, a means of navigating their personal journeys of faith, and a sense of protection against cultural and philosophical currents that threatened to undermine the absolute values on which they relied. However, dispensationalism's lack of academic respectability and intellectual prowess

---

[86] C.I. Scofield, (ed.), *The Scofield Reference Bible*, Authorized Version (New York: Oxford University Press, 1909).

[87] Marsden, *Fundamentalism and American Culture*, 119. Though Darby was a significant and undeniable force in the spread of dispensationalism throughout America, the version popularised by Scofield was not identical to Darby's version. C.C. Ryrie notes, 'If Scofield parroted anybody's scheme it was [Isaac] Watts', not Darby's.' See Ryrie, 76. See also Isaac Watts, 'The Harmony of All the Religions Which God ever prescribed to Men, and all his Dispensations towards them,' in *Works*, vol. II (Leeds: Edward Baines, 1800), 626–659.

[88] Though dispensationalists have not been alone among evangelicals in claiming the unity, coherence and perspicuity of the Bible, they have seen their dispensationalism as the logical result or evidence of those tenets. C.I. Scofield makes that connection clear in his introductory remarks to *The Scofield Reference Bible*, 'A Panoramic View of the Bible', v–vi.

[89] M.A. Noll, *Between Faith and Criticism: Evangelicals, Scholarship, and the Bible in America* (San Francisco: Harper and Row, 1986), 59. Noll claims that 'dispensationalism flourished in communities that distrusted professional scholarship. Most of its major proponents were neither academically trained nor professionally certified students of Scripture.'

eventually left it in need of assistance to combat the attacks of modernism. Thus, dispensationalism and the fundamentalism of which it was a part found an unlikely ally in the Reformed theologians of Princeton Theological Seminary.

Mark Noll records that Benjamin B. Warfield was 'especially antagonistic toward the defenders of revelational religious experience,' including 'the perfectionism of the "Higher Life" and Keswick movements. Yet, he shared with the fundamentalists a commitment to supernatural faith even though he questioned their methods.'[90] Noll goes on to observe that Warfield's prolific defence of biblical infallibility made him 'an important guide for conservative evangelicals in the twentieth century, even for those who do not share his Calvinism (he nevered wavered in rejecting the pretensions of 'free will'), his eschatology (he regarded premillennialism and dispensationalism as aberrations), or his views on science (he believed evolution could be reconciled with the inerrancy of early Genesis).'[91]

J. Gresham Machen was also suspicious of these theological trends. W. Stanford Reid recounts that 'when an attempt was made in the early days of the Presbyterian Church of America to change the Westminster Confession to allow more room for premillennialism, he opposed it.'[92] The opposition to the theological values of the revivalist and pietist tradition was not limited to Warfield.

However, the dispensationalist camp (as one expression of the broader millenarian movement) cooperated with the Princeton camp on the issue of biblical inerrancy and hermeneutics. On this issue, according to Sandeen, 'although the millenarians searched for a defender to match swords with the critics, they found none in their own ranks. But in the work of the theologians of Princeton Seminary inerrancy did find qualified defenders.'[93] For Christians feeling the spiritual intimidation of European theological influences that seemed determined to undermine the integrity of apostolic Christianity, the apologetic work of Benjamin B. Warfield and J. Gresham Machen provided dispensationalists, among other fundamentalist

---

[90] M.A. Noll, 'Warfield, Benjamin Breckinridge', in *EDT*, 1156. An example of Warfield's suspicion of both the piety and theological foundations of dispensationalism was his review of L.S. Chafer's book, *He That Is Spiritual* in *Princeton Theological Review* 17 (April 1919), 322–327. Keswick piety and dispensationalism were not identical, though the movements overlapped through conference speakers and shared an emphasis on a passive approach to sanctification. Warfield took aim at both Keswick spirituality and dispensationalism.

[91] Noll, 'Warfield, Benjamin Breckinridge', 1156.

[92] W.S. Reid, 'J. Gresham Machen', in D.F. Wells (ed.), *The Princeton Theology* (Grand Rapids: Baker, 1989), 103.

[93] Sandeen, 114.

Christians, a stabilizing sense of intellectual and spiritual power to undergird the credibility of their faith commitments. This informal alliance over the doctrine of Scripture became an intersection at which J.I. Packer would later find a receptive audience beyond the scope of his Reformed theology.

British evangelicalism was following a similar, though not identical trajectory in the early twentieth century. D.W. Bebbington observes,

> There was some reluctance to employ the term ['Fundamentalism'] in Britain, for it was felt to be alien, uncouth and pejorative. Yet some were prepared to wear the label. ... There was sympathy for the American Fundamentalist struggle and some exchange of personnel. It is therefore quite mistaken to hold (as it sometimes has been held) that Britain escaped a Fundamentalist controversy. Evangelicalism in Britain as well as in America suffered from fiercely contested debates in the 1920s.[94]
>
> Although the balance of contentious issues was rather different – evolution, for example, being more prominent in the United States – the occasions of controversy in themselves were identical.[95]

He also points out that an attitude of social passivism prevailed in British evangelical piety. 'The tendency to withdrawal was most marked among Evangelicals of a more conservative stamp. Anglicans of the Keswick School, by and large, needed little convincing that social reform lay beyond their province.'[96] Controversy within British evangelicalism was also keenly felt within the universities. This conflict is essential for understanding J.I. Packer's theological formation.

In the early 1890s plans were made for a national student Christian movement. In 1893 the first conference was held at Keswick and for several years thereafter. Previously independent, though cooperative and collegial, student groups at Cambridge and Oxford (CICCU and OICCU) began to work together. The Inter–Varsity Christian Union was the product, though the name was subsequently changed to the British College Christian Union (BCCU).[97] The BCCU was later called the Student Christian Movement (SCM).[98] Therein lay the future conflict.

The SCM became increasingly tolerant regarding its doctrinal stance and the doctrinal commitment required of its members. Those from the CICCU and OICCU protested, but according to Douglas Johnson, 'by 1910 it [the

---

[94] Bebbington, *Evangelicalism in Modern Britain*, 182.
[95] Ibid., 183.
[96] Ibid., 214.
[97] Johnson, 66–67.
[98] Ibid., 71.

SCM] had become sufficiently theologically comprehensive, by a change of its original policy basis, to be able to include most of the wide spectrum of theological traditions of the British churches, however far to the right or left these might be.'[99] The evangelical groups broke apart from SCM, though not without official resistance from the universities.

The Inter–Varsity Fellowship eventually emerged as the central organisation for CICCU, OICCU, and a rapidly expanding network of student Christian groups that eventually extended overseas. The IVF sought to maintain rigorous theological integrity through theological commitments that reflected its reaction against what its leadership perceived as dangerous laxity within the SCM. OICCU was never as strong as CICCU, twice merging back into the SCM then restarting in 1920 and 1928.[100]

The theological conflict between the IVF and the SCM widened as IVF insisted on an identity and membership marked by commitment to the deity of Jesus Christ, the authority of the Bible, the substitutionary nature of the atonement, and the spiritual lostness of all humanity.[101] Despite this intense interest in theological integrity, the IVF still retained an ethos that reflected its original emphasis on missions and its connection with the Keswick conferences. However, it was not theologically equipped for the apologetic battles in which it had become embroiled. D. Martyn Lloyd–Jones was to be a significant figure in addressing that need.[102]

When Lloyd–Jones was approached by Douglas Johnson about the possibility of speaking for the annual Inter–Varsity conference of 1935, he was initially suspicious of what he saw as an anthropocentric approach to evangelism and holiness by many English evangelicals. Iain H. Murray records, 'Some men prominent in the I.V.F., whom he had also met, confirmed his misgivings by their superficiality.'[103] Murray records that Lloyd–Jones accepted the invitation and afterward reflected that the conference was deficient in the overall seriousness, sensitivity to church history, and theological rigour that were so important to him.[104] Lloyd–Jones's involvement with the IVF continued and deepened, however.

---

[99] Ibid., 68.

[100] Ibid., 83–130.

[101] Barclay, *Whatever Happened to the Jesus Lane Lot?*, 78.

[102] I.H. Murray, *David Martyn Lloyd–Jones: The Fight of Faith 1939–1981*, II.227. Murray records, 'In the early 1950's ML–J was giving much time to the strengthening of doctrinal commitment with the IVF.'

[103] I.H. Murray, *David Martyn Lloyd–Jones: The First Forty Years 1899–1939*, vol. I (Edinburgh: Banner of Truth, 1982), 295.

[104] Ibid., 297–298.

Johnson recounts that he 'was elected President for the three opening years of the War [WWII].'[105]

Lloyd–Jones left an indelible imprint on the theological character of the IVF. This was, in turn, to mark the theology of J.I. Packer when he participated in the IVF at OICCU. Lloyd–Jones was an avid proponent of the Reformed, Princeton theology. He discovered the works of Benjamin B. Warfield first in a review in *The British Weekly*, but later came across them unintentionally when he visited the library at Knox Seminary during a 1932 stay in Toronto. Murray recounts Lloyd–Jones's 1952 review of Warfield as '"undoubtedly the greatest theologian of the past seventy years in the English–speaking world."'[106]

According to Murray, it was Lloyd–Jones's discovery that Douglas Johnson had already 'commenced to read Charles Hodge and B.B. Warfield' that helped soften him to the invitation to speak at the IVF conference.[107] Thereafter, even during his holidays, Lloyd–Jones's favourite reading consisted of Warfield, Charles Hodge, and J.C. Ryle.[108]

Lloyd–Jones represented and encouraged the IVF's desire to protect and foster doctrinal conservatism among British evangelicals. Though Keswick views on piety remained intact through the 1950s,[109] Lloyd–Jones sought from the 1940s on to instil the Reformed theology of the Puritans and the Princeton theologians into the institutional mindset of the IVF.

A more complete understanding of the evangelical theological agenda that constitutes the backdrop for J.I. Packer must take into account two significant intellectual features: the influence of scholasticism and the relationship between Scottish Common Sense philosophy and the Princeton theology.

2.1.3 Intellectual Features

2.1.3.1 SCHOLASTICISM

The earliest Protestant theologians may have departed from Roman Catholicism at significant junctures, but medieval Roman Catholicism left an imprint on Protestant theology through its theological method known as *scholasticism*. Henry H. Knight considers scholasticism to have provided

---

[105] Johnson, 200.

[106] Murray, I, 285, footnote 1, 'Review of Biblical and Theological Studies, B.B. Warfield, *The Inter–Varsity Magazine*, Summer, 1952, pp. 27–28.'

[107] Ibid., 296.

[108] Murray, II.53.

[109] Barclay, *Whatever Happened to the Jesus Lane Lot?*, 54–55. More will be said later about the influence of Packer's attack on Keswick piety through his 1955 review of S. Barabas's book *So Great Salvation*.

the means by which the religious conflict was continued intellectually after the Thirty Years War.[110] R.J. VanderMolen portrays the nature and effects of Protestant scholasticism as,

> a method of thinking developed in early Protestantism, which grew stronger in the seventeenth century and became a widely accepted way to create systematic Protestant theologies. Even though the major Protestant Reformers attacked the theology of the medieval schoolmen and demanded total reliance on Scripture, it was impossible either to purge all scholastic methods and attitudes derived from classical authors or to avoid conflicts that required intricate theological reasoning as well as biblical interpretation.
>
> Several factors account for the growth of Protestant scholasticism: formal education, confidence in reason, and religious controversy. Reliance on logical methods derived from Greek and Roman authors was not purged from sixteenth century educational institutions. Aristotle, for example, upon whom the medieval scholastics had relied, continued to be taught by Protestants: Melancthon at Wittenberg, Peter Martyr Vermigli at Oxford, Jerome Zanchi at Strassburg, Conrad Gesner at Zurich, Theodore Beza at Geneva. Though these teachers did not accept Thomas Aquinas's medieval scholastic theology, which also relied heavily on Aristotle's logic and philosophy, they did teach Aristotle's deductive logic and gave reason an important place in theology. … The dominant Reformed scholastics … were Beza, Vermigli, Adrianus Herebout, and, most importantly, Francis Turretin (1623–87). Turretin's *Institutio* became the standard work for modern Protestant scholastics, as it was used as a textbook to shape the modern Princeton Theology. Reformed scholasticism in this tradition led to what is generally labeled Calvinist orthodoxy.[111]

VanderMolen goes on to point out that 'there is strong evidence of Protestant scholasticism in the Canons of Dort, the Westminster Confession, and the Helvetic Confession of 1675.'[112] Thus, this intellectual trend within the Protestant Reformation extended its influence into and through these documents that have figured significantly into the ethos of the Reformed wing of modern evangelicalism.

---

[110] Knight, 23.

[111] R.J. VanderMolen, 'Scholasticism, Protestant', in *EDT*, 984–985.

[112] Ibid., 985.

2.1.3.2 COMMON SENSE REALISM AND THE PRINCETON THEOLOGY

The 'common sense' philosophy popularised in Scotland by Thomas Reid (1710–1796)[113] became an important intellectual resource for evangelical Christians. It provided a methodology that restored hope in the perspicuity of the Bible's message and the reasonableness of faith in its message. Reid contended that David Hume's philosophy posited a false disjunction between objects that are known and the ideas by which knowledge of them resides in the mind.[114] He further argued that ideas or perceptions of objects are perceptions of the objects themselves, not merely a mediating presence of the objects. Reid attempted to eliminate the grounds for scepticism of sense perceptions by arguing that human sense, or 'common sense,' is in fact innately capable of perceiving reality because the capability of perception corresponds to the reality that may be perceived.[115]

Reid's 'common sense' philosophy enjoyed a considerable length and breadth of influence, both inside and outside philosophical circles. S.A. Grave describes the phenomenon.

> The school of common sense, which derived from Reid, acquired with Dugald Stewart the stability of an institution. … Its influence spread far beyond philosophers to permeate Scottish intellectual life for several generations. During the first half of the nineteenth century it had a similar influence in America. In both countries it did more than supply a set of opinions; it established a way of thinking. Reid's ideas were introduced into France early in the nineteenth century by Pierre–Paul Royer–Collard;

---

[113] F. Copleston, *A History of Philosophy*, vol. IV, *Descartes to Leibniz* (Paramus, N.J.: Newman, 1958), 37–38.

[114] T. Reid, *An Inquiry into the Human Mind: On the Principles of Common Sense* (University Park, Pa.: Pennsylvania State University Press, 1997), 34. Reid claims that 'the triumph of ideas was completed by the Treatise of human nature, which discards spirits also, and leaves ideas and impressions as the sole existences in the universe.' He goes on to turn Hume's argument back on him by stating, 'It seemed very natural to think, that the Treatise of human nature required an author, and a very ingenious one too; but now we learn, that it is only a set of ideas which came together, and arranged themselves by certain associations and attractions' (35).

[115] S.A. Grave, 'Reid, Thomas', in P. Edwards (ed.), *The Encyclopedia of Philosophy*, vol. 7 (New York: Macmillan, 1967), 119–121. See also Reid, 261. Reid states, 'This Connexion which Nature hath established betwixt our Sensations and the conception and belief of external Objects, I express two ways: Either by saying that the Sensations suggest the objects by a natural principle of the Mind; or by saying that the Sensations are natural Signs of the Objects. These Expressions signify one and the same thing, and I do not pretend by them to account for this Connexion, but onely to affirm it as a fact that by the constitution of our nature there is such a Connexion.'

they were taken up by Victor Cousin and were used as weapons against the ascendancy of an extreme and doctrinaire empiricism. Reid was carefully studied in Italy and Belgium.[116]

D.W. Bebbington sees the emergence of Common Sense Realism as the next step of evangelicals in adopting and utilizing a product of Enlightenment philosophy as their foundational theological method.[117]
George M. Marsden describes how the philosophy of Common Sense Realism functioned in Princeton theology.

> They [the Old School Presbyterians who shaped the theological culture of Princeton Theological Seminary] tended to view truth in its purest form as precisely stated propositions. This applied not only to the [Westminster] *Confession*, but also to the infallible Scriptures that the *Confession* summarized. In either case truth was a stable entity, not historically relative, best expressed in written language that, at least potentially, would convey one message in all times and places. ...
>
> This view of things was particularly compatible with the Scottish Common Sense philosophy. No doubt it was not coincidental that this philosophy developed in Scotland where Presbyterianism was strong.[118] ...
>
> Here [referring to Archibald Alexander's appeal to the power of 'simple common sense' in understanding Scripture] and in other Common Sense statements we find the affirmation that basic truths are much the same for all persons in all times and places. This assumption is crucial to an understanding of the view of Christianity at Princeton and in fundamentalism generally.[119]

Common Sense Realism provided concurrently a basis for pragmatism and for rationalism in the practice of Christian faith. By concentrating on the power of pure inductive reasoning to achieve absolute truth and verify truth claims, it helped establish within evangelical culture a priority on the empirical verifiability of religious truth claims. This emphasis also served to present ultimate, religious truth as accessible to the common person. The ability to understand the rational infrastructure of the Christian faith was no longer seen as the exclusive domain of trained theologians. God's revealed truth and its practical implications could be discerned with confidence and precision in the lives of all reasonable, sincere seekers.

---

[116] Ibid., 121.
[117] Bebbington, *Evangelicalism in Modern Britain*, 59.
[118] Marsden, *Fundamentalism and American Culture*, 110.
[119] Ibid., 111.

Ironically, the evangelical by–products of Common Sense Realism – emphasis on the rational verification of truth and emphasis on simple, practical application of the Bible's message – were perpetuated through movements that, though originally related, would eventually veer away from each other in defining modern evangelicalism. The more rationalistic aspect grew through Scottish and Scots–Irish Presbyterianism to flourish in the United States as what came to be known as 'Old Side' Presbyterianism. The more pragmatic aspect of this Enlightenment era philosophy was expressed earlier in history in the revival movements led by figures such as John Wesley.

Mark A. Noll observes that the rationalistic strain was continued as Common Sense Realism became deeply imbedded in the assumptions and methods of the Princeton Theology. He states, 'The theologians at Princeton were among the American intellectuals who most consistently used the language and the categories of this philosophy even when, as later observers would contend, its tenets seemed to contradict Princeton commitments to Scripture and Reformed tradition.'[120]

The transmission of Common Sense Realism into Princeton Theology follows a clear line of tutelage. Noll records that 'it was brought to America from Scotland in its fullest form by the Rev. John Witherspoon, who became president of Princeton College in 1768 where he taught the teachers of the Princeton Theology.'[121] Witherspoon's student, William Graham, taught A.A. Alexander. Ashbel Green taught Charles Hodge and later, as president of Princeton College 'restored Witherspoon's text in *Moral Philosophy* to the position it had held when he was an undergraduate – as the culminating and integrating study of the undergraduate curriculum.'[122] Charles Hodge taught it to his son, A.A. Hodge. B.B. Warfield was instructed by James McCosh, 'the last great defender of the Scottish Philosophy who became president of Princeton College in 1868 as Warfield was beginning his undergraduate career.'[123]

These Princeton stalwarts made thoroughgoing application of this philosophy in their work. John Vander Stelt shows, for instance, how Charles Hodge developed a theology that 'is fundamentally determined by two all–pervasive and mutually dependent principles, namely, the method

---

[120] M.A. Noll, 'Introduction', in *The Princeton Theology, 1812–1921: Scripture, Science, and Theological Method from Archibald Alexander to Benjamin Breckinridge Warfield*, 30.

[121] Ibid., 31.

[122] Ibid., 32.

[123] Ibid. The entire lineage, as well as the citation, comes from Noll.

of scientific induction and the premise of biblical inspiration.'[124] Benjamin B. Warfield used Common Sense Realism to develop a supposedly airtight apologetic approach for 'the self–evidence of revelation, the objectivity of Christian dogma, and the infallibility of Scripture.'[125] Noll is careful to point out, however, that the Princeton theologians strove to remain faithful to Scripture and the Reformed tradition even when aspects did not fit perfectly with 'the mechanical categories of Common Sense. Among these elements is the Princeton stress on religious experience.'[126] Those experiential elements were emphasised even more, however, by others in evangelicalism's history.

Regarding the more pragmatic effects of Common Sense Realism, Bebbington claims that Wesley may not have made conscious use of Reid's philosophy, but still embraced the empiricist epistemology of the Enlightenment, especially its emphasis on rationality, in his approach to Scripture and the Christian life. However, Bebbington also sees Wesley as a leader in expressing the pragmatic dimensions of Enlightenment thought. Wesley's doctrine of assurance, for example, was grounded in the witness of the Spirit and a person's ability to discern that witness.[127] Bebbington goes on to argue that the empiricist orientation of revivalists accounted for the value they placed on experience as a catalytic factor in the experimentation process. They saw experience as essential to the advance of knowledge. Theological systems were viewed as dealing with abstract, metaphysical concepts that had little bearing on real life.[128] Bebbington also places Charles Simeon in the line of evangelicals who reflected Enlightenment pragmatism, as evidenced by his highly functional approach to church buildings.[129]

In the United States a divide grew between the rationalistic and the pragmatic emphases of Common Sense Realism. Thus the evangelical

---

[124] J.C. Vander Stelt, *Philosophy and Scripture: A Study in Old Princeton and Westminster Theology* (Marlton, N.J.: Mack, 1978), 123.

[125] Ibid., 182.

[126] Noll, *The Princeton Theology, 1812–1921*, 33.

[127] Bebbington, *Evangelicalism in Modern Britain*, 50, 54. See J. Wesley, Sermon 10 in A.C. Outler (ed.), *The Works of John Wesley*, Bicentennial Edition, vol. I (Nashville, Abingdon, 1984), 272. In discussing the witness of the Spirit to discern the 'marks' of being a child of God, Wesley says, 'Yet all this is no other than rational evidence: the "witness of our spirit", our reason or understanding. It all resolves into this: those who have these marks, they are the children of God. But we have these marks: therefore we are children of God.'

[128] Ibid., 57, 58.

[129] Ibid., 65.

tension between intellectual rigor and intense piety was perpetuated. George M. Marsden describes this division.

> The symbol of Presbyterian distinctiveness and unity was thus not a social–political program ... but doctrinal orthodoxy. Strict confessionalism was a major trait of the largest party of Scotch–Irish and Scottish Presbyters from their first appearance in the colonies. Presbyterianism in America, however, was from the outset fed by some other streams, not of Scottish but of English origin. English Presbyterianism itself had become tolerant of doctrinal diversity by the early eighteenth–century.[130]

This growing doctrinal tolerance eventually accounted for a widening chasm between confessionalists and revivalists, as represented in the 1741 split between 'New Side' and 'Old Side' Presbyterians and then the 'Old School/New School schism of 1837–38.'[131]

This division was the seedbed for the distinctive theological traditions that overlap to constitute the context for J.I. Packer's theological influence in the United States. The Reformed tradition of Puritan, Princetonian Calvinism continues 'Old School' or Princetonian confessionalism. A more amalgamated evangelicalism deriving from pietism and revivalism (found, for example in dispensationalism) carries on the 'New School' thought that emerged from New England Congregationalism while retaining a vestige of Calvinistic theology. These 'schools' model an ongoing tension within American evangelicalism; one side placing priority on the rational understanding of Scripture and the other side placing priority on the experience of redemption in Christian life. Packer's theological profile is well suited to speak into the convergence of these emphases with his use of both the Puritans and the Princetonians.

In Britain a similar tension was experienced in the latter half of the nineteenth century. Bebbington notes, '[T]he bulk of Evangelicals at mid–century retained their confidence in the Enlightenment appeal to evidences, scientific method and an orderly universe governed by cause and effect.'[132] He goes on to claim that English Congregationalism was internally disrupted during this period by a 'blurring of the edges of doctrine,'[133] adding that 'something of the incisiveness of Evangelical theology had been lost' as a result of humanitarian movements within the

---

[130] Marsden, 'Introduction: Reformed and American', 4.
[131] Ibid., 4–5.
[132] Bebbington, *Evangelicalism in Modern Britain*, 143.
[133] Ibid., 144.

Congregationalist church.[134] Thus the stage was set in both Britain and the United States for a form of pietism that was to make an indelible imprint on evangelicalism in both countries.

In the United States this tension between rationalism and pragmatism took place without the context of a national church and its sociological implications for religion. Hence, rather than seek to reconcile or even to cooperate with those who disagree, it was much easier for American evangelicals to divide and form new movements along these ideological lines.

On the British scene, however, the presence of the Anglican Church loomed over this tension, not always defining it but always at least casting its shadow. Though the conflict within British evangelicalism differed in some particulars from the conflict going on in American evangelicalism, it was nevertheless another version of the same tension between a predominantly rationalistic or a predominantly experiential approach to the Christian life.

2.2 American Evangelicalism as a Context for J.I. Packer

Contemporary American evangelicalism derives significant aspects of its character from the intellectual alliance of millenarianism (particularly dispensationalism) and Princeton theology against their common enemy, 'modernism,' in the late nineteenth and early twentieth centuries. British evangelicalism has contributed directly to this scenario. Professors at Princeton Theological Seminary (before J. Gresham Machen left to found Westminster Theological Seminary in 1929) contributed by becoming a mouthpiece for fundamentalism in this joint defence effort. This gave a decidedly apologetic thrust to the American evangelical ethos. To a lesser but not insignificant extent, both millenarianism and the Princeton school share Calvinistic roots.

Hodge, Warfield, and Machen were the most notable theological leaders of the Princeton school of thought in the nineteenth and early twentieth centuries. Hodge helped perpetuate the Calvinism of the Westminster Assembly in his *Systematic Theology*. Warfield placed the scientific assumptions and methodology of the Enlightenment at the core of Christian apologetics and epistemology, especially regarding the authority of the Bible. His book *The Inspiration and Authority of the Bible* served for decades as a stalwart defence of biblical inerrancy. Machen provided institutional leadership through the founding of Westminster Theological Seminary. He also responded to the terms of engagement set by modernism

---

[134] Ibid., 145.

in his book *Christianity and Liberalism* wherein he argued that Christian faith is necessarily grounded in the historical factuality of Jesus' birth, life, death and resurrection.

Since the founding of Westminster Theological Seminary in 1929 evangelicalism in America has evolved into different forms that still draw on the work and ethos of this theological tradition and its champions. The Reformed theological views of the Princeton/Westminster school have perhaps had less direct, ongoing influence on American evangelicalism than have the rationalistic assumptions and methods used by those theologians in the development of their Reformed theology. This intellectual feature of American evangelicalism as it moved into the 1940's offered a measure of intellectual continuity in the midst of denominational diversity and fragmentation. George Marsden observes that

> in the 1930's most of the few serious scholars who remained in fundamentalism had some connection with Machen. These inspired a new generation of fundamentalist intellectuals who began to emerge by the early 1940's. … Many of these scholars were associated with the National Association of Evangelicals (NAE), an agency founded in 1942, primarily to foster intrafundamentalist unity, to promote evangelism, and to try to regain a hearing in American life.[135]

Marsden also argues that 'twentieth–century American evangelicalism has had more unity than its denominational diversity might suggest. This degree of unity grows not only out of a common basic profession but also out of a considerable common heritage and experience.'[136] The rationalism of Princeton/Westminster theology survived as one of the unifying elements that helped American evangelicalism spread its influence despite various denominational and theological departures from Reformed theology. Yet, because this methodological basis provided intellectual credibility for a cross–section of American evangelicals, it can be seen as a significant reason that a theologian such as J.I. Packer has had a hearing in American

---

[135] G.M. Marsden, *Understanding Fundamentalism and Evangelicalism* (Grand Rapids: Eerdmans, 1991), 149. It is noteworthy that the NAE statement of faith does not involvement a commitment to Reformed theology, nor does it reflect a uniquely Reformed theological perspective. It is still widely used among evangelicals as a means of defining minimally acceptable theological commitment when working interdenominationally. For example, Denver Seminary, a well–known American evangelical school, accepts students from a wide spectrum of denominations and theological perspectives, requiring only that they subscribe to the NAE statement of faith.

[136] Ibid., 65.

evangelical circles other than those who fully identify with Reformed theology.

The influence of the Princeton/Westminster school of thought spread through Machen to Harold Ockenga and through Ockenga to Billy Graham.[137] Graham's rise to public notoriety placed him at the forefront of the evangelical desire for cultural influence. Though his public ministry was largely evangelistic, his vision launched the publication of *Christianity Today* under the editorship of Carl F.H. Henry, who acquired increasing recognition and influence as an evangelical intellectual. Henry, though not known as a Reformed theologian, nonetheless continued the rationalistic methodology of the Princeton/Westminster theologians and helped make it central to the ethos of a major segment of American evangelicalism. Henry gave full development to his own rationalistic epistemology and views of revelation in his seven–volume, *God, Revelation, and Authority*.[138] His theological work is more inclined toward philosophical apologetics than is Packer's work. Yet, Henry is perhaps the closest parallel to Packer as a theological leader within American evangelicalism.

This 'new evangelicalism' in the United States was poised for fresh intellectual leadership. Anderson comments, 'They looked across the great divide which fundamentalism had created between the mainline churches with their theological institutions and the independent churches and Bible colleges and determined to establish continuity with what they considered to be the roots of evangelical theology in the magisterial orthodoxy of the Reformers.'[139]

'New evangelicalism' wished to move away from the separatist mindset of fundamentalism while preserving its theological distinctives. Those theological distinctives needed deeper roots, however. The theological scene was ripe for Packer and his theology.

Summary

J.I. Packer has emerged from the theological context of British evangelicalism and served in the context of both British and American evangelicalism. This evangelicalism has its roots in the Protestant Reformation and was given some of its most distinguishable theological contours at the hands of English Puritanism through the Westminster

---

[137] Ibid., 183.

[138] C.F.H. Henry, *God, Revelation, and Authority*, six vols. (Waco, Tex.: Word, 1976-1983). Henry's rationalistic epistemology has been explored and analyzed by K.N. Jones, *Revelation and Reason in the Theology of Carl F. H. Henry, James I. Packer, and Ronald H. Nash*.

[139] Anderson, 'Evangelical Theology', 483.

Confession. It has been shaped by revivalism, pietism, rationalism, and controversy on both sides of the Atlantic. Though the British and American versions of this evangelicalism exhibit distinctive historical and theological nuances, their points of circumstantial interweaving and mutual influence have nurtured a unique evangelical environment in the United States. Since the early 1940s this environment has provided fertile soil in which J.I. Packer could sow his theological seed. The theological genesis and genetics of that seed will now be examined more closely.

Chapter 3

J.I. Packer's
Personal and Theological Development

Packer's personal spiritual journey and his theological development are intertwined. The incidents included in this account are those most relevant to understanding his theological anthropology, theological method, and theology of piety.[1] As much as possible, a chronological approach is taken. Some of the more formative events and relationships deserve extended treatment and are thus isolated anachronistically within the narrative.

3.1 The Early Years

Born 22 July 1926 in Gloucestershire, England, Packer was raised in the home of Anglican parents who regularly attended St. Catherine's parish church. At seven years of age he was chased out from the school grounds onto a busy street and was subsequently hit by a van, sustaining a serious fracture to the right–front side of his skull. While he was already becoming a lover of books and other intellectually stimulating pursuits, his accident prompted his parents toward extreme caution regarding his childhood activities. On his eleventh birthday, when many children received a bicycle, Packer's parents instead gave him a typewriter. This gift spurred the young Packer on toward his career as a writer.[2]

He was confirmed in the Anglican Church at age fourteen, though he was not a frequent attendee at Sunday school.[3] Among the earliest and most notable religious presences in his life was a young Anglican curate at St. Catherine's, Mark Green, who gave him personal preparation for confirmation. Brian Bone, a friend from school, sought unsuccessfully to sway Packer toward Unitarianism. C. S. Lewis, though not known by Packer on a personal level, made an imprint through his book *The*

---

[1]   A more complete account of his life is found in McGrath's biography.
[2]   McGrath, *To Know and Serve God*, 1–6.
[3]   Ibid., 7.

Screwtape Letters, which was introduced to Packer by one of his sixth–form English masters.[4]

Packer's wholehearted embrace of Christian faith resulted from a convergence of influences. Anglican upbringing and confirmation acquainted him with the formal structure of historic, Western, orthodox Christianity. Readings in Sigmund Freud, Carl Jung and Fyodor Dostoevsky moved him, though in different ways, to reflect more seriously on the possibility of an objective reality underlying the Christian faith.

3.2 Christian Conversion and Theological Formation

3.2.1 The Oxford Inter–Collegiate Christian Union

In Packer's final year before leaving to study at Oxford, his friend Eric Taylor began writing to him regarding his need for a personal faith in Jesus Christ, a faith that went beyond the level of formal belief. Taylor encouraged him to contact the Oxford Inter–Collegiate Christian Union (OICCU). Once he was in Oxford, Packer was approached by Ralph Hulme, the OICCU representative to Corpus Christi College. Through OICCU he attended a Sunday evening evangelistic service at St Aldate's Church on 22 October 1944 where he heard Earl Langston preach. At the end of the service he responded to Langston's invitation to make a personal commitment to Jesus Christ. His conversion took place in the same church where one of his heroes–to–be, the eminent Calvinist evangelist George Whitefield had made the same commitment in 1735.[5]

Ralph Hulme's influence continued in Packer's life as they worshipped together at St Aldate's Church, though Packer experienced both mixed sentiments about the quality of preaching in that congregation and a temporary resentment against the Church of England for what he perceived as its lack of emphasis on the type of personal faith he had embraced.[6] The OICCU was a significant source of spiritual formation for Packer during his university days. Ironically, during his time as an Oxford student the Keswick ethos of the OICCU was a magnet that at first attracted, then later repelled him.

Alister McGrath chronicles the popularity of the Keswick movement in the OICCU of the mid–1940's and its effect on the young James Packer.[7]

---

[4] Ibid., 8–9.
[5] Ibid., 10–18. The events and influences involved in Packer's conversion have been condensed from McGrath's detailed narrative.
[6] Ibid., 29.
[7] Ibid., 22–24.

The Keswick emphasis seemed to promise that, through total surrender of oneself to God, one could be rather immunised against the emotional turbulence and exhaustion of inner struggle against personal sin. A greater sense of intimacy with Jesus was offered as the fruit of this spiritual experience. Packer longed for this deliverance from his own struggles with sinful tendencies, yet grew in frustration at his apparent inability to attain victory.

3.2.2 Puritanism

While serving as junior librarian for the OICCU in 1946, Packer stumbled across several uncut volumes of writings by the Puritan, John Owen.[8] Captivated by the titles of addresses such as 'On Indwelling Sin in Believers' and 'On the Mortification of Sin in Believers,' Packer began to read Owen and found encouragement in Owen's portrayal of the Christian life. Though Owen treats the Christian experience as a life–long battle against indwelling sin, Packer found that, ironically, Owen's realism offered relief from the pressure attaining a (Keswick) spirituality that allegedly provided an easier path.[9] This introduction to Owen, according to Will Metzger, 'began a lifelong love affair with the Puritans.'[10]

Puritan theology began to shape Packer's thinking in other areas as well. As early as 1945 he developed an interest in the evangelist Charles G. Finney.[11] He found the Puritan approach to evangelism to be in stark contrast to Finney's approach. The Puritan's approach, Packer summarises, took seriously the Scripture's claims that we are 'dead' in our sins and that no individual can respond to God in saving faith until the Spirit of God sovereignly generates that faith.[12] This premise was later to become the heart of Packer's writings on evangelism.

---

[8] J.I. Packer, Vancouver, British Columbia, to D.J. Payne, Denver, Colorado, (17 July 2000).

[9] McGrath, *To Know and Serve God*, 25.

[10] Will Metzger, 'J.I. Packer: Surprised by Grace', in J. Woodbridge (ed.), *More Than Conquerors* (Chicago: Moody, 1992), 318. See also J.M. Houston, 'Knowing God: The Transmission of Reformed Theology', in *Doing Theology for the People of God*, 223. Houston comments in regard to the influence of the Puritans on Packer, 'Through them [the Puritans, especially Owen and Baxter] and their predecessor John Calvin, he saw the central objective of theology to be pastoral. In his many books, Dr. Packer has communicated consistently the same pastoral concern for the theological education of all the people of God. So this Puritan transmission continues.'

[11] Packer letter to the author, (17 July 2000).

[12] J.I. Packer, 'Puritan Evangelism', *The Banner of Truth* 1 (February 1957), 4–13.

Puritanism provided for Packer an early and relatively comprehensive paradigm for Christian faith and experience. He defends and defines Puritanism as follows.

> Puritanism ... was a total view of Christianity, Bible–based, church–centred, God–honouring, literate, orthodox, pastoral, and Reformational, that saw personal, domestic, professional, political, churchly, and economic existence as aspects of a single whole, and that called on everybody to order every department and every relationship of their life according to the Word of God, so that all would be sanctified and become 'holiness to the Lord.' Puritanism's spearhead activity was pastoral evangelism and nurture through preaching, catechizing, and counselling (which Puritans themselves called casuistry), and Puritan teaching harped constantly on the themes of self–knowledge, self–humbling, and repentance; faith in, and love for, Jesus Christ the Saviour, the necessity of regeneration, and of sanctification (holy living, by God's power) as proof of it; the need for conscientious conformity to all God's law, and for a disciplined use of the means of grace; and the blessedness of the assurance and joy from the Holy Spirit that all faithful believers under ordinary circumstances may know.[13]

Packer identifies three general contributions the Puritans have made to his life. These contributions illustrate how extensively they have impacted his thinking and, in particular, how theology and piety have interwoven for him as a result.

> [T]he Puritans have taught me to see and feel the transitoriness of this life, to think of it, with all its richness, as essentially the gymnasium and dressing–room where we are prepared for heaven, and to regard readiness to die as the first step in learning to live. ...
>
> The Puritans shaped my churchly identity, by imparting to me their vision of the wholeness of the work of God that they called reformation, and that we would more likely nowadays call renewal. ...
>
> The Puritans made me aware that all theology is also spirituality, in the sense that it has an influence, good or bad, positive or negative, on its recipients' relationship or lack of relationship to God. ...[14]

He notes, 'I for one ... owe more to Puritan writing than to any other theology I have ever read.'[15] Of all the Puritans, however, two stand out as his primary sources of influence, John Owen and Richard Baxter.

---

[13] J.I. Packer, 'Richard Baxter: A Man for All Ministries', in *Shorter Writings*, 4.24–25.

[14] Packer, *Among God's Giants*, 14–16.

3.2.2.1 JOHN OWEN

Packer considers John Owen (1616–1683) as the premier Puritan theologian. Owen's soteriology, especially his development of the doctrine of limited or particular atonement, has deeply marked Packer's theological system. He provided a lengthy, laudatory introduction to a modern edition of Owen's *The Death of Death in the Death of Christ*.[16] In his introduction to Owen's *Sin and Temptation* Packer identifies some key features of Owen's theological anthropology that will later be seen in his own anthropology. These features are, first, the priority of rationality as a characteristic of the image of God and, second, the role of understanding, will and affection as faculties whereby the image of God is a lived reality.[17] This priority on rationality is developed in both Owen and Packer as the necessary channel through which the Scriptures communicate the message of redemption.

Owen's soteriology has influenced Packer's approach to piety as well as anthropology. It has reinforced in Packer an Augustinian orientation to piety due to its emphasis on the ongoing power of indwelling sin in the life of the Christian and its emphasis on the need for radical dependence on God's grace. Packer reflects,

> At something of a crisis time soon after my conversion, John Owen helped me to be realistic (that is, neither myopic or despairing) about my continuing sinfulness and the discipline of self–suspicion and mortification to which, with all Christians, I am called. ... Suffice it to say that without Owen I might well have gone off my head or got bogged down in mystical fanaticism, and certainly my view of the Christian life would not be what it is today. ... Some years after that, Owen, under God, enabled me to see how consistent and unambiguous is the biblical witness to the sovereignty and particularity of Christ's redeeming love.[18]

The impact of Owen's work on Packer's theology, interestingly, began at and proceeded from an experiential starting point. The initial source of validation for Owen's thought was the way in which it addressed Packer's

---

[15] J.I. Packer, 'Why We Need the Puritans', in L. Ryken (ed.), *Worldly Saints: The Puritans as TheyReally Were* (Grand Rapids: Zondervan, 1986), xvi.

[16] J.I. Packer, Introduction to *The Death of Death in the Death of Christ*, by J. Owen (Carlisle, Pa.: Banner of Truth, 1959), 1–25. See also J.I. Packer, Introduction to *Sin and Temptation: The Challenge to Personal Godliness*, by J. Owen, J.M. Houston (ed.) (Portland: Multnomah, 1983), xxv.

[17] Packer, Introduction to *Sin and Temptation*, xix–xx.

[18] Packer, *Among God's Giants*, 12.

personal struggle of faith. This is ironic in light of the rationalistic nature of Packer's theological method, as will be seen later.

In his introduction to *Sin and Temptation*, Packer writes, 'I still think … that Owen did more than anyone else to make me as much of a moral, spiritual, and theological realist as I have so far become. He showed me that there is far more than I had known both to indwelling sin in believers and to God's gracious work of sanctification.'[19] Owen's theological foundations and their implications for piety converge powerfully for Packer, demonstrating Owen's dominance in Packer's Puritan heritage. He reflects, 'If our concern is with practical Christian living today, a Puritan model of godliness will most quickly expose the reason why our current spirituality is so shallow, namely the shallowness of our views of sin. And there is no question that among all the Puritan models, Owen's goes deepest at this point, and can make us realistic about sin most speedily.'[20]

Thus, the importance of Packer's encounter with Owen can hardly be overestimated. It was for him an entrance into the world of the Puritans who, along with their theological benefactors and descendants, became one of his primary theological points of reference during those formative years at Oxford.[21]

3.2.2.2 RICHARD BAXTER

Richard Baxter (1615–1691) is the other English Puritan whose work has most captured Packer's attention. Baxter's primary contribution to Packer is through his rigorous, pastoral approach to the Christian life. Packer's interest in Baxter was theological as well as pastoral. He went so far as to make Baxter's soteriology the subject of his Oxford DPhil thesis.[22]

In his DPhil thesis Packer finds much to commend in Baxter's thought, though he critiques Baxter's belief that redemption constitutes 'the ground for an offer of salvation to the world, on condition of faith.'[23] Baxter rejects

---

[19] Packer, Introduction to *Sin and Temptation*, xxix.

[20] Ibid., xxiv.

[21] M.A. Noll, 'The Last Puritan', *CT*, (16 September 1996), 51. Noll goes so far as to make the Puritans a critical link in the development of Packer's work. 'The link between Packer the scholar and the Packer the young Christian was his fascination with the Puritans. The Puritans provided for him a subject for doctoral studies, a model for Christian life, and (many years later) the subject matter for one of his most important books, A Quest for Godliness: The Puritan Vision for the Christian Life (1990).'

[22] J.I. Packer, 'The Redemption and Restoration of Man in the Thought of Richard Baxter.' DPhil thesis (University of Oxford, 1954).

[23] Ibid., 269.

the doctrine of limited atonement, understanding personal faith to be a result of election rather than of redemption.[24]

Packer finds that Baxter differs somewhat from the view of Moise Amyraut, however, by accepting a more Arminian view of Christ's atonement and, thereby, avoiding the inconsistencies involved in accepting 'a Calvinist view of the nature of the atonement with an Arminian view of its scope.'[25] According to Packer, Baxter 'denied that Christ's death was a case of penal substitution, affirming that its whole effect was to procure a new law of grace for the world, and insisted that faith is imputed for what under the new law it is – "evangelical righteousness" – and so is the proper ground of justification.'[26] Packer, therefore, differentiates Baxter from Amyraut, claiming,

> It is less than just to speak of him as one of Amyraldus' camp–followers. He was not. It was his 'political method' [which he adopted from Grotius, p. 457–458], his determination to make God's rectoral relationship regulative in his dogmatic construction, which led him independently to this view. ... As regards to the details of his system, Baxter stood alone.[27]

Still, Packer places himself in Baxter's lineage by identifying Baxter as a 'Puritan, practising and propagating the religion of St. Augustine on the basis of the theology of John Calvin.'[28]

Packer summarizes Baxter's influence on his approach to Christian spirituality and pastoral ministry as follows.

> Richard Baxter convinced me long ago that regular discursive meditation, in which as he quaintly put it you 'imitate the most powerful preacher you ever heard' in applying spiritual truth to yourself, as well as turning that truth into praise, is a vital discipline for spiritual health. ... Baxter also

---

[24] Ibid., 252, 263. See also Packer's introduction to Owen's *Sin and Temptation*, xxv. He recounts here that he became convinced that Bible teaches a 'particularistic' atonement when he read Owen's *The Death of Death in the Death of Christ* in 1953. His DPhil thesis on Baxter was completed in 1954. In the thesis he takes issue with Baxter on this point, suggesting that his own thinking was in transition during the writing of the thesis.

[25] Ibid., 460–461.

[26] Ibid., 459.

[27] Ibid., 462.

[28] J.I. Packer, 'Richard Baxter: A Man for All Ministries', 23. Packer goes on to comment, 'I do not think Baxter was always right, but I see him, as did the memorialists of 1875, as one of the most impressive of Christian thinkers, and there is just as much reason to honour him as such today as there was at that time' (26).

focused my vision of the ordained minister's pastoral office. ... From student days I have known that I was called to be a pastor according to Baxter's specifications.[29]

Despite strong disagreement on a soteriological point that Packer takes quite seriously (limited atonement), he has allied himself with Baxter's approach to piety (which encompasses his pastoral approach to theology). As with his use of Owen, this alliance with Baxter suggests that piety is an essential component of theology for Packer. Despite Packer's formal theological disagreements with aspects of Baxter's theology, he admires Baxter's willingness to selectively challenge conventional thought for the sake of his ministry convictions. Packer states, 'If Puritan theology is second–generation Calvinism, Baxter's theology is second–generation Puritanism. Baxter valued his heritage, but not blindly.'[30]

In Packer's treatment of Roman Catholicism (particularly in the late 1990s), he has modelled the irenic but discriminating manner to which he draws attention in Baxter. Packer notes, after quoting Baxter's admission that some Roman Catholics possessed genuine faith, 'Such honest Christian charity as these passages reflect seems unique in Puritanism.'[31]

Packer's work and writings leave no doubt that he has developed a deep appreciation for a wide range of Puritans and their writings.[32] Yet, he claims that he has read nothing in any other Puritan that is not in Owen or Baxter.[33]

3.2.3 John Charles Ryle

John Charles Ryle (1816–1900), Bishop of Liverpool, served as voice of confirmation for the Puritan theology that was moving Packer away from Keswick piety. Packer commented to Christopher Catherwood that 'in reading Bishop Ryle's book [*Holiness: Its Nature, Hindrances, Difficulties, and Roots*] ... he discovered that Ryle based much of his teaching on the Puritans.'[34] Packer refers to Ryle's book as a key influence in his thought,

---

[29] Packer, *Among God's Giants*, 13–14.

[30] Packer, 'The Redemption and Restoration of Man in the Thought of Richard Baxter', 35.

[31] Ibid., 90.

[32] Packer published fourteen papers related to the Puritan Studies conferences, eleven of which are directly related to Puritan thought. His first published article was 'The Puritan Treatment of Justification by Faith', *EvQ*, 24, no.3. See also Murray, II, 226. Packer joined with Raymond Johnston in requesting D. Martyn Lloyd–Jones's help to begin the Puritan and Reformed Studies Conference in 1950.

[33] J.I. Packer, interview by author, (2 July 1999). Vancouver: Regent College.

[34] Catherwood, *Five Evangelical Leaders*, 168.

claiming that it 'brings a great deal of Owen up to date.'[35] McGrath sees Ryle as having strengthened a theological bridge between the Puritans and Packer, i.e. Packer's understanding of the nature of sin in the Christian experience. Ryle criticised what he saw as the perfectionistic piety of his day,[36] claiming that 'a right knowledge of sin lies at the root of all saving Christianity'[37] and inherently precludes any expectation of living 'for years in unbroken and uninterrupted communion with God ...'[38] Ryle's Anglicanism also had implications for Packer. Catherwood notes regarding Ryle's overall contribution,

> Packer noticed that in the writings of Bishop Ryle, the two strands, Protestant and pietist – *had* interwoven. Ryle's books influenced him enormously and provided him with an Anglican evangelical framework of doctrine, pastoral care, and evangelism upon which to base his own thinking to the present. Because Ryle and the Puritans were Calvinists, Packer also inclined that way.[39]

Packer has clearly followed in Ryle's path in his combination of Calvinism within the Church of England.[40]

3.2.4 David Martyn Lloyd–Jones

In 1948 Packer received an invitation to teach Latin and Greek at Oak Hill College in London. McGrath observes that this year between his departure from Corpus Christi College, Oxford and his entrance to Wycliffe Hall provided several influential factors for his future. First, he established friendships with colleagues such as Alan Cole and Alan Stibbs, individuals who recognised his teaching ability and encouraged him in that direction. Second, students affirmed his teaching ability. Third, he was afforded the opportunity to sit under the preaching ministry of D. Martyn Lloyd–Jones at Westminster Chapel.[41]

Lloyd–Jones's affinity for the Puritans captured the hearts of Packer and his friend, Raymond Johnston. In 1949 Packer and Johnston approached

---

[35] J.I. Packer, 'Interview with J.I. Packer', *Discipleship Journal* (July 1982), 42.

[36] McGrath, *To Know and Serve God*, 77.

[37] J.C. Ryle, *Holiness: Its Nature, Hindrances, Difficulties, and Roots*, 1877; reprint of 1st ed. in *Faithfulness and Holiness: The Witness of J. C. Ryle*, by J.I. Packer (Wheaton: Crossway, 2002), 105.

[38] Ibid., 116.

[39] Catherwood, 170.

[40] W.H. Griffith–Thomas was another noteworthy figure in Anglican Calvinism. See Clifford, 81.

[41] McGrath, *To Know and Serve God*, 34–39.

him, proposing that he help them initiate a series of conferences on Puritan studies as part of the Tyndale Fellowship for Biblical Research. Lloyd–Jones responded enthusiastically.[42] This annual conference helped promote a growing interest in the Puritans among evangelicals and forged a close friendship and working relationship between Packer and Lloyd–Jones; a relationship that was to last until 1966.[43] While their personal relationship did not endure Packer's refusal to leave the Church of England when Lloyd–Jones called for evangelicals to do so, Lloyd–Jones's influence on Packer and his work has been active and evident ever since.

D. Martyn Lloyd–Jones's indelible imprint on Packer shows through when Packer calls Lloyd–Jones 'the greatest man I ever knew.'[44] Their joint passion for the Puritans and for reinvigorating British evangelicalism with Puritan ideas were but symptoms of the deeper theological bonds they shared. The Puritans were a powerful spiritual force in Lloyd–Jones's early Christian experience. Iain Murray recounts, 'Clearly in Baxter and the Puritans Dr Lloyd–Jones found an echo of something which he already knew in his own spirit. His own deepening sense of sin was a key to the interpretation of their "soberness and restraint."'[45] More specifically, Murray observes, Lloyd–Jones was heavily influenced by Richard Baxter and John Owen. 'In the course of time, Owen was to be preferred; but he always valued Baxter's *Christian* Directory.'[46] This not only explains Lloyd–Jones's enthusiastic support for the Puritan Studies Conference; it constitutes an interesting parallel to Packer's own preference for Baxter and Owen among the Puritans. Murray suggests that their relationship grew closer around 1953 when Packer read John Owen and informed Lloyd–Jones that he had become convinced of the doctrine of limited atonement, which prior to that time had been the only significant doctrinal difference between them.[47]

Lloyd–Jones and Packer were not without their theological differences. Tony Sargent notes that Lloyd–Jones was well known for 'his emphasis on the baptism of the Holy Spirit as an experience distinct from salvation.'[48] Lloyd–Jones believed, according to Packer, that the seal of the Spirit, the

---

[42] Ibid., 49–52.

[43] Ibid., 154–156.

[44] Packer, interview, (2 July 1999). Packer makes an almost identical comment in print. See J.I. Packer, 'David Martyn Lloyd–Jones', in *Shorter Writings*, 4.77.

[45] Murray, vol. I, 100.

[46] Ibid., 156.

[47] Murray, vol. II, 231.

[48] T. Sargent, *The Sacred Anointing: The Preaching of Dr. Martyn Lloyd–Jones* (Wheaton: Crossway, 1994), 41.

witness of the Spirit, and the baptism of the Spirit are all the same, providing a post–conversion experience of assurance.[49]

Sargent attributes Lloyd–Jones's preoccupation with the ministry of the Holy Spirit to two factors. First, the historical coincidence of his ministry with the rise of the Charismatic and Pentecostal movements combined powerfully with his keen interest in revival. 'His concerns caused him always to listen sympathetically, though objectively, to reports of anything which might savour of a genuine outpouring of the Holy Spirit.'[50] Second, his explorations into historical theology uncovered powerful experiences of the Holy Spirit in the lives of noteworthy figures such as Thomas Aquinas and Blaise Pascal. This historical search was generated by his own experience of the Spirit's ministry in the Welsh Calvinistic Methodist Church.[51] Packer attributes Lloyd–Jones's belief to the influence of the Puritan Thomas Goodwin.[52] Though Packer disagrees with Lloyd–Jones on the nature of the baptism of the Spirit,[53] the two seem to have converged around the Puritans on the importance of experiential theology. Lloyd–Jones embodied Puritan theology in his personal faith and his ministry. Packer identifies four Puritan characteristics in Lloyd–Jones's theology.

> First, his concept of theology as a rational, practical study corresponded perfectly to William Perkins' definition of it as 'the science of living blessedly for ever' and his view of the Bible as the source of theology … and of the system of thought that the Bible yields, was in entire accord with that classic of Puritan theology, the Westminster Confession. Second, his practice of preaching was altogether Puritan in its philosophy, method, and substance, even though it was entirely 20th century in its style and verbal form. … Third, the Doctor conceived Christian experience in Puritan terms. His understanding hinged on two principles: first, the primacy of the mind in man, as guide to his will and judge of his feelings; second, the indirectness of the work of the Holy Spirit, who teaches and moves us by first making us actively learn and then rousing us to move ourselves. … Finally, the Puritans, with Christians of every age till this century viewed dying well as the crown upon a godly life. Dr Lloyd–Jones often stressed in his preaching the need to be ready for death, and he told a colleague towards the close of his life that he saw it

---

[49] Packer, interview, (2 July 1999).
[50] Sargent, 41.
[51] Ibid., 43.
[52] Packer, interview, (2 July 1999).
[53] Ibid. See J.I. Packer, *Keep in Step with the Spirit* (Old Tappan, N.J.: Revell, 1984), 91. Packer contends that the baptism of the Spirit happens to all believers at the time of conversion.

as the final work of his ministry to make a good end. Thus he maintained
the Puritan view of things to the last.[54]

These same traits will be seen as salient features of Packer's theology as
well. It seems, then, that Lloyd–Jones had at least a confirming influence on
Packer's continued allegiance to the Puritans.

Benjamin B. Warfield constituted another point of theological
convergence for Lloyd–Jones and Packer. Murray attributes to Warfield the
strengthening of Lloyd–Jones's commitment to doctrine in his preaching.[55]
Ironically, Packer claims that Lloyd–Jones contributed nothing substantive
to his own theology, but that what he gained most from Lloyd–Jones was in
the area of preaching.[56] He claims, 'Nearly forty years on, it still seems to
me that all I have ever known about preaching was given me in the winter
of 1948–49, when I worshipped at Westminster Chapel with some
regularity.'[57] He cites three lessons he learned from Lloyd–Jones. First, the
business of the preacher is to let the Bible talk through him. Second, in the
act of preaching the preacher needs to be in such a spiritual condition that
he mediates God in the way he says what he says. Third, the preacher must
preach as one who is under the authority and power of his message.[58]
Lloyd–Jones's influence on Packer through his philosophy of preaching
bears Warfield's imprint.

---

[54] J.I. Packer, 'A Kind of Puritan', in *Shorter Writings*, 4.72–75.

[55] Murray, vol. II, 286–287. Murray states, 'We have already noted the usefulness of
such writers as James Denney and P.T. Forsyth to Dr Lloyd–Jones, yet, partly
because of the deficiency in their doctrine of Scripture and also because of weakness
in other areas of doctrine, the impression which they made upon him was neither so
profound nor so influential as that which he now received from Warfield. To
Warfield more than to anyone else he was to attribute a development in his thought
and ministry which occurred at this period. Hitherto Dr Lloyd–Jones' reputation was
built very largely on his evangelistic preaching. Intellectual though he was by
aptitude and training prior to this date, he showed no great interest in distinctly
doctrinal teaching or in the defence of the Faith against modern error. ... Warfield
gave him new insight into the necessity for doctrinal teaching. While not ceasing to
be an evangelist, he was now brought to the strong conviction that more was
required.'

[56] Packer, interview, (2 July 1999). See also Packer, 'David Martyn Lloyd–Jones' in A.
Spangler and C. Turner (eds.), *Heroes* (Ann Arbor: Servant, 1985), 77. Packer states
here, 'I am sure that there is more of him under my skin than there is of any other of
my human teachers. I do not mean that I ever thought of myself as his pupil, nor did
he ever see himself as my instructor; what I gained from him came by spiritual
osmosis, if the work of the Holy Spirit can be so described.'

[57] Packer, 'David Martyn Lloyd–Jones', 84.

[58] Packer, interview, (2 July 1999).

The influence that Lloyd–Jones had on Packer appears to extend beyond preaching, however. Packer calls Lloyd–Jones a 'brilliant diagnostician both spiritually and theologically.'[59] Lloyd–Jones brought with him into his pastoral ministry the mindset and methodology of his prior medical training. Packer finds in Lloyd–Jones an uncanny ability to discern the roots of spiritual malaise and prescribe a path toward healing; a casuistic method that Packer admires in many of the Puritans. Lloyd–Jones was not only a preaching mentor for Packer; he served Packer as a contemporary model of the Puritan theological method in the practice of ministry. Furthermore, Packer's embrace of the Puritan emphasis on 'experimental' or pastoral theology in his own theological work appears to have been reinforced by his relationship with Lloyd–Jones. It may also be argued that Lloyd–Jones strengthened Packer's vision and resolve for the Reformed tradition at a time when Reformed theology was decidedly a minority voice within British evangelicalism.

3.2.5 Princeton Theology

The formation of Packer's theology and piety was a process involving multiple influences: the Puritans, J.C. Ryle, D. Martyn Lloyd–Jones and the theologians of the old Princeton Theological Seminary. He states that by 1947 he was aware of Benjamin B. Warfield (1851–1921) and had been encouraged to read him. In unpublished correspondence Packer writes, 'There were some volumes of Warfield … including the two on perfectionism, in the OICCU library, and … the late Douglas Johnson[60] was exhorting all who had any aptitude for theology to read Warfield, and that his name was bandied around in the circle of IVF's Theological Students Fellowship and Tyndale Fellowship.'[61]

Charles H. Hodge (1797–1878) was professor of systematic theology at Princeton Theological Seminary. Hodges's three–volume *Systematic Theology* is, in Packer's judgment, one of the best modern systematisations of Calvinistic theology. In a personal interview with the author Packer

---

[59] Packer, 'A Kind of Puritan', 65.

[60] Douglas Johnson served as General Secretary of the IVF from 1924 (when it was still the Inter–Varsity Conference until 1928) until 1964. Though originally trained as a medical student, he provided leadership to the IVF in the theological struggles with the SCM and in procuring the involvement of D. Martyn Lloyd–Jones (see chapter II). See also Bebbington, *Evangelicalism in Modern Britain*, 259. Bebbington suggests that Johnson helped provide a link between the IVF and Princeton Theology, stating that Johnson 'was particularly devoted to the weighty Reformed theologians of America.'

[61] Packer letter to the author, (17 July 2000). See also, Barclay, *Whatever Happened to the Jesus Lane Lot?* 100,163.

mentioned that Hodge, along with Warfield and Louis Berkhof were recommended to him as the last and the best of evangelical theologians, though he feels that Hodge and Warfield were better exegetes than Berkhof.[62]

Though hesitant about some of the philosophical foundations upon which Hodge and Warfield built their theological systems, Packer admits to following their lead. He feels that these Princetonians were limited by the thinking of the people they were attempting to influence, especially scientifically and methodologically. Specifically, Packer expresses reservations about the way these theologians put their theology forward in the manner of Francis Bacon's scientific method, i.e. to put a question to the Bible, collect the facts, and then build a synthesis. Packer contends that this approach is limited because, first, it neglects the importance of a doctrine of Christian experience. Second, it assumes that a theologian could collect all the relevant facts before drawing a decision. Therefore, Packer feels that the Princetonian's apologetic concerns drove their methodology and yielded results that, while good, were incomplete.[63] As Packer's theological method is considered, it will be shown that he sends mixed messages about the value of this 'Baconian' theological method.

Despite his reservations, the Princetonians have wielded powerful influence over Packer's theological method and positions. He credits Warfield with being of most help to him in the area of apologetics.[64] It was on Warfield's philosophical foundation that he based his first major work *'Fundamentalism' and the Word of God.*[65] McGrath summarises the influence of the Puritans and Princetonians in Packer's theological development up to the time of this major publication.

> Taken together with his earlier writings on Puritanism (particularly its teaching on sanctification), the book [*'Fundamentalism' and the Word of God*] allows us to gain an insight into the type of theology which Packer was forging. At the risk of simplification, Packer's thought at this stage can be seen as a synthesis of aspects of Reformed thought from both the

---

[62] Packer, interview, (2 July 1999).

[63] Ibid.

[64] Ibid.

[65] McGrath, *To Know and Serve God*, 84,85. McGrath comments that in this book 'Packer provide[d] a clear and accessible statement of what is generally known as the "Old Princeton" or "Hodge–Warfield" position on the inspiration and authority of Scripture.' He goes on to say, 'The book can be seen as a distillation of the approaches to biblical authority and inspiration at Princeton Theological Seminary, New Jersey, during the nineteenth century, and particularly through the writings of Charles Hodge (1797–1878) and Benjamin B. Warfield (1851–1921).'

Old and the New World. English Puritanism (as found in John Owen and Richard Baxter) and the Old Princeton theology (as found in Charles Hodge and Benjamin B. Warfield) were brought together in Packer's vision of an academically rigorous yet pastorally relevant theology.[66]

The Princetonians, then, offered Packer a model of Reformed theology that expressed Calvinistic, Puritan foundations in terms more appropriate to the intellectual battles raging in evangelicalism during his own time.

During the time of Packer's early theological development the struggle continued between the IVF and the SCM. The practise and results of biblical higher criticism figured prominently into the controversy. In 1958 the SCM sponsored a debate over biblical authority, inviting Packer and Christopher Evans (dean of Corpus Christi College, Oxford) as participants.[67] This debate occurred the same year that Packer's book *'Fundamentalism' and the Word of God* was published. In the book he contends that higher criticism places human reason and subjectivity above the authority of Scripture and assumes that the text is filled with errors and contradictions due to its human character. Packer took this premise to be incompatible with submission to Scripture as the Word of God. He asserts, 'These "assured results of modern criticism" are simply popular hypotheses built on the inadmissible assumption that there may be untrue statements in Scripture.'[68]

Packer's colleague John Wenham attended the debate and many years later recounts, 'After Evans had spoken there was a time of questions at which Jim's response was ineffective. Unfortunately, he had never been subjected at an academic level to current critical teaching on the Bible and he didn't think it very important. The best answer to it, he considered, was a good grasp of reformed dogmatics along the lines of John Owen.'[69]

Packer's suspicion of biblical higher criticism wraps the process and the results into a single issue with a tight logical connection between them. The

---

[66] Ibid., 88–89.

[67] Ibid., 87–88.

[68] J.I. Packer, *'Fundamentalism' and the Word of God: Some Evangelical Principles* (London: Inter–Varsity, 1958), 141. See also Bebbington, *Evangelicalism in Modern Britain*, 260. Bebbington records F.F. Bruce's comment [in *Christian Graduate*, (March 1948), 16] that 'there is nothing in the pursuit of source–criticism in the Biblical field which is necessarily incompatible with the outlook of the I.V.F.' Bruce, as a New Testament scholar and participant in the IVF, illustrates a range of possible perspectives on this issue, depending on the assumptions operative within one's discipline.

[69] J. Wenham, *Facing Hell: The Story of a Nobody* (Carlisle: Paternoster, 1998), 138.

'human' dimensions of the text are of little or no relevance to the divinely intended function of the text. He contends,

> A century of criticism has certainly thrown some light on the human side of the Bible – its style, language, composition, history and culture; but whether it has brought the Church a better understanding of its divine message than Evangelicals of two, three and four hundred years ago possessed is more than doubtful. It is not at all clear that we today comprehend the plan of salvation, the doctrines of sin, election, atonement, justification, new birth and sanctification, the life of faith, the duties of churchmanship and the meaning of Church history, more clearly than did the Reformers, or the Puritans, or the leaders of the eighteenth–century revival. When it is claimed that modern criticism has greatly advanced our understanding of the Bible, the reply must be that it depends upon what is meant by the Bible; criticism has thrown much light on the human features of Scripture, but it has not greatly furthered our knowledge of the Word of God.[70]

Thus, Packer appears to see little hope for progress in dogma apart from progress in mastering Reformed teaching in the tradition of the Puritans. The Puritan, Reformed approach to Scripture he takes to be the epitome of 'biblical theology.' He comments, 'We welcome too the announced programme of the 'Biblical Theology' movement. If its sponsors carried it through, there would indeed be no controversy between Liberals and Evangelicals, for the former would be found on the evangelical side.'[71]

Yet, his reaction against Gabriel Hebert's advocacy of the Biblical Theology movement indicates that he equates Hebert's type of biblical theology with destructive higher criticism.[72] In 1964, however, he affirms Biblical Theology as Sir Edwyn Hoskyns practised it. Hoskins work, to Packer, supported the unity and coherence of Scripture. He describes the general state of British theology in the early twentieth century by stating, 'Hoskyns' work began a new era in British theology. For a generation now British biblical and theological study has proceeded on his principles, and seems likely to continue to do so. ... Here, as elsewhere, the British theologian holds that the most coherent view is the one most likely to be true.'[73] Apparently, then, he takes Hebert's approach to Biblical Theology to be something of an aberration.

---

[70] Packer, *'Fundamentalism' and the Word of God*, 112–113.
[71] Ibid., 152.
[72] Ibid., 142.
[73] Packer, 'British Theology in the First Half of the Twentieth Century', *Shorter Writings*, 4.325.

Seven years later in *God Has Spoken* he continues his attack on the suppositions of higher criticism, but appears to have softened his opinion about some aspects of its value.

> The situation is as paradoxical as it is pathetic, for critical scholarship has always claimed that its microscopic historical analysis of the books of Scripture gives the Church the Bible in a way in which the Church never had the Bible before, and in one sense this is perfectly true. Critical scholarship has sharpened the tools of biblical exposition and clarified the meaning of many biblical passages. It has given us commentaries of the highest value. It has invented a technique of analysing Scripture thematically without which the theological dictionaries and biblical theologies of the past sixty years could never have been written.[74]

Still, Packer approaches Scripture as one whose theology of Scripture precedes and determines his interaction with Scripture. The Puritans and the Princetonians (especially Warfield) clearly contributed to this settled approach.

3.2.6 Formal Education

The formation of Packer's theological outlook included formal education at Oxford as well as extra–curricular study. He received the BA in *Literae Humaniores* ('Classical Moderations') from Oxford (Corpus Christi) in 1948.[75] Returning to Oxford in 1949 after a year of teaching at Oak Hill College, he enrolled at Wycliffe Hall for theological study.[76] McGrath records, 'During the period 1935–70, Wycliffe Hall was widely regarded as a liberal Protestant college, with little genuine evangelical commitment.'[77] It is notable, though, that Packer's affinity for the Puritans was well–formed before he came to study at Wycliffe.[78] His commitment to Puritanism shaped his encounter with his formal study of theology.

Two individuals appear to have been of particular influence in shaping Packer's theological mind. Under Jim Hickinbotham's tutelage in the field

---

[74] J.I. Packer, *God Has Spoken: Revelation and the Bible* (London: Hodder and Stoughton, 1964), 12–13.

[75] McGrath, *To Know and Serve God*, 26–28.

[76] Ibid., 34–40.

[77] Ibid., 40.

[78] Ibid., 43. McGrath notes that Packer met John Gwyn–Thomas at his first meal at Wycliffe, immediately after which they had a stirring conversation about John Owen's view of mortification. He states, 'The conversation confirmed Packer's view of the realism of the Puritan world–view, and his growing determination to develop and apply it further.'

of patristics he moved from a general disregard to an appreciation for the Fathers of the Church.[79] F.W.L. MacCarthy–Willis–Bund of Balliol College supervised Packer in the discipline of analytical philosophy. He found Packer both interested and competent in the field. McGrath comments that 'MacCarthy was especially interested in classical and modern Thomism, which was on the verge of a revival at this stage ...'[80] Packer has since made significant use of Thomistic thought in his theology, as will be seen later. He received the BA in theology in 1950 and the MA/DPhil in 1954.[81]

3.3 Contributions

3.3.1 The Anglican Church

While Packer has consistently been a minority theological voice within the Church of England, he has exemplified its desire for unity. His relationship to the Anglican Church illustrates the value he places on both the unity of the church and on theological faithfulness. His willingness to hold these often polarised commitments in tension has been the source of two significant dilemmas he has faced. Both controversies were formative in his ministry.

The first dilemma resulted from his extensive involvement in the political and theological affairs of the Church of England in the 1950s and 1960s. Packer repeatedly sought to give voice to the basic tenets of Reformed, orthodox theology in his writing and speaking endeavours. His participation as a minority, evangelical voice in the process of considering the union of the Anglican and Methodist churches reinforced his identity as one committed to both his church and his theology. All along the way, however, he was championing his evangelical perspectives to the Anglican Church through his writing and speaking.[82]

---

[79]   Ibid., 44. McGrath states that 'At this stage, Packer tended to think of early Christian writers such as Augustine as at best "beginners" – enthusiastic but not particularly competent or helpful – and at worst enemies, in that their teaching and ministry led to the emergence of the Catholic Church.' He goes on to observe, 'One of the changes that Packer noticed taking place during his long career is his growing respect for these writers; he would now tend to think of them as "wise men", whose wisdom should be heeded.'

[80]   Ibid.

[81]   J.I. Packer, Personal Curriculum Vitae (15 February 1995) to D.J. Payne.

[82]   Examples of these writings are 'Episcopal Idol: A Consideration of *Honest to God*', T*he Evangelical Christian* (October 1963), 32–35; 'A Broad Church Reformation?' *London Quarterly and Holborn Review* (October 1964), 270–275; 'Wanted: A

In the 1960's and 1970's he became a key participant in the proposed Anglican–Methodist union commission as the lone, conservative, evangelical. John Wenham recounts the significance of the chairman's determination that Packer must be satisfied with any agreements and that Packer did most of the drafting of the commission's conclusions.[83] Though working from a decidedly minority theological perspective, Packer's theological reservations about the proposed union are reflected in the documents and factored into the demise of the proposal.[84] His concern that the historic message of the gospel remain the material centre for church unity can be observed in the amount of attention he has devoted to the nature of the gospel throughout his career. However, until the early 1970s his writings dealt with theological issues more from the perspective of their ecclesiastical context and implications than has been the case since his move to North America.

Not only did his presence as a conservative put him at odds with a majority of the leadership of the Anglican Church, but his strongly Reformed theology placed him in a unique role even within the British evangelical world. According to John Wenham 'he had made a name for himself not only by his '*Fundamentalism*' book, but also by his association with Martyn Lloyd–Jones in the promotion of Puritan and Reformed

---

Pattern for Union', in J.I. Packer (ed.), *All in Each Place: Towards Reunion in England* (Appleford: Marcham Manor, 1965), 17–40; 'The Status of the Articles', in H.E.W. Turner (ed.), *The Thirty–Nine Articles of the Church of England* (Oxford: Mowbray, 1964), 25–57; and *The Gospel in the Prayer Book* (Abingdon: Marcham, 1966). Later writings of the same purpose include *A Kind of Noah's Ark?*; *The Anglican Commitment to Inclusiveness*; and *The Evangelical Anglican Identity Problem: An Analysis*, Latimer Studies no. 1 (Oxford: Latimer House, 1978).

83 Wenham, 174.

84 Packer's hesitations are well captured in the following comment. 'The viewpoint [advocating a Anglican–Methodist union that downplayed the significance of theological differences] ... seems to them to forget the calling of the church of Christ to be "the pillar and bulwark of the truth" (I Tim. 3:15, R.S.V.) – that is, as the context shows, custodian of the revealed truth of the gospel. It forgets that the church's given unity, the unity which it already has in Christ, is unity *in this truth*, so that union schemes designed to make this unity visible must of necessity be based squarely upon this truth. It forgets that the church lives, not merely by love, and mutual forbearance, and generous recognition of the grace of God in others, but also, and indeed primarily, by obedience to the gospel of Christ. For the church stands under the gospel and is judged by the gospel, and if its public actions, confessional, liturgical, and disciplinary, are not unambiguously loyal to the gospel, it is actually unfaithful to its Lord. So the decisive question to ask about the Anglican–Methodist scheme is not whether it is generous enough in spirit, but whether it is evangelical enough in content.' 'Wanted: A Pattern for Union', 19.

studies.' Wenham continues, 'Both he [Lloyd–Jones] and Packer thought that a revival of Puritan theology and pastoral practice was the key to true renewal in the church.'[85]

Packer's reinvigorated emphasis on Puritan, Reformed theology evoked mixed reactions. Despite all those who followed their lead, the broader scope of evangelicals within the Anglican Church were not at all falling into line behind Packer and Lloyd–Jones. Gerald Bray reflects, 'In attempting to bring an Anglican neo–Puritanism into being, Dr Packer was heading for trouble ... This is basically because modern Anglican Evangelicalism is thoroughly "Arminian" in character, and is deeply marked by an amateurish do–it–yourself outlook which is its true uniting characteristic.'[86] Roger Beckwith confirmed that Packer's Calvinism is only one strand of the current evangelical movement in the Anglican Church, in which the 'rank and file' tend to think in more Arminian terms.[87] However, Beckwith suggests that Anglicanism, with its concern for unity and inclusiveness, accounts for the fact that Packer is more gracious to Arminians than many Calvinists tend to be.[88]

The second dilemma was his polarisation with D. Martyn Lloyd–Jones over whether evangelical Christians should withdraw from the Anglican Church as it became more accepting of theological viewpoints that many evangelicals found unacceptable. In 1966 Lloyd–Jones urged evangelicals to leave the Anglican Church, following the view that the church must be pure, i.e. composed only of those who could offer evidence of spiritual regeneration. Packer followed the lead of George Whitefield, Charles Simeon and J.C. Ryle in choosing to stay within the Anglican Church for the sake of facilitating reform.[89] Lloyd–Jones found this choice intolerable. It caused a rift between himself and Packer that resulted in a total cessation of contact for the rest of Lloyd–Jones's life. McGrath claims, 'To understand Packer, it is necessary to appreciate the tensions which intensified within English evangelicalism from this time onwards.'[90] His choice to remain within such an inclusive ecclesiastical body as a Reformed evangelical grows from his desire to identify and affirm common theological ground with theological adversaries while holding faithfully to his own theological priorities.[91]

---

[85] Wenham, 173.
[86] Bray, 360.
[87] R. Beckwith, interview by D.J. Payne, (12 January 1999).
[88] Ibid.
[89] McGrath, *To Know and Serve God*, 127.
[90] Ibid., 126.
[91] Examples of this attempt to balance faithfulness to evangelical theology with intradenominational and interdenominational understanding can be found in a

3.3.2 Regent College

Alister McGrath identifies at least six factors that discouraged Packer in England and precipitated his move: first, the devaluing of his Reformed, Puritan theological perspectives among younger Anglicans; second, his loss of credibility among free church evangelicals resulting from Lloyd–Jones' decision to ostracize him; third, his suspicion of the theological risk involved in the growing interest in hermeneutics; fourth, a burgeoning charismatic movement that brought with it a renewed version of the passive holiness he had worked so diligently so overturn through an emphasis on Puritan piety; fifth, the precarious standing of Trinity College, Bristol (where he taught) within the ranks of the Church of England, and; sixth, a strong desire to keep his theological work anchored in the life and worship of the church.[92] Regent College in Vancouver, British Columbia afforded Packer the opportunity to express his Puritan emphasis on experiential theology by its priority on theological education for the laity.[93]

Summary

It is curious that a British Anglican would gain such a hearing among American evangelicals. Packer's background has worked to his advantage in this regard. Roger Beckwith opined that because the Puritans were very practical in their theology, Packer has likewise been very concerned with theology that can be lived. Like the Puritans he has not restricted the aim of his theological to the academic realm. Beckwith went on to suggest that this may explain why Packer has never written a *magnum* opus but has focused the bulk of his writing for more popular audiences.[94]

Not only have Packer's style and priorities fit with the experiential, pragmatic ethos of American evangelicalism. The history of American evangelicalism, particularly the strains deriving from the Princeton and revivalist traditions, has also provided an intellectual context in which

---

number of Packer's more recent writings, such as 'Anglicanism Today: The Path To Renewal', in G. Egerton (ed.), *Anglican Essentials*(Toronto: Anglican Book Centre, 1995), 53–63 and 'Crosscurrents among Evangelicals', in C. Colson and R. neuhaus (eds.), *Evangelicals and Catholics Together: Toward A Common Mission* (London: Hodder and Stoughton, 1996), 147–174. The latter document is but one example of his participation in Catholic–Evangelical dialogue. Most notable and controversial has been his signing of the 'Evangelicals and Catholics Together' (ECT) document. His subsequent apologetic response to the controversy is also noteworthy; 'Why I Signed It', *CT*, (12 December 1994), 34–37.

92 McGrath, *To Know and Serve God*, 217–219,221.
93 Ibid., 226.
94 Beckwith, interview, (12 January 1999).

Packer's theological methods and priorities could gain a hearing. Mark Noll asserts, 'Packer has exerted that influence [on American evangelicalism] by combining characteristics that have rarely been joined together in America. In a word, he is an *educated, Reformed, Anglican evangelical,* with each of the four ascriptions vital as a counterweight to the other three.'[95] This unique combination has allowed Packer credibility with a cross–section of American evangelicals who may themselves be characterised by as few as one of these traits.

It may also seem unusual that a theologian associated with the Church of England would have such sway with American evangelicals when the Episcopal Church, U.S.A. has demonstrated increasing theological diversity, much to the disapproval of evangelicals both within and outside that communion. Packer's utilisation of Princetonian Reformed theology and public support for biblical inerrancy appear to have given him credibility with a broader American evangelical audience and provided him with a hearing on a wider range of theological issues. Additionally, it may have overridden suspicions that might be related to his Anglicanism.

Furthermore, his work in North America has not been as preoccupied with denominational and ecclesiastical issues as was his work prior to his migration to Canada. Noll notes in this regard, 'Packer's identification as an Anglican on the other side of the water has not loomed large in his North American career, where assistance to the Anglican Church of Canadian [sic] and the American Episcopal Church has not been nearly as visible as his contributions to transdenominational evangelicalism.'[96] Noll observes that Packer's influence in the United States has been of a somewhat more 'exegetical and theological' nature, whereas his influence in the United Kingdom leaned in a somewhat more 'historical and ecclesiastical' direction.[97]

Packer's biographer, Alister McGrath, observes, 'He is regularly cited by evangelical leaders and thinkers as one of the most important influences on their lives' and considers him to be 'one of the theological and spiritual giants of the twentieth century.'[98] The flood of accolades from prominent evangelical leaders derives from the support Packer has lent to theological causes close to the epicentre of evangelicalism's ethos, particularly in the United States. A recent American PhD thesis placed Packer alongside Carl F.H. Henry and Ronald H. Nash, arguing that a considerable degree of

---

[95] Noll, 'J.I. Packer and the Shaping of American Evangelicalism', 191.

[96] Ibid., 197.

[97] Ibid., 194. Noll substantiates this claim by reference to the numerous writings of each genre that were published in either the United Kingdom or the United States but not in the other.

[98] McGrath, *To Know and Serve God*, xi–xii.

methodological and epistemological similarity exists between their theologies. In this research K.N. Jones argues that 'Packer was England's post–World War II counterpart of Carl Henry in America, setting forth the nature and justification of an evangelical response to the philosophical watershed of the Enlightenment.'[99]

Packer has held consistently to the version of Reformed theology that he came to embrace in his early theological career. In a written response to the author's question about how his theology has changed over the years, he replied, 'My theology has no doubt broadened its base since 1947 but apart from getting clear on particular redemption in 1953 or 1954 [referencing in a marginal note his encounter with John Owen's *The Death of Death in the Death of Christ*] I don't think there has been any change in its structure, method or conclusions. Like Calvin, I was blessed in getting things basically right from the start.'[100]

The theological profile that has emerged is of one who is decidedly Augustinian[101] and Calvinistic.[102] In his Calvinism he is highly supportive of the interpretation given by the Westminster Confession and the pastoral/theological applications made by the English Puritans.[103] With each of these contributors he takes issue at various points. Those points of divergence will become obvious in the analysis of his theological anthropology, method, and piety.

---

[99] Jones, *Revelation and Reason in the Theology of Carl F. H. Henry, James I. Packer, and Ronald H. Nash*, 96.

[100] Packer, letter to author, (17 July 2000).

[101] J.I. Packer, 'The Christian and God's World', in *Shorter Writings*, 2.278. Packer says that 'surely he was right,' regarding Augustine's view of original sin. See also J.I. Packer, 'The "Wretched Man" Revisited: Another Look at Romans 7:14–25', in S.K. Soderlund and N.T. Wright (eds.), *Romans and the People of God: Essays in Honor of Gordon D. Fee on the Occasion of His 65th Birthday* (Grand Rapids: Eerdmans, 1999), 81. He refers to himself as 'a convinced and unrepentant Augustinian with regard to the 'wretched man [of Romans 7].'''

[102] J.I. Packer, 'Predestination and Sanctification', in *Shorter Writings*, 2.322. He states, 'I defend Calvinism as the purest version of Christian truth that the world has ever seen.'

[103] See J.I. Packer, 'Westminster and the Roller Coaster Ride', in *Shorter Writings*, 2.301.

Chapter 4

The Nature of Piety

J.I. Packer's approach to theology reflects his longstanding interest in piety. As shown in chapter three, Packer's personal experience of piety, first with Keswick and then with Puritan piety, preceded and influenced the further development of his theology. His theology of piety reflects the theological framework and emphases of Puritan Calvinism.

This and the following two chapters explore Packer's theology of piety by utilising his own terminology and organisational structure for the subject. The structure will be derived from his most comprehensive writing on piety, *A Passion for Holiness*, where he explains the nature of piety, the means of piety, and the experience of piety. Additional nuances and implications will be drawn from key features of his theology as found in his secondary works. Occasional reference will be made to aspects of his theological anthropology, but that subject will be more fully developed in chapter seven.

4.1 The Place of Piety in Packer's Thought

The subjects of piety, spirituality, and holiness (as defined in chapter one) reside at the heart of J.I. Packer's theological work, whatever the overt focus of his varied writings.[1] The influence of the seventeenth–century English Puritans is evident in this emphasis. He admits, 'It seems to me in retrospect that by virtue of this Puritan influence on me all my theological utterances from the start, on whatever theme, have really been spirituality (i.e., teaching for Christian living), and that I cannot now speak or write any other way.'[2] It will be seen that piety, for Packer, is related to the overarching subject of communion with God (another preoccupation that he attributes to the Puritans).[3] In his most well–known book, *Knowing God*, he posits a foundational connection between theology and piety by offering four descriptors of those who know God; they possess 'great energy for

---

[1] J.I. Packer, 'An Introduction to Systematic Spirituality', *Crux* 11 (March 1990), 2.

[2] Packer, *Among God's Giants*, 16.

[3] Ibid., 265–266.

God, great thoughts of God, great boldness for God, and great contentment in God.'[4] These traits resurface throughout his writings on piety.

4.1.1 Piety and Experience in Packer's Thought

Packer abandoned the Keswick expectation (as he interpreted it) that struggle with sin could be alleviated through passive reliance on the Holy Spirit. Instead, he experienced a liberating realism in his personal Christian experience when he embraced the expectation that the Holy Spirit empowers believers for obedience to Christ through vigorous engagement of the unavoidable, lifelong struggle with indwelling sin.[5] The Reformed piety he found in Owen and subsequently in other English Puritans affirmed his experience of spiritual struggle. Yet, in this new direction he found reassurance that his experience was neither abnormal nor an indicator of spiritual dereliction. Moreover, he found there other doctrines such as predestination that gave him hope and energy for the struggle.

Writing from a Reformed perspective, Howard Rice draws attention to the role of personality in the value that people assign to intellect or feelings in their spiritual experience.[6] Through the years, Packer has been highly critical of pieties that are overly preoccupied with the emotions,[7] even

---

[4]   J.I. Packer, *Knowing God* (London: Hodder and Stoughton, 1973), 23–27.

[5]   His theological reaction and response were first developed in '"Keswick" and the Reformed Doctrine of Sanctification'. As Packer developed his theological critique of the Keswick movement (at least as he understood it through the filter of his own experience and Steven Barabas's book, *So Great Salvation*) he contrasted the role and function of the Holy Spirit in Keswick and Reformed theology. 'Reformed theology teaches that the Spirit's sanctifying work is a hidden activity which manifests itself by its effects in consciousness and life' (160). 'When ... they [Keswick teachers] discuss how we may know God's will, they develop a mystical doctrine of personal communion with the Holy Ghost' (160). 'Keswick thus teaches that, instead of working through our conscious personal life, the Spirit stands over against it' (161). Packer's perspective on this point is consistent with that of the Westminster Confession (chapter xiii) on sanctification. 'In which war, although the remaining corruption for a time may much prevail, yet, *through the continual supply of strength from the sanctifying Spirit of Christ, the regenerate part doth overcome: and so the saints grow in grace, perfecting holiness in the fear of God*' [emphasis added]. Packer quotes this section of the Confession to introduce his essay, 'Sanctification – Puritan Teaching', in *The Christian Graduate* (December 1952), 125.

[6]   H.L. Rice, *Reformed Spirituality: An Introduction for Believers* (Louisville: Westminster/John Knox, 1991), 29.

[7]   Packer, *Keep in Step with the Spirit*, 172, 194. See also *A Passion for Holiness*, 168–169.

though he admits the significance of emotions in the Christian life.[8] Like Rice, he acknowledges the powerful influence of personality on piety.[9] However, nowhere in his writings does he acknowledge or attempt to interpret the influence of his own personality on his early experience of Keswick or Reformed piety. It would be worthwhile to consider how Packer's personality may have contributed to the formation of his theology of piety through the grid of those early encounters with Keswick and Reformed teachings. He recounts that in his early Christian experience, following Keswick teaching, he felt the need to repeatedly 'scrape my inside, figuratively speaking, to find things to yield to the Lord so as to make consecration complete.'[10] It is curious that he experienced such frustration with this form of introspective piety yet has become such a staunch advocate of Puritan piety which itself depends on rigorous introspection.

It may also be asked whether Packer did not, in practice, begin his critique of Keswick piety from an experiential starting point because it did not 'work' for him. The experiential origin of Packer's turn toward Puritan piety suggests an irony in his resistance to experience as a starting point for theological work. Indeed, experience appears to have been a significant starting point and criterion for his personal theological journey.

Packer's theology of piety must be seen in the light of his reaction to Keswick piety in his the earliest phase of his Christian experience. He has roundly criticized this viewpoint on the basis of Puritan Calvinism. Beginning with his 1955 review of Steven Barabas's overview of the Keswick movement he has been an outspoken critic of any piety in which he senses perfectionistic or passivistic tendencies.[11] At numerous points it

---

[8] Packer, *A Passion for Holiness*, 22–24.

[9] Ibid., 24–26.

[10] Packer, Introduction to *Sin and Temptation*, xxviii.

[11] As discussed in chapter two, the Keswick movement propagated a piety in which conscious struggle aimed directly against sin or at Christian maturity is seen as a rejection of God's grace for the Christian life and, consequently, ill–fated. The focus of Keswick piety is a direct reliance on the Holy Spirit to carry one through struggles with temptation and sin, with the promise that when every area of life has been completely surrendered to God, one can experience a regular sense of victory over those struggles. See Steven Barabas, *So Great Salvation: The History and Message of the Keswick Convention* (London: Marshall, Morgan and Scott, 1952). Packer's posits a similar criticism of Wesleyan piety, focusing primarily on what he deems unbiblical and unattainable promises of perfection in the present life due to a deficient view of both original and indwelling sin. Packer has expressed these views in, 'Augustinian and Wesleyan Views About Holiness' [audio cassette]. He attacks

will be asked whether Packer has accurately understood Keswick teaching, specifically, whether his criticisms of Keswick teaching (primarily as represented by Steven Barabas) may misrepresent Keswick intentions because he has interpreted them through the jadedness of his early experience with popular Keswick teaching.

4.1.2 Piety in Packer's Theological Structure

Packer develops his theology of piety under the doctrinal rubric of sanctification. His work most closely resembling a systematic theology is *Concise Theology*, which briefly addresses ninety–four doctrines in systematic fashion. In this volume his discussion of sanctification is immediately followed by consideration of three legally oriented themes: liberty (described in the first place as freedom 'from the law as a system of salvation'[12]), legalism, and antinomianism. This is consistent with the predominantly legal soteriology that will be seen later in Packer's forensic view of the atonement.

In his theological outline these legal themes that follow the discussion of sanctification are themselves followed by three existentially oriented themes: love, hope, and enterprise.[13] This reflects Packer's tendency to see the objective aspects of salvation in legal categories and to subordinate the subjective aspects to a distinct, separate, and dependent relationship. These soteriological aspects cohere by means of the doctrines of predestination and election. He states, 'Predestination … gives force to what the Bible says about sanctification in the Christian life.'[14] Sanctification, for Packer, is the goal, fruit, and proof of one's election.[15]

---

the Arminian theological basis of this position in 'Arminianisms', in *Shorter Writings*, 4.303.

[12] J.I. Packer, *Concise Theology: A Guide to Historic Christian Beliefs* (Wheaton: Tyndale House, 1993), 172. After formal, legal freedom comes freedom from the dominion of sin. This means that through regeneration and union with Christ 'the deepest desire of their heart now is to serve God by practicing righteousness.' The third type of freedom is 'from the superstition that treats matter and physical pleasure as intrinsically evil.' See also J.I. Packer, 'Liberty', in *NBD*, 732–734. In this article he expands on the theme by addressing its use in the Old Testament. 'Liberty is *from* slavery to powers that oppose God *for* the fulfillment of His claims upon one's life' (733). Regarding its New Testament usage he states, 'The divine law, as interpreted and exemplified by Christ Himself, remains a standard expressing Christ's will for His own freed bondservants (1 Cor. vii. 22)' (733).

[13] Packer, *Concise Theology*, table of contents, no page.

[14] J.I. Packer, 'Predestination and Sanctification', in *Shorter Writings*, 2.317.

[15] Ibid., 326.

Though he seeks to anchor piety within a Trinitarian framework, insisting on the unique and essential role of each Person in the Godhead for the realisation of evangelical spirituality,[16] the objective and subjective dimensions of piety find their integration elsewhere, that is, within a covenantal framework that is sustained by the doctrine of predestination. Covenantal predestination constitutes the framework for understanding the unique role of each Person of the Trinity in securing salvation and effecting holiness for the elect. He states, 'God's covenant commitment expresses eternal election; his covenant love to individual sinners flows from his choice of them to be his for ever in the peace of justification and the joy of glorification.'[17] He goes on to describe the roles and relationships within the Trinity as they function within the covenant of redemption.

> Scripture is explicit on the fact that from eternity, in light of human sin foreseen, a specific agreement existed between the Father and the Son that they would exalt each other in the following way: the Father would honour the Son by sending him to save lost sinners through a penal self–sacrifice leading to a cosmic reign in which the central activity would be the imparting to sinners through the Holy Spirit of the redemption he won for them; and the Son would honour the Father by becoming the Father's love–gift to sinners and by leading them through the Spirit to trust, love and glorify the Father on the model of his own obedience to the Father's will.[18]

The result of this covenant salvation, Packer states, is 'covenant piety, consisting of faith, repentance, love, joy, praise, hope, hatred of sin, desire for sanctity, a spirit of prayer, and readiness to battle the world, the flesh, and the devil in order to glorify God ...'[19]

Packer's *ordo salutis* begins with a sub– or infralapsarian view of predestination as indicated by his description of 'God's sovereign purpose for his world' as 'the purpose that led him to create, that sin then disrupted, and that his work of redemption is currently restoring.'[20] He treats the other

---

[16] Packer, 'Evangelical Foundations for Spirituality', 257. Here he states, 'Conscious acknowledgment of Jesus Christ as one's Saviour, of his Father as one's own Father through the grace of adoption, and of the Holy Spirit as Sustainer of this twofold fellowship, is of the essence of evangelical spirituality, and this Trinitarian framework sets it apart from anything else that is called spirituality anywhere in the church or in the world.'

[17] J.I. Packer, 'On Covenant Theology', in *Shorter Writings*, 1.11.

[18] Ibid., 15.

[19] Ibid., 14.

[20] Packer, *Concise Theology*, 37.

prominent soteriological themes in the following order: election, effectual
calling, illumination, regeneration, repentance, justification, adoption,
sanctification, and glorification.[21] His understanding of sanctification seems
to rest entirely on the sense in which it follows justification[22] and is
ultimately caused by predestination.[23] Packer presents sanctification as both
a gift and a task, but emphasises the gift dimension in a formal, not directly
experiential manner. It is the new position given to the Christian in Christ
(similar to justification) and the divine resources needed to embark
faithfully on the task.[24]

This forensically oriented theology has far–reaching ramifications for
understanding his treatment of holiness because of the relationship between
holiness and sanctification and because of where he places sanctification in
his *ordo salutis*. Hence, the first major issue that he addresses in *A Passion
for Holiness* is the nature of holiness or piety.

4.2 The Profile of Piety

As mentioned in chapter one, Packer defines true (i.e., biblical) piety as
godliness. He also relates it to the notion of holiness, stating, 'as the
maintaining of a state of separation from the world and consecratedness to
God, the New Testament calls it [piety] simply "holiness" (*hagiasmos,
hagiosyne*: see 1 Thes. iv.3; Heb. xii.14; 2 Cor. vii.1; 1 Thes. iii.13, *etc.*).'[25]
Likewise, he elaborates on the relationship between holiness and the
doctrine of sanctification.

---

[21] Ibid., table of contents, no page.

[22] L. Morris, *The Atonement: Its Meaning and Significance* (Leicester: Inter–Varsity,
1983), 40. Morris draws attention to the different senses in which sanctification is
used in the New Testament, contrasting known Pauline uses with that found in
Hebrews. Paul uses the concept to 'refer to the process of becoming holy, the
progressive growth in grace. But in Hebrews it is rather the initial act of being set
apart to be God's.' Packer places greater emphasis on the Pauline usage by placing
sanctification at a later point in the *ordo salutis*.

[23] J.I. Packer, *God's Plans for You* (Wheaton: Crossway, 2001), 128. Packer
acknowledges that texts such as Heb. 10:10,14,29 portray a 'positional sanctification'
that precedes the process of sanctification. Yet, this aspect of sanctification functions
more in the manner of justification for Packer. His dominant emphasis on
sanctification is on 'progressive sanctification.' See 'Predestination and
Sanctification.'

[24] Packer, 'Predestination and Sanctification', 320,326.

[25] Packer, 'Piety', 996.

But what exactly is holiness? … Consider first the word itself. *Holiness* is a noun that belongs with the adjective *holy* and the verb *sanctify*, which means to make holy. … *Holy* in both biblical languages means separated and set apart for God, consecrated and made over to him. In its application to people, God's 'holy ones' or 'saints,' the word implies both devotion and assimilation: devotion, in the sense of living a life of service to God; assimilation, in the sense of imitating, conforming to, and becoming like the God one serves. For Christians, this means taking God's moral law as our rule and God's incarnate Son as our model; this is where our analysis must start.[26]

In his unpublished lecture notes he defines sanctification as,

specifically the work of the indwelling Holy Spirit who reproduces in us the character–qualities of Jesus Christ, to whom we are vitally united (= the fruit of the Spirit, transformed outlook and habits of action and reaction), and who also energizes the dependent, faith–full, self–distrustful activity of love and good works in which Christian discipleship consists.[27]

He goes on in the same lecture to define 'biblical spirituality' as the

recognition of and response to the reality and power of God through Jesus Christ in the covenant of grace; and the first rule for practising biblical spirituality is: know the new world of which you are now part (i.e. the old world, made new by your new covenant relationship with God), know yourself as part of it, and learn to live in it according to your knowledge. … The second definition of spirituality is … living out the new life which God has wrought in you and constantly sustains in you; and the second rule for practising biblical spirituality is: know your own newness in Christ, and be natural in espressing (sic.) it and in negating all that is now unnatural to you.[28]

Sanctification, holiness, and biblical spirituality are interrelated in Packer's thought. There is no sanctification or true spirituality that does not involve or produce holiness. To be truly spiritual is to be growing in holiness and sanctification. Yet, the nature of this holiness can only be understood in light of the nature of that for which the believer is sanctified

---

[26] Packer, *A Passion for Holiness*, 19.

[27] J.I. Packer, 'Systematic Theology B, Man, Sin and Grace', section on 'The Reality of Salvation', 6.

[28] Ibid., 8–9.

or set apart, namely, the worshipful, loving, obedient imitation of God's character as exemplified in Jesus Christ.

It is significant that Packer also relates the themes of sanctification, holiness, and spirituality to the *imago Dei*. The following passage shows how he equates Christlikeness with the fulfilment of humanness as it is defined by the *imago Dei*.

> [A]s ministering servants of Jesus Christ we are required to be promoters and guardians of health and humanness among God's people, and we need spirituality for that. ... The Bible proclaims that humanness is more than just having a mind and a body; it is essentially a personal and relational ideal, the ideal of living in the image of God, which means being like Jesus Christ in creative love and service to our Father in heaven and our fellowmen on earth. When Scripture speaks of man as made in God's image and thus as being God's image–bearer, what it means is that each human individual is set apart from the animal creation by being equipped with the personal make–up, the conscious selfhood, feelings, brains, and capacity for love–relationships, without which Christ–like holiness would be impossible ... We may state the matter this way: structurally, God's image in us is a natural given fact, consisting of the rational powers of the human self, as such; substantively, however, God's image in us is an ongoing moral process, the fruit and expression of a supernatural character–change from self–centredness to God–centredness and from acquisitive pride to outgoing love – a change that only Christians undergo. So the conclusion of the matter is that the true and full image of God is precisely godliness – communion with God, and creativity under God, in the relational rationality and righteousness that spring from faith, and gratitude to one's Saviour, and the desire to please and honour God and to be a means of helping others; and the true goal of life is to know and receive and cooperate with God's grace in Christ, through which our potential for Christlikeness may be realised.[29]

Holiness (godliness) is the substance of the *imago Dei* in humanity and constitutes the goal of piety as it is restored in growth toward Christlikeness. Neither holiness nor humanness, for Packer, can be understood, defined, or experienced apart from Jesus Christ. He encapsulates this equation by stating, 'Genuine holiness is genuine Christlikeness.'[30]

---

[29] Packer, 'An Introduction to Systematic Spirituality', 3–4.
[30] Packer, *A Passion for Holiness*, 28.

4.2.1 In Relation to the Character of God

The material content of holiness is defined by God's moral character as expressed in God's 'communicable' attributes. Packer sets these attributes against the backdrop of God's 'incommunicable' attributes. [31] Specifically, he highlights God's

> *independence* (self–existence and self–sufficiency); His *immutability* (entire freedom from change, leading to entire consistency in action); His *infinity* (freedom from all limits of time and space: i.e., His eternity and omnipresence); and His *simplicity* (the fact that there are in Him no elements that can conflict, so that, unlike man, He cannot be torn different ways by divergent thought and desires). [32]

These attributes qualitatively differentiate God from humanity. God's 'communicable' attributes, on the other hand, are God's attributes that humans are called to reflect in their character and actions. These are

> qualities like God's spirituality, freedom, and omnipotence, along with all His moral attributes – goodness, truth, holiness, righteousness, etc. What was the principle of classification here? It was this – that when God made man, he *communicated* to him qualities corresponding to all these. This is what the Bible means when it tells us that God made man in His own image (Gen. 1:26f. – namely, that God made man a free spiritual being, a responsible moral agent with powers of choice and action, able to commune with Him and respond to Him, and by nature good, truthful, holy, upright (cf. Eccles. 7:29): in a word, *godly*.
> The moral qualities which belonged to the divine image were lost at the Fall; God's image in man has been universally defaced, for all mankind has in one way or another lapsed into ungodliness. [33]

Packer uses God's communicable attributes as the logical connection between holiness and the *imago Dei*. The *imago Dei* is essentially these moral attributes expressed in the context of relationship with God and other people.

In the discussion that follows the previous citation Packer elaborates on the communicable attributes of *wisdom*, *love*, and *light* and how each attribute affects piety. In human experience *wisdom* is the progressive

---

[31] Packer, *Knowing God*, 89. See also H. Bavinck, *The Doctrine of God*. Bavinck offers a more detailed treatment of God's attributes within the classifications of 'incommunicable' and 'communicable.'

[32] Ibid.

[33] Packer, *Knowing God*, 89–90.

influence of God's wisdom on human decisions. However, Packer challenges the expectation that God's wisdom can be experienced in ways that impart insight into the mysterious, inner–workings of providence. He also rejects the implication that a person lacks spiritual maturity if confusion is experienced regarding God's will.[34] The godly, wise Christian should abandon questions about the hidden reasons for events. Likewise, wise Christians resist the preoccupation with obtaining infallible guidance from God about decisions. Rather, spirituality or godliness is reflected in the application of wisdom wherein 'you simply try to see and do the right thing in the actual situation that presents itself.'[35] The life of godly wisdom 'consists in choosing the best means to the best end. … [I]t is not a sharing in all His knowledge, but a disposition to confess that He is wise, and to cleave to Him and live for Him in the light of His word through thick and thin.'[36] Wisdom contributes to a holiness that exists contentedly within the limitations of human finitude.

The divine attribute of impassibility is another connecting point between God's character and human holiness. In this case, however, he discusses divine impassibility, an attribute traditionally categorised as incommunicable, under the rubric of God's *love*. Though he supports the Anglican Thirty–nine Articles' affirmation that God is '"without body, parts, or passions,"'[37] Packer defines impassibility as if it were a communicable attribute that constitutes God's intrinsic holiness and humanity's obligation for holiness.

With Him 'there is no variation or shadow due to change' (James 1:17, RSV). Thus He is free from all limitations of time and natural processes, and remains eternally the same. God has no *passions* – this does not mean that He is unfeeling (impassive), or that there is nothing in Him that corresponds to emotions and affections in us, but that whereas human passions – specially the painful ones, fear, grief, regret, despair – are in a sense passive and involuntary, being called forth and constrained by circumstances not under our control, the corresponding attributes in God

---

[34] Ibid., 92.

[35] Ibid., 93.

[36] Ibid., 97. The question of how God's will is to be discerned has been a repeated concern for Packer over the years. See also 'Situations and Principles', in B. Kaye and G. Wenham (eds.), *Law, Morality and the Bible* (Downers Grove: InterVarsity, 1978), 151–167; 'Wisdom Along the Way', *Eternity* (April 1986), 19–23; 'Paths of Righteousness', *Eternity* (May 1986), 32–37; 'True Guidance', *Eternity* (June 1986), 36–39; *Knowing and Doing the Will of God* (Ann Arbor: Servant, 1995); and *God's Plans for You* (Wheaton: Crossway, 2001).

[37] Ibid., 109.

have the nature of deliberate, voluntary choices, and therefore are not of the same order as human passions at all. ... So, the love of God who is spirit is no fitful, fluctuating thing, as the love of man is, nor is it a mere impotent longing for things that may never be; it is, rather, a spontaneous determination of God's whole being in an attitude of benevolence and benefaction, an attitude freely chosen and firmly fixed.[38]

Divine impassibility defines the perfect, unchanging nature of God's love, as a communicable attribute, and how it functions as a criterion for human love and holiness.

Packer weaves a connection between God's love and the metaphor of God as *light*. This combination provides him with a theological mechanism for reconciling the wrathful judgment that derives from God's absolute righteousness with the love that God expresses toward people. He suggests that the biblical description of God as 'light' brings human sinfulness into a central role in the practise of piety. Through this 'light' God's holy character is reflected in the moral standard that Scripture communicates to humanity. He refers to God as 'light,' meaning 'holiness and purity, as measured by God's law'[39] Light and love, for Packer, are both central to God's character. He states, 'To say "God *is* light" is to imply that God's holiness finds expression in everything that He says and does. Similarly, the statement 'God *is* love' means that His love finds expression in everything that He says and does.'[40] God's light constitutes the perfect moral law and the standard for piety. God's love functions within the boundaries of that perfect moral law.

Light and love reflect the way in which God's holiness and love coexist and relate to each other. He states,

It is noteworthy that when John focuses the two sides of God's character by saying that he is both *light* and *love* (1John 1:5; 4:8) – not love without righteousness and purity, nor rectitude without kindness and compassion, but holy love, and loving holiness, and each quality to the highest degree – he offers each statement as summarizing what we learn from Jesus about God.[41]

---

[38] Ibid., 109–110.
[39] Ibid., 110.
[40] Ibid., 111.
[41] J.I. Packer, *Growing In Christ* (Wheaton: Crossway, 1994), 24. See also *A Passion for Holiness*, 59. '[T]he triune God is *light*. This means that he is holy – pure and perfect, loving all good and hating all evil. Also, it means that he constantly searches

The epistemological role of Jesus Christ in piety is to provide knowledge about God's moral purity and perfect love. Light and love unite in God's nature so as to demand that judgment and retribution for sin take place and to indicate that judgment and retribution are integral to God's love.

The themes of God as 'light' and 'love' express core assumptions of Packer's soteriology and piety; that God's perfect law has been violated, that God's moral character must be vindicated through retribution for sin, and that God in love provided a forensic, penal, substitutionary atonement for sin. He points out that 'the Bible insists throughout that this world which God in His goodness has made is a moral world, in which retribution is as basic a fact as breathing. ... God is not true to Himself unless He punishes sin.'[42] He further states that 'the heart of the justice which expresses God's nature is *retribution* ... To reward good with good, and evil with evil, is natural to God. So, when the New Testament speaks of the final judgment, it always represents it in terms of retribution.'[43] God's wrathful, punitive attitude toward sin occupies significant space in Packer's general theological works. In *Knowing God* he sets God's love and grace against the backdrop of God's hatred of sin. The themes of God's judgment, wrath, and jealousy occupy as much space in this book as do the themes of love and grace. The holiness to which humans are called is a direct reflection of the nature of God's holiness. He claims that holiness 'covers all the aspects of his transcendent greatness and moral perfection and thus is an attribute of all his attributes, pointing to the 'Godness' of God at every point. ... The core of the concept, however, is God's purity, which cannot tolerate any form of sin (Hab. 1:13) and thus obligates sinners to constant self–abasement in his presence (Isa. 6:5).'[44]

God's law, for Packer, is prominent in the human pursuit and experience of holiness as the background for his emphasis on God's wrath and human repentance. Love for God is defined by obedience to the law. God provides

---

out all that is in us, so that "everything is uncovered and laid bare before the eyes of him to whom we must give account" (Heb. 4:13).'

[42] Packer, *Knowing God*, 118. Packer acknowledges J. McLeod Campbell's criticism that penal substitution presents a false portrait of God as one who need not exercise mercy, but is compelled to punish. Packer responds to this charge in 'What Did the Cross Achieve?: The Logic of Penal Substitution', in *Shorter Writings*, 1.120, by saying that 'since the Bible says both that Christ's death was a penal substitution for God's people and also that it reveals God's love to sinful men as such, and since the Bible further declares that Christ is the Father's image, so that everything we learn of the Son's love is knowledge of the Father's love also, Campbell's complaint is unreal.'

[43] Ibid., 129.

[44] Packer, *Concise Theology*, 43.

light so that the divine Person may be illuminated as the source of all that is good. Thus, a fuller treatment of the relationship of holiness to God's law is warranted.

4.2.2 In Relation to the Law of God and Scripture

God's moral character is conveyed to humanity through God's law. Packer urges, 'Keep two truths in view. First, God's law **expresses his character**. It reflects his own behaviour; it alerts us to what he will love and hate to see in us. It is a recipe for holiness, consecrated conformity to God, which is (this is the second truth) God's law **fits human nature**.'[45] God's law, then, provides the standard for human holiness by expressing God's nature to humanity.

The Ten Commandments summarise the transcultural and transhistorical character of God's law for Packer. Jesus' life provides a perfect example of the heart of the law, as it is expressed in complete love for God and others. The New Testament writings provide authoritative exposition of the law as the rules of God's Kingdom as it extends past the political boundaries of Old Testament Israel.

> What is God's law? The Hebrew word *torah*, which is the basic term, means not legislated regulations as such ... but family instruction, which a father – in this case, the heavenly Father – gives to his children. All the directives for right living that God gave through his spokesmen in Old Testament times, the maxims of the wisdom books no less than the socio–political and liturgical legalities laid down through Moses and the diagnostic exhortations to righteousness voiced by the prophets, were in essence the Father's admonitions to his family (which is what Israel was: see Ex 4:22) and were centered [sic] on the Ten Commandments.

> The socio–political and liturgical laws, which were for Old Testament Israel exclusively, have lapsed. But the Decalogue, as interpreted by Jesus' two–commandment summary ('love God' and 'love your neighbor'[sic]; see Mt 22:37–40), stands as the all–time expression of God's moral will for his people.

> What then is the kingdom edition of the law? The kingdom of God (the new life of heaven on earth through the Holy Spirit) came into the world with Jesus, and now releases new moral power and energy in the lives of believers, whom Jesus called 'sons of the kingdom' (Mt 13:38). What I

---

[45] J.I. Packer, *The Ten Commandments* (Basingstoke/Abingdon: Chandos Press/Marcham, 1977), no page.

mean by the kingdom edition of the law is the exposition that Jesus and
the apostles give of the breadth and depth of God's requirements.[46]

In this approach to God's law Packer attempts to avoid a legalistic
application of moral principles while maintaining the binding character of
the Decalogue and its expression in the ethical teachings of the New
Testament. He brings God's law into his discussion of holiness by stating,
'Holiness sets its sights on absolute moral standards and unchanging moral
ideals, established by God himself. God's law defines the righteousness he
requires of believers.'[47] However, he does not see the authority of God's
law as restricted to believers.

Packer contends that God's law is applicable and binding for all people
equally, whether or not they are Christians, because the law is related to the
essence of humanity through the *imago Dei*.

> As rational persons, we were made to bear God's moral image – that
> is, our souls were made to 'run' on the practice of worship, law–keeping,
> truthfulness, honesty, discipline, self–control, and service to God and our
> fellows. If we abandon these practices, not only do we incur guilt before
> God; we also progressively destroy our own souls. Conscience atrophies,
> the sense of shame dries up, one's capacity for truthfulness, loyalty, and
> honesty is eaten away, one's character disintegrates. One not only
> becomes desperately miserable; one is steadily being de–humanised.[48]

This universal application is rooted in the assumption that human nature
is fulfilled only through conformity to God's law since God's very nature is
reflected in the structure of the law and human nature is contingent upon
God's nature through the *imago Dei*.[49]

For example, Packer uses the concepts of obedience, law, and human
purpose to posit a general principle regarding the function of authority in
society. He criticises what he sees as a general, cultural rejection of
authority, stating that 'there is such a thing as humanness and self–
fulfillment, which is true freedom, and which requires submission to an
adequate external authority, otherwise integration of one's life will never be
achieved.'[50] For example, in describing the pre–secularised situation in
England, Packer presents the nature of humanity as a criterion for the

---

[46] Packer, *A Passion for Holiness*, 176.
[47] Ibid., 175–176.
[48] Packer, *Knowing God*, 102–103.
[49] Packer, *Growing In Christ*, 280.
[50] J.I. Packer, 'Why is Authority a Dirty Word?' *Spectrum* (May 1977), 5.

importance of civil law.[51] All human responsibility to law is but an outgrowth of the innate accountability to God's law that is embedded in the *imago Dei*. It is important to note, though, that he also emphasises the spirit in which God's law is kept. God's law is never truly obeyed apart from love and worship of God.[52]

Packer points out that the thread of divine authority extends through the law and into the New Testament writings. This sets the stage for his understanding of the nature of Scripture as the communicative medium for God's law. Furthermore, it offers perspective on his insistence that biblical inerrancy is a logical necessity for the Christian life. The law demands a medium of communication that is adequate to the divine nature that it reflects and the human holiness that is its goal. To Packer, God's written communication to humanity must exist in perfect form (by whatever standards 'perfect' is to be understood) and must, at least theoretically, be comprehensible in a manner commensurate with its character. Moreover, the receptive apparatus of humanity must be of such composition that it is capable of apprehending this communication. Otherwise, the possibility of holiness is logically compromised. Packer's doctrine of Scripture, then, carries on the function and authority of God's law in human holiness. Moreover, it reflects the priority and significance of the faculty of reason in his theological anthropology, method, and piety.

Packer has become well known for his staunch defence of biblical infallibility and, particularly on the North American evangelical scene, the notion of biblical inerrancy. Beginning with *'Fundamentalism' and the Word of God*, in which he upheld the view of Scripture then being labelled as 'Fundamentalist' by British theologians such as Michael Ramsey and A. G. Hebert,[53] he has written numerous pieces throughout his career explaining and advocating the claim that Biblical inspiration and authority demand inerrancy. His case closely resembles the agenda of the 'old

---

[51] J.I. Packer, 'A Secular Way to Go', *Third Way* (April 1977), 3. He states, 'It was argued that the law must respect the rights, liberties and consciences of individuals, because all are made in the image of God, to live to him and one day to answer to him.'

[52] J.I. Packer, 'Good', in *NBD*, 483. 'Good works are good from three standpoints: they are done (i) in accordance with a right standard (the biblical law: 2 Tim. iii. 16f.); (ii) from a right motive (love and gratitude for redemption: 1 Thes. i. 3; Heb. vi. 10; *cf.* Rom. xii. 1ff.); (iii) with a right aim (God's glory: 1 Cor. x. 31; *cf.* 1 Cor. vi. 20; Mt. v. 16; 1 Pet. ii. 12). They take the form of works of love towards God and men, since "love is the fulfilling of the law" (Rom. xiii. 8–10; *cf.* Mt. xxii. 36–40).'

[53] Alister McGrath, Introduction to *The J.I. Packer Collection* (Downers Grove: InterVarsity, 1999), 17–18.

school' Princeton scholars Benjamin B. Warfield and J. Gresham Machen.[54]

This viewpoint propounded by Warfield, Machen, and Packer places distinct emphasis on the propositional character of God's self–revelation in Scripture. However, Packer recognizes a distinctly personal character in the truth revealed by God, challenging those such as Emil Brunner who seem to him to elevate personal revelation over propositional revelation or to polarize the two.[55] Packer claims, 'Truth in the Bible is a quality of persons primarily, and of propositions only secondarily: it means stability, reliability, firmness, trustworthiness, the quality of a person who is entirely self–consistent, sincere, realistic, and undeceived.'[56] This perspective allows him to see Scripture as communicating God's personal, holy character (particularly as it communicates God's law) and as constituting the relational moral framework by which humanity's integrity is defined and regulated.

---

[54] Packer, *'Fundamentalism' and the Word of God*, 25,77. He defends the same point in *Truth and Power: The Place of Scripture in the Christian Life* (Wheaton: Harold Shaw, 1996), 134. Among Packer's other writings in which he defends the inspiration and inerrancy of Scripture are: 'Revelation and Inspiration', in E.F. Kevan, A.M. Stibbs, and f. Davidson (eds.), *New Bible Commentary* (London: Inter–Varsity, 1954), 12–18; 'Contemporary Views of Revelation', in C.F.H. Henry (ed.), *Revelation and the Bible: Contemporary Evangelical Thought* (Grand Rapids: Baker, 1958), 89–104; 'The Bible and the Authority of Reason', *Churchman* 75 (October–December 1961), 207–219; *God Has Spoken: Revelation and the Bible* (London: Hodder and Stoughton, 1964); 'Biblical Authority, Hermeneutics and Inerrancy', in E.R. Geehan (ed.), *Jerusalem and Athens: Critical Discussions on the Theology and Apologetics of Cornelius Van Til* (Nutley, N.J.: Presbyterian and Reformed, 1971), 141–153; 'The Adequacy of Human Language', in N. Geisler (ed.), *Inerrancy* (Grand Rapids: Zondervan, 1980), 197–228; *God's Words: Studies of Key Bible Themes* (London: Inter–Varsity, 1981); 'Upholding the Unity of Scripture Today', *Journal of the Evangelical Theological Society* 25 (December 1982), 409–414; 'Infallible Scripture and the Role of Hermeneutics', in J.D. Woodbridge and D.A. Carson (eds.), *Scripture and Truth* (Grand Rapids: Zondervan, 1983), 325–358; 'John Calvin and the Inerrancy of Holy Scripture', in J.D. Hannah (ed.), *Inerrancy and the Church* (Chicago: Moody, 1984), 143–188; and 'Inerrancy and the Divinity and Humanity of the Bible', in J. Gregory (ed.), *Proceedings of the Conference of Biblical Inerrancy* (Nashville: Broadman, 1987), 135–142.

[55] Packer, 'Infallible Scripture and the Role of Hermeneutics', 334. Packer states, 'It is in fact best, because truest, to agree with Brunner that revelation is indeed essentially personal, and then go on to say that this is why it is and had to be propositional: no person can make himself known to another without telling him things, and the God of Scripture does in fact appear as one who tells people things constantly.'

[56] Packer, *Knowing God*, 102.

Packer bases holiness primarily on God's personal holiness and secondarily on the law as it expresses the nature of God's holiness in inerrant propositions. He offers the basis of this belief by bringing together the themes of Scriptural authority, God's law, and human nature as follows. 'When Christians affirm the authority of the Bible, meaning that biblical teaching reveals God's will and is the instrument of his rule over our lives, part of what they are claiming is that Scripture sets before us the factual and moral nature of things. God's law corresponds to created human nature, so that in fulfilling his requirements we fulfil ourselves.'[57]

His case for Scriptural authority as the basis for holiness includes the assertion of biblical infallibility or inerrancy. '[I]n the realm of belief, authority belongs to truth and truth only. ... I can make no sense – no reverent sense, anyway – of the idea, sometimes met, that God speaks his truth to us in and through false statements by biblical writers ... Accordingly, I have reasoned about the authority of Scripture on the assumption that it contains God–taught truth throughout.'[58]

The inerrancy of Scripture is the logical extension of combining Scriptural authority, God's law, and human nature in the way that Packer does. Without inerrant, propositional revelation in Scripture, all hope of holiness would collapse because the necessary communication from God is unreliable.

Packer follows a Puritan model in describing a precise communication of God's will to the human conscience through Scripture.

> But how can God's will be known? Can we tell His requirements with certainty and exactness? Is there any way out of the fogs of pious guesswork on this point into the clear light of certainty? Yes, said the Puritans, there is; the way out is to harness our consciences to the Holy Scriptures, in which the mind of God is fully revealed to us. To them, Scripture was ... written by the Holy Ghost through human agents in order to give the Church of every age clear direction on all matters of faith and life that could possibly arise. ... Certainly, seeing the relevant principles and applying them correctly in each case is in practice an arduous task; ignorance of Scripture, and misjudgment of situations, constantly lead us astray, and to be patient and humble enough to receive the Spirit's help is not easy either. But it remains true nonetheless that in principle Scripture provides clear and exact guidance for every detail and department of life, and if we come to Scripture teachably and expectantly

---

[57] Packer, *Truth and Power*, 15.
[58] Ibid., 46.

God Himself will seal on our minds and hearts a clear certainty as to how we should behave in each situation that faces us.[59]

A precise God – a God, that is, who has made a precise disclosure of His mind and will in Scripture, and who expects from His servants a corresponding preciseness of belief and behaviour – it was this view of God that created and controlled the historic Puritan outlook. The Bible itself led them to it. And we who share the Puritan estimate of Holy Scripture cannot excuse ourselves if we fail to show a diligence and conscientiousness equal to theirs in ordering our going according to God's written Word.[60]

Piety or holiness necessarily depend upon and involve an increasing precision in the quality of one's ethical perception and obedience. This level of precision in holiness depends also upon precise transmission of God's law to the human conscience. Scripture fulfils this role as it communicates God's revelation through precise, inerrant propositions.

Since holiness involves the restoration of the *imago Dei* in conformity to the character of Jesus Christ, the rational faculties necessary for comprehending and responding to the message of Scripture are therefore critical if the image is to be restored. Packer states, 'God is rational and unchanging, and all men in every generation, being made in God's image, are capable of being addressed by him.'[61] He reiterates the point by referring to 'the biblical position that God's speaking and God's image in man imply a human capacity to grasp and respond to his verbal address.'[62] Thus, the rational faculties necessary for recognition and response to that message are essential to the realisation of the restored image. Holiness, for Packer, depends upon an inerrant Scripture communicating God's Law with precision to the rational faculties. Precise knowledge of God's will and obedience to God's will is possible, and only possible, through this precise, rational formula.

4.2.3 In Relation to Soteriology

Packer's theology of piety reflects his Reformed soteriological framework. In his approach to systematic theology Packer treats the doctrine of piety or

---

[59] J.I. Packer, 'The Puritan Conscience', in *Faith and a Good Conscience* (London: The Puritan and Reformed Studies Conference), 23.
[60] Ibid., 24.
[61] J.I. Packer, 'The Adequacy of Human Language', in *Shorter Writings*, 3.27.
[62] Ibid., 39.

holiness, under the general heading of soteriology. Soteriology is developed under a broader heading of anthropology.[63] Piety reflects both the nature of the personhood that is restored in salvation and the particular manner in which salvation accomplishes this restoration.

4.2.3.1 PREDESTINATION AND ELECTION

Since he read John Owen's *The Death of Death in the Death of Christ* in 1953 Packer has held to strict, 'five–point' Calvinism.[64] He defines predestination as 'God's decision, made in eternity before the world and its inhabitants existed, regarding the final destiny of individual sinners. In fact, the New Testament uses the words predestination and election (the two are one), only of God's choice of particular sinners for salvation and eternal life (Rom. 8:29; Eph. 1:4–5, 11).'[65] His discussion of predestination occurs in the first section of his theological structure.

Having stated that predestination and election are one, he elaborates on the concept of election after he has addressed Christology and as he begins to address salvation. Election, he states, 'is a pastoral doctrine, brought in to help Christians see how great is the grace that saves them, and to move them to humility, confidence, joy, praise, faithfulness, and holiness in response.'[66] This way of treating predestination and election reflects both John Calvin's development of election under the rubric of Christ's grace[67] (though Packer treats it much earlier even in this section than Calvin does) and the Westminster Confession's placement of predestination toward the forefront of its theological outline.[68]

---

[63] In the second section of his systematic theology course at Regent College Packer arranges his topics in the following order: human nature, human sin, the person and place of Jesus Christ, reconciliation and justification, the person and the place of the Holy Spirit, the conversion complex, *systematic spirituality* [emphasis added], health and healing, sovereign grace and universalism, life together, and the hope of glory. 'Man, Sin and Grace', course description page. This order corresponds to the topical ordering in *Concise Theology*.

[64] Packer, Introduction to *The Death of Death in the Death of Christ*, by J. Owen, 1–25. Packer argues here, not only for the doctrine of particular atonement, but for the logical interdependence of 'five–point' Calvinism as articulated at the Synod of Dort.

[65] Packer, *Concise Theology*, 38.

[66] Ibid., 149–150.

[67] J. Calvin, *Institutes*, F.L. Battles (tr.) (Philadelphia: Westminster, 1949), III.xxi.

[68] *The Westminster Confession of Faith: An Authentic Modern Version* (Signal Mountain, Tn.: Summertown, 1979²), 7–8. The Westminster Confession treats the general theme of predestination and the specific theme of election together under the heading of God's Eternal Decrees.

The divine work of sanctification is sustained and assured by God's predestination and election. He claims,

> From all eternity, Paul declares, God has had a plan (*prothesis*) to save a Church, though in earlier times it was not fully made known (Eph. iii. 3–11). The aim of the plan is that men should be made God's adopted sons and be renewed in the image of Christ (Rom. viii. 29), and that the Church, the company of those so renewed, should grow to the fullness of Christ (Eph. iv. 13).[69]

His statement also indicates that he also attempts to relate ecclesiology to holiness, though this relationship is never as fully developed as individual factors.

A Calvinistic understanding of predestination and election provides, for Packer, the divine impetus and momentum, as well as the human motivation for sanctification. Contending that John Wesley misunderstood and misrepresented Calvinism as eliminating motivation for holiness,[70] Packer presents Calvinism as providing the greatest possible motivation for obedience in holiness. Only in this obedience, Packer claims, is real assurance of salvation to be found. He draws from John Owen to link election, holiness, and assurance of salvation.

> John Owen said it in these words:
> 'Faith, obedience and holiness are the inseparable fruits, effects and consequences of election. In whomsoever these things are wrought, he (that person) is obliged, according to the method of God in the gospel, to believe in his own election [no bibliographic reference given].' Why ought he to? Because his life is showing qualities which only the lives of the elect show. Thus they may know themselves to be one of God's elect because his life has been changed. And they ought to labour to make their

---

[69] J.I. Packer, 'Predestination', in *NBD*, 1026.

[70] Packer, 'Predestination and Sanctification', 325. Packer claims that Wesley was convinced 'the doctrine of election is constantly suspected of … not promoting holiness but of promoting carelessness.' In support, he cites Wesley, '"Question: What is the direct antidote to Methodism, the doctrine of heart holiness? Answer: Calvinism. All the devices of Satan for these fifty years have done far less toward stopping the work of God than that single doctrine. It strikes at the root of salvation from sin, previous to glory, putting it (salvation) on quite another issue."' Packer does not reference the source of this quote from Wesley.

election sure to himself in this way because of the joy this gives and the impulse in the life of godliness which springs from it.[71]

The doctrine of election, then, affords motivation for holiness so that Christians may verify their standing before God.

Packer offers four principles to combat the argument that a Calvinistic view of election destroys motivation for holiness. First, '*In Scripture sanctification is a goal of God's election*. Sanctification is what he selected us for [ref. Eph. 1:4].' Second, '*Sanctification is a fruit of God's election*.' Holiness is therefore initiated by God and produced inevitably in the elect whom God saves. Third, '*Sanctification is the only proof of one's election*.' Holiness is the instrumental validation for one's assurance of salvation. Fourth, '*Sanctification is advanced by the knowledge of your election*.' Motivation for pursuing holiness comes from grateful realisation of one's personal salvation.[72]

Packer appears to reflect John Calvin's approach to integrating justification and sanctification by placing adoption between them and referring to the role of the Spirit as the active agent.[73] However, he actually goes beyond Calvin by giving more prominent attention to predestination and election as the overarching factors.[74] This may not pose a material contradiction, but displays Packer's preference for the methodology of later Calvinism.

God's initiating and sustaining activity in election does not, however, mean that justification and sanctification are experienced or received in the same manner. Piety is affected by the different ways in which justification and sanctification are experienced. In another passage where he attempts to delineate the relationship between human responsibility and divine sovereignty in justification and sanctification, he appeals to the need for understanding God's strategy in election. With this understanding the Christian finds motivation for the active pursuit of holiness.

When we see what God through Christ and the Spirit is doing for us and in us, we shall be better placed to understand what it is that he calls us to

---

[71] Ibid.

[72] Ibid., 326. Emphases are Packer's.

[73] Packer, *Concise Theology*, 164–171.

[74] Calvin, *Institutes*, III.xi.6. Calvin gives greater attention to Jesus Christ as the locus of integration between justification and sanctification. He states, 'as Christ cannot be torn into parts, so these two which we perceive in him together and conjointly are inseparable – namely, righteousness and sanctification. Whomever, therefore, God receives into grace, on them he at the same time bestows the spirit of adoption (Rom. 8:15), by whose power he remakes them to his own image.'

do for him and with him. Here the distinction between justification and sanctification becomes important. As far as concerns the making of atonement for our sins, and the consequent pardoning and justifying of our person, the work is entirely and exclusively God's. When we confess ourselves lost sinners and cast ourselves on Christ to save us, we are acknowledging by our action that we contribute nothing to our new relationship with God save our need of it, and this is the exact truth. We get into God's favor, not by paying our way, but by accepting his gift of a blood–bought amnesty. However, *in sanctification, which is the work of God within us from which our holiness flows, we are called to cooperate actively with God. In order to do this as we should, we need to have some overall awareness of his purpose and strategy for our lives as a whole* [emphasis added].[75]

Packer's theology of piety depends on this distinction between monergism in justification and synergism in sanctification. Ultimately, he contends, it is God's grace that motivates and sustains the human effort required in sanctification. Citing 2 Peter 1:10, he refers to God's eternal decree of individual election as the motivation for Christians to validate their personal election to themselves through the pursuit of holiness. He states, 'Peter tells us we should be 'eager to make [our] calling and election sure' ... that is, certain to us.'[76] The believer is portrayed here as playing an important role in experiencing his or her own assurance of salvation through obedience.

4.2.3.2 ATONEMENT

Piety, for Packer, begins with and is continually dependent upon the appeasement of God's wrath against sin and its corollary, the need for forensic justice in light of the violation of God's law. Thus, he holds that Christ's substitutionary atonement for sin is of a forensic, penal character. He denies that other atonement motifs have equal status with the forensic, penal substitution model in defining the essence of Christ's salvific work. He states, 'It is a shallow fancy to imagine, as many scholars unhappily do, that this variety of language [regarding the nature and effects of Christ's death] must necessarily imply variation of thought.' He goes on to say that, 'when you are on top of the truth of propitiation, you can see the entire Bible in perspective, and you are in a position to take measure of vital matters which cannot be properly grasped on any other terms.'[77] He treats

---

[75] Packer, *A Passion for Holiness*, 44–45.
[76] Packer, *Concise Theology*, 150.
[77] Packer, *Knowing God*, 172.

the loving, relational result of salvation under the theme of adoption. Though he calls adoption 'the *highest privilege that the gospel offers*,' he places justification from sin in the role of 'the *primary* and *fundamental* blessing of the gospel.'[78]

Genuine biblical holiness, for Packer, begins with three assumptions. First, the nature of God's holiness is absolute moral purity. Second, humanity's sin and resulting legal guilt are the dual foci of its most radical problem. Third, Christ's death accomplished a forensic atonement for sin that appeased God's holy wrath against sin.[79]

The forensic, penal, substitutionary atonement of Christ for sin is not only one of Packer's favourite theological themes, it is an important foundation to his theology of piety. It relates closely to his understanding of sin, sin's impact on the *imago Dei*, and sin's consequent impact on humanity's relationship to God. His insistence on the substitutionary character of Christ's atonement follows the model developed by Anselm in *Cur Deus Homo*, wherein God's honour has been offended and, consequently, damages must be paid so that God's honour is restored.[80] However, Packer only takes over Anselm's general assumption that humanity has violated God and owes God a debt, then claims to follow Luther in making the violation of God's justice the fundamental issue.

> As Anselm expounded satisfaction, it was a matter of satisfying God's outraged honour, and that indeed is part of the truth. But when Luther came along, he broadened the idea of satisfaction to what he found in the Bible, and he made the right and true point that the satisfaction of Jesus Christ restores God's glory through Christ's enduring all penal retribution for sin. The satisfaction of Christ glorifies God the Father and wins

---

[78] Ibid., 186–187.

[79] Ibid., 170–171. 'No version of that [gospel] message goes deeper than that which declares man's root problem before God to be his sin, which evokes wrath, and God's basic provision for man to be propitiation, which out of wrath brings peace.' Guilt, for Packer, is primarily an issue of legal standing before God's law. See also Packer's article, 'Atonement', in D. Atkinson and D. Fields (eds.), *NDCEPT* (Leicester: Inter–Varsity, 1995), 174–177. Herein he explains Christ's atoning work by connecting sacrifice, redemption, reconciliation, propitiation, representation, and substitution. Each of these themes portray a unique aspect of the atonement that is fundamentally oriented by the law–divine wrath–appeasement motif (175).

[80] Anselm, *Cur Deus Homo?*, in *Basic Writings*, S.N. Deane (tr.) (LaSalle, Ill.: Opoen Court, 1962[2]), 202,205.

salvation for the sinner by being a satisfaction of God's justice. That is the thought Paul is expressing in Romans 3:25–26.[81]

This development constitutes the ground for Packer's emphasis on the penal character of Christ's substitutionary atonement. He states,

> To add this 'qualifier,' ['penal'] ... is to anchor the model of substitution (not exclusively, but regulatively) within the world of moral law, guilty conscience, and retributive justice. ... The notion which the phrase "penal substitution" expresses is that Jesus Christ our Lord, moved by a love that was determined to do everything necessary to save us, endured and exhausted the destructive divine judgement for which we were otherwise

---

[81] J.I. Packer, 'Sacrifice and Satisfaction', in *Shorter Writings*, 1.127–128. Packer clarifies his position by placing it against the backdrop of Faustus Socinus's criticism of the way 'Luther, Calvin, Zwingli, Melancthon and their reforming contemporaries' had stated Anselm's position and the subsequent responses of Reformed theologians such as Francis Turretin and Louis Berkhof. Socinus, according to Packer, resisted a substitutionary understanding of the atonement on the basis that the type of pardon supposedly granted by God is incongruous with our notions of satisfaction, justice, and morality. Reformed critics of Socinus, such as Turretin and Hodge, were well–intended but flawed in their defense against Socinus's attack, according to Packer. They assumed Socinus's frame of reference, 'a natural theology of human government, drawn from the world of contemporary legal and political thought.' This resulted is a defence of substitutionary atonement on the basis that God is like 'a sixteenth– or seventeenth–century monarch, head of both the legislature and the judiciary in his own realm but bound nonetheless to respect existing law and judicial practice at every point.' See Packer, 'What Did the Cross Achieve?: The Logic of Penal Substitution', 86–87. There he criticizes this Reformed defence as being 'defensive rather than declaratory, analytical and apologetic rather than doxological and kerygmatic.' See also J.I. Packer, 'The Redemption and Restoration of Man in the Thought of Richard Baxter,' 305. Packer's observation about the flaw in the Reformed defence against Socinus resembles his analysis of Richard Baxter's soteriology. Baxter, Packer contends, held a view of the atonement different from Calvin's view inasmuch as he held a different view of God's law. Calvin interpreted God's law as a reflection of God's inner character. Hence, it was impossible for God to change the law without denying God's own being. Baxter held to a view of God's law that reflected the notion found in human legal systems. God's law was external to God's self and could be changed. 'When man had fallen, and God purposed to glorify Himself by restoring him, He carried out His plan, not by satisfying the law, but by changing it. ... The penal law of works, with its sanction of death for sin, was enacted, not because it was a natural and necessary expression of the Divine character, but simply because efficient government required it. The demand for retribution was grounded in the nature of government rather than in the nature of God, and could be dispensed with if it seemed wise.'

inescapably destined, and so won us forgiveness, adoption and glory. To affirm penal substitution is to say that believers are in debt to Christ specifically for this, and that this is the mainspring of all their joy, peace and praise both now and for eternity.[82]

Packer attributes this retribution to the righteous character of God. Inasmuch, therefore, as righteousness is at the core of the *imago Dei*, sin causes human beings to lose the only basis for communion with God.

Since God's holiness is reflected in the law and human righteousness has been lost because God's law has been broken, only penal retribution can provide restoration of that communion. He states, 'Penal substitution, as an idea, presupposes a penalty (*poena*) due to us from God the Judge for wrong done and failure to meet his claims.'[83] God's righteousness demands that this violation be punished so that ultimate justice is accomplished and God's sovereignty remains intact. '[T]he retributive principle has his sanction, and indeed expresses the holiness, justice and goodness reflected in his law, and … death, spiritual as well as physical, the loss of the life of God as well as that of the body, is the rightful sentence which he has announced against us, and now prepares to inflict.'[84]

The retributive principle emerges from the nature of God's law as intrinsic to God's nature, thereby binding God, in a sense, to uphold the law and punish any offenses against it. Packer claims,

> The purity and uprightness of God's own character, and his judgments of value (what is good and worthwhile, and what is neither) are fixed and immutable. He cannot be other than hostile to individuals and communities that flout his law. He cannot do other than visit them sooner or later in displays of retributive judgment, so that all his rational creatures may see the glory of his moral inflexibility.[85]

---

[82] Packer, 'What Did the Cross Achieve?', 105.

[83] Ibid., 108.

[84] Ibid., 109. Packer attempts to defend this emphasis on retribution against the charge of polarizing God's wrath and God's love. He asserts that 'penal substitution is a Trinitarian model, for which the motivational unity of Father and Son is axiomatic' (118). He then refers to prominent passages that depict Christ's death for sin (Jn. 3:16, Rom. 5:8, and 1 Jn. 4:8–10) as if they self–evidently involve penal retribution. In this supposed 'motivational unity' he finds the reconciliation between God's love and wrath as expressed in the salvific satisfaction of God's wrath through the punishment of Christ for our sin.

[85] Packer, *A Passion for Holiness*, 135.

For the believer, this retribution is averted. Packer notes that 'through the redemption that is in Christ Jesus justice is done. Sin is punished as it deserves. But it is punished in the person of a substitute.'[86] Thus Packer views the predicament of humanity, due to sin, as most fundamentally a legal predicament that encompasses all other effects of sin.[87]

However, even for believers, for whom Christ's death has provided acquittal from the guilt that would otherwise incur God's retribution, Packer uses the language of retribution to describe God's corrective discipline for the purpose of holiness. He states, 'The unnatural act of backsliding, then, is always to be avoided, both because it provokes our holy heavenly Father to discipline and correct us in a punitive way (as is further explained in Heb 12:5–10), and also because, at some stage and in some measure, bitterness and misery are its ultimate and inescapable fruit.'[88]

Packer's doctrine of retribution wields such significant influence in his soteriology and piety because he relates humanity, made in the image of God, to God's nature through God's law; a relationship that is restored through a modified Anselmic understanding of the atonement.

Packer defends his position against the charge of being 'legal fiction,' that is, 'a form of words to which no reality corresponds,' by claiming that the atonement creates an independent, ontological reality that affects the relationship between believers and God. This is based on what he calls an 'ontological solidarity' between Christ and humanity in which Christ's righteousness is exchanged with our unrighteousness.[89] Packer follows Calvin's emphasis on the double–imputation involved between humanity's

---

[86] Packer, 'Sacrifice and Satisfaction', 128.

[87] Packer, 'What Did the Cross Achieve?' 100–101. Here he makes it clear that the penal substitution view of the atonement accounts for the manner in which other prominent theories of the atonement (e.g., Irenaeus's recapitulation theory, Peter Abelard's moral influence theory, and Gustaf Aulen's *Christus Victor* theory) view sin and its impact on humanity's relation to God. He states that the penal substitution view 'denies nothing asserted by the other two views save their assumption that they are complete. It agrees that there is biblical support for all they say, but it goes further. It grounds humanity's plight as victim of sin and Satan in the fact that, for all God's daily goodness to us, as sinners we stand under divine judgement, and our bondage to evil is the start of our sentence, and unless God's rejection of us is turned into acceptance we are lost for ever. On this view, Christ's death had its effect first on God, who was hereby *propitiated* (or, better, who hereby propitiated himself), and only because it had this effect did it become an overthrowing of the powers of darkness and a revealing of God's seeking and saving love.'

[88] Packer, *A Passion for Holiness*, 87.

[89] Packer, 'What Did the Cross Achieve?' 112.

sin and Christ's righteousness as the basis of justification before God,[90] making the penal, substitutionary character of the atonement the absolute basis of this justification. On any other ground, he claims, justification would indeed be legal fiction, no ontological change would take place between God and humans, and the moral order of the universe would be overturned.[91]

God's work of justification is at the heart of the Gospel for Packer. He accepts justification by faith as the material principle of the Reformation.[92] 'Justification is a judicial act of God pardoning sinners ... accepting them as just, and so putting permanently right their previously estranged relationship with himself. This justifying sentence is God's gift of righteousness (Rom. 5:15–17), his bestowal of a status of acceptance for Jesus' sake (2 Cor. 5:21).'[93] Christ's forensic, penal, substitutionary atonement for sin is the means by which justification takes place.

This forensic work of God is related to the existential restoration of the *imago Dei* through the doctrine of election in which God predetermines those who will be saved and works effectually to awaken them spiritually, regenerate their hearts and minds toward Jesus Christ, and progressively refashion their character into the perfect responsive righteousness that is the image of Christ.[94] 'It [justification] is thus a forensic term, denoting a judicial act of administering the law ... Justification thus settles the legal status of the person justified.'[95] Righteousness, therefore, is formal before it is functional or existential.

The more existential and functional aspects of renewal into the image of Christ come through the separate works of adoption and regeneration. Packer states, 'Justification is the basic blessing, on which adoption is the crowning blessing, to which justification clears the way. Adopted status belongs to all who receive Christ (John 1:12). The adopted status of believers means that in and through Christ God loves them as he loves his only–begotten Son and will share with them all the glory that is Christ's now (Rom. 8:17, 38–39).'[96] He goes on to link adoption with regeneration

---

[90]   Calvin, *Institutes*, II.xii.2.
[91]   J.I. Packer, 'Justification: Introductory Essay', in *Shorter Writings*, 1.142.
[92]   Ibid., 137.
[93]   Packer, *Concise Theology*, 164.
[94]   Packer, 'What Did the Cross Achieve?' 116.
[95]   J.I. Packer, 'Justification', in *EDT*, 593. In this article Packer distinguishes his position from Augustine and others by stating that 'there is no lexical ground for the view of Chrysostom, Augustine, and the medieval and Roman theologians that 'justify' means, or connotes as part of its meaning, '*make* righteous' (by subjective spiritual renewal)' 594.
[96]   Packer, *Concise Theology*, 167.

as 'two aspects of the salvation that Christ brings (John 1:12–13), but they are to be distinguished. Adoption is the bestowal of a relationship, while regeneration is the transformation of our moral nature.'[97] By delineating justification, atonement, adoption, and regeneration in this manner Packer is able to isolate the role of the atonement to the attainment of formal righteous standing before God and God's law. Thereby he defends his position against the charge of 'legal fiction' by defining legal fiction as the absence of any change in ontological reality between God and humans, rather than defining it as the absence of any existential impact of the atonement on humans.[98]

Sanctification builds on the forensic, atoning work of God through Jesus Christ to continue the restoration of the *imago Dei* in a progressive fashion.

> Sanctification, says the Westminster Shorter Catechism (Q.35), is 'the work of God's free grace, whereby we are renewed in the whole man after the image of God, and are enabled more and more to die unto sin, and live unto righteousness.' The concept is not of sin being totally eradicated (that is to claim too much) or merely counteracted (that is to say too little), but of a divinely wrought character change freeing us from sinful habits and forming in us Christlike affections, dispositions, and virtues.
>
> Sanctification is an ongoing transformation within a maintained consecration, and it engenders real righteousness within the frame of relational holiness. Relational sanctification, the state of being permanently set apart for God, flows from the cross, where God through Christ purchased and claimed us for himself (Acts 20:28; 26:18; Heb. 10:10).[99]

The placement and function that Packer assigns to sanctification within the *ordo salutis* carries significant implications for the relationship of anthropology to piety. He places sanctification in the *ordo salutis* as 'a link between regeneration and glorification.'[100]

---

[97] Ibid., 168.

[98] Packer prefers to define atonement as propitiation and expiation rather than in the wider sense of reconciliation. In drawing contemporary lessons from James Orr's theology he reveals the restricted way in which he defines atonement by listing it as a self-contained aspect of Christology, separate from the incarnation and resurrection. J.I. Packer, 'On From Orr: The Cultural Crisis, Rational Realism, and Incarnational Ontology', in *The J.I. Packer Collection*, 260.

[99] Packer, *Concise Theology*, 169.

[100] Packer, '"Keswick" and the Reformed Doctrine of Sanctification', *EvQ* 27 (1955), 154. Packer qualifies this statement in a footnote by claiming to follow Louis

Finding great significance in the order and the unique operation of each aspect of the *ordo salutis*, he repeatedly claims that Keswick piety fails to make these important distinctions. He sees Keswick piety as erroneously confusing sanctification with justification by treating sanctification as a gift that is to be passively received by faith apart from human effort. Keswick piety, he suggests, regards sanctification 'as a second and supplementary blessing' that is received from God by a second and subsequent act of faith. The Keswick *ordo salutis*, to Packer, appears to cohere around or be held together by the human act of faith. It appears to him to seriously underestimate the incapacitation of the will and overestimate a person's ability to exercise faith apart from the direct intervention of God's grace. Thus, he accuses Keswick piety of being inherently Pelagian.[101]

In comparison to the confusion of justification and sanctification that Packer senses in Keswick piety, he nevertheless maintains that sanctification is inextricably linked with justification. To Packer, the difference between his position and the Keswick position is that the organic connection or bond between justification and sanctification actually derives from God's sovereign election and the Holy Spirit's consequent work of regeneration rather than from a common means or criterion (i.e. faith) by which a person receives justification and sanctification. God's sovereign election makes salvation an integrated whole, but in practice the appropriate relationship of justification and sanctification can only be preserved if they function in a strictly sequential or linear process, each aspect with its own properties and requirements. Sanctification is experienced, says Packer, not as a gift to be received by a passive act of faith, but by trusting engagement of the regenerated will in active obedience as the will is empowered by the Holy Spirit.[102] Justification (and regeneration) is the temporal as well as logical prerequisite for sanctification.

> Regeneration was a momentary monergistic act of quickening the spiritually dead. As such, it was God's work alone. Sanctification, however, is in one sense synergistic – it is an ongoing cooperative process

---

Berkhof when he defines regeneration in the narrow sense of the implantation of new life and a new nature. He admits to departing from Calvin's broader emphasis on regeneration as encompassing 'the whole process of subjective renewal.' See also Packer's article, 'Regeneration', in *EDT*, 924–926.

[101] Ibid., 158.

[102] Packer, '"Keswick" and the Reformed Doctrine of Sanctification', 160. He states, 'Reformed theology links sanctification to regeneration, regarding it as the continuation of man's subjective renewal by the Holy Spirit; it represents both operations as centring on the will, and makes acts of repentance and faith their fruit and issue.'

in which regenerate persons, alive to God and freed from sin's dominion (Rom. 6:11,14–18), are required to exert themselves in sustained obedience. God's method of sanctification is neither activism (self–reliant activity) nor apathy (God–reliant passivity), but God–dependent effort (2 Cor. 7:1; Phil. 3:10–14; Heb. 12:14).[103]

This distinction, to Packer, avoids the charge of Pelagianism that he levels against Keswick piety because the distinction assumes the necessary condition of God's sovereign grace, based on individual election, as the only force[104] that can effectively overcome the depth of human depravity, initiating and sustaining a person's movement through the phases of the *ordo salutis*.

A tension repeatedly appears in Packer's theology as he attempts to present sanctification as both entirely the work of God and yet dependent on human activity. This struggle may be a result of both the definitive, *a priori* function he assigns to the doctrine of predestination in his *ordo salutis* and the linear manner in which the aspects of the *ordo salutis* must function in order to maintain this distinction between their respective modes of reception while holding to their organic unity.

In Packer's model, Christ's death for human sin influences sanctification in three ways. First, justification provides entrance into the journey toward restored, experiential holiness. Second, the power that God wielded over sin in Christ's death and resurrection becomes available to the Christian to overcome the power of indwelling sin in daily life.[105] Third, his death

---

[103] Packer, *Concise Theology*, 170–171.

[104] J.I. Packer, *Evangelism and the Sovereignty of God* (Downers Grove: InterVarsity, 1961), 15. Packer's theology of evangelism reflects his belief in irresistible grace when he says, 'You pray for the conversion of others. In what terms, now, do you intercede for them? ... I think that what you do is to pray in categorical terms that God will, quite simply and decisively, save them: that He will open the eyes of their understanding, soften their hard hearts, renew their natures, and move their wills to receive the Saviour. ... You would not dream of making it a point in your prayer that you are not asking God actually to bring them to faith, because you recognize that that is something He cannot do. Nothing of the sort! When you pray for unconverted people, you do so on the assumption that it is in God's power to bring them to faith. ... In your prayer, then ... you *know* that what makes men turn to God is God's own gracious work of drawing them to Himself ...' He also describes the irresistibility of grace in 'The Love of God: Universal and Particular', in *Shorter Writings*, 1.153, stating, 'to Calvinism election is God's resolve to save' and 'Calvinism holds that divine love does not stop short at graciously inviting, but that the triune God takes gracious action to ensure that the elect respond.'

[105] J.I. Packer, 'Sanctification – Puritan Teaching', *The Christian Graduate* (December 1952), 127–128.

provides a model of holiness for all to follow. Nowhere in his most extensive treatment of the effects of Jesus Christ's death on the cross ('What Did the Cross Achieve: The Logic of Penal Substitution') does Packer suggest that the cross has any direct bearing on sanctification. He brings the cross to bear on sanctification when he defends his penal, substitutionary view of the atonement against the charge of legal fiction by claiming that 'ontologically and objectively, in a manner transcending bounds of space and time, Christ has taken us with him into his death and through his death into his resurrection.'[106] Sanctification is not directly in view in this statement, however, thus presenting the resolution of legal guilt before God as the most direct and immediate impact of the cross.

Packer separates Christ's active and passive obedience in their impact on salvation.[107] He admits to following the way in which Richard Hooker, John Davenant, John Owen, and Richard Traill developed Calvin's doctrine of imputed righteousness in order to counter the perceived Arminian claim that personal faith counts for righteousness and forms the basis for God's justification. They 'drew a distinction between Christ's *active* obedience to God's law, in keeping its precepts, and his *passive* obedience to it, in undergoing its penalty, and insisted that our acceptance as righteous depends on the imputing to us of Christ's obedience in both its aspects.'[108]

In Packer's soteriology, Christ's active obedience during his life is necessary for salvation, but only on the basis of what his passive obedience accomplished. That is, his active obedience provided the validation,

---

[106] Packer, 'What Did the Cross Achieve?', 112.

[107] This compartmentalized view would contrast with, for example, that of T.F. Torrance who argues, following Irenaeus and Athanasius, that God the Son's assumption of human nature – even fallen human nature – was integral to the redemption of that fallen human nature. This broadens the purpose and effect of Jesus Christ's humanity in salvation. See T.F. Torrance, 'The Goodness and Dignity of Man', in T.A. Hart and D. Thimell (eds.), *Christ in Our Place: The Humanity of God in Christ for the Reconciliation of the World: Essays Presented to James Torrance* (Exeter: Paternoster, 1989), 379. Loren Wilkinson challenges Packer on the question of Jesus Christ's humanity as 'recapitulation,' arguing, *contra* Packer, that this was involved in the purpose of the incarnation. See L.E. Wilkinson, 'Immanuel and the Purpose of Creation', in *Doing Theology for the People of God: Studies in Honor of J.I. Packer*, 245–261.

[108] J.I. Packer, 'The Doctrine of Justification in Development and Decline Among the Puritans', in *By Schisms Rent Asunder* (London: The Puritan and Reformed Studies Conference, 1969), 21. Packer notes that though 'the distinction between active and passive obedience ... does not appear in the statement on justification in the Westminster Confession, nonetheless this statement is a classic indication of the precision and balance of thought ... learned in these exchanges [with Arminianism and Romanism]' (22).

integrity, and efficacy of the sacrifice for sin he made in his passive obedience.

> Jesus' sinlessness was necessary for our salvation. Had he not been 'a lamb without blemish or defect' his blood would not have been 'precious' (1 Peter 1:19). He would have needed a savior himself, and his death would not have redeemed us. His active obedience (perfect lifelong conformity to God's law for mankind, and to his revealed will for the Messiah) qualified Jesus to become our Savior by dying on the cross. Jesus' passive obedience (enduring the penalty of God's broken law as our sinless substitute) crowned his active obedience to secure the pardon and acceptance of those who put their faith in him ...[109]

His perfect obedience affects sanctification through the cross as God formally credits his righteousness to the account of the believer. Christ was protected from sharing in the fallenness of human nature by being 'made sin' (2 Corinthians 5:21) only in a representative capacity.[110] The cross, then, directly impacts sanctification only in a formal or legal manner. Yet, his Incarnation and general life of obedience (apart from enduring the cross) have no intrinsic saving effect in this strictly forensic, penal model of

---

[109] Packer, *Concise Theology*, 117. Packer perspective resembles Calvin's. Calvin portrays Christ's active obedience as effective only as it culminated in his passive obedience. He states, 'In short, from the time when he took on the form of a servant, he began to pay the price of liberation to redeem us. Yet to define the way of salvation more exactly, Scripture ascribes this as peculiar and proper to Christ's death.' See Calvin, *Institutes*, II.xvi.5.

[110] Packer, 'Justification', in *EDT*, 596. He states, 'By perfectly serving God, Christ perfectly kept the law (cf. Matt. 3:15). His obedience culminated in death (Phil. 2:8); he bore the penalty of the law in men's place (Gal. 3:13), to make propitiation for their sins (Rom. 3:25). On the ground of Christ's obedience, God does not impute sin, but imputes righteousness, to sinners who believe (Rom. 4:2–8; 5:19).' See also See J.I. Packer, 'The Uniqueness of Jesus Christ', in *Shorter Writings*, 1.78. When defending the importance of the Incarnation for justification, Packer states that 'his righteousness, that is his acceptance by the Father, which was maintained by his perfect obedience, is now extended to us for the taking.' This obedience, he goes on to suggest, is the basis of 'our subjective renewal – that is, according to Paul, our co–resurrection with Christ – as taking place "in Christ," through life–giving union and communion with the risen Lord.' See also Packer, 'Systematic Theology B, Man, Sin and Grace,' unpublished course notes, section on 'Christ in Christian Thought,' (Vancouver: Regent College, 1996), 5. Here he contends that though Christ's temptations and struggle were real, he was not capable of sinning because 'it was his nature to do the Father's will, and to resist and struggle with temptation till he had overcome it.'

redemption.[111] The existential impact (e.g. union with Christ and transformation) takes place in the form of discrete actions that result from the cross.

For Packer, Jesus' resurrection was involved in justification as a guarantee from God of the reality of the forgiveness offered in justification.[112] He separates Jesus Christ's saving work into two parts;

> his dealing with his Father on our behalf by offering himself in substitutionary satisfaction for our sins, and [the second is] his dealing with us on his Father's behalf by bestowing on us through faith the forgiveness which his death secured, and it is as important to distinguish these two parts as it is to hold them together. For a demonstration that part two is now possible because part one is finished, and for the actual implementing of part two, Jesus' resurrection is indeed essential, and so appears as an organic element in his work as a whole.[113]

---

[111] C. Gunton notes Augustine's influence on the notion that the Incarnation is oriented only toward sin. Gunton claims that this view connects Christ to the *imago Dei* only in relation to what is corrupted in humanity and logically restricts the Incarnation from being the means for the redemption of all creation. This stems, according to Gunton, from not interpreting the Creation Christologically and results in an inadequate basis for a theology of dominion. The place Packer assigns to dominion in the *imago Dei*, though significant, is indeed secondary or supportive and, thus, consistent with his view of the Incarnation in its relation to salvation. See Gunton, *Christ and Creation* (Grand Rapids: Eerdmans, 1992), 100.

[112] St. Paul connects justification and the resurrection in Rom. 4:25. Packer does not deal with this text in his most extensive treatments of justification, but mentions it while addressing the resurrection. 'It [the resurrection] guarantees the believer's present forgiveness and justification.' Packer, *Concise Theology*, 126. Otherwise, the closest Packer comes to relating the resurrection to justification is when (*Concise Theology*, 165) he contends that the object of justifying faith is 'Jesus Christ as crucified Savior and risen Lord (Rom. 4:23–25; 10:8–13).' He seems to hint at some role for the resurrection in justification when he says, 'justification is God's decisive acceptance of us for all eternity, the judgment of the last day brought forward in time to become a present fact.' J.I. Packer, 'Postscript: Dialogue and Justification', in J.I. Packer, R.T. Beckwith, and G.E. Duffield (eds.), *Across the Divide* (Appleford: Marcham, 1977), 62. The absence of any treatment of the resurrection in relationship to justification in writings such as, 'Justification in Protestant Theology', in J.I. Packer, M. Butterworth, S. Motyer, J. Atkinson, G.L. Bray, and D.H. Wheaton (eds.), *Here We Stand: Justification by Faith Today* (London: Hodder and Stoughton, 1986), 84–102; and 'Justification', in *EDT*, 593–597 suggests that it plays a limited (though not insignificant) role in his soteriology.

[113] Packer, 'What Did the Cross Achieve?', 102. Packer's reference to 'dealing with Father on our behalf' is reminiscent of J. McLeod Campbell, whom he references on

By so dividing Christ's saving work into two parts he assigns the resurrection to that aspect of the Christian experience that grows out of or depends upon justification. He states, '[T]he gospel proclaims a living, vindicated Saviour whose resurrection as the firstfruits of the new humanity is the basis as well as the pattern for ours ...'[114] The resurrection offers Christians encouragement that God's power displayed in the resurrection is available for their struggle against indwelling sin. Furthermore, the resurrection guarantees God's promises of final victory and deliverance. It is the basis of the Christian's hope.

Few aspects of Packer's theology are more influential in his understanding of the Christian life than his theology of the atonement. It is at this point that some pointed and interlocking questions may be asked about the coherence of his position. First, can he claim that his view of the atonement is not 'legal fiction' when the ontological change effected in the atonement must be followed by the existential force of adoption and regeneration? Second, can Jesus' work of forensic atonement achieve the ontological change Packer claims when Jesus shared in humanity's fallen condition only representatively? This is not to suggest that Jesus had to have a sin nature or in any way was personally sinful. However, it is curious that Packer goes to such pains to keep Jesus at a personal (and by implication, ontological) distance from that which most fundamentally separates humanity from God, then claims that his death provided an atonement whose effects are both legal and ontological. Packer ties these effects together by appealing to the interdependent nature of the components in his *ordo salutis*, which are held together by God's sovereign election. Yet, by placing the forensic, penal substitutionary atonement at the controlling position in salvation and by defining atonement merely in terms of God's law and holiness, he has created a formula for the Christian life in

---

p. 120 of this article. Packer and Campbell differ, however, in that Packer applies this equation only to the elect. Campbell contends that Christ died for all because God's love is equally central to God's nature, God's love prompting forgiveness and forgiveness prompting the atonement. Campbell reacts against the position of John Owen and Jonathan Edwards (whom Packer would follow) by claiming that 'they set forth justice as a necessary attribute of the divine nature, so that God must deal with *all men* according to its requirements, they represent mercy and love as not necessary, but arbitrary, and what, therefore, may find their expression in the history of *only some* men. For according to their system justice alone is expressed in the history of all men, that is to say, in the history of the non–elect, in their endurance of punishment; in the history of the elect, in Christ's enduring it for them. Mercy and love are expressed in the history of the elect alone.' See J. M. Campbell, *The Nature of the Atonement* (Edinburgh: Handsel, 1996²), 73.

[114] Ibid., 101.

which the existential effects of salvation are not intrinsic to the most vital aspect of Christ's saving work. Rather, they are the outgrowth (however, logically necessary) of that work. Packer's own paradigm for the Christian life, seen through the lens of the atonement, may be subject to a liability that would create the same result he challenges in other pieties that offer redemption without transformation.

The role of Christ's atonement in the Christian life depends largely on the nature of the human condition for which atonement is required. The nature of sin also determines the nature of the sanctification process as the believer responds to God's call for personal holiness on the basis of the atonement that has been made for sin. In addition to the atonement, then, Packer's understanding of sin is essential to his theology of the Christian life.

4.2.3.3 ORIGINAL AND INDWELLING SIN

The compelling and ongoing influence of original and indwelling sin are at the heart of Packer's soteriology and, consequently, shapes his theology of piety. He expresses more certainty about the character of original sin than about its origin.

> So the universal wilfulness that leads us to go our own way and do our thing is the instinct – we could even say the allergy – of original sin making itself felt. Original sin is a mystery. That means there is more in it than our minds can grasp, or more than God has told us, or maybe both. Certainly, the folly, discontent, ingratitude, thoughtlessness, irreverence, credulity, and arrogance of the first human sin, as narrated in Genesis 3, defy rational explanation. When Paul affirms everyone's solidarity with Adam in condemnation and subjection to sin and death ... he does not enlarge on how this is so. We have to say of original sin, therefore, that it is a perversion in us all that none of us fully understand.[115]

He claims to follow Augustine in defining original sin as pride.

> What drives the world? pride, plus pride's daughter, paranoia – the sense of being constantly threatened unless one can collar more power than one has at the moment. Augustine analyzed 'original sin' as pride (*superbia*), the passion to be 'top person,' independent, self–sufficient, big, strong and, thus, secure. And surely he was right. No profounder analysis is possible, for this is the very heart – the heart of the heart, we might say –

---

[115] J.I. Packer, 'Doing It My Way – Are We Born Rebels?', in J.N. Akers, J.H. Armstrong, and J.D. Woodbridge (eds.), *This We Believe: The Good News of Jesus Christ for the World* (Grand Rapids: Zondervan, 2000), 45.

of the 'play–God, fight–God, kill–God' syndrome that infected our race in Eden and rules the unregenerate still.[116]

This disposition of heart equates to an outright rejection of God's reign by refusing to obey God's law. He states, '*Sin* may be comprehensively defined as lack of conformity to the law of God in act, habit, attitude, outlook, disposition, motivation, and mode of existence.'[117] God's law so clearly expresses God's character that to disobey the law is to show despite to God.

Based on the assumption that Adam was representative of all humanity, the effects of the Fall involve all humanity in the curse of Adam's guilt.

> God made the first man the representative for all his posterity, just as he was to make Jesus Christ the representative for all God's elect (Rom. 5:15–19 with 8:29–30; 9:22–26). In each case the representative was to involve those whom he represented in the fruits of his personal action, whether for good or ill, just as a national leader involves his people in the consequences of his action … It would seem that the tree [of the knowledge of good and evil] bore this name because the issue was whether Adam would let God tell him what was good and bad for him or would seek to decide that for himself, in disregard of what God had said. By eating from this tree Adam would, in effect, be claiming that he could know and decide what was good and evil for him without any reference to God. … The results were that, first, the anti–God, self–aggrandizing mindset expressed in Adam's sin became part of him and of the moral nature that he passed on to his descendants (Gen. 6:5; Rom. 3:9–20). Second, Adam and Eve found themselves gripped by a sense of pollution and guilt that made them ashamed and fearful before God – with good reason. Third, they were cursed with expectations of pain and death, and they were expelled from Eden.[118]

---

[116] Packer, 'The Christian and God's World', in *Shorter Writings*, 2.278. Packer's definition of sin resembles Augustine's more closely than Calvin's. Calvin agrees with Augustine's declaration that sin is essentially pride, but develops his definition more fully in light of the temptation that precipitated Adam's sin. Calvin claims, 'Unfaithfulness, then, was the root of the Fall. But thereafter ambition and pride, together with ungratefulness, arose, because Adam by seeking more than was granted him shamefully spurned God's great bounty, which had been lavished upon him.' See Calvin, *Institutes*, II.ii.4.

[117] Packer, *Concise Theology*, 82.

[118] Ibid., 79–80.

Though Packer admits that '[o]riginal sin is a mystery,' and 'a perversion in us all that none of us fully understand,'[119] he is not so restrained about its effects. Those effects are best understood in light of God's intentions for humanity as expressed in creation. 'The doctrine of original sin ... explains to us that life as we live it and observe it in others is not life as our Creator meant it to be.'[120] Packer and Thomas Howard highlight the tragedy of sin by contrasting it to the humanity that God intended. They state, '[I]t is sin that dehumanizes, and it is only in the matrix of holiness that authentic humanness takes shape.'[121]

By contrasting original sin to God's original intentions for humanity Packer sees it as alien to fundamental human nature, yet affecting all people.

> The assertion of original sin means not that sin belongs to human nature as God made it (God made mankind upright, Eccles. 7:29), nor that sin is involved in the processes of reproduction and birth (the uncleanness connected with menstruation, semen, and childbirth in Leviticus 12 and 15 was typical and ceremonial only, not moral and real), but that (a) sinfulness marks everyone from birth, and is there in the form of a motivationally twisted heart, prior to any actual sins; (b) this inner sinfulness is the root and source of all actual sins; (c) it derives to us in a real though mysterious way from Adam, our first representative before God.[122]

He also resists speculation about the nature of sin's transmission from generation to generation (in contrast to Augustine, but similar to Calvin).[123]

---

[119] Packer, 'Doing It My Way – Are We Born Rebels?', 45.

[120] Ibid., 47.

[121] J.I. Packer and T. Howard, *Christianity: The True Humanism* (Berkhamsted: Word, 1985), 50.

[122] Packer, *Concise Theology*, 83.

[123] Calvin likewise stops short of speculation about how sin is transmitted, simply affirming that sin is such a corruption of human nature in Adam that it is transmitted to all his descendants. 'Therefore, all of us, who have descended from impure seed, are born infected with the contagion of sin. ... We must surely hold that Adam was not only the progenitor but, as it were, the root of human nature; and that therefore in his corruption mankind deserved to be vitiated.' Also, 'the beginning of corruption in Adam was such that it was conveyed in a perpetual stream from the ancestors into their descendants. For the contagion does not take its origin from the substance of the flesh or soul, but because it had been so ordained by God that the first man should at one and the same time have and lose, both for himself and for his descendants, the gifts that God had bestowed upon him.' See Calvin, *Institutes*, II.ii.6,7. In these passages can be found hints at both a representative and a traducian view of sin's

The effects of sin extend to all areas of human life and incapacitate all people from acceptable, moral response to God. Packer states,

> The phrase *total depravity* is commonly used to make explicit the implications of original sin. It signifies a corruption of our moral and spiritual nature that is total not in degree (for no one is as bad as he or she might be) but in extent. It declares that no part of us is untouched by sin, and therefore no action of ours is as good as it should be, and consequently nothing in us or about us ever appears meritorious in God's eyes. ... Total depravity entails total inability, that is, the state of not having it in oneself to respond to God and his Word in a sincere and wholehearted way (John 6:44; Rom. 8:7–8). Paul calls this unresponsiveness of the fallen heart a state of death ...[124]

This depravity or death is experienced as captivity to sin. He states, 'We have no natural ability to discern and choose God's way because we have no natural inclination Godward; our hearts are in bondage to sin, and only the grace of regeneration can free us from that slavery.'[125] This inherited sinfulness is the source of the actual, ongoing sin in the life of every person.

---

transmission. Yet, Calvin never clearly declares either of these. Augustine suggests that sin is transmitted seminally when he speaks of 'the debt which the contagion of carnal generation contracted.' See Augustine, *On Original Sin* in P. Schaff (ed.), *A Select Library of the Nicene and Post–Nicene Fathers of the Christian: St. Augusting: Anti–Pelagian Writings*, vol. V, P. Holmes and R.E. Wallis (trs.), (Grand Rapids: Eerdmans, 1978[2]), 37.250. Augustine compares the transmission of sin through human generations to the reproduction of wild olive seeds by both wild and cultivated olive trees, then goes on to defend Christ's sinlessness on the basis that Mary was never 'injected' with 'the cause of lust (45., 253).' See also *On the Trinity* in P. Schaff (ed.), *A Select Library of the Nicene and Post–Nicene Fathers of the Christian Church: St. Augustine: On the Holy Trinity, Doctrinal Treatises, Moral Treatises*, vol. III, A.W. Haddan (tr.), (Grand Rapids: Eerdmans, 1983[2]), 13.18.23., 180.

[124] Packer, *Concise Theology*, 83–84.

[125] Ibid., 86. Packer wholeheartedly subscribes to Luther's perspective in *The Bondage of the Will*. Along with O.R. Johnston, Packer translated Luther's work and wrote a lengthy, laudatory introduction. Here they summarise and clarify Luther's polemic as vying against 'the ideal of rational autonomy and self–sufficiency in theology – the ideal of philosophers and Scholastic theologians, to find out and know God by the use of their own unaided reason. ... Man's part, therefore, is to humble his proud mind, to renounce the sinful self–sufficiency which prompts him to treat himself as the measure of all things, to confess the blindness of his corrupt heart, and thankfully to receive the enlightening Word of God. Man is by nature as completely unable to know God as to please God; let him face the fact and admit it! ... This is the point of

Central to both Packer's theology of piety and his anthropology is the notion that sin's influence continues throughout the course of human life and is never fully overcome, even in the life of the Christian.

> Like Isaiah in the temple, so with Christians everywhere. The more vividly they see how holy God is, the more poignantly they feel how sinful and corrupt they are themselves. Because spiritual advance thus enlarges insight into the depth of one's own fallenness, those going forward in holiness often feel they are going backward. Their deepened awareness of how sinful they still are, despite their longing to serve God flawlessly, weighs them down.[126]

The effect of this indwelling sin is that every person experiences an innate, lifelong, and insurmountable inclination toward sin. This view, characteristic of Calvinistic theology, constitutes a point of differentiation from some other evangelical views wherein sin is seen as a disposition that can be experientially overcome.[127] Though these other views do not take a

---

Luther's polemic against reason' J.I. Packer and O.R. Johnston, Introduction to M. Luther, *The Bondage of the Will* (London: James Clarke and Co., 1957), reprint (Grand Rapids: Revell, 1999), 45–47. This understanding of Luther's argument illustrates the relationship in which Packer places the will and the reason. The will is that which is most directly in bondage to sin. The reason, as a result, is incapable of knowing God apart from God's intervention. In this schema God's aid must be directed at the will in order for the reason to know God.

[126] Packer, *A Passion for Holiness*, 221.

[127] J.I. Packer, 'Holiness Movement', in *NDT*, 314. Packer uses the Wesleyan, Keswick, and Pentecostal movements as examples of piety that derived from Wesley's teaching that 'God roots all sin out of Christian hearts in this life, so that motivationally Christians become all love. ... It was held to be wrought instantaneously in response to earnest seeking, and to be attested immediately by the inner witness of the Holy Spirit. ... Christians will advance spiritually after being sanctified, as they did before, but with an altered experience, since their hearts are now ablaze with love to God and man, and nothing else. Unwise, inept and misconceived action can still occur, but motivationally the sanctified are sinless.' Charles G. Finney was in the lineage of those who Packer rebuts. Finney held to the possibility of complete sanctification by defining it as the total consecration of the will. Finney states in reference to sanctification that 'holiness consists, not at all in the constitution of body or mind; but that it belongs, strictly, only to the will or heart, and consists in obedience of will to the law of God, as it lies revealed in the intellect; that it is expressed in one word, love.' See C.G. Finney, *Lectures on Systematic Theology*, 403. However, Finney takes issue with the charge of 'perfectionism,' claiming that entire sanctification is something utterly different. The error of perfectionism, Finney asserts, results as a reaction to teaching that denies the

uniform expression, Packer goes to great pains to contend that they either reflect a Pelagian spirit or practice an erroneous biblical exegesis that is influenced by naïve optimism. In fact, he levels both of these criticisms against his earliest and most longstanding theological target, Keswick piety.[128]

For the sake of comparison, Packer's rather pessimistic portrayal of indwelling sin and his contentions against Keswick and Wesleyan piety must be juxtaposed to Calvin's comment on 1 John 3:9 wherein Calvin seems to suggest the possibility of a considerable degree of victory over sin. Calvin states,

> *And he cannot sin.* Here the Apostle ascends higher, for he plainly declares that the hearts of the godly are so effectually governed by the Spirit of God, that through an inflexible disposition they follow his guidance. ... [H]e not only shews that we cannot sin, but also that the power of the Spirit is so effectual, that it necessarily retains us in continual obedience to righteousness. Nor is this the only passage of Scripture which teaches us that the will is so formed that it cannot be otherwise than right.[129]

---

possibility of entire sanctification. When no hope of deliverance of sin is offered, those earnestly seeking it are ultimately estranged from their churches and pastors. This estrangement, then, subjects them the temptations of antinomianism in an effort to find release. See C.G. Finney, *Principles of Sanctification*, 110f. Packer draws upon B.B. Warfield's analysis of theological developments that appear to be versions of 'perfectionism' as Warfield combated them in *Perfectionism*, vols. 7 and 8, *The Works of Benjamin B. Warfield*. Most directly relevant to the piety that Packer criticises are Warfield's critiques of the 'Higher Life' and 'Victorious Life' movements (pp. 463–610, reprint ed.) in which he examines the foundations laid for Keswick piety by Hannah Whitall Smith, Robert Pearsall Smith, and Charles G. Trumbull. See Packer's footnotes to Warfield in '"Keswick" and the Reformed Doctrine of Sanctification', 153,165.

[128] Packer, '"Keswick" and the Reformed Doctrine of Sanctification', 154,158,166. Though Packer accuses Keswick piety of Pelagianism, at least at the tacit and functional levels, he finds it to combine a modified Augustinian view of sin (a sinful nature without a sinful will, p. 159) with a misplacement of sanctification in the *ordo salutis* (p. 154) and a misunderstanding of the Christian's apprehension of the Holy Spirit's role (p. 160), such that the sin nature is not eradicated, simply circumvented or 'counteracted.'

[129] J. Calvin, *Commentaries on the Catholic Epistles*, J. Owen (tr.), (Grand Rapids: Eerdmans, 1948[2]), 213.

It may be asked whether Packer, in reaction against Keswick and Wesleyan piety, has actually gone further than Calvin in his portrayal of the power of indwelling sin vis–à–vis God's grace in sanctification.

The ongoing power of indwelling sin in the life of the Christian relates to Packer's view of how the saving work of Christ affects the human condition, both formally and existentially. The formal aspect of restoration is accomplished entirely and all–at–once through the atonement while the existential aspect is restored or realized only partially and progressively through the process of sanctification.

Late in his theological career Packer still maintained this contention through his exegesis of Romans 7:14–25.[130] The concept of the 'wretched man' constitutes for Packer a definitive model of sin's function in the ongoing experience of every Christian. He maintains that the 'wretched man' is the Apostle Paul's description of his own ongoing experience as a Christian, thus denoting the residing and unavoidable presence and power of sin. In fact, he argues, the Holy Spirit's work of regeneration and sanctification exacerbate the sense of dissonance and 'wretchedness' in the life of the Christian. He anchors this position in Augustine's theology.

In the fifth century, facing the Pelagian claim that power to keep God's law remains universal, despite sin, Augustine came to think that the 'wretched man' is Paul as he writes Romans, showing by means of his self–assessment that we must rely every moment on God's mercy and grace for salvation, inasmuch as our attempted obedience always fall[s] short. By contrast, Pelagians then and since have taken the 'wretched man' to be someone other than a Christian. ...

In the sixteenth century, confronted by theologies that referred this whole passage to preconversion existence and denied that desires to sin are sinful when not yielded to, Luther, Calvin, and all the magisterial Reformers except Bucer and Musculus invoked the passage as exegeted by Augustine to show that there is sin in the best Christians' best works: all that we do, however good by comparison with what we once did and others do still, falls short of perfection, both motivational and substantive, and so cannot gain merit in God's sight.[131]

---

[130] Packer, 'The "Wretched Man" Revisited', 70–81. Interestingly, this essay defending the Reformed understanding of indwelling sin is part of a *Festschrift* to Packer's colleague Gordon D. Fee. Packer concludes the essay, '*Pace* my honored colleague Gordon Fee, then, I remain a convinced and unrepentant Augustianian with regard to the "wretched man"' (p. 81).

[131] Ibid., 71.

This experience of 'wretchedness,' that is, the struggle with indwelling sin is the experience of every believer. The nature of this struggle must be understood, however, if Packer's full meaning is to be captured.

The state of 'wretchedness,' as Packer understands the Apostle Paul's description, is not necessarily a state of perpetual misery or defeat. In order to describe it, he attempts to dispel 'three common misconceptions.' First, he claims, Paul was primarily attempting to describe his frustration at having come to understand, after the fact, sin's deceptive force on him. 'Paul's text delineates a state of frustration at this repeated discovery, rather than of unavailing struggle remembered as such.'[132] Second, the state of 'wretchedness' that Paul describes does not denote complete or absolute moral failure. 'Paul is not telling us that the life of the 'wretched man' is as bad as it could be, only that it is not as good as it should be, and that because the man delights in the law and longs to keep it perfectly his continued inability to do so troubles him acutely.'[133] Third, he suggests, Paul was not in this passage proposing any particular method of spiritual growth or offering insight into how this struggle might be overcome. Rather, he [Paul] is merely affirming the value of God's law even though its holy demands prompt this keen awareness of sinfulness and struggle.[134]

The nature of this struggle with indwelling sin is the active, personal context of spiritual growth and constitutes one reason that hope is a central theme in the Christian experience.

> There is no sinless perfection in this life. Sinless perfection is part of the hope of glory. Here, the best the Lord enables us to do is less than perfect, and we must constantly ask God to forgive what is defective. ... If you have understood the second half of Romans 7 where we see Paul at his best, reaching out after perfection and then lamenting that his reach exceeds his grasp, you will appreciate what I am saying. However much we use the means of grace, we shall never cease to be in this life hell–deserving sinners living daily by pardon.[135]

Packer portrays indwelling sin as 'desire,' corresponding to his insistence that sin's most devastating, corrupting effect is on the will. He develops this definition of indwelling sin in terms of a typical, growing Christian's personal experience. 'Discerning sinful desires in themselves despite their longing to be sin–free, and finding that in their quest for total

---

[132] Ibid., 77.
[133] Ibid.
[134] Ibid., 78.
[135] J.I. Packer, 'The Means of Growth', in *Shorter Writings*, 2.291.

righteousness their reach exceeds their grasp, they will live in tension and distress at their frustrating infirmities (cf. Rom. 7:14–25).'[136]

Indwelling sin or the 'sin nature' and 'flesh' are synonymous with the biblical concept of *sarx* (e.g. Roman 8:5) for Packer, though he qualifies what 'flesh' does and does not imply. In explaining the reference to the 'flesh' (NRSV) or 'sinful nature' (NIV) in Romans 7:25, he comments,

> 'Sinful nature' is not a happy rendering of 'flesh,' though it is hard to find a better. 'Nature' suggests that sin is the 'real me,' which in a regenerate believer is not the case. 'Flesh' in Paul has to do with the person, not just that person's body, and points to the reality of desire misdirected toward earthly and self–serving objectives rather than the service of God. Sin, personified as a tyrant in 3:9; 5:21; 6:12,14,23, is the chameleon energy that thus misdirects. 'Sinful streak' and 'corrupt and deviant conation' would hardly do in a general–purposes translation of the Bible, but both phrases have a semantic field nearer to what Paul means by 'flesh.'[137]

In one of his more popular–level works he more cryptically defines and qualifies the 'flesh' as 'the sinful self,' thus differentiating between indwelling sin and one's essential personhood.[138] Paul's use of *sarx* in Romans 8:5 portrays, for Packer, the regenerate person's struggle with sin. He clarifies his understanding of 'flesh' by referring to the manner in which the Apostle Paul contrasts flesh with Spirit. 'As "flesh" in Paul is always some aspect of life under the old order, so "spirit" – always when used of God's Spirit and almost always when used of the human spirit, the self to which the divine Spirit ministers – points to the life of the new order.'[139] In this context he again uses his favoured phrase of *one's reach exceeding one's grasp* to portray the implications of this concept.[140]

The effect of indwelling sin is a continual battle between opposing forces in the life of the Christian. Yet, the continual reaching toward holiness indicates that between these opposing forces the regenerate life is preeminent and provides ultimate hope of deliverance.

> God unites the individual to the risen Lord in such a way that the dispositional drives of Christ's perfect human character – the inner urgings, that is, to honour, adore, love, obey, serve and please God, and to benefit others for both their sake and his sake – are reproduced at the

---

[136] Packer, 'Evangelical Foundations for Spirituality', 265.

[137] Packer, 'The "Wretched Man" Revisited', 73.

[138] Packer, *Growing in Christ*, 187.

[139] J.I. Packer, 'The Holy Spirit and His Work', in *Shorter Writings*, 1.230.

[140] Packer, *Keep in Step with the Spirit*, 128.

motivational centre of that individual's being. And they are reproduced, in face of the contrary egocentric cravings of fallen nature, in a dominant way, so that the Christian, though still troubled and tormented by the urgings of indwelling sin, is no longer ruled by those urgings in the way that was true before.[141]

Regeneration does not, however, eliminate inclinations toward sin. As a result of sin, human nature is capable of multiple and incongruent facets. He cautions,

> A widespread but misleading line of teaching tells us that Christians have two natures: an old one and a new one. They must obey the latter while denying the former. ... The misleading thing here is not the reminder that we are called to holiness and not to sin, but that the idea of 'nature' is not being used as it is used both in life and in Scripture (see, for example, Rom 2:14; Eph 2:3). The point is that 'nature' means the whole of what we are, and the whole of what we are is expressed in the various actions and reactions that make up our life. To envisage two 'natures,' two distinct sets of desires, neither of which masters me till I choose to let it, is unreal and bewildering, because it leaves out so much of what actually goes on inside me.[142]

Thus, for Packer, the presence and power of indwelling sin is the cause for continual, vigilant spiritual battle. However, it also draws attention to the promise of final victory and freedom as a motivation for the pursuit of holiness.

The issue of indwelling sin also includes the question of how, to Packer, indwelling sin or the sinful nature relates to the biblical concepts of 'natural' and 'spiritual.' Scripture compares *psychikos* ('those who are unspiritual' – NRSV) and *pneumatikos* ('those who are spiritual' – NRSV) in 1 Corinthians 2:14,15.[143] The critical question is how Packer relates these

---

[141] Packer, 'Evangelical Foundations for Spirituality', 259.

[142] Packer, *A Passion for Holiness*, 83–84. Packer never directly identifies the source of this 'widespread but misleading line of teaching,' though it bears the marks of his criticism of Keswick and Wesleyan piety, along with those whom he thinks posit a false polarization of flesh and spirit. See pp. 110–112.

[143] G.D. Fee notes the 'considerable debate' over why Paul used the term *psychikoi* instead of *sarx* to pose a contrast with *pneumatikoi*. He concludes that, despite the debatable points, 'the ... description demonstrates that it refers to those who do not have the Spirit, and thus to the merely human. ... More likely it comes out of his own [Paul's] Jewish background , where the Greek noun *psyche* has been used to translate Heb. *nepes*, which often simply denotes humanity in its natural, physical existence.

concepts and, specifically, what he understands to be implied in the way the Apostle Paul contrasts them. The contrast between 'spiritual' and 'unspiritual,' to Packer, pertains to the ability to apprehend God's revealed truth, rather than implying levels of spiritual maturity or commitment. Packer uses 1 Corinthians 2:14 as his keynote text for his chapter on the subject of illumination in *Concise Theology*.[144]

He interprets the *psychikos* ("unspiritual") as the unregenerate who do not possess the Holy Spirit and, hence, have not comprehended 'the reality and relevance of those activities of the triune God to which Scripture testifies.'[145] Packer uses 'spiritual' as a simple descriptor of believers, not to denote a level of spiritual maturity among believers or to polarize the incorporeal and corporeal aspects of human life and nature. To be 'unspiritual,' conversely, is to be unregenerate.

Packer proceeds to describe the *sarkinois* ('people of the flesh') of 1 Corinthians 3:1 as immature, worldly Christians. He refers to them as 'double–minded, halfhearted, world–dominated, sin–indulging believers ('carnal' folk, 'men of the flesh ... babes in Christ' as Paul calls them in 1 Corinthians 3:1).'[146] To Packer, Paul was identifying the type of ministry required for these people because they were behaving as if they were unregenerate. In this manner, he attempts to avoid a view of 'spiritual' that encourages a passive approach to the Christian life[147] and a view of 'unspiritual' that separates faith from repentance and obedience.[148] Packer vigorously rejects any piety in which 'spiritual' somehow indicates a mode

---

This seems to be his present point. With this term he is designating people who are not now, nor have they ever been believers.' *The First Epistle to the Corinthians*, NICNT (Grand Rapids: Eerdmans, 1987), 116.

[144] Packer, *Concise Theology*, 154.

[145] Ibid. See also *Keep in Step with the Spirit*, 238. He takes this text to be Paul's confirmation that 'only through the Spirit do our sin–darkened minds gain sure knowledge of divine things ...'

[146] Packer, *Keep in Step with the Spirit*, 150. In three other places, Packer reiterates this point that those addressed in 1 Cor. 3:1 are in fact Christians who are 'babyish and carnal, behaving in ways that for Christians are inconsistent (31),' characterised by 'moral carelessness (114),' unspiritual babes in Christ, unable to take solid food' (203).

[147] Ibid., 155–157.

[148] J.I. Packer, 'Understanding the Lordship Controversy', in *Shorter Writings*, 2.213. See also *Keep in Step with the Spirit*, 151, where he criticises the Keswick suggestion that one can choose 'to be a "carnal Christian" – that is, one who receives Christ as Saviour but not as Sanctifier ...'

of relating to the Holy Spirit that circumvents or terminates the struggle against indwelling sin.[149]

The Apostle Paul's contrast of the unspiritual and spiritual persons appears to correlate in Packer's thought to the contrast of the 'old' and 'new;' for example, *palaion anthropon* ('old self' – NRSV and NIV) and *ton neon ton anakainoumenon* ('new self'– NRSV and NIV) in Colossians 3:9, 10.

> Putting off and putting on is the language of changing clothes, and when the NIV renders 'man' as 'self' it misses some of the meaning; what the Christian has put off is solidarity with Adam, and what he puts on is Christ, or solidarity with Christ, as the source and principle of his new life (cf. Rom. 13:14; Gal. 3:28).
>
> Each image entails the thought of a totally fresh beginning: one has ceased to be what one was, and has commenced to be what previously one was not. Paul then charts the course of this newness in terms of being restored as God's image (Col. 3:10), serving righteousness and God as bondslaves of both (Rom. 6:16–23), and bringing forth the fruit of the Spirit (Gal. 5:22–25) ... Motivationally, within the heart, the change is an implanting in us of the inclinations of Christ's perfect humanity through

---

[149] The most well–developed theological exposition of this view was offered by L.S. Chafer in *He That Is Spiritual: A Classic Study of the Biblical Doctrine of Spirituality* (n.p.: Our Hope Publisher, 1918). Though not formally or institutionally connected to the Keswick movement, the Dispensationalist theological tradition inherited, systematised, and perpetuated by Chafer drew heavily upon the ethos of the Keswick movement through Bible teachers such as C.I. Scofield and W.H. Griffith-Thomas. Chafer understood 'spiritual' in two different senses. The first sense simply treats the difference between 'natural' and 'spiritual' in 1 Cor. 2:14 as the difference between the unregenerate and the regenerate inasmuch as the regenerate have the Holy Spirit's indwelling presence as a result of having personally accepted Christ in order to secure salvation from sin and consequent eternal blessing (pp. 22, 118 in reprint ed.). The second sense is somewhat more discrete, deriving from an exegesis of 1 Cor. 3:1–15 in which he develops the notion of three types of people in the world; the unregenerate, i.e. non–Christians, Christians who are worldly or 'carnal' and 'unspiritual,' and Christians who are utterly and consciously submissive to God and, hence, 'spiritual.' In this sense 'spiritual' denotes one who has a particular and advanced type of relationship with the Holy Spirit. Chafer is another who advocated a form of piety that appears to Packer to be both passive and a modified form of perfectionism. Chafer states that '... true spirituality means, for the time, not wishing to sin ... but this does not imply the eradication of the ability to sin: it means rather that, because of the energizing power of God, a complete victory for the present time is possible' (131).

our ingrafting into him: this produces in us a mind–set and lifestyle that is not explicable in terms of what we were before.[150]

Thus, being 'unspiritual' and defined by the 'old' characterise an unregenerate condition in which the sinful, Adamic nature dominates one's life. 'Spiritual' and 'new' both mark the condition in which the Holy Spirit has brought understanding of the gospel and implanted the life of Christ in a person, bringing with it an entirely new and dominant (though not exclusive or unidirectional) set of desires. It is not clear, however, how Packer reconciles his view that human nature is a unified whole with his claim that sin can still be so powerfully embedded in the will after regeneration, especially when the will (volition, desire) is at the very heart of the material *imago Dei*, the concept that defines human nature.

Packer's use of the term 'regeneration' adds further insight into his view of the 'old' self.

> Regeneration in Christ changes the disposition from lawless, Godless, self–seeking (Rom. 3:9–18; 8:7) which dominates man in Adam into one of trust and love, of repentance for past rebelliousness and unbelief, and loving compliance with God's law henceforth. It enlightens the blinded mind to discern spiritual realities ... and liberates and energizes the enslaved will for free obedience to God (Rom. 6:14,17–22; Phil. 2:13). ... The regenerate man has forever ceased to be the man he was; his old life is over and a new life has begun; he is a new creature in Christ, buried with him out of reach of condemnation and raised with him into a new life of righteousness (see Rom. 6:3–11; II Cor. 5:17; Col. 3:9–11).[151]

Here the 'old' self of Romans 5 and 6 seems to be synonymous with the 'old' self in 2 Corinthians 5:17. Packer also refers to this self as the 'carnal' self, 'that is to say self–will, self–assertion, the Adamic syndrome, the sinful, egocentric, behavior–pattern which one has been developing from birth, the recurring irrational impulse to do anything rather obey God and embrace what one knows to be right.'[152] This self is utterly unresponsive to God and incapable of fulfilling the *imago Dei* due to the 'death' or enslavement of the will to sin. Accordingly, he denounces the notion of free will in much the same way that Luther did.

> Free will ... has been defined by Christian teachers from the second century on as the ability to choose all the moral options that a situation

---

[150] Packer, 'Evangelical Foundations for Spirituality', 264, 265.

[151] J.I. Packer, 'Regeneration', in *EDT*, 924.

[152] Packer, Introduction to *Sin and Temptation*, xxvi–xxvii.

offers, and Augustine affirmed against Pelagius and most of the Greek Fathers that original sin has robbed us of free will in this sense. We have no natural ability to discern and choose God's way because we have no natural inclination Godward; our hearts are in bondage to sin, and only the grace of regeneration can free us from that slavery. This, for substance, was what Paul taught in Romans 6:16–23; only the *freed* will (Paul says, the freed person) freely and heartily chooses righteousness.[153]

This enslavement of the will necessitates regeneration before any progress in sanctification occurs.

In the regenerate or 'new' humanity Packer still sees the presence and power of indwelling sin. However, indwelling sin no longer has absolute power over the regenerate person. Though there is no escape from this struggle in the present life, but there is assistance from the ministry of Holy Spirit. He states his understanding of the Spirit's role in relation to the Christian's battle with sin. 'The Father and the Son have given us the Spirit, we might say, so that he may give us back to the Father and the Son by sovereignly inducing us to give ourselves back, as the free and resolute determination of hearts now freed from sin's dominion.'[154]

The reality and power of indwelling sin, even in Christians, was the subject of one of Packer's earliest controversies. He reacted against a Keswick perspective, which he understood to offer a state of perpetual victory over indwelling sin through an act or moment of self–denial and total consecration to God. He personally moved to the view that the believer's commitment to God is expressed in a vigorous struggle against the power of sin and that victory over sin is never more than partial this side of the eschaton. In Packer's view, shaped predominantly by his study of John Owen, J.C. Ryle, and B.B. Warfield,[155] the role of the Holy Spirit is to energize the believer's will to do battle against indwelling sin rather than bring the battle to an end through conscious reliance on the Holy Spirit.[156]

---

[153] Packer, *Concise Theology*, 86.

[154] Packer, *A Passion for Holiness*, 228.

[155] McGrath, *To Know and Serve God*, 77, 88, 89, 91.

[156] J.I. Packer, '"Keswick" and the Reformed Doctrine of Sanctification', 160–161. He states, 'Reformed theology teaches that the Spirit's sanctifying work is a hidden activity which manifests itself by its effects in consciousness and life: evoking and working through the Christian's use of his own faculties, the Spirit enlightens him to know God's truth and causes him to love and to do it. ... Keswick ... teaches that, instead of working through our conscious personal life, the Spirit stands over against it. His indwelling means that He is present, not to empower us for action, but merely to tell us what we ought to do ...'

At the heart of Packer's critique of the Keswick position on sanctification was that it does not recognise the fallenness of the will; nor does it see the need for God's regenerative work to apply to the will. He summarises this sentiment by stating, 'Now we can see the essential difference and root disagreement between the Reformed and Keswick doctrines of sanctification. *Keswick teaching is Pelagian through and through.* There is no hint in *So Great Salvation* [by Steven Barabas] that God's sovereignty extends to the will, or that His sanctifying activity in any way affects the will.'[157]

Thus, Packer's focus on the fallenness of the will emerges again as central to his understanding of human nature, regardless of whether he has properly understood Barabas and the Keswick position.[158] It is the will that must be first be regenerated in order for the other aspects of humanity to experience restoration. Keswick, in Packer's view, does not assume utter dependence on God for the liberation of the will in order to respond to God for sanctification.[159]

4.2.4 In Relation to the Image of God in Jesus Christ

Holiness, for J.I. Packer, can never be fully understood or realised by humanity apart from a perfect, human model of that holiness. Jesus Christ, the incarnate Son of God provides that essential model. It is not unusual to find Jesus Christ occupying a central role in paradigms of holiness, though there is variety in how that role is conceived.[160]

---

[157] Ibid., 158.

[158] Barabas's own words offer a different impression than Packer gives. Barabas states, 'The effect of sin may be traced in the impairment of voluntary power, and in the enfeebling of all moral energy, as well as in the hardening and deadening of the spiritual sense.' See Barabas, *So Great Salvation*, 45.

[159] Packer, '"Keswick" and the Reformed Doctrine of Sanctification', 158.

[160] See Rice, *Reformed Spirituality*, 66. Rice appeals to Calvin's image of union with Christ in order to describe holiness in the Reformed tradition. 'This mystical union of the believer with Christ is the real heart of holiness in the Reformed tradition; it appears throughout Reformed literature and speaks powerfully of a sense of Christ living within us. ... Unlike some medieval forms of spirituality which spoke of union with God, Reformed spirituality has centered on union with Christ.' Packer embraces the concept of 'union with Christ' but emphasises union as the cause from which holiness or sanctification is the effect. 'It is out of our union by the Spirit, through faith, with the Christ who died for us and whom first we trust for justification (Romans 3–5), that our subsequent life of holiness is lived (Romans 6–8)' (*Keep in Step with the Spirit*, 105). Calvin goes further than Packer in what he acknowledges about the intrinsic value of Jesus' human body for salvation. Calvin argues that 'this [eternal] *life* is placed *in his flesh*, that it may be drawn out of it. ...' He continues, '[F]or as the eternal Word of God is the fountain of *life*, (John i.4), so his flesh, as a

Packer's theology of holiness, however, emphasises Jesus Christ first as the provider of a forensic, substitutionary atonement and consequent justification before God. On that basis Christ provides the moral model for sanctification as the believer is united with him, then prompted and enabled by the Holy Spirit to follow Christ's model in obeying God's law. Jesus is the one who is to be followed and imitated because he perfectly conformed to God's character by perfectly obeying God's law. The character of sanctification or holiness, then, is human conformity to Jesus Christ's conformity to God's law.

Packer exerts considerable effort to clarify the nature of this law–keeping holiness that is experienced by imitating Jesus. Fearing that the emphasis on law might give the mistaken impression of a legalistic holiness, he points to the divine love at the heart of holiness. One of the seven principles of holiness he articulates in both *A Passion for Holiness* and *Keep in Step with the Spirit* is, 'The heart of holiness is the spirit of love.'[161]

> Love knows itself to be blind and to need the law as its eyes. Jesus embodies love to God and others. He was, we might say, love incarnate. The nature of love may be learned by watching him. Law–keeping love is the epitome of holiness, though love in any other sense negates it. Law–keeping love is God's prescription for the fulfilling of our humanity. Any alternative to it pulls us, more or less, out of our proper human shape. Grace restores and perfects nature by teaching us to truly love.[162]

> As Jesus was law incarnate, so he was love incarnate, and following his way of self–giving is holiness in its purest and most perfect expression. Hard, harsh, cold–hearted holiness is a contradiction in terms. Love to God as prescribed in Matthew 22:37, citing Deuteronomy 6:5, and as voiced in Psalm 18, and love to neighbor as defined in 1 Corinthians 13:4–7 and illustrated in Jesus' story of the Samaritan (Luke 10:29–37) is, by contrast, the very heartbeat of holiness.[163]

---

channel, conveys to us that *life* which dwells intrinsically, as we say, in his Divinity.' See J. Calvin, *Commentary on the Gospel According to John*, W. Pringle (tr.), vol. I (Grand Rapids: Eerdmans, 1956), 262. Calvin's more nuanced development of the value of Jesus' Incarnation allows for union with Christ to depend intrinsically on the brokenness of his humanity. In Packer's thought, the Incarnation takes on a more utilitarian role vis–à–vis the Cross and serves as a moral model of humble, loving obedience to God.

[161] Packer, *A Passion for Holiness*, 177. See also *Keep in Step with the Spirit*, 114.

[162] Ibid.

[163] Packer, *Keep in Step with the Spirit*, 114–115.

The fulcrum of this argument is Packer's presentation of Jesus as the combination of 'law incarnate' and 'love incarnate.' This love does not circumvent the structure of the law but depends on that structure for its substance and orientation.

Holiness as progressive transformation into the moral image of Jesus Christ becomes an authentic possibility only on the basis of a new ontological relationship with God that is established through participation in the crucifixion and resurrection of Christ. As a result of this particular or individualised atonement[164] and Jesus' resurrection,[165] the Holy Spirit unites the believer with Christ. Packer claims,

> The root of holiness is cocrucifixion and coresurrection with Jesus Christ. ... [T]his means that an end has been put to the sin–dominated lives they were living before. Also, they have been raised with him to walk in newness of life; this means that the power that wrought Jesus' resurrection is now at work in them, causing them to live differently because in truth they are different at the center of their being in what Paul in Romans 7:22 calls 'my inmost self' and Peter in 1 Peter 3:4 calls 'the hidden person of the heart.'[166]

He explains how this union with Christ in his death and resurrection actually connects the formal and experiential dimensions of holiness. 'Heart–hostility to God, which is natural to all the unregenerate, makes holiness impossible for them (Rom. 8:7–8). The taproot of holiness is love for God and his law, which the Holy Spirit imparts by uniting us to Christ in his death and resurrection.'[167] From the formal, legal relationship with God emerges the subjective aspect of the Spirit's active work in the

---

[164] Packer, 'What Did the Cross Achieve?', 116. Here Packer reiterates the argument that he makes in his introduction to J. Owen's *The Death of Death in the Death of Christ*, i.e. that the logic of a truly efficacious atonement forces one to conclude either that Christ died only for specific individuals (God's elect) or that all will ultimately be saved (universalism). Packer's understanding of the nature of the substitution that Christ made presupposes God's election of the individuals for whom Christ died and who will necessarily be drawn to persevering faith in Christ. See also *Concise Theology*, 137–139.

[165] Ibid., 112. He asserts that 'in a manner transcending bounds of space and time, Christ has taken us with him into his death and through his death into his resurrection.'

[166] Packer, *Keep in Step with the Spirit* , 106–107. Never does Packer relate the cross to the existential work of sanctification or holiness except as the soteriological ground or provision for sanctification. The cross and the notion of co–crucifixion are only presented as formally, never as directly related to sanctification in an ontological or existential sense.

[167] Packer, *A Passion for Holiness*, 172.

believer toward the personal experience of holiness, i.e. responsive, imitative conformity to the pattern of Jesus' prior conformity to God's law.

Thus, Jesus' life of obedience most directly provides a moral model for the restored *imago Dei* through his perfect conformity to God's law. Packer claims that 'holiness is the healthy growth of morally misshapen humans toward the moral image of Jesus Christ, the perfect man.'[168] This moral image pertains to that which is central to human nature.

> Concerning *Jesus* ... he is the yardstick at the level of motivation and attitudes of what it means to be fully human. Concerning *ourselves*, the claim is that only as we set ourselves to imitate Christ at this level are we fulfilling and developing (as distinct from violating and diminishing) our own nature, which is already much diminished through sin; and only in this way can we find true joy ...[169]

The faculty of volition appears as central to human nature, this time under the rubric of 'motivation.' Jesus Christ offers the perfect example of humanity at its motivational core.

As Packer contends in his numerous diatribes against Keswick and other perfectionistic versions of holiness, this transformation is progressive, not instantaneous. The progressive nature of holiness means that it is learned through personal struggle, not imparted to a passive recipient. Here, Jesus models not only the goal of holiness but also the process of holiness. He states, 'As Jesus "learned obedience from what he suffered" (Heb. 5:8) – learned what obedience requires, costs, and involves through the experience of actually doing his Father's will up to and in his passion – so Christians must, and do, learn ... holiness from their battles for purity of heart and righteousness of life.'[170]

The difference between the holiness that can be experienced by fallen humans and Jesus' own holiness is that Jesus' obedience did not involve transformation from personal sinfulness. Rather, Jesus battled against his human instincts toward self–preservation while sinful humans battle against their indwelling sin. Thus, Jesus did not experience the struggle against sin in exactly the same manner as sinners do.

Christ perfectly embodied conformity to God's law and personally reflected God's being. However, Packer never mentions what Jesus' humility, submissiveness, and self–forgetfulness say about the nature of

---

[168] Packer, *A Passion for Holiness*, 165. See also Packer, 'Evangelical Foundations for Spirituality', 265. 'Motivationally, within the heart, the change is an implanting in us of the inclinations of Christ's perfect humanity through our ingrafting into him ...'

[169] J.I. Packer, 'Jesus Christ the Lord', in *Shorter Writings*, 1.35.

[170] Packer, *A Passion for Holiness*, 15.

God.[171] This rather telling omission makes Christ's humility appear rather utilitarian in service toward the goal of showing humanity how to glorify the Father, but not necessarily revealing anything about the nature of God. Inasmuch as humility is essential to being Christ–like, Packer is consistent, however, with his own understanding of the nature of the Trinity and his belief in the Son's eternal subordination to the Father.[172]

A potential problem arises, however, when he attempts to be Christological in his epistemology. If the Son reveals the exact nature of the Father and his 'moral perfections' are seen most clearly on the cross, then this sacrificial humility seems to be in conflict with the Father's nature unless the Father's nature also includes this trait.[173] This, too, portrays the compartmentalised manner in which Packer relates Christology to holiness. If Christ's death on the cross was not the full presence of God in sin and for the redemption of sin, the existential power of sin would seem to be one step removed from the transforming power of redemption.

Packer does, however, find Jesus Christ to be the connection between created and redeemed humanity. He is the model for humanness as well as holiness, thus providing the bridge between anthropology and piety. Packer allies humanness and holiness so closely, for both Jesus Christ and the rest of humanity, that humanness and holiness are interdependent. Packer claims, 'Holiness has to do with my humanness.' He then elaborates.

> And what is human godliness, the godliness that is true holiness, as seen in Jesus? It is simply human life lived as the Creator intended – in other words, it is perfect and ideal humanness, an existence in which the elements of the human person are completely united in a totally God–honoring and nature–fulfilling way. (Since God made humanity for himself, godliness naturally fulfils human nature at the deepest level. As

---

[171] Packer's attempt to reconcile the *kenosis* assumes that it is somehow pitted against divine nature. See K. Barth, *Church Dogmatics*, I.2., G.W. Bromiley and T.F. Torrance (eds.), (Edinburgh: T & T Clark, 1980), 37–38. By contrast, Barth speaks of the *kenosis* as an 'externalisation' of 'the knowability of God' and a veiling of God's majesty which is unveiled in the resurrection. Barth's approach locates the polarisation within the epistemological process of humanity, resolved by the resurrection, rather than within the nature of divine attributes, which must then be resolved by exploring the psychology of Jesus.

[172] Packer interview, (2 July 1999).

[173] Gunton, *Christ and Creation*, 83. Gunton's perspective on the nature of God (admittedly following Barth, *Church Dogmatics*, IV.1.) illuminates the reason that Packer must go to such pains to explain the *kenosis*. Gunton argues that being and act may not be separated in the nature of God and that Christ's self–emptying is an 'expression of the divine being rather than its depotentiation.'

experience proves, no contentment can match the contentment of obeying God, however costly this may prove.)

Human lives that are lived differently from this, however, though human in a biological and functional sense, are less than fully human in terms of their quality. Holiness and humanness are correlative terms and mutual implicates ... To the extent that I fall short of the first, I fall short of the second as well.

All members of our fallen race who, because they do not know Jesus Christ, still live under the power of that self–deifying, anti–God syndrome in our spiritual system which the Bible calls sin, are living lives that are qualitatively subhuman. [174]

Thus, the only way in which the *imago Dei* can have abiding character and implications for all humanity is for the *imago Dei* to be the horizon of holiness for which all are created and to which all are called.

No question exists about Packer's belief in the centrality and exclusiveness of Jesus Christ in and for salvation.[175] The issues that must be explored for an adequate understanding of his approach to piety have more to do with the nature of a person's appropriation of Jesus Christ. The nature of faith and repentance must be examined as requirements for receiving and experiencing salvation from God. In addition, Packer's thought must be clarified regarding the relationship between conscious faith and repentance toward Jesus Christ and the knowledge of God in general.

Summary

J.I. Packer's theology of the Christian life follows a distinct anthropological and soteriological trajectory. The Christian life is a life of godliness or holiness as defined by God's law. This genuine, biblical piety is a life of heartfelt obedience to God's law which in turn depends upon inerrant, propositional communication of God's will through Scripture and also on the human faculty of reason to comprehend that self–revelation. Holiness, true piety, is humanity restored to God's original intentions as expressed in

---

[174] Packer, *A Passion for Holiness*, 26–27.

[175] In addition to his more well–known books, Packer has developed these claims in numerous articles such as; 'Jesus Christ: the Only Saviour', in G. Egerton, (ed.), *Anglican Essentials: Reclaiming Faith within the Anglican Church of Canada* (Toronto: Anglican Book Centre, 1995), 98–110; 'The Uniqueness of Jesus Christ', *Churchman* 92 (1978), 101–111; 'The Love of God: Universal and Particular', in T.R. Schreiner and B.A. Ware (eds.), *The Grace of God, the Bondage of the Will* (Grand Rapids: Baker, 1995), 413–428; and 'The Problem of Universalism Today', *Theology Review* 5 (November 1969), 16–24.

the *imago Dei*. However, this restoration is obstructed by the pervasive and tragic effects of original and indwelling sin, even in the life of the Christian. God provides and effects forgiveness and restored legal standing for the elect through Jesus Christ's penal, substitutionary atonement for sin in his death on the cross. This formal justification before God then leads to sanctification, the existential transformation of the believer's character into the image of Jesus Christ, who in his own obedience provided the model of godliness for which God intended humanity. Sanctification is enabled by God but demands ongoing, strenuous struggle in faith that God is working in and through the Christian's efforts to bring about deep, genuine, and lasting transformation.

Chapter 5

The Means of Piety

The origins and development of J.I. Packer's work in the area of piety reflect the controversy that has laced the history of Protestant Christianity on this subject.[1] At the heart of this dispute lie distinct understandings of the fundamental nature of holiness, particularly, how holiness fits within a soteriological schema. The soteriological framework of piety sets the tone for the manner in which piety is to be pursued.

5.1 Divine Activity

In light of his insistence that sanctification is synergistic without being Pelagian, it is necessary to further develop Packer's thought regarding the relationship between the divine and human roles in sanctification. His efforts to resolve the tension rest on the assumptions of God's grace as the initiating and enabling factor and the active agency of the Holy Spirit as the medium through whom that grace is experienced in the process of sanctification.

This manner of describing a theocentric orientation toward holiness (or 'evangelical spirituality') is illustrated when Packer explains the experiential implications of repentance. He describes this in two ways. First, evangelical spirituality involves particular disciplines that express a radical and sweeping turnabout from egocentricity toward God in a person's allegiance. These disciplines emerge in an individual's experience as a gift of God's grace.

> Being under grace, the Christian is freed from sin (Rom. 6:14–7:6; Gal. 5:13–25; cf. John 8:31–36); the motivational theocentricity of the heart set free will prompt the actions that form the habits of Christ–likeness that constitute the Spirit's fruit (Gal. 5:22f.), and thus the holiness of radical

---

[1] Packer, 'Evangelical Foundations for Spirituality', 255,256. Packer defends spirituality as a theological discipline when he claims that 'ethics and spirituality should be viewed as departments of theology and be controlled by the truths of theology and, on the other hand, theology should always have an eye to the ethical and devotional implications of its theses, since God's truth is given to be practiced.'

repentance (daily abandonment of self–centred self–will), childlike humility (daily listening to what God says in his Word, and daily submission to what he sends in his providence), and love to God and humans that honours and serves both, will increasingly appear. This thorough–going intellectual and moral theocentricity, whereby Christians come to live no longer for themselves but for him who died and rose to save them (cf. 2 Cor. 5:15), is first God's gift and then the Christian's task, and as such it is the foundation not only of sound ethics but also of true spirituality.[2]

Second, though not under the heading of theocentricity, he emphasises the Trinitarian nature of spirituality and the importance of rightly remembering and responding to each member of the Trinity in the practise of spirituality.[3] The Christian experience of salvation, as it is expressed in the themes of spirituality, piety, and holiness must be anchored in the Trinitarian personhood of God and in God's prevenient work. All human responsibilities take a decidedly secondary status. The roles of the Father and the Son are elaborated under numerous other headings in his theology. The role of the Spirit is seen most prominently as it relates to the means of piety.

---

[2] Ibid., 258–260.

[3] Ibid., 259–261. Interestingly, Packer opines that an anemic Trinitarianism in spirituality is being helpfully challenged by a combination of 'post–Barthian theology with charismatic experientialism.' He also shows sympathy with the understanding of the Trinity as *perichoresis*, suggesting that the conciliar work of Nicaea and Constantinople provides more than just an antidote to Arianism. '[I]t is in fact the joyful proclamation that, as a Puritan somewhere put it, and as John's gospel shows, "God himself is a sweet society," and that the purpose first of creation and then of redemption was to extend that fellowship of love by bringing creatures into it.' Packer does not explain what he means by 'post–Bartian theology' but, despite his many misgivings concerning Barth's doctrine of Scripture and Christology, Packer nonetheless applauds Barth's insistence on the relationality of the Trinity and the implications for piety. Likewise, despite Packer's repeated cautions and corrections regarding the charismatic movement, he recognises the validity of the movement's concerns for a vibrant dependence on the Holy Spirit. See *Keep in Step with the Spirit*, 232, where, after lengthy criticism he warns, 'The charismatic movement is a God–sent gadfly to goad the whole church into seeking more of totality before the Lord than most Christians today seem to know. Face the challenge!' T.F. Torrance suggests that 'with the aid of the *homoousion* and the *perichoresis* our understanding of God's self–revelation to us is lifted up from the economic Trinity to the ontological Trinity, yet, paradoxically, without leaving the economic Trinity behind.' See T.F. Torrance, *The Christian Doctrine of God: One Being Three Persons* (Edinburgh: T & T Clark, 1996), 110.

5.1.1 The Holy Spirit

The importance of the Holy Spirit in Packer's understanding of piety is evidenced by the diversity of his writings on the subject as well as by the role of pneumatology in his approach to theology. Though he repeatedly addresses the subject of the Holy Spirit with regard to the charismatic movement, ecclesiology, and the doctrine of Scripture,[4] his most frequently addressed concern is the Spirit's role in the Christian life. He develops the pneumatological implications of holiness in his most extended treatment of the doctrine of the Holy Spirit, *Keep in Step with the Spirit.*

Packer summarises the Scripture's portrayal of the Holy Spirit's ministry in ways that have immediate bearing on the subject of holiness. In the Old Testament, he states, 'revealing and enabling are the activities mainly stressed.'[5] 'Tripersonal thinking about God surfaces in the NT constantly ...'[6] He delineates eight points regarding the Holy Spirit's ministry as it began at Pentecost.

> In this ministry the Spirit 1. *reveals* Jesus' reality and the truth about him ... 2. *unites* believers to Christ in regenerative, life–giving co–resurrection ... 3. *assures* believers that they are children and heirs of God ... 4. *mediates fellowship* with the Father and the Son of a kind that is already heaven's life begun ... 5. *transforms* believers progressively through prayer and conflict with sin into Christ's moral and spiritual likeness ... 6. *gives gifts* – that is, witnessing and serving abilities – for expressing Christ in the believing community that is his body ... 7. *prays*

---

[4] Packer addresses the theology and phenomena of the charismatic movement in 'The Empowered Christian Life', in G.S. Grief and K.N. Springer (eds.), *The Kingdom and the Power: Are Healing and the Spiritual Gifts Used By Jesus and the Early Church Meant for the Church Today?: A Biblical Look At How to Bring the Gospel to the World Today* (Ventura, Calif.: Regal, 1993) 207-215, 'Theological Reflections on the Charismatic Movement', *Churchman* 1 and 2 (1980); and 'Piety on Fire', *CT*, (12 May 1989), 18–23. His ecclesiological writings on the Holy Spirit include 'The Holy Spirit in the Book of Common Prayer', in S. Harris (ed.), *The Holy Spirit* (Charlotteville: St. Peter, 1993; and 'The Holy Spirit and the Local Congregation', *Churchman* 78 (June 1964). The Holy Spirit's role in relation to Scripture is developed in 'The Holy Spirit – And Authority', *The Almond Branch* (1962), 9–12; 'The Inspiration and Infallibility of Scripture', Symposium of Articles from *TSF Bulletin* (n.d.), 16–18; 'The Spirit with the Word: The Reformational Revivalism of George Whitefield', in *The Bible, the Reformation and the Church*; 'The Holy Spirit and His Work', *Crux* 23 (June 1987), 2–17, and 'Revelation and Inspiration', in *The New Bible Commentary.*

[5] J.I. Packer, 'Holy Spirit', in *NDT*, 316.

[6] Ibid., 317.

effectively in and for believers in Christ who feel unable to pray properly for themselves ... 8. *prompts missionary action* to make Christ known ... and *pastoral decision* for consolidating Christ's church.[7]

In other writings he also notes the role of the Spirit in enabling worship and strengthening Christians in suffering.[8]

Packer traces his pneumatology to the Calvinistic theology he learned from the Puritans early in his Christian experience, claiming, 'I stumbled during my student days on what was then literally buried treasure, namely the classic teaching on the Holy Spirit given by Calvin, the English Puritans, and Jonathan Edwards.'[9] He goes on to call Calvin '*the* theologian of the Holy Spirit in the post–apostolic Christian church, with the Puritans and Edwards in close support.'[10] The doctrine of the Holy Spirit is a point at which he departs slightly from Augustine. He claims that Augustine emphasised internal grace in a manner that 'blocked serious pneumatology for years.'[11] He attributes to Puritans such as John Owen the full development of the Spirit's ministry in sanctification 'as an ongoing pilgrimage and battle in which by 'God's free grace ... we are renewed in the whole man after the image of God, and are enabled more and more to die unto sin, and live unto righteousness' (Westminster Shorter Catechism, q. 35).'[12] Yet, he does not entirely endorse all Puritan thought on the subject. He disagrees with Puritans such as Thomas Goodwin and Thomas Brooks in their belief that there is an interval of time between a person's initial belief and the sealing by the Holy Spirit (Ephesians 1:13). To Packer, the Holy Spirit is the seal, not the sealer, and is given for that purpose

---

[7]   Ibid.

[8]   J.I. Packer, 'On Being Serious about the Holy Spirit', in *Shorter Writings*, 1.207.

[9]   J.I. Packer, 'The Holy Spirit and His Work', in *Shorter Writings*, 1.213.

[10] Ibid. He attributes his opinion of Calvin thought on the Holy Spirit to B.B. Warfield's influence through his book *Calvin and Augustine*.

[11] Packer, 'Holy Spirit', *NDT*, 317–318. See also his article entitled 'Holy Spirit,' in D. Atkinson and D. Fields (eds.), *NDCEPT* (Leicester: Inter–Varsity, 1995), 446, where he challenges Augustine's depiction of the Trinity as lover, beloved, and love as having 'the unintended effect of depersonalizing the Spirit in Western minds (for love, as such, is obviously not a distinct person), so that Western theology and devotion outside the evangelical tradition ... have repeatedly lapsed into legalism, moralism, sacramentalism and formal "churchianity" for want of appreciating the personal, life–giving ministry of the Spirit in those whom he indwells and empowers.'

[12] Ibid., 318.

immediately upon belief.[13] It was this point upon which he also disagreed with his early mentor, D. Martyn Lloyd–Jones.[14]

Perhaps the most significant feature of Packer's pneumatology as it relates to piety is that the Holy Spirit is not to be the direct object of the believer's attention. Rather, the Spirit draws attention to the Son, Jesus Christ, enabling faith in him then prompting responses of obedience as the believer's character is shaped into the image of Christ. This was a central aspect of Packer's critique of Keswick piety.

> Reformed theology teaches that the Spirit's sanctifying work is a hidden activity which manifests itself by its effects in consciousness and life: evoking and working through the Christian's use of his own faculties, the Spirit enlightens him to know God's truth and causes him to love and to do it. ... [In Keswick piety, on the other hand] Consecrated Christians must 'cultivate the habit of asking the Spirit to illuminate our minds, suggest our thoughts, and direct our speech' [Barabas, *So Great Salvation*, 142]. Keswick thus teaches that, instead of working through our conscious personal life, the Spirit stands over against it.[15]

Fittingly, then, Packer refers to the Holy Spirit as the 'Shy Sovereign.' '[I]t is the Spirit's way to keep out of direct view, like a shy child hiding behind the door. So Christians never know the Spirit in the way they know the Son, and we can be led astray by questioning that suggests we do.'[16] The Spirit's work in a Christian's life is validated, therefore, not by a sense of the numinous but by the objective phenomena of conviction of sin, obedient love for God, and the fruit of the Spirit. He makes this case in his early work, *The Spirit Within You*, which he co–authored with Alan Stibbs, stating,

> [I]t is the continuing work of the Spirit of revelation to produce in those of whom He takes possession deep conviction of sin (cf. Jn. 16:8) ...
>
> It is also the present work of the Spirit, whom Christ as Saviour gives to His people, to work out in them the results of what Christ has wrought for them, and to make the enjoyment of salvation and progress in sanctification a practical reality in their experience.
>
> The way of life is 'by the Spirit' to 'put to death the deeds of the body'; this, before anything else, is what it means to be 'led by the Spirit of God' (Rom. 8:13f.). Again, it is through examining ourselves by these

---

[13] Ibid., 319.

[14] J.I. Packer, 'D. Martyn Lloyd–Jones: A Kind of Puritan', in *Shorter Writings*, 4.75.

[15] Packer, '"Keswick" and the Reformed Doctrine of Sanctification', 160–161.

[16] J.I. Packer, 'Shy Sovereign', in *Shorter Writings*, 1.203.

practical standards that we may discover how far we are actually experiencing the divinely–intended consequences of God's gift to us in Christ of His indwelling Spirit.

Internally our nature and heart's attitude to God are changed; for sin – the anti–God impulse which was previously our ruling 'drive' – is dethroned, and our deepest urge henceforth is to seek, and love, and know, and serve, and praise, and please, God. This is the first and decisive step in God's work of ironing out the distortions and twists that have marred His image in us hitherto.

It is only in the pathway of obedience that the active co–operation of the Spirit is experienced.[17]

Packer's pneumatology intersects his anthropology as the Spirit works to redeem human faculties without commandeering them.

The Holy Spirit's ministry serves for Packer also as the existential remedy to the seemingly sterile and abstract implications of a strictly forensic view of the atonement. He states,

> If this further element of the Gospel of salvation in Christ is not fully grasped, serious consequences may ensue. In the first place, the justification thus enjoyed in God's sight may appear to be – some, indeed, caricature it as – a mere pretence, a legal fiction, making no vital and practical difference to the person on whom it is conferred. The full truth, however, is that once a sinner is thus put right with God he is immediately given the life–giving Spirit.[18]

Thus, in Packer's soteriology the Holy Spirit's ministry allows him to portray the atonement primarily in legal terms while still retaining a vital, existential impact. In this schema human nature is changed, not through any connection with the Incarnation, but strictly through the work of the Holy Spirit in mediating God's life to Christians on the basis of Christ's atoning work.

---

[17] J.I. Packer and A.M. Stibbs, *The Spirit Within You: The Church's Neglected Possession*, Christian Foundations series, vol. 18 (London: Hodder and Stoughton, 1967), 18.23, 24, 24, 47, 51 (respectively).

[18] Ibid., 16.

It is noteworthy that in the preponderance of Packer's writings on the Holy Spirit he overtly uses what he considers to be various aberrations on the subject as a foil for developing his own Reformed view. Keswick and Wesleyan theology are his most frequent targets[19] as representatives of

---

[19] Though Packer frequently criticises John Wesley and the Wesleyan view of holiness, e.g. 'Augustinian and Wesleyan Views About Holiness,' audio cassette (Edinburgh: Rutherford House, n.d.), Packer's writings offer evidence of rather limited interaction with Wesley's writings. In 'Arminianisms', in *Shorter Writings* he refers to Wesley's *The Doctrine of Original Sin according to Scripture, Reason and Experience* (4.283) and *Thoughts on Christ's Imputed Righteousness* (4.300). In *Among God's Giants* he refers to 'the private oddities of John Wesley's theology, which he miscalled Arminianism out of deference to the Wesley family tradition but which is better categorised as inconsistent Calvinism' (56). He lists Wesley's journal in a footnote for this statement. Footnote references to Wesley in *Keep in Step with the Spirit* (274) include secondary sources by R. Newton Flew (*The Idea of Perfection in Christian Theology*), Harald Lindstrom (*Wesley and Sanctification*), Albert Outler (*John Wesley*), and W.E. Sangster (*The Path to Perfection*). He refers to Wesley's *Notes on the New Testament* when he analyses Wesley's interpretation of Romans 7 and to Wesley's sermons on Wesley's view of the nature of sin. In 'Theological Reflections on the Charismatic Movement,' in *Shorter Writings* he references Wesley's 'A Plain Account of Christian Perfection' and *The Letters of the Rev. John Wesley* regarding Wesley's doctrine of entire sanctification (2.115–116). In *Keep in Step with the Spirit* he traces the charismatic idea of Spirit–baptism as a second–stage in the Christian life back to Wesley's doctrine of entire sanctification, though he does directly state that Wesley himself associated Spirit–baptism and entire sanctification (228). In *Evangelism and the Sovereignty of God* he refers to Wesley's famous conversation with Charles Simeon concerning which of them was a Calvinist and which an Arminian (13). In *Keep in Step with the Spirit* (132–145) he discusses 'Wesleyan Perfectionism.' He identifies the core of Wesley's view as a modified Augustinianism in which sin is seen in terms of a person's conscious motivations (132) and as a substance that can be removed (141). According to Packer, Wesley's idea of perfection did not relate to absolute moral perfection but to 'a state of wholeheartedly going on with God in obedient worship and service that are fueled by love and love alone' (135). Packer levels numerous accusations against Wesley. First, Wesley elevated an experiential goal to doctrinal status (137). Second, Wesley adopted a notion of perfection from the Greek Fathers and used his Aldersgate experience as a premise to argue that perfection takes place instantaneously in the same manner as justification (138). Third, Wesley confuses the eschatological consummation of sanctification with the penultimate experience of sanctification (140). Fourth, the pastoral implications of Wesley's doctrine are unrealistic and, hence, unedifying. Fifth, Wesley erroneously interprets the inner–personal conflict described in Romans 7:7–25 as referring to Paul's pre–Christian experience, thus posing a contradiction between the two halves of verse 25 where Paul speaks simultaneously of his inner conflict and of his gratitude to God for the promise of

belief in a two–stage approach to sanctification that offers false hope of escaping from the struggle with sin. To a lesser extent, but still repeatedly and somewhat more sympathetically, he addresses the charismatic movement. He applauds its desire for passionate intimacy with God but cautions against its preoccupation with ecstatic experience rather than holiness in character.[20] This criticism (though irenic) is most fully developed in *Keep in Step with the Spirit*, throughout which the Holy Spirit's ministry is described with the intent of correcting these supposedly spurious viewpoints.

The *manner* of the Spirit's ministry has been a repeated concern for Packer. Yet, he attests that the primary issue is the *effects* of the Spirit's ministry. He portrays the Spirit as the 'shy' member of the Trinity whose primary focus is the Son, Jesus Christ. '[B]ecause God is gracious,' Packer states, 'he may ... deepen our life in the Spirit even when our ideas about this life are nonexistent or quite wrong, provided only that we are truly and wholeheartedly seeking his face and wanting to come closer to him.'[21] He goes on to concede that 'countless sinners truly experience the saving grace of Jesus Christ and the transforming power of the Holy Spirit while their notions about both are erratic and largely incorrect. ... All the same, however, we would appreciate the Spirit's work much more, and maybe avoid some pitfalls concerning it, if our thoughts about the Spirit himself were clearer ...'[22] Still, he goes to great lengths to define what the Spirit's ministry is *not*. Any emphasis on the experience of the Spirit, for Packer, is suspect and unhelpful as a criterion for the reality of God's presence and power in a person's life unless the experience is formally validated by the Scripture and the fruit of a person's life.

One of the most significant roles of the Holy Spirit, in Packer's pneumatology, is to provide assurance of salvation. He repeatedly places

---

deliverance through Jesus Christ (143–145). Packer calls Keswick teaching a 'modified version of the Wesleyan view' (145). He compares Keswick and Wesleyan views by stating that, 'while rejecting the claim to sinlessness of heart as perfectionist heresy, Keswick teachers proclaimed sinlessness of acts in the sense of conscious deliverance from all known wrong. Though they broke with Wesley's belief that God gives perfect love in this life, they held to his concept of "sin properly so called (that is, a voluntary transgression of a known law) [Outler, *John Wesley*, 287]" and in terms of it depicted the Christian life as potentially one of total and endless victory over every form of temptation and moral weakness' (148).

[20] In addition to Packer's previously noted writings in which he addresses the charismatic movement, he also devotes considerable attention to it in chapters five and six of *Keep in Step with the Spirit*.

[21] Packer, *Keep in Step with the Spirit*, 19.

[22] Ibid., 20.

the subject of assurance under the heading of the Holy Spirit's work, as is common in Puritan thought.[23] Regardless of how faith is involved from the human side, Packer points out that assurance is ultimately provided by God through the agency of the Holy Spirit.

Packer identifies two senses in which the concept of assurance appears in Scripture. In the first sense God provides objective grounding for the believer's faith through specific, decisive, historical acts such as the resurrection of Jesus Christ and other miracles. To illustrate this sense he refers to Acts 17:31 and the translation of πίστις as 'assurance' (KJV) or 'confidence' (RV), referring to 'objectively adequate grounds for belief.'[24] In the second sense the believer is provided with a personal, subjective conviction regarding the truthfulness of God's saving intentions and abilities as evidenced in the acts mentioned in the first sense. For this sense he refers to the repeated use of *plerophoria* (e.g. in Colossians 2:2) and particularly its passive verbal form (e.g. in Romans 14:5). 'This passive points to the fact that Christian assurance is not an expression of human optimism or presumption, but a persuasion from God.'[25] In both senses he emphasizes that God is the source of assurance, objectively and subjectively.

The Holy Spirit's role, for Packer, culminates in the transformation of the Christian's character into the image of Jesus Christ. He states, 'The life generated by the Holy Spirit in Christians is one in which the behavioural uprightness and beauty lost at the Fall of Adam begin to be restored.'[26] He summarises this objective by comparing the Spirit's work with Christ's work.

> In short, as the Christian's whole life is life in Christ in terms of its meaning, centre, and direction, so the Christian's whole life is life in the Spirit from the standpoint of his knowledge, disposition, and ability to love and serve. Putting off the old man and putting on the new man, which God renews (Eph. 4:20–24; Col. 3:9–10), and being new created in Christ (2 Cor. 5:17) corresponds in Paul to new birth in John, and though Paul nowhere says this explicitly, it is plain that the initial inward renewal is the Spirit's work, as is the living that expresses it. ... Everything that is

---

[23] Packer, 'The Witness of the Spirit: The Puritan Teaching', in *The Wisdom of Our Fathers* (London: The Puritan and Reformed Studies Conference, 1956), 11. He opens his discussion of the Puritan view of assurance by stating that 'the work of the Holy Spirit is the field in which the Puritans' most valuable contributions to the Church's theological heritage were made ...'

[24] J.I. Packer, 'Assurance', in *NBD*, 100.

[25] Ibid.

[26] Packer, 'The Holy Spirit', in *NDCEPT*, 446.

good, right, positive, and valuable, comes from Christ through the Spirit.[27]

The Spirit brings about a comprehensive transformation of the believer into the moral image of Christ, which is the goal of salvation.

Finally, Packer depends on pneumatology to defend his piety against the charge of being synergistic. As previously stated, he follows what he calls the Puritan view of sanctification by referring to the role of the Holy Spirit as the 'first cause' and human effort as the 'second cause.'[28] His articulation of the relationship between the Spirit's work and human effort presents additional insight into the relationship of the *imago Dei* to the nature of piety.

> In this sanctifying process the Spirit exerts his power, not by suspending or overriding the ordinary operations of mind and body by ecstatic takeover, as non–human agencies are understood to do in shamanism, in the trances of spiritist mediums, and in New Age channelling, but in bringing about a directed use of our natural powers in obedient, creative service of God, motivated by gratitude and a purpose of glorifying him for the grace he has given. …
>
> [T]he directional, relational and habitual changes that the Spirit induces by thus applying the word, however much they exceed what would be possible without him, are wrought with and through the believer's active co–operation in responsive and prayerful moral endeavor. The image of God that is being restored – namely, Christlike holiness (Eph. 4:24; 4:32–5:2) – comes about without any violence being done to the rational, relational and reverential powers of the believer.[29]

In this description Packer shows his belief that the *imago Dei* and the holiness it involves are experienced in and by the human faculties and introduce nothing alien to the structure of the human soul except the righteous character of Christ and right standing before God.

---

[27] Packer, 'The Holy Spirit and His Work', 231.
[28] Packer, 'Sanctification – Puritan Teaching', 126.
[29] Packer, 'Holy Spirit', *NDCEPT*, 447.

5.1.2 *Grace*

Though the subject of grace receives comparatively sparse attention as a discrete theme in Packer's writings,[30] it can be argued that grace occupies a central role in his understanding of piety. *Concise Theology* has no heading under which he directly addresses grace, yet all themes related to soteriology and ecclesiology are organised under the general heading of 'God Revealed As Lord Of Grace.'[31] Sanctification is one chapter under that heading and is subtitled 'The Christian Grows in Grace.'[32] Grace is specifically mentioned in that chapter only twice; first when he quotes Q.35 of the Westminster Shorter Catechism[33] to define sanctification and second when he states that, 'God calls his children to sanctity and graciously gives what he commands (1 Thess. 4:4; 5:23).'[34] That grace is a central assumption in Packer's theology (and, in particular, his theology of piety) while receiving relatively little overt treatment may be due to the fact that it is logically subsumed under the doctrine of election. He summarises, 'This divine choice is an expression of free and sovereign grace ...'[35] Grace is the functional expression of election toward God's sovereignly chosen outcomes. While Packer opts to direct primary attention to the doctrine of election, a certain understanding of grace pervades the operation of his theology of piety.

Packer's assumption that salvation depends ultimately and entirely on God's grace serves as a reminder of three premises: the exclusively divine source of salvation, humanity's absolute dependence on God for the realisation of salvation, and the promise that salvation emerges from a benevolent God. Describing grace theologically in his lecture course, Packer offers a brief historical overview of how grace was viewed by Augustine, in semi–pelagianism, in sacramentalism, and by the Reformers.

He appears to differ from Augustine and adhere to the Reformers on the precise meaning of grace. Packer claims that to Augustine, grace meant, 'God gives the faith and love he commands, so enabling us to merit [salvation], yet without guaranteeing preservation.' [36] To the Reformers

---

[30] The only work in his bibliography that explicitly address the topic of grace is *Great Grace: A 31–Day Devotional*, B. Feia (comp.), (Ann Arbor: Servant, 1997). Even this piece is merely a compilation of extracts from other works.

[31] Packer, *Concise Theology*, table of contents, no page.

[32] Ibid.

[33] Ibid., 169. 'Sanctification, says the Westminster Shorter Catechism (Q.35), is "the work of God's free grace, whereby we are renewed in the whole man after the image of God, and are enabled more and more to die unto sin, and live unto righteousness."'

[34] Ibid., 170.

[35] Packer, *Concise Theology*, 149.

[36] Packer, 'Systematic Theology B, Man, Sin and Grace', section on 'Grace,' 1.

grace meant that, 'God gives faith, whereby we are freely justified for Christ's sake and preserved to glory though we never deserve it.'[37] He entitles his own description of grace as 'dimensions,' depicting it in collaborative terms that in his view are often falsely polarised. In his unpublished lecture notes he offers an exhortation as well as definitions.

> Avoid false antitheses. Grace is
> both personal favour and powerful action (1 Cor. 15:10)
> both God's for us and God in us and through Christ (Rom. 8:31; Col. 1:27)
> both God's presence and his energy
> both prevenient and cooperating (Augustine's distinction: making us both will and work, Phil. 2:12 f.) ...
> both free (i.e. undeserved and unelicited) and tied (in the sense that God commits himself to complete the work of grace he started, Phil. 1:6f.)
> both persuasive, by rational means, and immediate (the Puritans said, physical) in changing hearts.[38]

These polarities, though he sees them as integrated, are expressed in a manner that makes grace appear forceful, even if tacit. Grace is both formal acquittal in justification and active, continuous empowerment in sanctification.

Packer depicts the process of growth (progressive sanctification) as growth in grace. He states, 'The general idea of growth covers change, development, enlarging, gaining strength and showing energy, advancing, deepening, ripening, and maturing. What, precisely, is the nature of growth in grace?' [39] To answer this question he concludes, '[J.C.] Ryle is surely right in all this, and we treat his understanding of growth in grace as growth in graces, that is, transformation of character ...'[40] That is, growth in grace results in the progressive development of Christian virtues.

For Packer, salvation is initiated, sustained, and completed by grace. Justification, regeneration, and adoption are instantaneous in nature and initiate the Christian pilgrimage.[41] In his understanding of regeneration he admits departing from Calvin, who 'used the term 'regeneration' to cover man's whole subjective renewal, including conversion and sanctification.'[42] Sanctification, on the other hand, is progressive. Glorification is the

---

[37] Ibid., 2.
[38] Ibid., 1.
[39] Packer, *A Passion for Holiness*, 160.
[40] Ibid., 162.
[41] Packer, *Concise Theology*, 157–158,164–168.
[42] Packer, 'Regeneration', 925.

eschatological culmination of progressive sanctification.[43] All aspects
depend entirely on God's grace, but as shown in his previously cited
explanation of synergism, sanctification is the sole aspect that requires
active, human effort – even struggle – in trusting response to God's call and
promise.

5.2 Human Responsibility

Packer carefully portrays the role of human effort toward holiness as being
essential, though merely responsive to God's role. Having reacted
adamantly to Keswick piety in his early Christian experience, Packer has
maintained throughout his theological career that holiness involves
intentional and vigorous struggle to obey against the ongoing influence of
indwelling sin. However, he sees his own emphasis on synergistic
sanctification as qualitatively different from the Keswick emphasis and
immune to the charge of Pelagianism because Keswick, in his view,
reverses the order of God's activity and human responsibility in
sanctification.

He structures his approach to human responsibility in holiness around
three elements: doctrine, experience, and practice.

Doctrine. This refers to the truth and wisdom that we may constantly
receive from God through Bible study, Bible–based meditation (not the
same thing, be it said), and the ministry of the biblical Word.
Experience. This means the many–sided fellowship with God to which
divine truth and wisdom lead when brought to bear on our lives: the faith,
the penitence, the renewed sense of sin, the restored joy of salvation, the
distress at our repeated failure to be for Christ all that we wanted to be,
the sorrow we feel at others' need and misery as we pray for them, the
delight we feel when others are blessed …
Practice. This involves setting oneself to obey the truth and follow the
path of wisdom in one's relationships, one's day–to–day self–
management, one's family involvement, one's church commitment, one's
role in the community, one's wage–earning employment, and so on.[44]

---

[43] Ibid., 170. Packer states, 'Paul's use of *glory* in 2 Corinthians 3:18 shows that for
him sanctification of character is glorification begun. Then the physical
transformation that gives us a body like Christ's, one that will match our totally
transformed character and be a perfect means of expressing it, will be glorification
completed (Phil. 3:20–21; 1 Cor. 15:49–53).'

[44] Packer, *A Passion for Holiness*, 61–62. Chapter eight will address Packer's
methodological assumption that doctrine can be sequentially separated from

In these themes he attempts to encompass the cognitive, affective, and concrete domains of human experience.

Prior to and sustaining each aspect is a vigorous emphasis on worship and prayer. Praise and gratitude emerge as the basic human responsibilities in piety, without which there will be no true integration of heart and obedience. He states,

> The life of true holiness is rooted in the soil of awed adoration. It does not grow elsewhere. That which grows elsewhere is not true holiness, whatever it is.[45]
>
> It is important to be clear that, as praise to God for his transcendent greatness is the doxological basis of holiness, so commitment to spend one's life expressing gratitude for God's grace, every way one can, is its devotional basis.[46]
>
> [A] life commitment, deliberate, zealous, and daily renewed, to glorify the Lord Jesus is the dedicatory basis of holiness. There is no holiness without a Christ–centered, Christ–seeking, Christ–serving, Christ–adoring heart.[47]

Even this adoration of God, however, presupposes a fundamental change of heart toward God and what Packer calls, 'holiness as the redirecting of desire.'[48]

Prayer is a crucial link between holiness and worship. Packer pulls these themes together by stating that,

> holiness is viewed first and foremost as the detaching of desire from created things in order to attach it through Christ to the Creator, for expression and satisfaction in and through God–centered prayer. Important as the outward life of justice, integrity, and neighbor–love is, the inner life of pure–hearted prayer is held (surely rightly) to be far more important. ... Prayer is thus the top priority in the life of holiness. Indeed, only insofar as prayer is the breath, heartbeat, and energy source of one's inner being can one be said to be living a life of holiness at all.[49]

---

experience. Though he admits that experience shapes interpretation, his suspicion of experience leads him to relegate experience to a clearly separate and subordinate role in the hermeneutical process and the theology that it produces.

[45] Ibid., 73.

[46] Ibid., 77.

[47] Ibid., 81.

[48] Ibid., 98.

[49] Ibid.

In addition to this emphasis on the private dimension of piety, Packer seeks to provide balance with attention to the social or corporate dimensions of piety.[50] However, his statement that holiness detaches desire from created things introduces a tension with the otherwise creation – affirming emphases found within his piety.[51]

5.2.1 Faith

Though Packer addresses the subject of faith in a variety of writings, he discusses faith in *Concise Theology* only under other rubrics and never as an isolated topic.[52] He perceives that the Keswick movement made faith into an autonomous capacity that can be possessed apart from God's prior enabling through grace.[53] In contrast, he insists, Reformed theology considers faith as a fruit of a regenerated will and is impossible apart from regeneration. 'Keswick,' he contends, 'represents both [sanctification and justification] as external to the will, and makes acts of consecration (repentance) and faith – which, it is assumed, man is antecedently free to perform – the condition of their bestowal and the mode of their reception.'[54] This act of detaching faith from the will appears to Packer to allow faith to function as if it were self–sufficient.

It has already been shown how Packer maintains that both justification and sanctification depend entirely upon God's sovereignty even though they are apprehended in different ways. The importance of human effort and responsibility for obedience are placed under the rubric of sanctification, while justification is received through a purely passive act of faith. Though he sees faith and obedience as intrinsically related,[55] the

---

[50] J.I. Packer, 'Fellowship: The Theological Basis', *Christian Graduate* (September 1963), 8. He states, 'We should not, therefore, think of our fellowship with other Christians as a spiritual luxury, an optional addition to the exercises of private devotion. We should recognize rather that such fellowship is a spiritual necessity; for God has made us in such a way that our fellowship with Him is fed by our fellowship with fellow–Christians, and requires to be so fed constantly for its own deepening and enrichment.' See also *Knowing Christianity*, 147–156.

[51] Packer and Howard, *Christianity: The True Humanism*, 161–183.

[52] In *Concise Theology* Packer addresses faith under headings such as 'Works,' 'Repentance,' and 'Justification.'

[53] See Barabas, *So Great Salvation*, 30. Barabas contends that 'God never issues a command that He does not give us grace to fulfil.' A certain prevenience of God's grace would seem to undergird this claim. It seems entirely plausible that Keswick assumed God's grace as the enablement of the faith that it enjoins for the realisation of sanctification.

[54] Packer, '"Keswick" and the Reformed Doctrine of Sanctification', 160.

[55] Packer, 'Understanding the Lordship Controversy', 211.

question must be raised whether dividing response to God into these categories and placing human effort in the sanctification category offers the impression that sanctification is somehow less dependent on God's grace than justification.

It must be asked, then, whether Packer and the Keswick movement may have missed each other by representing the nature of grace and the responsibility to obey in different ways and with different results. In Packer's thought, sanctification is not accomplished apart from human effort, regardless of the credit given to God's grace as the initiating and sustaining factor. Functionally, God's grace is incomplete without the assistance of human works. In Keswick piety, as Packer understands it, both justification and sanctification are received by faith. To Packer, however, Keswick piety dilutes the significance of human responsibility in sanctification in two ways; first, by characterising all moral effort as futile and, second, by polarizing moral effort and reliance in faith upon the Holy Spirit for sanctification.[56]

Later in his theological career Packer refined his diatribe against the Keswick understanding of faith when he addressed the debate over 'Lordship salvation' that proved divisive within some sectors of American evangelicalism, particularly in the 1970s and 1980s.[57] In his brief article

---

[56] See Barabas, *So Great Salvation*, 95. Barabas offers a subtle clarification regarding human effort, calling into question Packer's criticism and his overall charge of passivity. Barabas states, 'When the believer realizes and accepts by faith God's provision for sin – the identification of believers with Christ in His death to sin, and the gift of the Holy Spirit as the indwelling Agent of sanctification – he ceases from his own struggles to live a holy life, and enters the "rest of faith." This, however, Keswick teaches, is not rest from spiritual conflict and temptation, but rest *in* temptation, the heart rest of those who have learned the secret of perfect and constant victory over temptation.'

[57] The phrase 'Lordship salvation' denotes the question concerning whether a person can experience salvation by granting mere cognitive agreement to the claim that Jesus Christ's death paid the penalty for one's sins and asking God to forgive one's sins on that basis. Those who believe that this is the case hold that an eternal future in heaven is thereby secured regardless of whether the person actually repents of sin and intends to follow Jesus Christ as a disciple. Those who oppose this position argue (though with varying degrees of intensity) that saving faith necessarily involves repentance and a commitment to follow Jesus Christ as Lord. Those who follow the first position are frequently found within circles marked by Dispensationalist theology. Dispensationalist theologians such as Zane C. Hodges in *Absolutely Free!: A Biblical Reply to Lordship Salvation* (Grand Rapids: Zondervan, 1989) and C.C. Ryrie in *So Great Salvation: What It Means to Believe in Jesus Christ* (Wheaton: Victor, 1989) provide popular theological arguments for this position. The 'Lordship' view is supported vigorously by Packer and by J.F. MacArthur, Jr. in *The Gospel*

'Understanding the Lordship Debate' he portrays the notion that faith can lead to salvation apart from repentance and discipleship as being novel and utterly out of character with historic, Reformed soteriology.[58] This debate afforded Packer the opportunity to apply his critique of Keswick theology to a Dispensationalist definition of faith with which Keswick developed significant affinities.

When he discusses the nature of faith Packer explains the relationship of faith to justification and the Reformation tenet of *sola fide* by carefully distinguishing between faith as the 'instrumental means' of justification (which he asserts) and faith as the 'ground' of justification (which he denies).

> Paul regards faith, not as itself our justifying righteousness, but rather as the outstretched hand which receives righteousness by receiving Christ. In Hab. 2:4 (cited in Rom. 1:17; Gal. 3:11) Paul finds, implicit in the promise that the godly man ('the just') would enjoy God's continued favor ('live') through his trustful loyalty to God (which is Habakkuk's point in the context), the more fundamental assertion that only through

---

According to Jesus: What Does Jesus Mean When He Says 'Follow Me'? (Grand Rapids: Zondervan, 1988). MacArthur, though a Dispensationalist himself, takes a more Reformed view of the nature of faith and its relationship to repentance, obedience, and discipleship.

[58] J.I. Packer, 'Understanding the Lordship Controversy', 211. Packer writes in reference to Zane Hodges's book, 'If ten years ago, you had told me that I would live to see literate evangelicals, some with doctorates and a seminary teaching record, arguing for the reality of an eternal salvation, divinely guaranteed, that may have in it no repentance, no behavioral change, no practical acknowledgment of Christ as Lord of one's life, and no perseverance in faith, I would have told you that you were out of your mind.' He goes on to argue, 'Hodges' argumentation had already in essence appeared in the Scofield Bible and the writings of Lewis Sperry Chafer and Charles Ryrie.' This view is, to Packer, an 'intellectualism' akin to that found in the soteriology of Karl Barth and actually 'less than faith,' incapable of effecting salvation. It may be asked whether he properly interprets Barth when he states that for Barth, 'faith is simply believing that because of Christ's death and resurrection one is already justified and an heir of eternal life, as is everybody else.' Barth himself, however, seems to see radical and pervasive implications for those who accept God's reconciliation when he claims, 'Faith is simply following, following its object. Faith is going a way which is marked out and prepared. ... It is simply man's active decision for it, his acceptance of it, his active participation in it.' Barth goes on to state that faith 'is the act in which man does that which this object demands, that which is proper to him in face of this object ... The "object" of faith ... is Jesus Christ, in whom God has accomplished the reconciliation of the world ... with Himself ...' See K. Barth, *Church Dogmatics*, IV.1., 742.

faith does any man ever come to be viewed by God as just, and hence as entitled to life, at all.[59]

Though qualified as being the instrumental means, Packer nonetheless stresses the absolute necessity of faith for salvation.[60]

He contends that the fruit of faith is intrinsic to faith itself, observing that 'the Hebrew noun corresponding to '*aman* ('*emuna*, rendered *pistis* in the LXX), regularly denotes faithfulness, and *pistis* occasionally bears this sense in the NT ...'[61] This line of thought is developed further when he states that 'the nature of faith, according to the NT, is to live by the truth it receives; faith, resting on God's promise, gives thanks for God's grace by working for God's glory.'[62] Faith, in the biblical sense, necessarily involves or leads to acting in confidence on what one claims to believe.[63]

The only appropriate faith response to the gospel, then, is one that includes the conscious intention to turn away from what one has previously

---

[59] Packer, 'Justification', in *EDT*, 596. Packer notes the use of the Greek prepositions *ek* in Romans 3:30 and *dia* in Romans 3:25 to modify *pisteos* in an instrumental sense.

[60] Packer, 'The Redemption and Restoration of Man in the Thought of Richard Baxter'. Packer criticized Richard Baxter for confusing these functions of faith vis-à-vis justification. He states, 'Baxter understood the sinner's justification by grace as follows ... His initial act of faith, forsaking sin and receiving Christ, is an act of compliance with the precept of the Divine law now in force, the law of grace which commands all men everywhere to repent and promises an amnesty to those who do. It is thus an act of righteousness, and God imputes it to him as such' (289). He also claims, '[F]aith in Baxter's doctrinal scheme is the condition, not the discovery, of justification, and consists in an act of will, a hearty self–committal to the rule of the Redeemer' (423).

[61] Packer, 'Faith', in *EDT*, 399.

[62] Ibid., 400.

[63] Packer, *Growing in Christ*, 19–20. He states, 'But the [Apostles'] Creed's opening words, "I believe in God," render a Greek phrase coined by the writers of the New Testament, meaning literally: "I *am believing into* God." That is to say, over and above believing certain truths *about* God, I am living in a relation of commitment *to* God in trust and union. When I say "I believe in God," I am professing my conviction that God has invited me to this commitment, and declaring that I have accepted this invitation. ... Whereas 'belief' suggests bare opinion, "faith," whether in a car, a patent medicine, a protégé, a doctor, a marriage partner, or what have you, is a matter of treating the person or thing as trustworthy and committing yourself accordingly. ... And I show faith in God by bowing to his claim to rule and manage me; by receiving Jesus Christ, his Son, as my own Lord and Savior; and by relying on his promise to bless me here and hereafter. This is the meaning of response to the offer and demand of the Creed.'

trusted and followed instead of Jesus Christ. It is impossible, in Packer's view, to truly believe the gospel or trust Jesus Christ without both the commitment and the intention of being a disciple, that is, of obeying Jesus Christ and living out the implications of the gospel as best one understands them. Thus, his claim that faith encompasses obedience would seem to create a dilemma when he insists on a distinction between monergistic justification and synergistic sanctification. On these terms, either justification would need to be just as synergistic as sanctification or sanctification would need to be just as monergistic as justification.

The role of faith raises again the issue of assurance of salvation. The English Puritans have left an obvious imprint on Packer's approach to assurance.[64] Numerous Puritans were well known for their keen interest in the subject.[65] They believed that it is possible to be falsely assured of one's election unto salvation. Consequently, it is both possible and necessary to validate one's election and achieve true assurance through a 'practical syllogism' that began with the major premise that salvation produced particular evidences in those who are truly God's elect. Packer observes,

> Conscience says Thomas Goodwin, is 'one part of practical reason', and the Puritan theologians, still following Aquinas – for they never hesitated to borrow from mediaeval writers when they judged their teaching to be scriptural – all depict the reasonings of conscience as taking the form of a *practical syllogism*: that is, an inference from two premises, major and minor, concerning either our duty ... or our state before God ...[66]

---

[64] Packer, *Among God's Giants*, 236. 'The Puritans speak of assurance sometimes as a fruit of faith, sometimes as a quality of faith; they talk both of assurance growing out of faith and of faith growing into assurance. Assurance, to them, is faith that is full grown and come of age. There can be faith without assurance, but where assurance is present it is present as an aspect of faith, organically related to it, not as something distinct and separable from it.'

[65] See R.T. Kendall, *Calvin and English Calvinism to 1649*, 8. Kendall takes particular note of the influence of William Perkins and William Ames in fostering a self–defeating preoccupation with personal assurance by means of the 'practical syllogism' to determine one's elect status. Karl Barth finds the preoccupation with assurance to be a departure from Reformed theology's original emphasis on salvation as God's gift. 'It was an outside and apocryphal interest which won the day when in the second or third generations [of Reformed theology] (with Beza first, if I am not mistaken, and later and above all with the English Presbyterians) the question of the "assurance of salvation" took the chief place and became regulative for the whole of the Reformed doctrine.' See *The Word of God and the Word of Man*, 265.

[66] J.I. Packer, 'The Puritan Conscience', in *Faith and a Good Conscience* (London: The Puritan and Reformed Studies Conference, 1962), 20.

Each individual bears the burden of proof for the minor premise regarding the presence and validity of the fruit of salvation in their lives so that they can discern the reality of their election.

Packer follows this syllogistic approach to assurance through the conscience when he warns,

> Self–deception is, however, a danger here, for strong persuasions of a saving relationship with God may be strong delusions of demonic origin. Inward assurance must therefore be checked by external moral and spiritual tests (*cf.* Tit.i. 16). John's Epistles deal directly with this. John specifies right belief about Christ, love to Christians, and righteous conduct as objective signs of being a child of God and knowing Him savingly … Those who find these signs in themselves may assure (lit. persuade) their hearts in the presence of God when a sense of guilt makes them doubt His favour (1 Jn. iii. 19). But absence of these signs shows that any assurance felt is delusive …[67]

Though Packer contends that faith adequate for the assurance of salvation derives from God's election and depends upon the ministry of the Holy Spirit, the experience of assurance depends on individual discernment through this syllogism.

Synergism emerges again in that he seeks to uphold an ultimate (perhaps *formal*) theocentricism to piety while enjoining a *functionally* anthropocentric model. Packer's model exhibits strong anthropocentric traits in the area of assurance by being highly individualistic. Though he commendably seeks to turn the believer's attention toward Christ, Packer rarely if ever mentions the role of the church as a resource for assurance.

The first step Packer identifies for gaining assurance of salvation 'is to make sure that the person we wish to help understands the meaning of sin, Christ's atoning death, repentance, and faith, and has personally sought to turn from a life of self–will to trust the living Christ as his Saviour and Master.'[68] The rational faculties of reason and volition, respectively, are engaged in this first step.

The second step focuses on experiential introspection, 'to make him aware of the reality of the Spirit's indwelling.'[69]

---

[67] Packer, 'Assurance', 100. See also, Packer, *Among God's Giants*, 153–154. Here he rejects the criticism that the Puritans' emphasis on the practical syllogism focuses believers inappropriately on their own sinfulness and away from Christ. Nevertheless, his approach remains highly introspective in its starting point.

[68] Packer and Stibbs, *The Spirit Within You*, 90.

[69] Ibid.

Ways of doing this are by asking such questions as these: Has Jesus Christ been glorified before the eyes of your spirit? Have you come to adore Him as your Lord and your God? Have you come to glory in the cross, and to see that your only hope lies in the fact that Jesus died for you? Has the thought that Jesus is alive taken hold of your mind, so that you know you can talk to Him and have fellowship with Him anywhere, and you know too that you go through life under His eye and in His company? Does your heart warm to the thought that He is on the throne of the universe, and will one day triumph visibly over all who now oppose Him? It is not nature but the indwelling Spirit that begets such a sense of the glory of Christ.[70]

Packer continues the lengthy list of indicators, including a recognition of being undeserving of God's love, a desire to call God 'Father,' inclination toward the Bible, rearrangement of priorities, and submission to God's discipline.

Most significantly, perhaps, he also designates a sense of 'inner conflict' as a mark of the Spirit's presence and work. 'Only those who are indwelt by the Spirit ever experience such a conflict, for only they are set to serve God whole–heartedly in the first instance. Only they therefore find within themselves the state of affairs described by St. Paul [in Galatians 5:17] …'[71] Packer recognises the risks of individualised introspection and denounces it if a person's focus stops at that point. However, he insists that it is a prerequisite for being able to appreciate and fully respond to God's saving grace.[72]

Packer acknowledges that a great paradox resides here, especially for Christians possessed of a sensitive conscience. Those who are truly indwelt by the Holy Spirit experience a greater measure of torment, for they are more keenly and painfully aware of their failings and can feel most insecure before God.[73] He attempts to resolve this existential dilemma by emphasising the formal promise of assurance. 'By this means, spontaneously, those interrogated may come into the state described in Hebrews 10:22 as 'full assurance of faith' – that state, that is, in which they find within themselves the certainty that Christ is theirs, and they are Christ's, for ever.'[74] This way of deferring to what he perceives as the

---

[70] Ibid.

[71] Ibid., 91.

[72] Packer, *Among God's Giants*, 153–154.

[73] Packer, *A Passion for Holiness*, 151. Packer claims that a Christian's discovery of pervasive shortcomings and mixed motives calls for 'constantly renewed repentance' and is 'unquestionably depressing.'

[74] Packer and Stibbs, *The Spirit Within You*, 92.

stated claim of Scripture seems to be Packer's way of avoiding the conundrum introduced by seeking assurance through a process that he admits can lead a Christian to self–doubt before God.

Packer's model for finding assurance of salvation reflects the pneumatology he articulates in his criticism of the Keswick movement. That is, he seeks to direct the believer's attention toward Christ (after attending to the character of one's life, particularly one's sinfulness), assuming that the Spirit then provides assurance through that focus. In Keswick piety, he argues, attention is focused directly on the Spirit. It may rightly be asked of Packer, however, whether his Puritan model of assurance is ultimately any less subjective than the Keswick model because of its introspective, individualistic character and its lack of emphasis on the role of the church. While the Scriptures do indeed indicate that the presence of the Holy Spirit produces discernable marks in a person's life (Galatians 5:22,24), it seems tenuous to assert that individuals may properly discern the ministry of the Holy Spirit for assurance of salvation by starting with a rigorous and individualistic process of self–scrutiny. Moreover, that very process appears to work against those most inclined to use it, possibly driving them into a vortex of guilt and pushing the assurance they seek further and further from their grasp.

5.2.2 Repentance

As the previous section indicates, Packer perceives faith to be a comprehensive response to God, that is, a response that involves the whole person. This response, which alone places a person into a saving relationship with God, is a marshalling and orientation of the reason, volition, and affection toward Jesus Christ as one's sole hope and source of salvation, both in this life and the next. Contending against Zane Hodges's attempt to separate faith and repentance, Packer defines true faith. 'By contrast, faith according to reformational teaching is a whole–souled reality with an affectional and volitional aspect as well as an intellectual one. It is, as the seventeenth–century analysts put it, *notitia* (factual knowledge), *assensus* (glad acceptance), and *fiducia* (personal trust in a personal Savior, as well as in His promises).'[75] Saving faith, for Packer, can never be reduced to the response of any one faculty such as the reason. This approach constitutes the basis for making repentance integral to the nature of true, saving faith.

The theme of repentance rises to prominence in Packer's thought not only because of his Reformed theology and the influence of competing theological forces that attempt to dissociate it from faith, but also because

---

[75] Packer, 'Understanding the Lordship Controversy', 212.

of cultural trends that have influenced Western Christianity toward preoccupation with superficial issues such as entertainment and self–help programs.[76] He contends that the need for emphasising repentance is more acute in contexts where the public is obsessed with the proliferation of resources that attempt to address humanity's deepest needs, either through tawdry distractions or humanistic philosophies. This contention invites further clarification about the nature of repentance.

First, Packer understands repentance as a radical redirection of all the faculties such that outwardly discernable change takes place in a person's lifestyle. He portrays repentance as

> changing one's mind so that one's views, values, goals, and ways are changed and one's whole life is lived differently. The change is radical, both inwardly and outwardly; mind and judgment, will and affections, behavior and life–style, motives and purposes, are all involved. Repenting means starting to live a new life.[77]

> The term is a personal and relational one. It signifies going back on what one was doing before, and renouncing the misbehavior by which one's life or one's relationship was being harmed. In the Bible, repentance is a theological term, pointing to an abandonment of those courses of action in which one defied God by embracing what he dislikes and forbids.[78]

It appears in these descriptions that Packer conceives repentance as equally internal and external. True internal repentance will result in external change.

Second, it must be noted that though repentance is integrally related to faith, it can be analysed psychologically as following the cognitive aspect of faith and soteriologically as following the regeneration of the will. In the following passage he describes the relationship between repentance and faith. Repentance is defined with reference to that from which one turns. Faith is defined with reference to the object toward which one turns.

> Repentance is a fruit of faith, which is itself a fruit of regeneration. But in actual life, repentance is inseparable from faith, being the negative aspect (faith is the positive aspect) of turning to Christ as Lord and Savior. The idea that there can be saving faith without repentance, and that one can be

---

[76] Packer, *A Passion for Holiness*, 143–144.
[77] Ibid., 162.
[78] Ibid., 122–123.

justified by embracing Christ as Savior while refusing him as Lord, is a destructive delusion.[79]

Accordingly, though repentance is tightly connected to the faith that brings a person into the experience of relationship with God, its subsequence to regeneration implies that 'repenting in the full sense of the word – actually changing ... – is only possible for Christians, believers who have been set free from sin's dominion and made alive to God.'[80]

In his unpublished course notes he describes repentance as, 'Turning to God from sin and self–will, so <u>changing</u> (cf. Ps. 51:4–10). Repentance is a fruit of faith; both are fruits of regeneration. Remorse, conviction of sin and self–reproach are steps to repentance, maybe, but less than repentance.'[81] This claim prepares the way for his claim that repentance must be practised even after the point of conscious entrance into relationship with God. 'Christians are called to a life of habitual repentance, as a discipline integral to healthy holy living.'[82] Repentance is at the heart of the entire Christian experience.

Repentance and faith adhere for Packer under the concept of conversion. He refers to the Hebrew *šûb* and the Greek *strepho* word groups as denoting the idea of turning around or turning back, especially with regard to God's covenant and its obligations on both individuals and nations.[83] His discussion of conversion sounds remarkably similar to his discussion of repentance. In its Old Testament usage he notes that 'a true turning to God under any circumstances will involve inward self–humbling, a real change of heart, and a sincere seeking after the Lord ... and will be accompanied by a new clarity of knowledge of His being and His ways ...'[84] In the New Testament, Packer claims, conversion

> consists of an exercise of repentance and faith, which Christ and Paul link together as summing up between them the moral demand of the gospel (Mk.i. 15; Acts xx. 21). Repentance means a change of mind and heart towards God; faith means belief of His word and trust in His Christ; conversion covers both. Thus we find both repentance and faith linked

---

[79] Packer, *Concise Theology*, 163. The first part of Packer's statement parallels Calvin's claim that 'repentance not only constantly follows faith, but is also born of faith.' See *Institutes*, III.iii.1.

[80] Packer, *A Passion for Holiness*, 123.

[81] Packer, 'Systematic Theology B, Man, Sin and Grace', section on 'Conversion Complex', 5.

[82] Packer, *A Passion for Holiness*, 121.

[83] J.I. Packer, 'Conversion', in *NBD*, 250–251.

[84] Ibid., 251.

with conversion, as the narrower with the wider concept (repentance and conversion, Acts iii. 19, xxvi. 20; faith and conversion, Acts xi. 21).[85]

He contends that 'faith and repentance as principles of daily living' are 'marks of conversion.'[86] He claims to follow Calvin by portraying conversion as both initiation and sustenance of the Christian life.

There has to be for all of us some form of entry into the converted state, in which none of us is found by nature. ... But there is more: following on from 'the hour I first believed,' conversion must now become a lifelong process. Conversion has been defined from this standpoint as a matter of giving as much as you know of yourself to as much as you know of God. This means that as our knowledge of God and ourselves grows (and the two grow together), so our conversion needs to be repeated and extended constantly.

To think in these terms is to catch up with John Calvin, who both referred explicitly to the 'sudden conversion' (*subita conversio*) [Preface, *Commentary on the Psalms*] ... and also in his *Institutes of the Christian Religion* [III.iii.5] set forth a concept of conversion as the practice of lifelong active repentance, the fruit of faith, springing from a renewed heart ...[87]

By encompassing repentance and faith under the rubric of conversion, Packer bolsters his case that salvation demands a lifelong response of the whole person. Conversion, he argues, carries the explicit theological overtones of union with Christ without which there is no freedom from sin, even at the formal or forensic level.[88]

---

[85] Ibid.

[86] Packer, *Growing in Christ*, 108. See also S.B. Ferguson, *John Owen on the Christian Life* (Edinburgh: Banner of Truth, 1987), 34–35. Ferguson contends that for Calvin, 'repentance and regeneration ... were not the inauguration of the Christian life so much as its continuing character, namely the mortification of sin and vivification in Christ' [*Institutes*, III.iii.1.]. However, Ferguson continues, 'Owen denotes different things when he employs the same language. Repentance for him is not penitence as a Christian grace, but, more narrowly, the initial turning from sin which is associated with conversion.' Packer seems to understand repentance and faith as both the initiation and the continuance of the Christian life.

[87] Packer, *A Passion for Holiness*, 139–140. However, Packer's way of relating conversion, repentance, and faith differs slightly from Calvin. In the very passage Packer mentions (*Institutes*, III.iii.5.) Calvin refers to repentance as the more comprehensive concept, stating that 'the whole of conversion to God is understood under the term "repentance."'

[88] Packer, 'Conversion', 251.

The fact that Packer links repentance to faith is certainly significant for his understanding of piety. Perhaps more significant, however, is the manner and nature of the connection he posits. First, it must be asked whether he is justified in so frequently identifying repentance with its negative rather than its positive orientation. Since the biblical evidence, by Packer's own admission, depicts repentance as oriented *toward* a certain horizon as well as *away from* another, he could be expected to produce criteria for emphasising the negative dimension over the positive dimension. It is entirely possible that this corresponds to the role he sees for the presence and power of indwelling sin in the life of the Christian. Naturally, if personal struggle with indwelling sin is a ubiquitous, existential reality, repentance must occupy a place of equal force in a person's piety if any degree of growth in holiness is to occur. This presupposes, though, that his portrayal of indwelling sin accords with the biblical witness.

Second, it must be asked whether Packer's definitions of faith and repentance are consistent with the way he understands the psychological faculties to function in respect to soteriology. Specifically, he refuses to concede that the intellectual or cognitive dimension of faith (assent to the truth of the Gospel) is sufficient for salvation apart from the volitional dimension (repentance).

> Faith must be defined, just as it must be exercised, in terms of its object. ... Surely it is undeniable that God has joined faith and repentance, in the sense of change of life, as the two facets of response to Christ, and has made it clear that turning to Christ means turning from sin and letting ungodliness go. Surely it is undeniable that in the New Testament true faith is not only knowing facts about Jesus, but coming to him in personal trust to worship, love, and serve him.[89]

In one respect this appears consistent with his claim that the will is the centre of relationship with God and had the primary or operative role in the

---

[89] J.I. Packer, 'Evangelicals and the Way of Salvation', in *Shorter Writings*, 1.196. See also, 'On from Orr: The Cultural Crisis, Rational Realism, and Incarnational Ontology', in A. McGrath (ed.), *The J.I. Packer Collection* (Downers Grove: InterVarsity, 1999), 264. He claims here that 'it is the way of fundamentalism to follow the path of contentious orthodoxy, as if the mercy of God in Christ automatically rests on persons who are notionally correct and is just as automatically withheld from those who fall short of notional correctness on any point of substance. But this concept of, in effect, justification, not by works, but by words – words, that is, of notional soundness and precision – is near to being a cultic heresy in its own right ...'

Fall. Yet, he insists, the restoration of the will depends on the illumination of the intellect regarding the propositional truth of the gospel. When he suggests that salvation is not necessarily contingent upon precise comprehension of the Gospel message,[90] it would appear that he assumes some disjunction between the intellect and the will in salvation. It appears inconsistent then, for Packer to allow that while intellectual faith cannot save apart from the turning of the will toward obeying Christ, volitional faith may save a person without total intellectual comprehension of the gospel.

5.2.3 Mortification and Vivification

Mortification and vivification are the logical extensions of faith and repentance for Packer, though he does not discuss these themes to the same extent that he discusses faith and repentance. Mortification carries the reorientation and turning involved in repentance a step further toward the removal of sin from the believer's inclinations and practices. It constitutes the ongoing function of repentance in sanctification. Vivification cultivates the new life of regeneration into habitual responses of obedience and worship. Both mortification and vivification presuppose that repentance and faith extend throughout a Christian's lifetime.

In his emphasis on repentance Packer goes beyond Calvin and relies more on the Puritans for what he considers to be a balanced view of piety. He claims, 'Whereas Calvin regularly referred to Christian holiness as progress in faith and fortitude, the Puritans characteristically depicted it as an increasing measure of deliverance from sin.'[91] The advantage of the Puritans, to Packer, is that they more fully address the problem of indwelling sin and its power against the Christian.

While he sees the Puritans as generally modelling a healthy, though often unrecognised, balance between the positive and negative aspects of piety,

---

[90] J.I. Packer, 'Knowing Notions or Knowing God?' *Pastoral Renewal* (March 1982), 65–68.

[91] Packer, *A Passion for Holiness*, 107. Nonetheless, Calvin clearly includes mortification and vivification as aspects of repentance that are essential to holiness (*Institutes*, III.iii.8). Calvin calls self–denial and self–renunciation 'the sum of the Christian life [*Institutes*, III.vii.]' and discusses mortification under this heading. Specifically, Calvin uses the term 'mortification' in reference to the self–denial necessary for developing true love for those who are difficult to love [III.vii.7.]. See also Ferguson, *John Owen on the Christian Life*, 73. 'This, then, is the ground–plan of Owen's teaching on Christian living. The embryo of regeneration develops in accordance with its own nature in the vivification of spiritual life, and the mortification of sin.'

he considers their emphasis on the negative aspect a much needed corrective to a common negligence of sin.

> The Puritans have always had a bad press. Their emphasis on each Christian's lifelong war to the death with 'besetting' (habitual) sins has sometimes been dismissed as Manichean ... morbid ... and morally unreal ... But all of this is factually incorrect, and the idea that fighting sin was all the Puritan saints ever thought about is quite wrong. ... It was not all harping on a single note. Yet it is true that a drumbeat stress on detecting, resisting, and overcoming sin's downdrag appears everywhere. ... The solemn business of self–scrutiny and suffering, inward and outward, as one strives and struggles against sin is only one side of it. But in an age in which self–ignorance, secular–mindedness, moral slackness and downright sin are as common among Christians as they are today, it is doubtless from the stern side of Puritanism – the side that forces on us realism about our sinfulness and our sins – that we have most to learn.[92]

In his introductory comments to J. Owen's *Sin and Temptation*, he observes, 'Ungodliness, unrighteousness, unbelief, and heresy are sin's natural forms of self–expression. Sin pervades and pollutes the whole man.' He concludes, 'Christian living must therefore be founded on self–abhorrence and self–distrust because of indwelling sin's presence and power.'[93] Thus, true repentance depends upon an introspective and suspicious approach toward one's spiritual condition, with a view to discovering, repenting of, and mortifying sin. For Packer, the presence and function of indwelling sin necessarily leads to a preoccupation with one's personal sinfulness in order for any progress toward holiness to be realised. Thus, mortification depends on the practice of regular introspection.[94]

---

[92] Ibid., 108–109.

[93] Packer, Introduction to *Sin and Temptation*, xx.

[94] See W. Pannenberg, *Christian Spirituality* (Philadelphia: Westminster, 1983),13–30. Pannenberg critiques the Reformation preoccupation with sin by labelling it as 'penitential piety' and claiming that it fails to grasp the scope of God's forgiveness and obscures the power of grace and gratitude in the Christian experience. He advocates instead a 'eucharistic piety' (31–49), wherein sin is recognised but is overshadowed by a sense of gratitude for forgiving grace. See also K. Stendahl, 'The Apostle Paul and the Introspective Conscience of the West', *Journal for the Scientific Study of Religion* 1 (April 1962), 262. Stendahl attributes this preoccupation with introspection to a misinterpretation of the Apostle Paul's comments concerning his struggle with sin, mostly at the hands of Augustine and Martin Luther. He states, 'While it is true that Luther found in Paul's writings a solution to the painful dilemma of his conscience, it is equally clear that Paul himself had written these

This emphasis on habitual repentance stems from Packer's view of God's law and its role in defining the contours of Christian obedience. He states, 'The self–knowledge in which a Christian's repentance is rooted comes from the law. It is a result of being made to face God's prescribed moral standards for us his creatures.'[95] His first premise is that God's law is absolute and uncompromising in its moral demands. Second, he notes that the nature of sinfulness, even in regenerate persons, is such that it affects even the deepest level of one's motivations and is never fully purged in this life. Thus, no act is ever utterly devoid of some sin. He claims, 'God searches our hearts as well as weighing our actions. For this reason, guilt for sin extends to deficiencies in our motives and our purposes, as well as in our performance.'[96] Thus, since every day of a Christian's life is filled with actions, decisions, intentions, and goals, each of which is morally flawed and offensive to God's glory and falls short of the demands of God's law, it behoves all Christians to take initiative daily in searching their consciences for any sign of sin.[97]

Godly Christians have always been marked by a two–sided perception of the numinous. On the one hand, the transcendent glory of God's purity and love, as focused in the plan of salvation, fascinates them. On the other hand, the transcendent glory of God's sovereignty, as focused in the divine threat of judgment for impiety, alarms them. This characteristically Christian sense of the mercy and the terror (fear) of the Lord is the seed–bed in which awareness grows that lifelong repentance is a 'must' of holy living. That awareness will not grow under any other conditions. Where it is lacking, any supposed sanctity will prove on inspection to be flawed by complacency about oneself and short–sightedness about sin.[98]

Because sin, both of omission and of commission, in motive, aim, thought, desire, wish, and fantasy even if not in outward action, is a daily event in Christians' lives ... regular repentance is an abiding necessity.[99]

---

saving statements as answers to quite different problems, far removed from those raised by an introspective conscience.' He goes on to claim, 'It is first with Augustine that Paul's thoughts are made to transcend the limitations of their original setting. And they do so precisely under the pressure of human introspection and of a deepened awareness of the ethical dilemma.'

[95] Packer, *A Passion for Holiness*, 150.
[96] Ibid., 135.
[97] Ibid., 134–140.
[98] Ibid., 132.
[99] Ibid., 136.

This process Packer refers to as 'weeding out.' He cites with admiration the model of the Puritan John Bradford who made a habit of regularly cataloguing his sins and of signing his correspondence with descriptors such as 'hypocrite,' 'unthankful sinner,' 'most miserable,' and 'half–hearted.'[100] Packer's approach to repentance, then, assumes the priority of God's law in defining God's character. It assumes that God's grace cannot be rightly understood and God rightly worshipped apart from prior, personal reflection on one's sinfulness.[101] It assumes that though a Christian may already have experienced God's grace, awareness of and appreciation for that grace will necessarily atrophy unless a keen awareness of personal sin is aggressively sought.

Repentance (mortification), involving confrontation, reflection, and turning from personal sin, occupies such a significant place in piety for Packer that he makes it a gauge of spiritual health. 'The further one goes in holy living, the more sin one will find in the attitudes of one's own heart, needing to be dealt with in this way. As the single–mindedness of our inward devotion is the real index of the quality of our discipleship, so the thoroughness of our daily repentance is the real index of the quality of our devotion.'[102] Repentant mortification does not provide or accomplish all that is needed for healthy, growing communion with God. It merely prepares the way for that communion to be further pursued through the disciplines of vivification.

---

[100] Ibid., 126, 138.

[101] R.S. Wallace, *Calvin's Doctrine of the Christian Life* (Grand Rapids: Eerdmans, 1959), 226. Wallace suggests that to Calvin, 'This self–examination must not be a spasmodic and momentary feature of our Christian experience but should be a duty which we perform diligently each morning and evening [Sermon on Deut. 9:6–7]. And when our sins are brought to mind we must think about them and "let the bitterness of them dwell within" in order that we may be driven not to despair but to increased watchfulness over our lives [Sermon on Deut. 6:15–19].' See also J. Calvin. *Sermons on Deuteronomy* (Edinburgh: Banner of Truth, 1987²), 293. In his sermon on Deuteronomy 6:15–19 Calvin exhorts, 'And thereby we be taught, that when we have done any fault, we must bethink us of it, to the intent we may do no more so. And instead of taking occasion to grudge at GOD through impatience: we must humble our selves the more under his awe'. In his sermon on Deuteronomy 9:6–7 he says, 'Yea and if we will yield him the due praise of his grace: we must come to the acknowledgement of our sins. And that must not be done for once only, but every of us must give himself to examination both evening and morning, and upon the knowledge of one fault, we must go to the sifting out of an other. True it is that in this case there is no measure, neither can we be too circumspect' (382). [Spelling modernized by the author]

[102] Packer, *A Passion for Holiness*, 144.

Packer finds the interdependence of mortification and vivification to be articulated most persuasively by the English Puritans and John Calvin. He develops them under the heading 'Holiness as the Overcoming of Sin's Downdrag.'[103] John Owen provides for Packer the connection between the nature of mortification and the nature of Christ's provision for it. He states that for Owen,

> Mortification is more than the mere suppression, or counteraction, of sinful impulse. It is nothing less than a gradual eradication of it. … The sin that indwells the believer was killed in principle on the cross; Christ's death will in time be its death. It was dethroned in fact by regeneration, and now, with the Spirit's aid, the Christian is to spend his lifetime draining its lifeblood (Rom. 8:13).[104]
> Simply stated, sanctification's 'positive side is *vivification*, the growing and maturing of the new man; its negative side is *mortification*, the weakening and killing of the old man.'[105]

Packer attempts to integrate the distinctives of Calvin and the Puritans into what he considers a balanced view. Yet his tone appears more reflective of the Puritans due to his emphasis on the pervasive struggle with indwelling sin.

He uses the word 'vivification' less frequently, emphasising instead the Christian's responsibility for obedient response to God's grace. He states, 'Holiness means, among other things, forming good habits, breaking bad habits, resisting temptations to sin, and controlling yourself when provoked. No one ever managed to do any of these things without effort and conflict.'[106] Parallel to his emphasis on human responsibility, he highlights the power of God that is available for this obedience.

---

[103] Ibid., 106. He states, 'With Calvin, they [primarily referring to the English Puritans, though he also includes some who went to New England] analyzed God's work of sanctifying sinners as, on the negative side, *mortification*, the progressive killing of sin as it manifests itself in each rebellious and self–indulging habit, plus, on the positive side, *vivification*, the inculcating and strengthening in us of all Christ–like habits ("graces") …'

[104] Packer, *Among God's Giants*, 262. He also comments, 'It ought to be said … that this dichotomised scheme of sanctification as a matter of vivifying our graces and mortifying our sins, which Owen sets forth with such masterful and searching brilliance, is not in any way peculiar to him. It is conventional Puritan teaching, going back through Calvin to Romans 6 and Colossians 2:20–3:17' (264).

[105] Ibid., 261.

[106] Packer, *A Passion for Holiness*, 174.

Christ's personal victory over sin through his death on the cross constitutes the ground of holiness while the believer's union with Christ through faith is the pathway along which the power for holiness comes to the believer. Packer affirms this formula, though he refuses to define the exact nature of the process.

Jesus' point [in John 15:4–5,9–10] is that he himself must be the focus of his followers' lives. By faith in him they are already united with him in such a way that his life really, although mysteriously, flows through them (they are branches in him, the vine). Now they are to look to him as their source of power to serve, listen to him to find what form that service should take, cultivate his company as they go about his business, and bask in the certainty of his ongoing love.[107] Here Packer appears to utilise Calvin's emphasis on union with Christ and make it the basis of both the Christian's obligation to obey and Christ's provision of power to obey.[108]

Despite his efforts to affirm Christ's power for mortification and vivification in the believer's life, Packer does not appear to provide a theological and existential foundation adequate to that process. First, he only links Christ's death directly with justification. In his two most significant writings on the cross, 'What Did the Cross Achieve?'[109] and 'Sacrifice and Satisfaction,'[110] he makes no mention of sanctification. In the first of those writings his nine–point summary of the cross's achievement includes only a reference to positional righteousness in Christ, a guarantee of 'preservation to glory,' and the call 'to trust, to worship, to love and to serve.'[111] The closest link he makes between the cross and sanctification is his statement that justification is 'the context of sanctification.' He explains that to mean that growth in holiness involves continual need for the cleansing of the blood of Christ.[112] That is to say, the forgiveness of sins procured by Christ on the cross is the ongoing source of forgiveness for the

---

[107] Ibid., 193.

[108] R.C. Gleason, *John Calvin and John Owen on Mortification: A Comparative Study in Reformed Spirituality*, Studies in Church History series, vol. III (New York: Peter Lang, 1995), 147. Gleason compares Owen's view of mortification with that of Calvin, claiming that 'for both Calvin and Owen, union with Christ is the means through which Christ's benefits are channeled.' He also notes, 'Both [Calvin and Owen] follow the three–fold structure of the soul. Mortification begins with the mind which in turn instructs the will and, thereby, informs the affections which cause a change in behavior' (148). This will be seen in chapter seven to be consistent with Packer's anthropological structure and how it influences piety in his thought.

[109] Packer, 'What Did the Cross Achieve?' 85–123.

[110] Packer, 'Sacrifice and Satisfaction', 125–136.

[111] Packer, 'What Did the Cross Achieve?' 121.

[112] Packer, 'Predestination and Sanctification', 322.

Christian. The cross contributes to the mortification of sin by dealing with sin in principle, that is, by destroying or taking away its definitive role in human experience.

Second, his description of the believer's union with Christ places more emphasis on the movement of the believer toward Christ after the cross than on the movement of Christ toward all people in the Incarnation. The latter movement is not excluded, but neither is it commensurate with the believer's movement toward Christ, simply because in Packer's Christology the Son of God enters the human experience up to and not including the sinful nature. Justification tends to be his primary concern in relation to the cross.

Human responsibility in holiness does not end with faith, repentance, mortification, and vivification, however. Packer places these specific activities under the overarching call for endurance, wherein he incorporates the subject of eschatology into piety.

5.2.4 Endurance

Packer mentions that there are over seventy occurrences of *hupomone*, *hupomeno*, *makrothumia*, and *makrothumeo* in order to substantiate the claim that 'endurance is a major New Testament theme.'[113] This fits with his repeated emphasis on the Christian life as a life of struggle and diligent effort against constant hostility from the world, the flesh, and the Devil. 'Christian maturity,' he states, 'which is holiness full–grown, is the promised end–product of another hard–gaining discipline, namely *endurance* – both passive (*patience*) and active (*perseverance*).'[114] Three

---

[113] Packer, *A Passion for Holiness*, 240. He observes regarding these words, 'The two pairs are virtually synonymous, though the verbal form of the one (*hupomone, hupomeno*) gives the thought of standing firm under pressure while the verbal form of the other (*makrothumia, makrothumeo*) suggests rather staying cool under provocation and not quickly cracking. In fact, the two ideas shade into each other, and the habit of endurance calls for both.'

[114] Ibid. See also Wallace, *Calvin's Doctrine of the Christian Life*, 325. Wallace notes that, for Calvin, '[t]here is a state of achieved victory over sin and whole–hearted surrender which by the grace of God may be called "perfection".' Wallace finds statements in Calvin's commentaries and sermons that seem to imply the possibility of a Christian's will being in utter harmony with God's will, though a struggle against sin still takes place. Yet, Wallace observes, 'Calvin at times speaks as if this achievement of victory over sin can become a settled and stable state' [326]. Calvin's emphasis on progress and struggle in sanctification pervades his thought on the possibility of 'perfection.' Nevertheless, he appears more optimistic than Packer, whose doctrine of sanctification has been shaped by his reaction against the 'perfectionism' of Keswick and Wesleyan perspectives.

elements recur prominently in Packer's development of the concept of endurance in the Christian life: divine enabling, suffering, and hope.

Consistent with his manner of relating election, justification, and sanctification, Packer makes endurance completely dependent upon God's grace to initiate the desire for it and grant the energy to pursue it. Endurance influences holiness, for Packer, as the spiritual strength and determination needed for long term faithfulness to God. However, endurance is also a Christian responsibility. He points out that the patience involved in endurance is a fruit of the Spirit (Galatians 5:22–23) and is thus 'not a natural endowment but a supernatural gift, a grace of character which God imparts to those whom he is transforming into the likeness of Christ.'[115]

The active aspect of endurance, perseverance, points directly to the influence of God's election, providing assurance and hope that God will certainly bring to fruition the saving work begun in the life of those who are truly regenerate. This aspect, too, draws attention to God's grace as the operative factor in endurance. Packer states, 'Perseverance means persistence under discouragement and contrary pressure. The assertion that believers persevere in faith and obedience despite everything is true, but the reason is that Jesus Christ through the Spirit persists in preserving them.'[116] The role of endurance in Packer's understanding of piety directly reflects his soteriological commitment to the Calvinism expressed at the Synod of Dort. Lifelong endurance in faithful growth is an indicator of a person's election and regeneration.

The context of endurance is suffering, without which endurance would have no virtue and no capacity for glorifying God. When discussing endurance in *A Passion for Holiness* he explains, 'God's faithfulness consists in his unwillingness that his children should lose any of the depths of fellowship with himself that he has in store for them. So he afflicts us to make us lean harder on him, in order that his purpose of drawing us into closest fellowship with himself may be fulfilled.'[117]

The theme of suffering is so important in Packer's piety that he portrays 'suffering Christianly' as 'an integral aspect of biblical holiness.'[118] In the context of suffering, God's glory is displayed as Christians are confronted with their sinfulness and their natural inability and disinclination to follow God apart from God's grace. In suffering, their affections are distilled of distractions and idols then purified in attentive focus on their Lord.

---

[115] Ibid.
[116] Packer, *Concise Theology*, 241.
[117] Packer, *A Passion for Holiness*, 268.
[118] Ibid., 250.

In his treatment of suffering Packer's Christology resurfaces as a model for piety. Jesus' own holiness is a model to emulate in that he was willing 'to suffer all kinds of pain for his Father's glory and others' good. One facet of holiness in Jesus' disciples is willingness to be led along a parallel path.'[119] In this statement there is an indication of how Packer allows his theology of the Incarnation to shape his understanding of piety. He does not understand humanness to be fulfilled in disembodied or escapist terms, but in the sometimes harsh realities of created, fallen existence where Jesus lived out the perfect image of God in suffering. The model of Jesus demonstrates to Packer that perseverance is not stoicism.[120]

Summary

In J.I. Packer's theology the Christian life involves a marked transition from a monergistic mode of justification, wherein God does all the work and the believer's responsibility is repentance and faith, to a synergistic mode of sanctification that relies primarily on God's grace administered to the believer through the agency of the Holy Spirit, yet still demands intentional responses of obedience. As God is both the initiator and sustainer of the entire process of salvation, sanctification constituting an integrated yet logically distinct link in the sequence, Packer seeks to avoid charges of Pelagianism that he levels against versions of the Christian life that do not draw those lines quite as clearly. In these formulations he seeks to be faithful to the biblical texts that enjoin the Christian's conscious effort while honouring the priority of God's role in the Christian experience.

---

[119] Ibid., 266.
[120] Ibid., 244.

Chapter 6

The Experience of Piety

As holiness is rightly pursued, its effects are outwardly manifest in changed values, relationships, and activities. He persists in rejecting the notion that holiness is a merely mystical experience, a withdrawal from relationships, or an avoidance of struggle with sin and temptation. The 'earthliness' of piety is illustrated in his claim that holiness is influenced by unique personality factors. Every individual's experience of piety will be unique to some extent, depending on the mix of those factors.[1]

Packer's clearest, most comprehensive description of the effects and functioning of piety is found in *A Passion for Holiness*. He suggests five signs of

> spiritual growth – growth in the graces of Christian character, and in intimacy with God ... *Sign one* is a growing delight in praising God, with an increasing distaste for being praised oneself. ... *Sign two* is a growing instinct for caring and giving, with a more pronounced dislike of the self–absorption that constantly takes without either caring or giving. ... *Sign three* is a growing passion for personal righteousness, with more acute distress at the godlessness and immorality of the world around, and a keener discernment of Satan's strategy of opposition, distraction, and deception for ensuring that people neither believe nor live right. ... *Sign four* is a growing zeal for God's cause, with more willingness to take unpopular action to further it. ... *Sign five* is a greater patience and willingness to wait for God and bow to his will, with a deeper abhorrence

---

[1] Packer, *A Passion for Holiness*, 183, 184. 'The precise quality of change involved in people's growth in grace is always conditioned by their natural make–up.' Then later he states, 'The partial moderating of some choleric's furious temper, or the partial melting of some phlegmatic's chilly aloofness, or the partial curing of some sanguine's zany irresponsibility, or the partial deliverance of some melancholic from the paralyzing obsession of despair, may well argue a greater measure of growth in grace ... than is present in more sturdy, forthcoming, realistic, energetic saints who never had to cope with these particular flaws in themselves.'

of what masquerades as the bold faith, but is really the childish immaturity, that tries to force God's hand. [2]

A shorter, but similar list of descriptors can be found in his article, 'The Means of Growth.' Here he describes four 'dimensions of growth,' each of which 'will increasingly appear in us if we are growing in grace.' Those dimensions are *worship* ('praising God'), *endurance, love,* and *contending* ('for God's truth against error').[3] Two important assumptions undergird his profile of spiritual growth. First, spiritual progress involves frustration because it must overcome resistance. Second, spiritual growth involves renewal of the motivation.

6.1 Progress through Struggle

Though the most salient object of the Christian's hope may be the unmediated experience of God's presence, the longing for conformity to Christ's image is also the occasion for Christians to experience acute dissonance.

> Seeing themselves as travellers on the way home, they will live by hope – hope, quite specifically, of meeting their beloved Saviour face to face, and being with him for ever. Discerning sinful desires in themselves despite their longing to be sin–free, and finding that in their quest for total righteousness their reach exceeds their grasp, they will live in tension and distress at their frustrating infirmities (cf. Rom. 7:14–25).[4]

This dissonance is exacerbated as they grow in holiness because, becoming more sensitive to God's heart, they become more keenly and painfully aware of their shortcomings. This is the heart of the paradox that Packer admits in his view of holiness.

> Clearer perceptions of God's purity have a reflex effect, as if that purity were a light shining into the recesses of the self and showing up all that has been lurking in the dark there. As a result, Christians come to see in themselves sinful motives and attitudes, failures, shortcomings, and deficiencies, of which they were unaware before, simply because until now their consciences had not assessed their conduct by so bright a light from God. … Because spiritual advance thus enlarges insight into the depths of one's own fallenness, those going forward in holiness often feel they are going backward. Their deepened awareness of how sinful they

---

[2] Ibid., 188–189.
[3] Packer, 'The Means of Growth', 289–290.
[4] Packer, 'Evangelical Foundations for Spirituality', 265.

still are, despite their longing to serve God flawlessly, weighs them down.[5]

The other side of the paradox is increasing delight in God and in living responsively to God's law. The attention that Packer gives to sin in his theology of piety helps account for the persistence presence of frustration in the Christian experience.

6.2 Renewed Motivation

Renewal of the Christian's motivation is a prominent goal of piety for Packer because the will is at the core of the *imago Dei* and because sin has its most radical impact on the will. Any impact that Jesus Christ's soteriological work has on human nature must therefore address these issues. Packer brings these themes together and points out the effect of salvation on the motivation.

> What happens [in conversion] is that in a sovereign act of grace that the New Testament theologizes as birth from God (John 1:13; 13:5–8; James 1:18; 1 Peter 1:23; 1 John 3:9; 5:1,4), co–resurrection with Christ (Rom. 6:4–11; Eph. 2:1–10; Col. 2:13; 3:1–11), new creation in Christ (2 Cor. 5:17; Gal. 6:5) and regeneration (Titus 3:5) … God unites the individual to the risen Lord in such a way that the dispositional drives of Christ's perfect human character – the inner urgings, that is, to honour, adore, love, obey, serve and please God, and to benefit others for both their sake and his sake – are now reproduced at the motivational centre of that individual's being. And they are reproduced, in face of the contrary egocentric cravings of fallen nature, in a dominant way, so that the Christian, though still troubled and tormented by the urgings of indwelling sin, is no longer ruled by those urgings in the way that was true before.[6]

This metamorphosis, as previously indicated, is neither instantaneous nor total in this lifetime. Rather, the change takes place through progressive mastery of the motivation by redeemed impulses.

Jesus' perfect nature provides both the template and the source for the renewal of a Christian's motivation. For Packer, this occurs as a direct result of a union with Christ that God brings about through a unilateral act of grace. Packer elaborates on the nature of this union and its effect on the Christian's motivation. 'Motivationally, within the heart, the change is an

---

[5] Packer, *A Passion for Holiness*, 220–221.
[6] Packer, 'Evangelical Foundations for Spirituality', 258–259.

implanting in us of the inclinations of Christ's perfect humanity through our ingrafting into him: this produces in us a mind–set and lifestyle that is not explicable in terms of what we were before.'[7] Packer also describes this union as solidarity with Christ when he explains Paul's images of putting on the new person (Colossians 3:10) and clothing oneself with the Lord Jesus Christ (Romans 13:14).[8]

6.3 Engagement with Creation

Anthropology and piety, for J.I. Packer, involve a positive relationship to the created order, even in its fallen state. His anthropology emerges from a theology of creation that supports a world–affirming piety. The following passage offers an overview of his perspective on the Christian's relationship to the created order.

> Since it is his world, we are not its owners, free to do as we like with it, but its stewards, answerable to him for the way we handle its resources. And since it is his world, we must not depreciate it. Much religion has built on the idea that the material order – reality as experienced through the body, along with the body that experiences it – is evil, and therefore to be refused and ignored as far as possible. This view, which dehumanizes its devotees, has sometimes called itself Christian, but it is really as un–Christian as can be. For matter, being made by God, was and *is* good in his eyes (Genesis 1:31), and so should be so in ours (1 Timothy 4:4). We serve God by using and enjoying temporal things gratefully, with a sense of their value to him, their Maker, and of his generosity in giving them to us. It is an ungodly and, indeed, inhuman super–spirituality which seeks to serve the Creator by depreciating any part of his creation.[9]

Packer affirms the 'cultural mandate,' by which he means 'mankind's obligation to develop a pattern of corporate life that honours the Creator by embodying true moral and spiritual values and so furthers the realizing of all the joyful potential of human life in God's world.'[10] He rejects any

---

[7] Ibid., 265.

[8] Ibid., 264. He states, 'Putting off and putting on is the language of changing clothes, and when the NIV renders "man" as "self" it misses some of the meaning; what the Christian has put off is solidarity with Adam, and what he puts on is Christ, or solidarity with Christ, as the source and principle of his new life ...'

[9] Packer, *Growing in Christ*, 37.

[10] Packer, 'The Christian and God's World', 276. Packer's emphasis and language here is similar to that used in the Dutch Reformed tradition by theologians such as Abraham Kuyper. However, Packer does not attribute these concepts to anyone in the

notions that creation is inherently corrupt or that the life of faithful relationship with God is inhibited by engagement with the created order. 'Enjoying our bodies while we can, as opposed to despising them (which is Platonism at best, Manicheism at worst, and super–spiritual conceit either way), is part of the discipline of gratitude to our Creator.'[11] A godly relationship with the created order finds expression, for Packer, under the rubrics of health, culture, and politics.

Physical health is to be considered a gift from God to be enjoyed and valued, but only within the context of a broader understanding of health that is defined by God's intentions for human righteousness in relationship with God. Comparing the Christian view of physical health with a strictly humanistic view, he claims that the humanist will reduce the questions of sickness and death to issues of physical pathology. The Christian view, in contrast, involves 'a picture which includes the whole of our experience, leaving nothing out, and which shows that it all has meaning in terms of God's own goals.'[12] Thus, as health includes the physical dimension but encompasses much more, '*ill health of the person is more than ill health of the body.*'[13] He elaborates, 'In short, health and virtue coincide; health is wholeness, and wholeness is integration in the practice of love and righteousness.'[14] Physical health, though it derives value from the original intentions of God in creating a perfect world, takes on a decidedly secondary status in Packer's view of health and holiness.

True or complete health, for Packer, is a matter of holiness. He claims, 'Wholeness comes wholly through holiness.'[15] Through this integration of health and holiness Packer brings his understanding of sanctification into

---

Dutch Reformed tradition. He rarely makes reference to that strain of Calvinism, except when criticising G.C. Berkouwer in reference to the doctrine of Scripture. While he lists works from the Dutch Reformed tradition in the bibliographies for his systematic theology course notes at Regent College, he teaches another complete course entitled 'Calvin and the Calvinist Tradition' in which the syllabus contains not a single reference to the Dutch Reformed tradition. The syllabus contains four pages of notes on Calvin's teachings, followed by twenty–five pages of notes on Puritan Calvinism.

[11] J.I. Packer, *Hot Tub Religion* (Wheaton: Tyndale House, 1987), 63. See also Packer, *Among God's Giants*, 341. Packer defends the Puritans against the charge of being Manichean, claiming that 'the picture is entirely mistaken: like Calvin before them, the Puritans affirmed the duty of appreciating the goodness and delights of the material creation, and forbade only such immoderate and disorderly enjoyment of these gifts as would steal one's heart from the Giver.'

[12] Packer and Howard, *Christianity: The True Humanism*, 117.

[13] Ibid., 130.

[14] Ibid.

[15] Ibid.

view. 'To be 'sanctified' is to be restored to that place lost by Adam of belonging wholly to God, and thus to be enjoying the very thing that human life was made for in the first place. It is to be clean, alive, free, strong, and glad – even, says Christianity, on my death bed or in Belsen or Gulag or in the Black Hole of Calcutta.'[16]

He goes on to argue that since health is fundamentally a matter of living as a citizen of God's Kingdom through right relationship with Jesus Christ, moral virtue lies at the heart of health.

Suffering fits under the rubric of health as an important aspect of piety in Packer's theology. 'Suffering,' he claims, 'is in the mind of the sufferer, and may conveniently be defined as getting what you do not want while wanting what you do not get.'[17] Suffering, the various ways in which the conditions for embodied wholeness are absent, serves as a reminder of sin's effects and an encouragement to live by hope in God's promises of full restoration in the Kingdom. Packer claims that *'trust in God through the experience of ill health and suffering humanizes.* It does so by ripening us spiritually, for humanness and godliness are correlative concepts in the Christian view of things.'[18] Suffering accomplishes this goal by prompting prayer and bringing humility.[19]

Pleasure is the other side of suffering in Packer's theology of piety. He defends Calvin and the Puritans by insisting that his readers see their 'integration of pleasure into godliness.'[20] He attributes many of the

---

[16] Ibid., 131. Packer illustrates his view of health when he contrasts the 'health' of those whom modern culture recognises as psychologically or physically desirable specimens of humanity. He rather backhandedly admits that those who possess physical beauty (calling it 'a gift most gratefully to be prized') and some measure of psychological health do indeed possess something of value. Yet, he insists, these are only of relative value while qualities such as the fruit of the Holy Spirit (Gal. 5:22–23), as well as 'generosity and courage and honesty … good–humor and selflessness … purity of heart and sympathy and stamina and kindness … are the qualities that crown us with glory' (133). Such are the marks of those who are healthy and whole even when all other forms of embodied health are missing and the most extreme forms of deprivation are present.

[17] Packer, *A Passion for Holiness*, 249.

[18] Packer and Howard, *Christianity: The True Humanism*, 128.

[19] Ibid., 129.

[20] Packer, *Hot Tub Religion*, 80. Packer claims that 'Calvin affirms (against Augustine!) that not to use for pleasure created realities that afford pleasure is ingratitude to their Creator' (79). In defending Calvin and the Puritans he first offers a brief historical summary and explanation of Christianity's perpetual struggle with the tension between denying and affirming the created world and its delights. He cites (79) the decadence of the Graeco–Roman world as the catalyst for the largely negative attitudes found in 'the New Testament and the patristics writings' and

contemporary Christian hesitations about pleasure to revivalism and the piety it engendered.

> However, not all evangelicals followed Calvin and the Puritans in their integration of pleasure into godliness. Revivalism bred a narrow and negative other–worldliness, and in eighteenth– and nineteenth–century Britain and America many pietistic evangelicals made a point of embracing an ostentatiously frugal version of the bourgeois life–style as a witness against luxury and profligate living. ... Pietism seldom goes beyond surface–level criticism of the ways of the world, primarily because it tends to be world–denying rather than world–affirming. ... So Protestant pietists, mainstream and free church alike, entered the twentieth century with a less positive theology of pleasure than other Christians held and, one suspects, a less robust enjoyment of it in consequence.[21]

However, this positive theology of pleasure must be seasoned by the realisation that pleasure is innately 'Janus–faced: as a human reality it may be good and holy, or it may be sinful and vile.'[22] Furthermore, it must be clarified in its relationship to self–denial. These perspectives are necessary in order for pleasure to be part of true holiness.

Christians must be guided by a 'two–world perspective that views the next life as more important than this one and understands life here as essentially preparation and training for life hereafter.' He enjoins an 'other–worldliness' as the counterweight to his recognition of the value of temporal pleasure. In this 'other–worldliness' the Christian holds this life loosely, enjoying and appreciating it as a gift from God but with the tentativeness of a traveller who has not yet reached home.[23]

The human interest in culture, Packer concludes, is rooted in anthropology. It is the desire of people 'to be wholly awake to their own humanness.'[24] Though Packer and Thomas Howard claim that through the influence of the gospel 'Christianity transcends culture,' 'generates

---

'carried into the Middle Ages.' 'But then,' he claims, 'through the Reformers' and Puritans' insistence on the sanctity of secular life, the biblical theology of pleasure finally broke surface, and most of Christendom has recognized it by now.'

[21] Ibid., 80–81. To the author's knowledge Packer nowhere identifies the individuals within 'revivalism' who he thinks promoted this 'world–denying' piety.

[22] J.I. Packer, 'Leisure and Life–style: Leisure, Pleasure, and Treasure', in *Shorter Writings*, 2.390.

[23] Packer, *Hot Tub Religion*, 90.

[24] Packer and Howard, *Christianity: The True Humanism*, 162.

culture,' and 'critiques culture,'[25] they find biblical justification for interest in culture, not in direct biblical statements or allusions to cultural matters, but in the creation mandate to exercise dominion over the earth.

A life that is fully responsive to God, therefore, includes an interest in culture. Along with Thomas Howard he asserts,

> Christians have always believed in the goodness of creation, and historically the cultivating of the created order (which is what the word *culture* on Christian lips signifies) ... All created things reflect eternal realities and embody divine values (as Plato with uncanny intuition had gropingly guessed), and we are to study and value them accordingly. Also, we are to serve God by developing their latent capacities – which is what the creating of a civilization, with its arts, sciences, pooled know–how, and cooperative patterns of learning, acquiring, and distributing, really amount to. The picture of Adam set to tend God's garden says it all; for gardens are cultivated by planned hard work based on acquired knowledge of natural growth processes which the gardener seeks to direct and control. ... Thus, the Christian estimate of cultural activity is that, far from being an irrelevance or a snare or a sin, it is one of the ways in which we serve both our neighbor and our Maker.[26]

They continue by placing cultural growth in the context of the Christian's comprehensive responsibility for personal vocation and righteousness.

> [I]n addition to being called to faith, hope, love, righteousness, worship, and witness – Christians have a vocation to develop taste (that is, a sense of fitness and value), to become civilized themselves, and to play as positive a part as they can in the ongoing civilizing process around them. Redemption is God's restoring of what he created. And his commands to the redeemed, though now applying in a redemptive context (signalised sometimes by calling them 'kingdom ethics'), are in essence the laws of creation, of which those embodied in the Decalogue number ten and the 'cultural mandate' is an eleventh.[27]
>
> It [the Bible] does not, to be sure, teach us standards of beauty or ideal voting patterns, any more than it teaches us how to use a knife and fork or to split atoms or to compose music. But it charges us to use our creativity to devise a pattern of life that will fitly express the substance of our godliness, for this is what subduing the earth, tending God's garden, and

---

25 Ibid., 169,175,178.
26 Ibid., 177.
27 Ibid.

having dominion over the creatures means. It thus belongs to the Christian vocation to be world–affirming.[28]

Ultimately, Packer and Howard present Jesus as the model of how culture is to be engaged, which returns to Packer's insistence on Jesus as the complete model for Christian piety because he is the model of complete humanity.[29]

The cultural dimensions of piety, for Packer, include engagement with the political dimension of life, but in a manner that validates the temporal only in light of the eternal. Nevertheless, he affirms the significance of the temporal, created world, even in its fallen state, and applauds efforts to make the world a more hospitable place through influencing political and other social processes. On one hand, Packer eschews piety whose 'goals reduce the Christian faith from a pilgrim path to heaven to a socio–political scheme for this present world. This scheme is often referred to as establishing God's kingdom on earth by ending society's collective sins of racism, economic and cultural exploitation, class division, and denial of human rights.'[30]

On the other hand he criticises those who define holiness only in other–worldly terms.

> These people [some whom Packer labels as 'Protestant absolutists,' often of a quite conservative bent and preferring to be called 'evangelicals'] are *pietistic* in their concern about achieving holiness, avoiding sin, winning souls, practicing fellowship with Christians, and opposing all the forces of anti–Christianity on the personal level. Pietistic inhibitions take the form of political passivity and unwillingness to be involved in any level of civil government.[31]

---

[28] Ibid., 178.

[29] Ibid., 183. He states, 'But if we want to exert a genuinely humanizing influence, programs or no programs, we must embody and model true humanness as our Master did; there is, in God's ordering of things, no other way to do it. We influence others culturally either by this means or not at all.'

[30] J.I. Packer, *Knowing Christianity*, 182.

[31] Ibid., 185. Again, Packer does not make clear who he has in mind, though it would seem that he may be making specific reference to the Keswick movement and general reference to late nineteenth– and early twentieth–century revivalists who promoted millennialism and reacted against those who strove to change social structures.

A third approach he rejects is what he calls '[t]he political imperialism of some Christian biblicists.'[32] These, in Packer's view, often prefer the label 'fundamentalist' to 'evangelical' and understand biblical imperatives to imply 'no hesitation in announcing objectives and plunging into the hurly–burly of the political world in order to gain them.'[33] Though he strongly supports transformational political involvement, Packer warns against an 'uncompromising fighting stance' and 'the temptation to view the democratic power game as the modern equivalent of holy war in the Old Testament, in which God called upon his people to overthrow the heathen and take their kingdom by force.'[34]

Packer's denouncement of these three attitudes toward the political implications of piety incorporates various emphases of his anthropology. Against the first strategy, 'reductionism,' he points out the spiritual incompleteness of human beings, even those in a redeemed state.[35]

In response to the second strategy, 'pietism,' he alludes to the relational structure of his anthropology, criticising 'individualism that resolves all social problems into personal problems.'[36] This individualism constitutes an anthropological deficiency in that it fails to recognise that sin produces alienation at the social level and must therefore be addressed at that level.

Against the third strategy, 'imperialism,' Packer offers the challenge that it does not recognise the basic worth and rights of all people, whatever their political persuasions. His critique reflects his theology of the *imago Dei* in which the dignity of all people is grounded and which remains even in the aftermath of the Fall. Modern, pluralistic environments demand recognition that people 'count.'[37]

6.4 Hope

Jesus' model for piety combines the themes of suffering and hope. Packer points out this link when he asserts, '[T]he fact that Jesus is our model in holy endurance shows that the channel through which power to endure flows, subjectively speaking, is *hope*, which as we saw is faith's forward

---

[32] Ibid., 186.

[33] Ibid., 187.

[34] Ibid.

[35] Ibid., 184. He claims that 'all Christians are called [to] ... the relieving of human misery every way one can. But it is all to be done in the service of a Christ whose kingdom is not of this world and who requires humanity to understand this life, with its joys and riches on the one hand and its hardships and sorrows on the other, as a moral and spiritual training ground, a preparatory discipline for eternity.'

[36] Ibid., 185.

[37] Ibid., 187.

look [Hebrews] (11:1).'[38] Hope stands out in numerous of Packer's writings as the predicate of his favourite description of the Christian life: one's reach exceeding one's grasp. For example, this is what he thinks the Apostle Paul has in mind when he speaks of 'wretchedness' in Romans 7:24. As he discusses the Apostle Paul's treatment of this condition he refers to hope as the sustaining force for the struggling Christian. 'The thanksgiving [in 7:25] proclaims, not present justification or present enabling, as the other views would require, but personal Christian hope, the theme of chapters 5 and 6, soon to be taken up again in chapter 8.'[39] Hope is the stabilizing and energizing resource for Christians as they endure internal as well as external opposition to their quest for faithfulness to God.

Packer ties his theology of hope into his Christology even further by anchoring hope in the doctrines of the Incarnation, Resurrection, and Ascension. He contends that though the Resurrection is often homiletically used as an apologetic device by moving directly from the Resurrection as a historical fact to the current experience of the Risen Christ, the Resurrection is more appropriately and theologically related to the Ascension.

The Incarnation, Resurrection, and Ascension belong together theologically for Packer and provide hope for Christian piety through Jesus' humility and suffering in Incarnation, his glorification and victory over death in Resurrection, and his intercession for Christians in his Ascension.[40] He points to this relationship and some of its implications for piety when he states,

> Jesus took our flesh and lived as one of us enduring all the routine demands, the fatigue, the pressure, and the suffering that mark our mortal lives. He died as one of us, in weakness, grief, pain, and apparent defeat. But thereby he defeated death in his own death, and rose again, bringing our mortal flesh with him to immortality. This is the reason for all the Christian hilarity at Easter: Death, our worst enemy, has been conquered, and with that enemy, all our despair. Hope therefore rises. And when Jesus ascended, so the gospel teaches, he took human flesh with him into the impenetrable glory and mystery of the Holy Trinity itself. This guarantees that he will do the same for our flesh, yours and mine, one

---

[38] Packer, *A Passion for Holiness*, 246.
[39] Packer, 'The "Wretched Man" Revisited', 76.
[40] Ibid., 128. Packer lists Christ's ministry of intercession for believers as a 'fact' that has been established by the Ascension.

day. ... Christian hope grasps hold of this fact every time a Christian prays.[41]

This statement is the closest Packer ever comes to acknowledging an organic relationship between the Incarnation and salvation, that is, a connection beyond the utilitarian function of providing Jesus with a human body and a perfect nature so that his death would be efficacious in satisfying the demands of God's law. Nevertheless, even when he admits that Jesus' takes our humanity into his own and 'enlivens' it,[42] he is careful to differentiate that from the atonement, which was strictly forensic. Christ's act of taking humanity into the life of God saves the whole person from death. This, however, is a separate theological act from the atonement, which strictly addressed sin and guilt in relation to God's law.[43]

The Incarnation provides hope by offering a model and motivation for endurance in suffering through Jesus' solidarity with the sufferer. The Ascension fully integrates the solidarity between Jesus and humanity into the Trinity. The Resurrection provides hope by promising the restoration of all things. This eschatological strand figures prominently into Packer's resistance to pieties that promise forms of perfectionism in this life. Pieties that offer a route to faithfulness without trial and struggle ignore, in Packer's view, the need for the hope provided by the eschatological trajectory of the Incarnation, Resurrection, and Ascension.

The Resurrection creates and sustains the Christian's hope by directing the believer's attention heavenward. Packer uses the concept of Heaven as encompassing both the intermediate, disembodied state and the embodied state that will be experienced when all things are made new.

> *Heaven* ... is the Bible term for God's home (Ps. 33:13–14; Matt. 6:9) where his throne is (Ps. 2:4); the place of his presence to which the glorified Christ has returned (Acts 1:11); where the church militant and triumphant now unites for worship (Heb. 12:22–25); and where one day Christ's people will be with their Savior forever (John 17:5,24; 1 Thess. 4:16–17). ... At some future point, at the time of Christ's return for judgment, it will take the form of a reconstructed cosmos (2 Pet. 3:13; Rev. 21:1). To think of heaven as a place is more right than wrong, though the word could mislead. Heaven appears in Scripture as a spatial reality that touches and interpenetrates all created space.[44]

---

41 Packer and Howard, *Christianity: The True Humanism*, 99.
42 Packer interview, (2 July 1999).
43 Ibid.
44 Packer, *Concise Theology*, 264.

His reference to Hebrews 12 indicates that he believes the intermediate state of believers to involve conscious activity in God's presence. However, believers will not be fully integrated into the experience of Heaven until they experience resurrection. Packer states, 'A resurrection body adapted to heaven's life awaits us (2 Cor. 5::1–8), and in that body we shall see the Father and the Son (Matt. 5:8; 1 John 3:2).'[45]

It seems that this general way of conceiving Heaven allows Packer to retain what appears to be a rather quasi–Platonic emphasis on the disembodied aspects of human existence. This may help account for a recurring tension between two themes within Packer's thought. On one hand he denounces body–soul dualism, insisting that human life involves embodiment and functionality within the context of creation. He states,

> The embodiment of the soul is integral to God's design for mankind. Through the body ... we are to experience our environment, enjoy and control things around us, and relate to other people. ... The Christian hope is not redemption *from* the body but redemption *of* the body. We look forward to our participation in Christ's resurrection in and through the resurrection of our own bodies.[46]

He seeks to provide a balanced perspective by encouraging Christians to hold to this present life loosely, in anticipation of Christ's reconciliation of all things.[47] Specifically, he suggests four principles: duty to God, neighbour–love, freedom, and openness to God, as providing an appropriate balance between the tension of embracing temporal, created existence while having one's ultimate affections set on God's Kingdom.[48]

The hope provided by Jesus' incarnation, resurrection, and ascension is poignant for Packer because it stands in relief against the spectre of death and all that death represents. The hope of heaven, states Packer, 'allows us to approach our own mortality with a forthright boldness that is unique to Christian believers and stands in stark contrast to the common attitude in Western society.'[49] He even speaks as if it were God's intentions that humanity's temporal state involve brokenness and frustration when he says, 'And it is good to know that God's aim in giving us second–rate physical frames here is to prepare us for managing better bodies hereafter.'[50] Packer links this hope of heaven to the Ascension, asserting, 'And because Jesus

---

[45] Ibid., 265.

[46] Ibid., 75.

[47] Packer and Howard, *Christianity: The True Humanism*, 105–108.

[48] Packer, 'Leisure and Life–style: Leisure, Pleasure, and Treasure', 386–387.

[49] Packer, *Knowing Christianity*, 242–243.

[50] Packer, *Growing in Christ*, 84.

has ascended to heaven we can be sure that we, too, have a hope of heaven.'[51]

Richard Baxter provides Packer with a praiseworthy example of how hope functions vis–à–vis the certainty of death. Death should be a lens through which one examines and evaluates the affairs and involvements of this life, thereby learning to hold them loosely.[52] Packer extols Baxter's 'heavenly–mindedness' as a spiritual virtue that contrasts sharply with the spiritual shortsightedness and dullness that is induced by the distractions of modern, technological culture and the distorting effects of original sin.[53] Thus, heaven provides the horizon that not only sustains the Christian's hope by promising restoration of brokenness and freedom from sin in the future, but also clarifies and purifies spiritual values during this life. In this manner hope relates to faithfulness in Packer's thought.

The hope of being like Jesus Christ is a particularly salient aspect of the promise of resurrection, for Packer. This claim culminates his discussion in his most direct treatment of resurrection as a hope for humanity.[54] Packer exhorts potential spiritual seekers,

> Ask God to show you how Jesus' life, body and soul, was the only fully human life that has ever been lived, and keep looking at Jesus, as you meet him in the Gospels, till you can see it. Then the prospect of being like him – that, and no less – will seem to you the noblest and most magnificent destiny possible, and by embracing it you will become a true disciple.[55]

He also presents Jesus' transfiguration as the projection of restored humanity, stating, 'It was a transition too from humanity as it is in us now

---

[51] Packer, *Knowing Christianity*, 242.

[52] J.I. Packer, 'Richard Baxter on Heaven, Hope and Holiness', in *Shorter Writings*, 4.267.

[53] Ibid., 269. Packer states, '[B]ecause original sin has twisted all our desires in an egocentric direction, and because our technologically oriented culture shrinks our souls and erodes our capacity for moral and spiritual discernment, we imagine that the hunger of our hearts will be satisfied by sexual activity, aesthetic experience, making money, gaining and using power, or something similar, and we dismiss the idea that God and heaven are what our hearts seek as old–fashioned, unenlightened fantasy.' He continues, 'Meditating on heaven is a headclearing, heartwarming, invigorating discipline, hard work and ungratifying to the flesh, no doubt, but very enriching to the spirit. So Baxter had proved in his own life, and so he presented the matter to the Christian world' (270).

[54] Packer, *Growing in Christ*, 85.

[55] Ibid., 86.

to what it will be on Resurrection Day (Phil. 3:20–21).'[56] His overall presentation raises a question, however, about how clearly he delineates the pre–resurrection Jesus from the resurrected, glorified Jesus as the model for holiness and restored humanity.

He clearly portrays the resurrected Jesus as the model when he refers to 'the planned and promised supernaturalizing of our inner life through our sharing in Christ's risen life,'[57] but states elsewhere, 'For Christians this [holiness] means taking God's moral law as our rule and God's incarnate Son as our model ...'[58] Packer's presentation of the resurrected, glorified Christ as the model of restored humanity is more consistent with his utilitarian view of the Incarnation.[59] However, when he gives the impression that the pre–resurrected Christ is the model for holiness the connection between holiness and restored humanity is rather strained.

Summary

J.I. Packer's theology of piety reflects his longstanding battle with Keswick and, to a lesser extent, Wesleyan piety. His earliest personal Christian experience, marked by frustration with Keswick piety then liberation through the influence of John Owen and other Reformed theologians, has left lingering marks on his theological framework. Augustine's view of original and indwelling sin, John Calvin's soteriological framework, and the English Puritans' understanding of the outworking of piety are definitive in Packer's theology of piety. Other significant factors that affect his theology of piety are his placement of predestination at the forefront of his theological system, his forensic and penal view of the atonement, and

---

[56] Packer, *Concise Theology*, 123.

[57] Packer, *A Passion for Holiness*, 171–172.

[58] Ibid., 19. He makes the identical statement in 'Holiness: What It Is, Why It Matters', *Faith and Renewal* (March/April 1993), 4.

[59] See Irenaeus, *Against Heresies* in A. Roberts and J. Donaldson (eds.), *The Ante–Nicene Fathers: Translations of The Writings of the Fathers Down to A.D. 325: The Apostolic Fathers*, vol. I (New York: Charles Scribner's Sons, 1913[2]), III.18.7. In contrast, Irenaeus viewed the Incarnation as a recapitulation of all that God had intended for humanity. 'God recapitulated in Himself the ancient formation of man, that He might kill sin, deprive death of its power, and vivify man; and therefore His works are true.' In Irenaeus's model, God dealt with sin directly or organically through the entire life of Christ. Irenaeus states, 'For it behoved Him who was to destroy sin, and redeem man under the power of death, that He should Himself be made that very same thing which he was, that is, man; who had been drawn by sin into bondage, but was held by death, so that sin should be destroyed by man, and man should go forth from death.'

his restricted view of how the Son of God relates to humanity through the Incarnation. These factors create a situation in which he must go to great pains to integrate the formal and the existential aspects of salvation. Packer's emphasis on the power of indwelling sin seems to cast a shadow over the prospect of experiencing God's grace as a vibrant, liberating force in piety. His particular emphases may indeed contribute to the notion that piety is a rather grim endeavour, all his noteworthy protests and expositions notwithstanding.

Against the backdrop of a pietistic evangelical culture that has prioritised the eternal over the temporal, Packer offers a clearly world–affirming corrective. He strives to recapture a theology of creation that seems missing from the theological framework of much pietistic American evangelicalism. In this regard he has attempted to steer a course away from unhealthy imbalances in this piety. It remains to be seen, though, whether his theological anthropology is adequate to the piety he presents.

Chapter 7

Theological Anthropology

J.I. Packer portrays salvation as the restoration of fallen humanity. His understanding of the nature of piety and the process whereby it is attained is shaped by his understanding of the nature of humanity, both before and after the Fall. It is necessary, then, to examine more closely the theological anthropology that undergirds his theology of piety. Packer's theological anthropology will be developed through an exploration of his understanding of the *imago Dei* and the Incarnation.

Anthropology has occupied a somewhat ambivalent place in theology. The value or role assigned to anthropology within a theological structure has ramifications for other aspects of that structure as well as for the piety that it shapes. In recent years theologians from a variety of traditions have developed approaches to ethics and spirituality by using the doctrine of the *imago Dei* as a starting point or framework.[1] Yet, these affirmations are sometimes subject to suspicion. The influence of Pelagianism and non–Christian sources on the doctrine of humanity has made some theologians cautious in approaching this subject.[2] Likewise, theologians who have

---

[1] H. Thielicke makes the doctrine of the *imago Dei* foundational to his approach to ethics in *Theological Ethics*, vol. I *Foundations*, W.H. Lazareth (ed.), J.W. Doberstein (tr.), (Grand Rapids: Eerdmans, 1979). The *imago Dei* also constitutes the primary point of reference for the Christian experience in works such as R. Macauley and J. Barrs, *Being Human: The Nature of Spiritual Experience* (Downers Grove: InterVarsity, 1978); H.R. Dunning, *Reflecting the Divine Image: Christian Ethics in Wesleyan Perspective* (Downers Grove: InterVarsity, 1998), and Kenneth Boa, *Conformed to His Image: Biblical and Practical Approaches to Spiritual Formation* Grand Rapids: Zondervan, 2001).

[2] See A.A. Hoekema, *Created in God's Image* (Grand Rapids: Eerdmans, 1986), 4. Hoekema puts forth such a warning even as he prepares to defend the importance of the doctrine of humanity. 'We must remember, however, that often non–Christian notions have crept into so–called Christian anthropologies. ... The results of this mismating of two diverse anthropologies are, unfortunately, with us to this day. ... It is therefore important for us to have the right understanding of man. As we try to arrive at a proper Christian understanding, we should keep in mind such questions as ... Are there still remnants of non–Christian anthropology in our thinking about man?'

emphasised the humanity of Jesus Christ to the exclusion or compromise of his deity have been the object of evangelical critique.[3] The work of Friedrich Schleiermacher has made a prominent contribution to this suspicion.

Schleiermacher felt that the rationalist tendencies of the Enlightenment were unduly influencing theology toward an overemphasis on abstract doctrine and moralism. In reaction he followed Romanticism by focusing on the human experience of God as the essence of religion.[4] By granting to these existential, anthropological concerns a definitive role in theology Schleiermacher encouraged piety that prioritises the phenomenon of religious experience as the source of religious authority.

Schleiermacher's anthropocentric theological orientation seems to have gone hand in hand with his contention that some tenets of historic orthodoxy such as the virgin birth and crucifixion of Jesus have subjective but not objective significance in the life of faith.[5] Thus, according to Philip E. Hughes, he is 'often called the father of liberal Protestant theology.'[6] Due, at least in part to Schleiermacher's influence, Christians with a high view of biblical authority (of whom evangelicals are a subset) have been careful lest an overemphasis on anthropological questions eclipse the primacy, objectivity, and binding authority of God's self–revelation as interpreted in the traditionally accepted framework of orthodox (not necessarily Orthodox) doctrine. They have been wary of any theology that would seem to elevate human experience as the standard for discerning truth.

The doctrine of the 'image and likeness of God,' the *imago Dei*, is a central component of theological anthropology. It has been a subject of longstanding dispute in the history of theology. Debates about the nature of the *imago Dei* have been generated, at least in part, by the fact that the Bible never explicitly defines or describes the phrase. The nature of the *imago Dei* has historically been treated as foundational to understanding the nature of the soul as well as the value and teleology of human existence, especially in relationship to the rest of creation.

---

[3]   Packer, 'The Uniqueness of Jesus Christ', 79. Packer criticises Ritschl, Harnack, and Schweitzer for reducing Jesus' uniqueness to his impact.

[4]   W.A. Hoffecker, 'Schleiermacher, Friedrich Daniel Ernst', in *EDT*, 981–982. See also Hughes, *The True Image*, 355. Schleiermacher begins his discussion of the nature of dogmatics by examining the nature of religious experience. He claims that 'piety is feeling' and repeatedly returns to the notions of 'absolute dependence' and 'self–consciousness' as being the medium through which the truthfulness of religion is validated. See also F. Schleiermacher, *The Christian Faith*, 8,36ff.

[5]   Hughes, *The True Image*, 219,220,356.

[6]   Ibid., 981.

Theological anthropology also encompasses Christological considerations. The New Testament portrays Jesus Christ as the image of God (Colossians 1:15) and representation of God (Hebrews 1:3) as well as depicting salvation as conformity to the image of the Son (Romans 8:29). David Cairns sees the image and likeness of God as integrated in Jesus Christ who, as such, provides the model for restored humanity. He states, 'The New Testament doctrine pictures the image as a likeness to Christ, a likeness for which God has planned our being, a likeness into which we must be restored by the grace of God in Christ. ... It is not possible to say that the Old Testament doctrine of the image is not to be found in the New Testament. It is found quite explicitly in ... the letter of St. James [3:9].'[7]

This link between the Old Testament notion of the *imago Dei* and the New Testament's reference to the image of Christ raises several questions in regard to the restoration of humanity in salvation and the experience of that restoration in piety. For example, what was the nature of Jesus Christ's humanity? What was the relationship of Jesus' human nature to human nature in general, especially to fallen human nature? How does Jesus' humanity relate to salvation? How does humanity's restoration into the image of Christ relate to the *imago Dei* in Genesis? The nature of the *imago Dei* will be the starting point from which these other questions will be considered.

7.1 The *Imago Dei* in Historical Perspective

The interpretive history of the *imago Dei* provides a context for understanding J.I. Packer's interpretation of the *imago Dei*.[8] Any assignment of theological significance to the *imago Dei* must first take into account that many details are veiled in the biblical creation account where the phrase is found. The phrases 'image of God' or 'likeness of God' are found in only three passages: Genesis; 1:26–27, 5:1, and 9:6. In each of these texts the concept seems to carry significant implications (sometimes derived from the context) but appears to rest on undeveloped assumptions. This ambiguity has led theologians through the centuries to debate not only the nature of the image but also whether the 'image' (*tselem*) of God and the 'likeness' (*d'mût*) of God are synonymous or distinct. R.S. Anderson attempts a resolution by suggesting that the point of the Genesis texts was

---

[7] David Cairns, *The Image of God in Man* (London: SCM Press, 1973²), 38.
[8] A complete survey of the history of interpreting the *imago Dei* is beyond the scope of this book but can easily be found in the capable work of others referenced in this chapter. I shall mention here only those features of this history that seem most directly related to and illuminative of Packer's anthropology.

to focus on God as both the origin and destiny of humanity.[9] Yet, centuries of theological reflection have tended to define the concepts in a more anthropocentric fashion.

Stanley J. Grenz and John R. Franke draw attention to a general pattern of interpreting the *imago Dei* in the Western theological tradition. They claim,

> Perhaps the most long–standing interpretation of the *imago* sees it as a structure of the human person. In this understanding, the divine image consists of the properties that constitute human beings as human with special emphasis placed on the capacity for rationality coupled with our moral nature. This view is widespread in the writings of the church fathers and the medieval scholastic theologians. It was challenged to some extent in the Protestant Reformation, regained ascendancy in Protestant orthodox theology, and continues to be influential in those traditions influenced by scholastic traditions.[10]

The view that the *imago Dei* is closely related to rationality, more specifically to the faculty of reason, is significant for the examination of Packer's anthropology.[11] David Cairns concludes that the tendency to place priority on humanity's reason as providing a connection with divinity goes back to Heraclitus, from whom it proceeded through the Stoics and Philo of Alexandria, then into early Christian thinkers. It subsequently became the

---

[9] R.S. Anderson, 'Anthropology, Christian', in A. McGrath (ed.), *The Blackwell Encyclopedia of Modern Christian Thought* (Oxford: Blackwell, 1993), 5. 'The creation of the human out of the dust of the ground is simultaneously a formation of the human through a divine "breathing" of the breath of life (Gen. 2:7). The Bible does not inform us as to how or when this occurred, only that the human is uniquely formed as the creature bearing the divine image and oriented to God. Whether the formation of the human body took place through a process of evolution … or was directly created by God is a question not answered by Scripture. What we are told is that the destiny of the human is under divine determination, even as the origin of the human was through divine agency.'

[10] S.J. Grenz and J.R. Franke, *Beyond Foundationalism: Shaping Theology in a Postmodern Context* (Louisville, Ky.: Westminster John Knox, 2001), 197. See also F. LeRon Shults, *Reforming Theological Anthropology: After the Philosophical Turn to Relationality* (Grand Rapids: Eerdmans, 2003) for an extensive history of the interpretation of the *imago Dei* in Western theology.

[11] Rationality and reason are taken in this study to be synonymous unless otherwise noted. While rationality may have broader connotations, including the intellectual, volitional, and affective faculties, Cairns uses 'rationality' and 'reason' interchangeably (66).

dominant view of the most influential theologians of the Western church through the time of Thomas Aquinas.[12]

The work of Augustine of Hippo (354–430) provides one of the most substantial resources for Packer's anthropology. Grenz attributes to Augustine the vast influence of rationalism on theological anthropology throughout the history of Western theology. He claims, 'Although a modern invention ['the concept of the centered self'], its genesis lies in Augustine's highly innovative 'turn inward.' His attempt to find God at the foundation of his mind and will launched a centuries–long quest to establish the self as the stable, abiding reality that constitutes the individual human being.'[13]

Augustine connects the mind or reason with the image and likeness of God. He states, 'We behold the face of the earth furnished with terrestrial creatures, and man, created after Thy image and likeness, in that very image and likeness of Thee (that is, the power of reason and understanding) on account of which he was set over all irrational creatures.'[14] It is significant that Augustine seems to treat 'image' and the 'likeness' as synonyms.[15]

---

[12] Cairns, *The Image of God in Man*, 66. 'Christian thinkers up to and including St Thomas are in part dependent on this pre–Christian thought, regarding the image predominantly as rationality, though Augustine and Aquinas do not define it in the Stoic manner, and are free from any tendency to regard the image as a spark of the divine in man.' For Philo of Alexandria, Cairns claims, 'The logos is God's thought displayed in the whole system of the universe. It can be conceived of in two aspects – first, in its relation to the mind of the creator. The logos was present in his mind before the created world came into being. And, second, the logos can be seen in the created universe, for it is the principle of rationality and cohesion in the world. The logos there expresses visibly the mind of the creator, just as a cathedral is the visible expression of the architect's mind' (p. 74). See also C.H. Dodd, *The Bible and the Greeks* (London: Hodder and Stoughton, 1935). Dodd provides insight into the influence of Hellenistic thought on early interpretations of the Genesis creation account. He addresses the issues of how, within Hellenistic Judaism, *logos* was seen to function as the agent of creation, relate to God as the source of creation, and relate to God as *nous*. These discussions provide a foundation for later questions about how the humanity (*sarx*) of Jesus, as the Son and *logos* of God, related to God the Father as *nous*.

[13] S.J. Grenz, *The Social God and the Relational Self: A Trinitarian Theology of the Imago Dei* (Louisville, Ky.: Westminster John Knox, 2001), 16.

[14] Augustine, *Confessions* in P. Schaff (ed.), *A Select Library of the Nicene and Post-Nicene Fathers of the Christian Church: The Confessions and Letters of St. Augustin*, vol. I (Grand Rapids: Eerdmans, 1979²), 13:32.

[15] B. Babacz, *St. Augustine's Theory of Knowledge: A Contemporary Analysis* (Lewiston, N.Y.: Edwin Mellen, 1981), 22. Babacz states, 'A common patristic view is that man was originally created in God's image and likeness, but after the fall he

Augustine assigns the function of knowing God to the mind since it is made in God's image and constitutes the closest link between humanity and God. The mind is the epistemological means of access to the immaterial world, while the senses offer access to the material world.[16] Neoplatonic sources such as Plotinus provided Augustine with a model for seeing the human body as necessary, though subordinate, to the needs of the soul.[17] Bruce Bubacz notes that, 'The two realms are united in human beings, whom Augustine treats as having an inner and an outer aspect.'[18] Babacz also notes that 'Augustine draws a parallel between the inner–man's imaging God and the outer–man's imaging the inner–man.'[19] Augustine finds the harmony of human existence in a type of master–servant relationship between mind and body. 'Whatever sets man above the beast, whether we call it "mind" or "spirit" or, more correctly both, since we find both terms in Scriptures, if this rules over and commands the other parts that make up man, then man's life is in perfect order.'[20]

Though the mind is central to his view of the *imago Dei*, it is essential to note that for Augustine, sin originated in the will.[21] He claims that 'the free choice of the will is the cause of our committing evil.'[22] Through sin the

---

lost His likeness but not His image. Augustine rejected this view on purely philosophical grounds.'

[16] D.J. Hoitenga, Jr. *Faith and Reason from Plato to Plantinga: An Introduction to Reformed Epistemology* (Albany: State University of New York Press, 1991), 75.

[17] Babacz, *St. Augustine's Theory of Knowledge*, 19. Augustine's dependence on Neoplatonism was certainly not uncritical. See also J.E. Sullivan, *The Image of God: The Doctrine of St. Augustine and Its Influence* (Dubuque, Iowa: Priory, 1963), 14,20. Sullivan points out numerous instances in which Augustine's thought parallels Neoplatonic thought forms, particularly 'the principle that images have reality only insofar as they have contact with the intelligible ideas in the divine mind.' However, he also notices that Augustine broke with Plotinus's concept of image in denying that 'equality with an examplar and the imaging of the examplar are mutually exclusive notes.'

[18] Ibid.

[19] Ibid., 22–23.

[20] Augustine, *The Free Choice of the Will* in R.P. Russell (tr.), *The Fathers of the Church*, vol. 59, *Saint Augustine: The Teacher, The Free Choice of the Will, Grace and Free Will* (Washington, D.C.: Catholic University of America, 1968), 88.

[21] Augustine, *Reply to Faustus the Manichaean*, in P. Schaff *A Select Library of the Nicene and Post–Nicene Fathers: St. Augustine: The Writings Against the Manichaeans and Against Donatists*, vol. IV (Grand Rapids: Eerdmans, 1983²), XXII.22. 'The origin of sin is in the will; therefore in the will is also the origin of evil, both in the sense of acting against a just precept, and in the sense of suffering under a just sentence.'

[22] Augustine, *Confessions*, 7.3, 165.

imago Dei is damaged, but not utterly lost. Rather, it resides in some form such that it can be recovered or renewed. He states that the *imago Dei* 'lost righteousness and true holiness by sinning, through which that image became defaced and tarnished; and this it recovers when it is formed again and renewed.'[23] However, Augustine focuses the renewal process, not directly on the place of sin's origin (the will) but on the place of sin's effect (the mind). He states, 'This renewal, then, and forming again of the mind, is wrought either after God, or after the image of God, But it is said to be after God, in order that it may not be supposed to be after another creature; and to be after God, in order that this renewing may be understood to take place in that wherein is the image of God, *i.e.* in the mind.'[24]

This distinction between the will and the mind appears in Packer's anthropology when he describes the renewal of the *imago Dei* as dependent on the mind's reception of God's saving message so that the will is liberated to respond obediently to God. The equation appears sensible when mind and will are treated as integrated functions; the will being perverted through the deception of the mind, then the will being converted through the renewal of the mind. However, the use of these categories can also create the impression that mind and will are discrete functions, not equally and inherently sinful and, hence, not equally in need of redemption.

Augustine is well–known for his attempt to find evidence of God's Trinitarian nature in various human 'trinities,' such as the triads of *intellect, memory, will* and *lover, beloved, and love*. David Cairns observes,

> In his great work on the Trinity, Augustine spends almost half his time in an attempt to discover the divine image in man and see wherein it consists. … From revelation it is known that God is a Trinity, and also that man is in the image of God. Augustine is therefore entitled, as far as logic goes, to the conjecture, that the image in man may also be a trinity. And if this conjecture be true, then a study of this derivative trinity may throw some light upon the nature of the God who created it.[25]

Cairns believes that Augustine locates the *imago Dei* in human rationality, but finds that his various human 'trinities' are subordinate and subservient to the 'capacity to understand and behold *God*.'[26] Augustine refers to 'the principal part of the human mind, by which it knows or can know God, in order that we may find therein an image of God.' He understood 'memory' as the cumulative impressions residing in the mind as

---

[23] Augustine, *On the Trinity*, 14.16.
[24] Ibid., 195–196.
[25] Cairns, *The Image of God in Man*, 99.
[26] Ibid., 102–103.

a result of experiences. 'So it is that we bear these images in the deep recesses of the memory as witnesses, so to speak, of things previously experienced by the senses.'[27] He perceives intellect to be the knowledge held and used consciously.[28] The will, to Augustine, is the motive power or movement of the human agent on the basis of what is known.[29]

It is not clear whether Augustine saw these human 'trinities' as corresponding ontologically to the nature of God, but the epistemological capability they provide is the heart of the *imago Dei*. He brings together his discussion of image, trinity, and mind as follows.

> But we have come now to that argument in which we have undertaken to consider the noblest part of the human mind, by which it knows or can know God, in order that we may find in it the image of God. For although the human mind is not of the same nature with God, yet the image of that nature than which none is better, is to be sought and found in us, in that than which our nature also has nothing better. But the mind must first be considered as it is in itself, before it becomes partaker of God; and His image must be found in it. For, as we have said, although worn out and defaced by losing the participation of God, yet the image of God still remains. For it is His image in this very point, that it is capable of Him, and can be partaker of Him; which so great good is only made possible by its being His image. Well, then, the mind remembers, understands, loves itself; if we discern this, we discern a trinity, not yet indeed God, but now at last an image of God.[30]
>
> This trinity, then, of the mind is not therefore the image of God, because the mind remembers itself, and understands and loves itself; but because it can also remember, understand, and love Him by whom it was made.[31]

For Augustine, the *imago Dei* provides humanity with epistemological and relational capacities for God through the interrelated functioning of discrete faculties.

Augustine compares the sense in which humanity and Jesus are the *imago Dei* by resisting the claim that humanity is only 'after' the image while Jesus 'is' the image. Both, he insists, *are* the *imago Dei*. The difference, however, is that humanity's bearing of the *imago Dei* depends upon, focuses upon, and reflects the plurality of number within the Trinity,

---

[27] Augustine, *The Teacher*, 53.

[28] Ibid., 53–54.

[29] Ibid., *Confessions*, 7.3, 165.

[30] Ibid., *On the Trinity*, 14.8.11., 189.

[31] Ibid., 14.12.15., 191.

whereas for the Son the *imago Dei* points to equality of essence with the Person of the Father. The concept of 'likeness' carries the relativity of relationship between God and humanity, thus allowing Augustine to see a direct correspondence between God and humanity while reserving strict ontological identification only for the Son.[32]

Calvin resists the tendency to differentiate between 'image' and 'likeness,' referring to the common Hebrew practice of explaining a concept by repeating it with the use of synonyms.[33] He strives for an anthropology in which humanity is seen as the unity of body and soul. Yet he tends to assign priority to the immaterial dimensions of humanity when attempting to describe how the various aspects and phenomena of human existence relate to the *imago Dei*. He insists that 'it be regarded as a settled principle that the image of God, which is seen or glows in these outwards marks, is spiritual.'[34] Calvin makes no clear distinction between soul and spirit, treating them as synonymous ideas. The soul or spirit includes the whole range of immaterial dimensions that characterize humans. The soul or spirit does not constitute the whole essence of humanity, but exists in subordinate relationship to the image or likeness of God, which is the most comprehensive anthropological designation.

Thus Calvin resists the tendency to present human faculties as the essence of the *imago Dei*. Yet, he still sees the faculties as integrally related to the image because of their relationship to the soul, which is subordinate to the image. Reason and intelligence do not belong to the body, but to the soul.[35] He refuses to reduce the essence of humanity to nothing more than the soul. Nevertheless 'the primary seat of the divine image was in the mind and heart, or in the soul and its powers.'[36] Faculties exist as the means by which humanity reflects God's glory. Moreover, the *imago Dei* cannot be rightly or fully conceived apart from the faculties and their doxological function.[37] He claims that 'in order that we may know of what parts this

---

[32] Ibid., 7.6.12., 113.

[33] Calvin, *Institutes*, I.xv.3. See also Calvin's comments on Genesis 1:26 in *Commentaries on the First Book of Genesis Called Genesis*, J. King (tr.), *Calvin's Commentaries*, vol. I (Grand Rapids: Eerdmans, 1948), 94.

[34] Calvin, *Institutes*, I.xv.3.

[35] Ibid.

[36] Ibid. He repeats this viewpoint in his commentary on Genesis 1:26 (95). 'The chief seat of the Divine image was in his mind and heart, where it was eminent: yet was there no part of him in which some scintillations of it did not shine forth.'

[37] Ibid., I.xv.4, 189. He claims that 'we do not have a full definition of "image" if we do not see more plainly those faculties in which man excels, and in which he ought to be thought the reflection of God's glory.'

image consists, it is of value to discuss the faculties of the soul.'[38] He goes on to claim that 'the human soul consists of two faculties, understanding and will.'[39] His point of departure from those who proposed a more static, rationalistic view of the *imago Dei* is his emphasis on the image as relationship with God expressed through grateful, worshipful, obedient response.[40]

T.F. Torrance claims that Calvin's anthropology has often been inappropriately interpreted through the eyes of the rigid Aristotelian categories that Calvin went to pains to avoid.[41] Calvin actually moved away from the scholastic emphasis on the image as a static gradation or analogy of being toward an emphasis on the image as dynamic expression of continuous response to the will of God.[42] Through this dynamic response, humanity is reshaped in the moral image of God, which is 'true holiness and righteousness.'[43]

Though it might appear that in some ways Calvin hardly differs from those who define the *imago Dei* in rationalistic terms, he distinguishes his own position when he challenges Augustine, claiming that 'Augustine, beyond all others, speculates with excessive refinement, for the purpose of fabricating a Trinity in man.'[44]

> Now God's image is the perfect excellence of human nature which shone in Adam before his defection, but was subsequently so vitiated and almost blotted out that nothing remains after the ruin except what is confused, mutilated, and disease–ridden. ... Yet in order that we may know of what parts this image consists, it is of value to discuss the faculties of the soul. For that speculation of Augustine, that the soul is the reflection of the Trinity because in it reside the understanding, will, and memory, is by no means sound. Nor is there any probability in the opinion of those who locate God's likeness in the dominion given to man, as if in this mark alone he resembled God, that he was established as heir and possessor of all things; whereas God's image is properly to be sought within him, not outside him, indeed, it is an inner good of the soul.[45]

---

[38] Ibid, 190.

[39] Ibid., I.xv.7, 194.

[40] T.F. Torrance, *Calvin's Doctrine of Man* (London: Butterworth, 1952), 46,59,64.

[41] Ibid., 7.

[42] Ibid., 29, 30, 64, 65.

[43] Calvin, *Institutes*, III.iii..9, 601.

[44] Calvin, *Commentaries on the First Book of Moses Called Genesis*, 93.

[45] Calvin, *Institutes*, I.xv.4. In his commentary on Genesis, Calvin deals with Genesis 1:26 by identifying Chrysostom as one who held to the 'dominion' view, though

The essence of the image for Calvin is humanity's reflecting of the glory of God in communion with God and others.[46]

Torrance proposes a corrective to the perception that Calvin's dependence on the framework of scholastic, rationalistic anthropology implies an anthropocentric character to his understanding of the *imago Dei*. Certainly, Calvin insists that righteousness within the context of relationship with God relies heavily on the faculties of understanding and will. Likewise, though he seeks to differentiate the soul from the essence of the *imago Dei*, the soul is the location wherein the image is realised. However, Torrance contends that Calvin is ultimately not anthropocentric in his view of the *imago Dei* because he carefully differentiates between its subjective and objective dimensions. Torrance observes,

> There are times when Calvin appears to say that the *imago dei* is equivalent to man's reason and understanding, but on examination that never turns out to be the case. It is always to the *light* of the understanding that he points, which is man's life as a child of God and which can only be maintained in him by thankfully responding to God's grace, and that response is thought of as part of the *imago–light* which God intends to be in his soul. There is then in Calvin's doctrine of the *imago dei* an objective basis which is the act of God's pure grace, and which may indeed be identified with Christ Himself. … On the subjective side, however, the *imago dei* has to do with man's response to grace.[47]

Through this subjective–objective distinction in the *imago Dei*, Calvin is able to relocate the essence of the image in the personhood of God while using the categories of faculty psychology and a Platonic understanding of the soul[48] to explain how the subjective dimension of the image functions in realising its objective character. Still, his insistence that the image is an interior feature of the human soul leaves the impression of a predominantly anthropocentric orientation to his view of the *imago Dei*.

Another means by which Calvin attempts to avoid a thoroughgoing anthropocentrism in his view of the *imago Dei* is the incorporation of the Incarnation into his anthropology, making Jesus Christ the central or defining expression of the *imago Dei* in humanity.

Calvin insists that dominion is a 'portion, though very small, of the image of God.' *The First Book of Moses Called Genesis*, 94. Augustine is actually more specific in his comparison of the Trinity and the *imago Dei*, stating that in the mind alone is man the image of the Trinity. See Augustine, *On the Trinity*, 15.7.

[46] Torrance, *Calvin's Doctrine of Man*, 45.

[47] Ibid., 69–70.

[48] Calvin, *Institutes*, I.xv.6.

Now we are to see what Paul chiefly comprehends under this renewal. In the first place he posits knowledge, then pure righteousness and holiness. From this we infer that, to begin with, God's image was visible in the light of the mind, in the uprightness of the heart, and in the soundness of all the parts. ... Now we see how Christ is the most perfect image of God; if we are conformed to it, we are so restored that with true piety, righteousness, purity, and intelligence we bear God's image.[49]

In this passage Jesus Christ, as the *imago Dei*, provides the foundation for understanding the nature of the image in terms of holiness. Torrance points out that for Calvin, the Incarnation is integral to the *imago Dei* because the image only reveals God by reflection and God's self–revelation always takes place through God's Word. Humanity's ability to reflect God as the *imago Dei* is connected to and reliant upon Jesus Christ as the Incarnate Word and image of God.[50] The image, for Calvin, is like a mirror in which the glory of God is actively displayed as humanity responds in obedience. The perfection of God's glory is found in Christ, not in the soul or the faculties.[51]

Calvin provides the foundation for a close connection between theological anthropology and piety by contending that the meaning of the *imago Dei* becomes clear only as it is restored in salvation. 'Since the image of God has been destroyed in us by the fall, we may judge from its restoration what it originally had been. Paul says that we are transformed into the image of God by the gospel. And, according to him, spiritual regeneration is nothing else than the restoration of the same image (Col. iii. 10, and Eph. iv. 23.)'[52]

He goes on to refer to this restoration as *synecdoche*, not excluding other factors from the *imago Dei* but encompassing the various means by which it may be expressed, e.g. in dominion over creation. Thus, by placing the locus of the image primarily in Christ, Calvin also incorporates an eschatological and teleological dimension into the *imago Dei*. Ultimately, the *imago Dei* is outside humanity as the horizon toward which humanity is called for its fulfilment. This is the anthropological foundation for Calvin's assertion that sanctification is the progressive restoration of the *imago Dei*.[53]

---

[49] Ibid., I.xv.4.

[50] Torrance, *Calvin's Doctrine of Man*, 36, 37.

[51] Ibid., 53.

[52] Calvin, *Commentaries on the First Book of Moses Called Genesis*, 94.

[53] Calvin, *Institutes*, III.iii.9.. He states, 'And indeed, this restoration does not take place in one moment or one day or one year; but through continual and sometimes even slow advances God wipes out in his elect the corruptions of the flesh, cleanses

J.I. Packer's theological anthropology also reflects the influence of the English Puritans, most notably Richard Baxter and John Owen. The views of Baxter and Owen on the *imago Dei* will be presented when Packer's own views are discussed so that the comparison will be more obvious. It will now be shown how J.I. Packer develops his own theological anthropology and how he compares to the historical development of this area of theology.

7.2 The *Imago Dei* in J.I. Packer's Theology

J.I. Packer claims that he feels called to be a 'communicator,' not an 'originator' in his theological work, that is, he seeks merely to preserve and transmit what God has said.[54] Accordingly, he does not attempt to make an original contribution to theological anthropology, but draws from his favourite theological sources to construct a working model of the *imago Dei* that decisively shapes and is reflected in his understanding of Christology, soteriology, and the Christian life. He makes no distinction between the 'image' and 'likeness' of God but uses 'image' as the comprehensive concept that includes the issues that some have attributed to the 'likeness.'[55] Though not without criticism or alteration, he admits the influence of Augustine, Aquinas, Calvin, and the Puritans on his theological anthropology.

7.2.1 *The* Imago Dei *as Responsive Righteousness*
Packer's language, like Calvin's, could be taken to imply that the *imago Dei* is static and anchored in the human person. 'The human animal ... is

---

them of guilt, consecrates them to himself as temples renewing all their minds to true purity that they may practice repentance throughout their lives and know that this warfare will end only at death. ... Now this is not to deny a place for growth; rather I say, the closer any man comes to the likeness of God, the more the image of God shines in him. In order that believers may reach this goal, God assigns to them a race of repentance, which they are to run throughout their lives.' See also Torrance, *Calvin's Doctrine of Man*, 61.

[54] Packer interview, (2 July 1999).

[55] Packer, 'Conscience, Choice and Character', in B. Kaye and G. Wenham (eds.), *Law, Morality and the Bible* (Downers Grove: InterVarsity, 1978), 191. In a footnote Packer affirms Derek Kidner's view in *Genesis*, Tyndale Old Testament Commentaries, 'The words *image* and *likeness* reinforce one another: there is no "and" between the phrases, and Scripture does not use them as technically distinct expressions, as some theologians have done, whereby the "image" is man's indelible constitution as a rational and morally responsible being, and the "likeness" is that spiritual accord with the will of God which was lost at the Fall' (50f.).

noble,' he states, because of 'his personal constitution.'[56] His claim that every person 'bears God's image' sounds as if the *imago Dei* is in some sense a person's possession.[57] Yet, he parts ways with the structure of medieval theology by holding the *imago Dei* to be dynamic, not static. He believes the essence of the *imago Dei* to be righteousness, i.e. response to God in terms of His revealed will (obedience and worship).[58] Thus, he aligns his position with Calvin's.[59]

Responsive righteousness, the essence of the *imago Dei*, is defined and perfectly exemplified by Jesus Christ, not only in his humanity but also as the Son, the second member of the Trinity. Humans are to reflect the image of God in the same manner that the Son worships and will forever worship the Father. This order within the Trinity anchors and guides the piety that emerges as the *imago Dei* is restored in humanity through Jesus Christ. Packer states,

> Part of the revealed mystery of the Godhead is that the three persons stand in a fixed relation to each other. The Son appears in the gospels, not as an independent divine person, but as a dependent one, who thinks and acts only and wholly as the Father directs. ... Though co–equal with the Father in eternity, power, and glory, it is natural to Him to play the Son's part, and find all His joy in doing His Father's will, just as it is natural to the first person of the Trinity to plan and initiate the works of the Godhead and natural to the third person to proceed from the Father and the Son to do their joint bidding. Thus the obedience of the God–man to the Father while He was on earth was not a new relationship occasioned by the incarnation, but the continuation in time of the eternal relationship between the Son and the Father in heaven. As in heaven, so on earth, the Son was utterly dependent upon the Father's will.[60]

---

[56] Packer, 'Conscience, Choice and Character', 169–170.

[57] Ibid., 170.

[58] Packer interview, (2 July 1999).

[59] Packer, 'Conscience, Choice and Character', 170. In this text Packer describes Calvin's view of the image of God as 'knowledge of God in righteousness and holiness.'

[60] Packer, *Knowing God*, 54–55. See K. Giles, *The Trinity and Subordinationism: The Doctrine of God and the Contemporary Gender Debate* (Downers Grove: InterVarsity, 2002), 16–28. Giles discusses the historical development and contemporary significance of the debate over subordinationism within the Trinity. He claims that 'the most popular expression of subordinationism found in contemporary evangelical literature rejects ontological subordinationism, arguing that the Son is only eternally subordinated in role or function. ... Role or functional

The Son obeys and worships the Father because the Father is *arche* in the economic and the ontological Trinity. Packer recognises that Western theology does not emphasise the ontological Trinity in the same manner as Eastern Orthodoxy does. Yet, he claims that the economic Trinity reflects the ontological Trinity.[61] There is no deception, he contends, in the way the Bible depicts the Persons of the Godhead. They are presented realistically. Their attitudinal and operational dimensions are one. The Son is eternally subordinate because in creation the Father created 'through' the Son and in the eschaton the Father will receive glory 'through' the Son.[62] Regeneration, which makes us like Christ, makes us want to do what He does, i.e. obey and worship the Father.

In these claims Packer appears to go further than Calvin, who portrays the uniqueness of the Father, Son, and Spirit as interpenetrating and interdependent. Though challenging the claim of ontological subordination, not functional subordination, Calvin emphasises, for example, that 'the name 'God' ... is sometimes applied to the Father par excellence because he is the fountainhead and beginning of deity – and this is done to denote the simple unity of essence.'[63] Calvin also points out that 'there is comprehended under the name of 'Father' the unique essence of God which is common to both.'[64] The correspondence that Packer claims between the economic and ontological aspects of the Trinity make it difficult to see how he can escape the implications of ontological subordinationism. He appeals to the Son's eternal subordination to the Father as the resolution to the *kenotic* problem, stating,

> that since the Son's nature is not to take initiatives but to follow his Father's promptings, his reason for not doing certain things, or bringing to conscious knowledge certain facts was simply that he knew that his Father did not wish this done. In other words, Jesus' human limitations should be explained in terms, not of the special conditions of the incarnation, but of the eternal life of the Trinity.[65]

---

subordinationism is based on the premise that the Son and, likewise, women can be permanently subordinated in function or role without in any way undermining their personal worth or equality. Role subordinationism, we are told, does not imply inferiority. This is generally true, but once the note of permanency is introduced and competence is excluded, this is not true' (17).

[61] Packer interview, (2 July 1999).

[62] Ibid.

[63] Calvin, *Institutes*, I.xiii.23.

[64] Ibid., I.xiii.25.

[65] J.I. Packer, 'A Modern View of Jesus', in *Shorter Writings*, 1.72.

Packer does not refer to the Spirit's role in Jesus' life to address the *kenosis*. Thus, he creates an anthropological framework for piety in which the absolute necessity of the Spirit's work is not obvious in his logic, regardless of the amount of attention he gives the subject.

This Christological and Trinitarian framework clarifies what Packer means by 'responsive.' That is, the *imago Dei* is fulfilled as humans repond in obedience to God after the pattern of the Son's obedience to the Father. The *imago Dei* is seen fully in Jesus Christ, 'the true image of God in his humanity as well as in his divinity.'[66]

7.2.2 The Imago Dei *as Rational, Relational, and Representational*

Responsive righteousness, the most basic definition of the *imago Dei* for Packer, is expressed as humans *represent* God's holy character in the context of *relationships*. In claiming that 'life, we know, is essentially relationships,' he offers the innate human need for relationships as a clear expression of the divine–human relational structure that stems from the *imago Dei*.[67] He conceives the representational aspect as a dynamic expression of the divine image through human endowments. 'God's image must be thought of not just as something static and given, like a tattoo that stays on me whether I like it or not, but also as a condition which is more or less achieved according to how I use my God–given capacities.'[68] However, Packer emphasizes rationality as the integrative motif for both the representation of God and relationship with God. Thus, he goes beyond

---

[66] Packer, *Concise Theology*, 72. Packer stated in his interview with the author (2 July 1999) that he sees a distinction between the way in which humans and Jesus Christ are the *imago Dei*. He sees humans as made *in* the image but Christ *as* the image. See also P.E. Hughes, who supports this distinction in *The True Image*, 16. While Packer appeals to this distinction so as to preserve the Christological orientation of *imago Dei*, it must be realised that this is a theological distinction that is not clearly derived from the language of the relevant texts. See G.J. Wenham, *Genesis 1–15* (Waco: Word, 1987), 29,32. Wenham argues that the Hebrew prepositions ב ('in, like') and כ ('as, like') in Genesis 1:26 indicate that humanity is the image and likeness of God in a derivative rather than identical sense. G.D. Fee seems to take a similar approach when interpreting 1 Cor. 11:7, but translates Paul to say, 'that man is God's "image,"' going on then to assume that Paul meant 'in God's image.' See *The First Epistle to the Corinthians*, 515–516. 2 Cor. 4:4 and Col. 1:15 both refer to Jesus Christ as the image of God by using the intransitive verb (*estin eikon*). F.F. Bruce states of Col. 1:15, 'To say that Christ is the image of God is to say that in him the nature and being of God have been perfectly revealed.' See *The Epistles to the Colossians, to Philemon, and to the Ephesians*, 57. P.E. Hughes takes the same interpretation of 2 Cor. 4:4. See *The Second Epistle to the Corinthians*, 130.

[67] Packer, 'A Christian View of Man', in *Shorter Writings*, 2.171.

[68] J.I. Packer, *For Man's Sake* (Exeter: Paternoster, 1978), 12.

other theologians who have tended to emphasise either rationality or relationality as the dominant description of the *imago Dei*.[69]

Human beings *represent* a *rational* God and *relate* to God by means of that rationality. This triad of representation, rationality, and relationship constitutes the framework in which the *imago Dei* is fulfilled in human existence. Rationality provides moral definition to human existence as the medium through which God's character is reflected. This moral dimension provides motivation and guidance for the act of reflecting God's character in the varied forms of dominion over creation. Human teleology thus derives from the outworking of this dominion along the moral lines established by God's character. Responsive relationship, primarily with God and secondarily with other people, provides the context in which the righteousness at the heart of the divine image is fulfilled. Packer's elucidation of this interrelationship is worth quoting at length.

> Human dignity, yours and mine, and that of every human being without exception, flows from the fact that we are made in the image of God, as Genesis 1:26 and 5:1–2 affirm.
>
> What does that mean? we ask. Clearly, the basic idea is that human beings are like God in a way that other animate creatures are not. … The *imago Dei* relationship relates not to our physical but to our personal nature, and this at four levels.
>
> First, God, whom Genesis 1 and all Scripture presents as rational, made us rational, able to form concepts, think thoughts, carry through trains of reasoning, make and execute plans, live for goals, distinguish right from wrong and beautiful from ugly, and relate to other intelligent beings. This rationality is what makes us moral beings, and it is the basis for all other dimensions of Godlikeness, whether those given in our creation or those achieved through our redemption.
>
> Second, God the Creator made us sub–creators under him, able and needing to find fulfillment in the creativity of art, science, technology,

---

[69] Packer, 'Systematic Theology B, Man, Sin and Grace', section on 'Nature and Sin', 2. Packer calls the *imago Dei* 'a key notion, guaranteeing our <u>addressability</u> and <u>answerability</u>.' He goes on to comment that the *imago* is 'not structure or potentiality alone [*contra* Luther and Barth]' and that 'more balanced is the view of Brunner, Hoekema, etc. that sinners are not God's image <u>functionally</u> though they remain so <u>structurally</u>.' An example of a Reformed theologian who holds a predominantly representational view of the divine image is H. Fernhout, 'Man: The Image and Glory of God' in A.H. DeGraaf and J.H. Olthuis (eds.), *Toward a Biblical View of Man* (Toronto: Association for the Advancement of Christian Scholarship, 1978). A predominantly relational view of the divine image is found in K.Barth, *Church Dogmatics*, III.1.2.

construction, scholarship, and the bringing of order out of various sorts of chaos.

Third, God as Lord made us his stewards, that is, deputy managers–bailiffs, as the English say, or factors, to put it in Scotch – to have dominion over the estate which is his world. This role, which presupposes our rationality and creativity, is the special theme of Psalm 8. Man's unique privilege is to harness, develop and use the resources of God's world, not only making animate creatures and vegetation his food, but tapping the resources of raw materials and energy, in order to create culture for two ends which God has inseparably linked – his honour, and our joy. Such cultural activity is natural and instinctive to us.

Finally, God who himself is good (truthful, faithful, wise, generous, loving, patient, just, valuing whatever has moral, intellectual or aesthetic worth and hating all that negates such worth) originally made man good in the sense of naturally and spontaneously righteous. Righteousness in man means active response to God by doing what he loves and commands and avoiding what he hates and forbids. God has a moral character, as you and I have, and there are specific types of action which he approves and others which he disapproves.

Human nature as created has a teleological structure such that its fulfillment (which subjectively means our conscious contentment and joy) only occurs as we consciously do, and limit ourselves to doing, what we know that God approves. ...

What Christians say about the image of God in mankind, therefore, with some variety of vocabulary but substantial unity of sentiment, is that while we retain the image formally and structurally, and in terms of actual dominion over the created order, we have lost it materially and morally, and in terms of personal righteousness before our Creator.[70]

The manner in which Packer connects the themes of rationality, creativity, stewardship, and righteousness demonstrates the priority he gives to rationality, relationship, and righteousness in his overall anthropology.

Rationality, relationship, and righteousness are meaningfully expressed through humanity's engagement in responsible stewardship over creation. However, Packer presents this engagement in a manner that suggests it is secondary to the reflection of God's rational and righteous character, i.e. the expression of God's character in relationship, and the innate capacities that sustain that reflection. He clarifies how these primary aspects relate to the secondary aspects.

---

[70] Packer, 'A Christian View of Man', 173–174.

Genesis 1:1–25 sets forth God as personal, rational (having intelligence and will, able to form plans and execute them), creative, competent to control the world he has made, and morally admirable, in that all he creates is good. Plainly, God's image will include all these qualities. Verses 28–30 show God blessing newly created humans (that must mean telling them their privilege and destiny) and setting them to rule creation as his representatives and deputies. The human capacity for communication and relationship with both God and other humans, and the God–given dominion over the lower creation … thus appear as further facets of the image.

God's image in man at Creation, then, consisted (a) in man's being a 'soul' or 'spirit' (Gen. 2:7, where the NIV correctly says "living being;" Eccles. 12:7), that is, a personal, self–conscious, Godlike creature with a Godlike capacity for knowledge, thought, and action; (b) in man's being morally upright … (c) in man's environmental dominion. Usually, and reasonably, it is added that (d) man's God–given immortality and (e) the human body, through which we experience reality, express ourselves, and exercise our dominion, belong to the image too.

The body belongs to the image, not directly, since God … does not have one, but indirectly, inasmuch as the God–like activities of exercising dominion over the material creation and demonstrating affection to other rational beings make our embodiment necessary. There is no fully human life without a functioning body, whether here or hereafter.[71]

It could be argued that in Packer's schema God's rationality and God's righteousness occupy equal status in defining the nature of God and, hence, in the *imago Dei* that humanity is called to reflect.

The *imago Dei* obviously involves a relationship to creation and to others in Packer's thought. These aspects of the *imago* are of secondary importance to the personal righteousness that is to be expressed in individual relationship with God. However, he presents them as important outgrowths of that primary relationship. The way in which Packer structures these elements in anthropology and emphasises them in piety reflects the way he relates the doctrine of the Incarnation to the doctrine of Creation. Colin Gunton points out that the extent to which a piety can fully integrate the theme of dominion (i.e. going beyond merely acknowledging its importance to making it integral to piety) depends in part on the extent to which Christ's reign over creation is emphasised as an aspect of the Incarnation.[72] Packer does not directly relate the Incarnation to the creation

---

[71] Packer, *Concise Theology*, 71–72.
[72] Gunton, *Christ and Creation*, 20–22,25.

account because of his emphasis on the Incarnation as oriented only toward sin and the restoration of corrupted humanity. Though he makes the Christian's relationship to creation an important feature of piety, his logic only supports relating it to piety in a secondary manner, i.e. as a matter of obedience to the dominion mandate. However, unless Christ is presented as integrally involved as Lord of creation, whether or not sin had entered the world, there is no theological basis upon which a direct relationship to creation itself is integral to piety.[73]

Furthermore, though Packer attributes great value to human community and relationships, they ultimately occupy the same status in his anthropology as creation, i.e. secondary (though important) expressions of individual righteousness in relationship with God. When the *imago Dei* is thus defined individualistically, the role of community is logically restricted in its ability to fulfil personhood. Grenz contends, 'The image of God does not lie in the individual life per se but in the relationality of persons in community. The relational life of God who is triune comes to representation in the communal fellowship of the participants in the new humanity.'[74] Packer certainly stresses the importance of the church, both in theology and in practise, even going so far as to claim that 'the fellowship of sharing with one another' is '*a spiritual necessity.*'[75] Life in the church is not presented, however, as itself a direct fulfilment of the *imago Dei*. Nor does Packer directly relate anthropology to ecclesiology. Rather, the community of faith is 'first vertical before it can be horizontal' and is portrayed as an essential resource for the fulfilling God's call to individual righteousness.[76] The relationship between the individual and corporate dimensions of the *imago Dei* in the church are tightly interwoven, but the individual aspect takes priority. Obviously, this individualised anthropology leads to and supports his emphasis on personal or individual holiness, even though individual holiness has strong social ramifications.

In addition to representing Packer's basic anthropological triad of representation, rationality, and relationship, the preceding texts offer clarification on three additional areas that affect his anthropology. Rationality, for Packer, is more than simply reason or cognition. It also encompasses moral sense, purposefulness, communicative capacities, and volition. He understands unfallen rationality as reason, will, and affection functioning in proper relationship. He admits and embraces the sources of this paradigm.

---

[73] Ibid., 100.

[74] Grenz, *The Social God and the Relational Self*, 305.

[75] J.I. Packer, 'Body Life', in *Shorter Writings*, 2.13.

[76] Ibid., 13–14.

The Puritans' understanding of human nature, which underlies their account of its renovation by grace, was expounded in the psychological vocabulary which, since Augustine had introduced it from Neoplatonism and Aquinas standardised it from Aristotle, had been universal in Christian thought. The Puritans considered it admirably suited to express the biblical doctrine. On this view, the components of personality were: *reason ... will ... and affections.* ... Man was made a rational animal, to live to God for His glory. Reason should prescribe action to this end and the will should execute its commands, while affection, spontaneously evoked, was to animate and spur him to wholehearted activity. ... When man fell, his will threw off reason's yoke and enslaved itself to the sensitive appetite and affections. ... Now, sanctification is that part of the work of recreating him in Christ's image which is done on earth (the other part is glorification). Sanctification progressively restores his rationality and makes him a man again.[77]

Packer makes repeated use of these psychological faculties in his understanding of how human nature is restored to holiness through sanctification.

Packer understands 'soul' and 'spirit' to be synonymous, rejecting a trichotomous view of personhood. His view of human personhood is closer to the dichotomous view of the soul found in 'substance–dualism' theories.[78] He states, 'We are body and soul/spirit, ensouled bodies or embodied souls.'[79] The human body is not an essential aspect of the *imago*

---

[77] Packer, 'Sanctification – Puritan Teaching', 126.

[78] A contemporary exposition of substance–dualism can be found in J.P. Moreland, 'A Defense of a Substance Dualist View of the Soul', in J.P. Moreland and D.M. Diocchi (eds.), *Christian Perspectives on Being Human: A Multidisciplinary Approach to Integration* (Grand Rapids: Baker, 1993), 55–85 and J.P. Moreland, 'Spiritual Formation and the Nature of the Soul', *Christian Education Journal* 4, no. 2 (2000), 25–43. Moreland sees 'spirit' as a subcategory of 'soul' and as the means whereby humans relate personally to God. He makes the functioning of a relationship with God dependent on the existence of certain capacities that are resident within the 'spirit.' The physical capabilities through which this relationship is experienced exist only as 'second–order' capacities. If physical impairment (e.g. brain damage) impedes the experience of conscious relationship with God, the prospect of relationship nevertheless remains as a 'first–order' capacity awaiting restoration in the eschaton.

[79] Packer, 'Systematic Theology B, Man, Sin and Grace', section on 'Nature and Sin', 2.

Dei, but is necessary to the full functioning and expression of the material aspects of the image.[80]

Packer attempts to combine his three major emphases into an integrated profile of the *imago Dei*.

That God originally made humankind in his own image as the crown of his creation – to procreate, to exercise dominion, and to enjoy the world's abundance, in grateful responsive communion with his Maker – is shown, repetitiously for emphasis, in Genesis 1:26–29. In past discussions as to what precisely constitutes the image, there have been different emphases. Some have highlighted rationality, meaning our power to think, remember, and plan. Some have pointed to relationality, meaning our power to love other people interactively, as God loves us interactively. Others have focused on rulerhood, meaning our dominion over the rest of the created order. And it has been debated whether the primary thought that the image idea expresses is of being God's deputy, ruling and managing his world, or of being holy and upright in action, as God himself is. *Genesis 1:1–25 yields a basis for all these notions, so the way of wisdom is surely to combine them; from this combination of substantive, relational, and functional features the original dignity of*

---

[80] In his unpublished course notes ('Systematic Theology B, Man, Sin and Grace', section on 'Nature and Sin', 2–3) he offers 'The Meaning of Humanness' as a major heading under which he treats the body/soul/spirit question and the *imago Dei* as separate sub–headings. In his understanding of 'soul' and 'body' Packer reflects the influence of Augustine who struggled with Neo–Platonism by considering the soul to be created, even though immortal, and sought to legitimise the body while keeping it in a secondary, subservient position to the primary objectives of the soul. See also H. Chadwick, *Augustine* (Oxford: Oxford University Press, 1986), 98–99. Chadwick observes, 'Augustine refused to identify the body with the root of evil. On the other hand he thought it illusion to suppose that man's highest good is attainable in this life and may be found in his magnificent social or cultural or technological achievements. Man's highest good lies in eternal life in and with God. This does not entail a rejection of this life's values; but it does make them relative.' See also Packer, 'Conscience, Choice and Character', 169. Here Packer describes his own approach to the tension between the material and immaterial aspects of human existence by stating that 'Having within me something both of ape and angel, I can all too easily lose my cosmic balance, so to speak, and lapse into incoherent oscillation beween [sic] seeing myself as no less than God, a spirit having absolute value in myself and settling the value of everything else by its relation to me, and seeing myself as no more than an animal, whose true life consists wholly in eating, drinking, rutting and seeking pleasures for mind and body till tomorrow I die. I often catch myself slipping one way or the other.'

human beings as God's image–bearers at once becomes plain [emphasis added].[81]

This attempt to integrate various interpretations of the *imago Dei* displays the breadth of theological sources that have shaped Packer's anthropology. All aspects do not have the same role, however. Righteousness in relationship is the material aspect of the *imago*. Rationality is the structural aspect. Representation is the functional aspect. Ironically, rationality seems to occupy the position of greatest influence since without it the other aspects of the *imago Dei* could not be realised.

Packer's understanding of the *imago Dei* parallels John Owen's emphases on righteousness expressed in obedient relationship, the subordination of dominion to righteousness, and the doxological intent of the entire human enterprise. Owen states,

'God made man in his own image;' that is, in such a rectitude of nature as represented his righteousness and holiness – in such a state and condition as had a reflection on it of his *power* and *rule*. The former was the substance of it – the latter a necessary consequent thereof. This representation, I say, of God, in power and rule, was not that image of God wherein man was created, but a consequent of it. ... Because he was made in the image of God, this dominion and rule were granted unto him. ... Three things God designed in this communication of his image unto our nature ... The *first* was, that he might therein make a *representation of his holiness and righteousness* among his creatures. This was not done in any other of them. ... The *second* was, that it might be a means of rendering actual glory unto him from all other parts of the creation. Without this, which is as the animating life and form of the whole, the other creatures are but as a dead thing. They could not any way declare the glory of God, but passively and objectively. ... The *third* was, that it might be a means to bring man unto that *eternal enjoyment* of Himself, which he was fitted for and designed unto. For this was to be done in a way of obedience.[82]

Owen does not mention rationality as part of the *imago Dei* in the same way that Packer does. Yet the similarities between Owen and Packer are obvious when they prioritise the righteous character and the doxological purpose of God's intentions for humanity. When Owen states that 'the whole rational soul of man since the fall, and by the entrance of sin, is

---

[81] J.I. Packer, 'Doing It My Way: Are We Born Rebels?' 48–49.
[82] J. Owen, *The Works of John Owen, D. D.*, W.H. Goold (ed.), (Edinburgh, T & T Clark, 1862), I.182–183.

weakened, impaired, vitiated, in all its faculties and all their operations about their proper and natural objects,'[83] it appears that for him as for Packer, rationality is the controlling factor in the *imago Dei* .

Though Richard Baxter focuses on reason or intellect working together with the will to direct the other faculties, he attributes to reason the premier position of guidance.[84] The *imago Dei*, according to Baxter, is the human soul and is comprised of three faculties, 'vital and executive power, understanding, and will.'[85] The human soul derives its nature from the nature and attributes of God.[86]

In his doctoral thesis Packer comments on Baxter's view of the intellect in its relationship to rationality as a whole and to the other individual faculties.

> But this end [the knowledge of God] is only attainable insofar as man behaves rationally, and will and affection follow the dictates of intellect. Where intellect is the slave of sense, God can neither be known, nor loved, nor obeyed. In fallen man, however ... intellect is a mere figurehead; sense has usurped the government and become the power behind the throne, and the appearance of a rationality is a sham. ... Rational self–control must be restored. All the inferior faculties must be brought into subjection to the intellect and so to the law of Christ which demands this subjection.[87]

In this passage Packer sees Baxter elevating the intellect to a dominant role in relationship to the other faculties. Packer's way of articulating the

---

[83] J. Owen, 'Corruption or Deprivation of the Mind by Sin', in *Works*, W.H. Goold (ed.), (London: Banner of Truth, 1965[2]), III.3.iii.

[84] R. Baxter, *The Practical Works of Richard Baxter* (London: George Virtue, 1838), II.I.i.12. 'My sense and bodily faculties are naturally to be subjected to the guidance of my reason and the command of my will, as the superior faculties. For one is common to brutes, and the other proper to rational creatures; and rational agents are more excellent than brutes; and the most excellent should rule. Reason can see further than sense; and the wisest is most fit to govern. ... The sum is, that man is a living wight, having an active and executive power, with an understanding to guide it, and a will to command it ...' Baxter proceeds to develop the implications of this basic anthropology in terms of humanity's established dominion over the created world, followed by the responsibilities of relatedness to other people.

[85] Ibid., II.5.31.

[86] Ibid., II.5.29. Baxter states here that we can conceive of God's attributes by analogy from our essential faculties.

[87] Packer, 'The Redemption and Restoration of Man in the Thought of Richard Baxter', 336–337.

relationship of intellect to the other faculties bears a clear resemblance to Baxter's.

7.2.3 *Implications of the Structural and Material* Imago Dei

7.2.3.1 CONSCIENCE

Chapter six showed the function of conscience in holiness and the relationship of conscience to the nature and function of Scripture in piety. Anthropologically, Packer sees the mind as the foundation for conscience. He defines conscience (admitting that he personally follows Thomas Aquinas) as 'man's mind making moral judgments.' He goes on to explain that

> as God's moral judgments should control our acts and will actually settle our destiny, so our conscience functions in the style of a voice within actually addressing us to command or forbid, approve or disapprove, justify or condemn. ... From the standpoint of standards, it is truer to say that conscience is a capacity for hearing God's voice, rather than an actual hearing of it in each verdict that conscience passes.[88]

Conscience depends not merely upon the rational faculties, but on the particular faculty of reason to contribute to the structural dimension of the *imago Dei*. Conscience is the potential for, and channel of communication between Creator and creature, but must not be taken as identical with God's communication. Packer aligns himself with the general Puritan view of conscience.

> Conscience, to them [the Puritans], signified a man's knowledge of himself as standing in God's presence ... Conscience was the court (*forum*) in which God's justifying sentence was spoken. Conscience was the soil in which alone true faith, hope, peace, and joy could grow. Conscience was a facet of the much–defaced image of God in which man was made; and vital Christianity ... was rooted directly in the apprehensions and exercises of conscience under the searching address of God's quick and powerful word, and the enlightenment of his Holy Spirit. So the Reformers held; and the Puritans, too.[89]

Without conscience there would be no possibility that the *imago Dei* could be realised. Through the faculty of reason the conscience is a necessary though insufficient condition for relational righteousness and the

---

[88] Packer, 'Conscience, Choice and Character', 175.
[89] Packer, *Among God's Giants*, 141.

fulfilment of the *imago Dei*. Conscience is an instrument by which rationality (the structural dimension) enables relational righteousness (the material dimension) and doxological representation (the functional dimension) through precise response to the will of God as known from God's law and as expressed in the inerrant, rational propositions of Scripture.

7.2.3.2 THE LAW OF GOD AND SCRIPTURE

The function of God's law in piety depends upon both the capacity of conscience and the medium of Scripture, the latter of which communicates God's will to the mind, through the conscience, in order to enable volitional response. The anthropological significance of this equation is that Packer rests his entire view of Scripture on the premise that the human mind corresponds to God's mind.[90] This assumption gives rise to his conviction that in and through the Bible God offers self–revelation that is comprehensible to humans on the basis of the *imago Dei*. He comments, 'Included in that image are rationality, relationality, and the capacity for righteousness that consists of receiving and responding to God's revelation. We are able to know God because we are thinking, feeling, relating, loving beings, just as he is himself.'[91]

These interconnected themes constitute the basis for Packer's theological method in which the doctrine of Scripture stands at the forefront.[92] Though he demurs from the strictly Thomistic notion of an analogy between divine

---

[90] J.I. Packer, 'The Adequacy of Human Language', in *Shorter Writings*, 3.27–40. In this article Packer connects the theory of the verbal, plenary inspiration of Scripture with the nature of the mind as its receptor by positing the rational nature of the *imago Dei* in humans as constituting the possibility of meaningful communication between the divine mind and the human mind. He makes several remarks that indicate this connection. 'By depicting God as the first language user (1:3,6, et. al.), Genesis shows us that human thought and speech have their counterparts and archetypes in him' (38).' Also, ' … the biblical position that God's speaking and God's image in man imply a human capacity to grasp and respond to his verbal address …'

[91] Packer, *Knowing Christianity*, 57–58.

[92] In *Concise Theology* Packer departs from Calvin's organisational pattern by beginning with the subjects of Scripture, Interpretation, General Revelation, Guilt, Inward Witness, Authority, and Knowledge. He then follows with the doctrine of God, which begins Calvin's system. This switch is typical of those who follow Scholastic Calvinism of the seventeenth century. See Grenz and Franke, *Beyond Foundationalism*, 103. They observe, 'In scholastic theological treatises, the doctrine of scripture is routinely treated first among the theological *loci* for the purpose of establishing scripture as the sole source and foundation on which the theological enterprise is based.'

and human nature,[93] he finds that the prospect of intelligible communication between God and humans stems from the *imago Dei*, that is, 'the biblical position that God's speaking and God's image in man imply a capacity to grasp and respond to his verbal address.'[94] He claims, 'The final proof that human language can speak intelligibly of God is that God has actually spoken intelligibly about himself in it. This intelligibility flows from the so–called anthropomorphism (manlikeness) of his account of himself. But such anthropomorphism is primarily a witness to the essential theomorphism (Godlikeness) of man.'[95]

Correspondence between God's rationality and human rationality provides the basis for intelligible reception of God's self–revelation. Yet, it does not imply an unencumbered human ability to comprehend God's revelation. Sin has affected the correspondence between divine and human rationality, such that relationship with God is impossible to unaided human rationality. He states, 'Spiritual understanding – that is, the discernment of the reality of God, his ways with humankind, his present will, and one's own relationship to him now and for the future – will not, however, reach us from the text until the veil is removed from our hearts and we are able to share the writer's passion to know and please and honor God (2 Cor. 3:16; 1 Cor. 2:14).'[96]

In this statement Packer uses the terms 'spiritual understanding' and 'heart' rather generically to depict the rationality necessary for restored relationship with God. The restoration of relationship with God (holiness/piety) and the *imago Dei* takes place, however, through a particular, multi–directional interplay between God and the psychological faculties as the restoration of rationality.

Holiness and the restored *imago Dei* depend upon apprehension of the message of Scripture. Yet, the message of Scripture does not restore rationality by a direct effect upon the will. It affects the mind or reason first. Scripture authoritatively and inerrantly reflects the mind and will of God for human life. This restoration process is so dependent on Scripture that the process would be crippled were Scripture not inerrantly conveying the propositional message of salvation from God's mind through the human

---

[93] Packer, 'The Adequacy of Human Language', 47. Packer argues that neither the analogy of attribution nor the analogy of proportionality offer accurate knowledge of God. However, he maintains that the Bible's depictions of God as '"father," "loving," "wise," and "just,"' are true of humanity analogically in that they are true 'up to a certain point.' That is, 'only *some* of the implications of the normal use of these predicates, therefore, carry over.'

[94] Ibid., 39.

[95] Ibid.

[96] Packer, *Concise Theology*, 6–7.

mind to the human will. Thus, biblical inerrancy is for Packer a critical and logical necessity for the possibility of human salvation,[97] though he stops short of claiming that personal belief in biblical inerrancy is essential to an individual's salvation.[98]

In a personal interview Packer stated to the author that he prefers to think of the rational faculties as functioning in an integrated manner, he nevertheless confesses to following Thomas Aquinas in holding that the intellect takes the lead. The human person is 'more or less disintegrated,' says Packer. Furthermore, it is a matter of experience that the mind should lead but instead becomes a 'slave of blind desire' that is inordinate because it has no rational control and is dominated by feelings. Irrationality is *prima facia* evidence of this disintegration.[99] The overall structure of Packer's anthropology and his specific admission of the priority of the intellect seem to work against his stated vision of an integrated functioning of the faculties.

---

[97] Biblical inerrancy, to Packer, derives from its source in the mind and character of God. In *'Fundamentalism' and the Word of God*, his first significant exposition of this theme, he defended both 'inerrancy' and 'infallibility' by developing the views B.B. Warfield expressed in *The Inspiration and Authority of the Bible*. Many years later he anchored himself in that earlier perspective by stating that 'there is nothing in it that I have ever wished to withdraw ['Inerrancy and the Divinity and Humanity of the Bible', in *Shorter Writings*, 3.169.].' See also *Truth and Power*, 102. Here, he briefly defines inerrancy as follows. 'Inerrancy, meaning the full truth and trustworthiness of what the Bible tells us, is entailed, that is, necessarily and inescapably implied, by the God–givenness of what is written.' The implications of biblical inerrancy are far–reaching to Packer. It supports the ability of the Bible to exercise authority over all human opinions and actions. He claims that 'without inerrancy the structure of biblical authority as evangelicals conceive it collapses' (101). He defends inerrancy as being utterly compatible with the divine–human character of the Bible by comparing it to the divine–human character of Jesus. See 'Inerrancy and the Divinity and Humanity of the Bible', in *Shorter Writings*, 3.169. 'In both cases,' he states, 'you have a mysterious union of divine and human. In both cases, you have perfection, as a result, in human form.'

[98] Packer, *Truth and Power*, 104–105. Packer recognizes that there are thoroughgoing evangelicals who do not hold to biblical inerrancy. He simply believes that their position is inadequate for the theological enterprise and the Christian experience.

[99] Packer interview, (2 July 1999). Packer does not, however, 'reify' mind or will, preferring to speak of 'specific' emotions and affections, not of emotion or affection abstractly. He compares the functioning human self to a 'ball of wax.' It is dynamic, not abstract. He prioritises the 'concrete' reality of mind, emotions, and will because he feels that is the Bible's way of talking about humans and because that is true to the way psychology talks about human life, i.e. thinking, feeling, and doing.

For Packer, the corruption of the will through sin contributes to the dysfunction of human rationality. As a result of this dysfunction, the faculty of reason is crippled in its ability to properly comprehend God's revelation. His definition and description of reason illuminate the relationship between the broader corruption of human rationality and the impact of that corruption on reason.

> In ordinary speech, reason means, first and fundamentally, the power of abstract, analytical thinking. ... [M]an is the only animate being that can form an abstract idea, construct a definition, analyse a concept, make a generalization, classify, draw inferences, make deductions, conceive hypotheses and means to verify them – in short, do all the things that we lump together under the umbrella–word *ratiocination*. Reason is the faculty whereby man *ratiocinates*. ... The object of reason's quest, in a word, is truth. And the fundamental notion of truth is that of correspondence between man's thoughts and that which is objectively the case.[100]

By connecting the function of reason to the question of truth, he does not suggest that the truth to which reason can attain is all the truth that is necessary for holiness. The truth of reason is, however, a necessary level or gradation of truth that is prerequisite to the intimate, personal truth involved in relationship with God.

He goes on to claim that sin affects the restoration of relationship with God by blinding reason through the corruption of the heart, that is, through the affective and volitional aspects of rationality.

> Fallen man's reason is blind through sin, so that no amount of reasoning unaided by the Holy Spirit can find out God. Fallen man's reason is, moreover, the servant of a sinful heart, which does not like to retain God in its knowledge (Rom. 1:28), and labours accordingly to turn the light of general revelation into darkness. ... Fallen man cannot of himself escape bondage to sin. Sin he must, whatever he does. It is not in him to acknowledge God's authority; it is not in him to receive God's truth when it is presented to him. ... What can cure his condition? Only *regeneration*.[101]

The blindness to which Packer refers, though pervasive, simply keeps the mind from recognising God's truth for what it is. For Packer, sin has crippled the outworking of the *imago Dei* and thwarted its purposes by

---

[100] J.I. Packer, 'The Bible and the Authority of Reason', in *Shorter Writings*, 3.55,56.
[101] Ibid., 3.63.

corrupting every aspect of human rationality. It is significant, though, that in his theology sin appears to have negatively affected the capacity of reason to understand God's revelation through the avenue of the 'heart' or 'will.'

Packer never offers biblical grounds for utilising the categories of faculty psychology to understand human rationality. Rather, he appeals to experience and observation as the basis for this paradigm. The effect of this approach is that, despite his attempts to portray the functions of reason, volition, and affection in an integrated manner, these discrete categories create a scenario in which sin affects each faculty in a different manner. The volitional faculty appears to be more active in its rebellion against God while the faculty of reason appears to be more passive or unresponsive ('blind') in its state of rebellion. The moral misdirection taken by the reason results from the influence of the fallen will. Despite his refusal to 'reify' the faculties, Packer's schema nevertheless assumes some degree of reification when sin originates in the will, then spreads to the other faculties and disables them.

The psychological faculties are related to the *imago Dei* in a manner that seems to make the material content of the image contingent upon them. He states,

> When Scripture speaks of man as made in God's image and thus as being God's image–bearer, what it means is that each human individual is set apart from the animal creation by being equipped with the personal make–up, the conscious selfhood, feelings, brains, and capacity for love–relationships, *without which Christ–like holiness would be impossible* [emphasis added] … But Scripture also speaks of the new creation of believing sinners, and defines this as the motivational and dispositional renewing of us in Christ by the Holy Spirit, and assures us that it is only through new creation that Christlike holiness ever becomes actual.[102]

In Packer's schema holiness depends upon the renewal of the will, which in turn depends on the illumination of the mind. Holiness and the *imago Dei* depend on fundamental change in the will as the epicentre of personhood. An impasse results, however, when Packer portrays the will as being at the mercy of the mind's illuminated apprehension of God's revelation in Scripture and, at the same time, claims that the Holy Spirit must first regenerate the will, breaking down its innate resistance to God, in order to heal the blindness the mind.

---

[102] Packer, 'An Introduction to Systematic Spirituality', 4.

Packer appears to believe that sin has incapacitated the mind or reason just as thoroughly as any other aspect of rationality. He comments, '[T]hough I do not join Barth in his denial of general revelation through the created order, I … affirm, as he did, the total inability of the fallen human mind to think correctly about God, and gain true knowledge about him, apart from the instruction of Holy Scripture mediated by the illumination of the Holy Spirit.'[103] The moral predicament of the mind or reason implies that its restoration depends upon the illumination of the Spirit. Through the spiritually illuminated mind, then, God regenerates the will.

This creates a confused relationship between illumination and regeneration. In *Concise Theology* he treats the subjects of illumination and regeneration back–to–back and in that order. In his explanation of regeneration he claims that 'the ordinary context of new birth is one of effectual calling – that is, confrontation with the gospel and illumination as to its truth and significance as a message from God to oneself.'[104] He contends that 'illumination … starts before conversion with a growing grasp of the truth about Jesus and a growing sense of being measured and exposed by it.'[105] Immediately thereafter he discusses conversion under the heading of regeneration. Yet, he claims that the sinfulness of the will is responsible for the bondage experienced in all other aspects of human personhood. He states, 'We have no natural ability to discern and choose God's way because we have no natural inclination Godward; our hearts are in bondage to sin, and only the grace of regeneration can free us from that slavery.'[106] Thus, the spiritual inability of the mind is a result of the sinful will, creating a situation in which the will must be regenerated before the mind can be renewed. Yet, the regeneration of the will depends on the illumination of the mind. Thus, regeneration of the will and illumination of the mind each appear to depend on the prior work of the other.

Illumination of the mind regarding the meaning of Scripture assumes the presence of a structural correspondence between God's mind and the human mind. Though the mind or reason is totally darkened by sin, the Spirit's illumination depends on the assumption that humanity shares analogically in God's rationality. The Spirit's illumination, therefore, assumes this innate rational structure within humans in order for God's revelation to be received. He observes that

---

[103] Ibid., 5.
[104] Packer, *Concise Theology*, 158.
[105] Ibid., 155.
[106] Ibid., 86.

Understanding of what Scripture means when applied to us – that is, of what God in Scripture is saying to and about us – comes only through the work of the sovereign Holy Spirit, who alone enables us to apprehend what God is and see what we are in His eyes. ... But this Spirit–given understanding comes by a rational process that can be stated, analyzed, and tested at each point.[107]

God who gave His Word in the form of the rational narration, exposition, reflection, and devotion that Holy Scripture is, now prompts the making and receiving of rational application of it.[108]

By separating the faculty of reason from the other faculties, Packer is able to offer a unique description of how sin affects the mind vis–à–vis the will. That is, the structure of the mind remains intact even though it is utterly unable to comprehend the inner truth of God's revelation in a 'saving' manner. The incapacity is actually a wilful spiritual blindness that is removed when the will is regenerated.[109] Yet again, the regeneration of the will depends on the illumination of the mind, thus creating a perplexing sequence.

Packer's anthropology is reflected in the role he assigns to God's law and Scripture in holiness and the restoration of the *imago Dei*. The precise moral nature of God's law and the precise epistemological nature of Scripture as a communicative medium for God's moral will correspond to the highly rationalistic role they play in holiness and the restoration of the *imago Dei*. The mind emerges as the gatekeeper for the other faculties, without which holiness, the heart of the *imago Dei*, cannot be realised. Logically, this would have severe theological implications for those whose faculties are impaired. Since Packer places holiness at the heart of the *imago Dei*, places the psychological faculties at the control centre of the *imago Dei*, and anchors human dignity in the *imago Dei*, the possibility of

---

[107] Packer, 'Infallible Scripture and the Role of Hermeneutics', 337.

[108] Ibid., 347.

[109] Koranteng–Pipim, 'The Role of the Holy Spirit in Biblical Interpretation', 331–338. He concludes that Packer holds to a 'hermeneutic of the elect' in which the Holy Spirit's ministry of illumination is restricted to the elect, even though he recognises a distinction between 'saving illumination' and 'common illumination.' In common illumination the Holy Spirit moves with general beneficence to enhance the lives of unbelievers but without the intention of bringing them to salvation. The saving illumination that brings salvation to the elect 'changes sinners' hearts and brings to them a knowledge of the way back to God' (334). Koranteng–Pipim is careful to note that Packer does not claim that the non–elect are unable to understand Scripture's message at a purely propositional level but must have the Spirit's illumination in order to understand in such a way that the heart is changed.

human dignity and a relationship with God would seem to be compromised for those with impaired faculties. The logic of Packer's anthropology at this point seems quite anthropocentric.

7.2.3.3 EXPERIENTIAL PHENOMENA

Obviously, Packer appeals to the *imago Dei* as the source of humanity's unique dignity, purpose and place in creation. From his four–dimensional structure of rationality, creativity, dominion, and righteousness he develops the implications of humanness as it is restored in salvation and expressed in daily life. Along with Thomas Howard he argues that, 'rightly understood, Christianity is the true humanism, since it has for its purpose the forming and freeing and exalting of our true humanness.'[110] Packer and Howard contend that humans inevitably strive after identity, freedom, companionship, peace, truth, beauty, goodness, love, esteem, joy, and meaning. They even add such 'fugitive items' as play, conflict, and worship to the list of goals that the intrinsic impetus of humanity pursues.[111]

Packer takes Psalm 8 as the starting point of his exposition of the *imago Dei*. The wonder expressed by the Psalmist allows Packer to begin his anthropology phenomenologically. He asks, 'Well, what is man? I start my argument by picking up that question as it relates to each human individual. It is an escapable question which no one who thinks at all can avoid asking about himself or herself. We find ourselves to be self–transcendent, because we are self–conscious and self–aware.'[112] He goes on to quote Shakespeare's *Hamlet* in elucidating his point.

> 'What a piece of work is man! how noble in reason! how infinite in faculty (i.e., ability)! in form, in moving, how express and admirable! in action how like an angel! in apprehension how like a god! the beauty of the world! the paragon of animals!' Here Hamlet says brilliantly what Psalm 8 adumbrates and Christians have always said about man: namely, that he is a kind of cosmic amphibian. He has both a body and a mind and so has links with both apes and angels; he stands between animals who have no minds like his and angels who have no bodies like his.
>
> This is the classic Christian hierarchical view according to which the creatures are ranked in tiers, so to speak, below the Creator, at different levels of intrinsic complexity and significance in the cosmic order.[113]

---

[110] Packer and Howard, *Christianity: The True Humanism*, 50.
[111] Ibid., 37.
[112] Packer, 'A Christian View of Man', 169.
[113] Ibid., 170.

It is this grand vision of humanity that stands, for Packer, in stark contrast to the depths to which humanity has been depraved. The gravity of sin's impact on humanity is seen most poignantly against the backdrop of the glory for which humans were originally created.

In developing the implications of the *imago Dei* Packer elucidates the themes of dignity, destiny, and freedom. The *imago* is the source of the unique worth of human beings, above and beyond all the rest of God's creation. This value transcends any utilitarian purposes that may be imposed. The destiny of human beings is bound up in the call to responsive obedience to God. In this alone is human fulfilment possible. The distinctively moral dimension of human life grows from the freedom for self–determination that God has granted to humans. Notwithstanding the influence of other factors on human choice and the limitations of human choosing, God has made humans accountable and authentic with this freedom to shape their lives.[114]

The value of embodied existence finds its source, for Packer, in the *imago Dei*. Even early in his theological work he decries the 'Manichean' leanings of Christians who define holiness

> in terms of abstinence from needless traffic with created things. Nothing is gained from the study of anything here below, and the less interest one has in the world around one the better for one's soul. Such 'spirituality' is in no way Christian; yet it constantly appears in the Christian Church. ... But the Manichean attitude is altogether wrong. God forbids Christians to lose interest in His world. He made man to rule the created order; man is set in it to have dominion over it and to use it for God's glory, and therefore he may, and must, study its contents and its problems.[115]

Affirmation of embodied existence includes affirmation of one's relationship with one's self. In contrast to the suspicion of self–love sometimes found in those who hold to a radical view of sin, Packer states that 'a proper self–love is a further facet of God's image in us, for he too seeks his own felicity. The assertion, common nowadays, that one cannot robustly love either God or one's neighbor unless one robustly loves oneself is, both psychologically and theologically, a deep truth.'[116]

---

[114] Packer, 'Conscience, Choice and Character', 171–172.
[115] Packer, *'Fundamentalism' and the Word of God*, 132–134.
[116] Packer, 'Conscience, Choice and Character', 181.

7.3 Christological Anthropology in J.I. Packer's Theology

The anthropological implications of the Incarnation play a significant role in shaping piety for Packer. Holiness is defined as conformity to the moral character of Jesus Christ, who is the perfect *imago Dei*.[117] Since Packer defines God's character fundamentally in terms of moral purity, the human access to holiness (the restored *imago Dei*) provided by the incarnate Son of God takes place forensically. Through the forensic atonement Jesus Christ opened the way for sinners to be holy without personally touching the sinful human nature from which he redeems them.

7.3.1 Incarnation

Packer understands the Incarnation to mean 'that the second Person took to himself all that is involved in being human, personally and physically, in such a sense that all the elements of our experience became archetypally and inclusively his.'[118] From this starting point he sets the doctrine of the Incarnation within the context of the Trinity.

> Trinity and Incarnation belong together. The doctrine of the Trinity declares that the man Jesus is truly divine; that of the Incarnation declares that the divine Jesus is truly human. Together they proclaim the full reality of the Savior whom the New Testament sets forth, the Son who came from the Father's side at the Father's will to become the sinner's substitute on the cross.[119]

He fully accepts the conclusions of the councils of Nicea and Chalcedon and refers to them as substantiating the full divinity (Nicea) and the full humanity (Chalcedon) of Jesus Christ.[120] His reference to the Chalcedonian formula has particular bearing on the relationship of anthropology to piety. '[A]ll the qualities and powers that are in us, as well as all the qualities and

---

[117] J.I. Packer, 'Jesus Christ the Lord', in *Shorter Writings*, 1.35. Packer states, 'Concerning *Jesus*, it is claimed, that he is the yardstick at the level of motivation and attitudes of what it means to be fully human. Concerning *ourselves,* the claim is that only as we set ourselves to imitate Christ at this level are we fulfilling and developing (as distinct from violating and diminishing) our own human nature, which is already much diminished through sin; and only in this way can we find true joy, which is always integrally bound up with a sense of fulfilment.'

[118] Packer, 'Systematic Theology B, Man, Sin and Grace', section on 'Christ in Christian Thought', 4.

[119] Packer, *Concise Theology*, 104.

[120] Ibid., 104–105.

powers that are in God, were, are, and ever will be really and distinguishably present in the one person of the man from Galilee.'[121]

The Trinitarian and covenantal aspects of Packer's Christology are seen in the way he links the Father's act of sending the Son to fulfil the 'covenant of redemption.' He states, '[T]he unchanging cooperative pattern is that the second and third Persons identify with the purpose of the first so that the Son becomes the Father's executive and the Spirit acts as the agent of both. It is the Son's nature and joy to do his Father's will (John 4:34). Regarding redemption, the Father's will for the Son is sometimes called the covenant of redemption ...'[122] He cites article VIII.1 of the Westminster Confession to explain his understanding of this covenant. He explains how Jesus fits within the broader aspects of his covenantal theology by stating, 'Salvation is covenant salvation: justification and adoption, regeneration and sanctification are covenant mercies; election was God's choice of future members of his covenant community, the church; baptism and the Lord's Supper, corresponding to circumcision and Passover, are covenant ordinances; God's law is covenant law, and keeping it is the truest expression of gratitude for covenant grace and of loyalty to our covenant God.'[123] He notes Jesus' role as '"the mediator of a new covenant" (Heb. 9:15;12:24) – that is, the initiator of a new relationship of conscious peace with God ...'[124] It was Christ's atoning death that 'ratified the inauguration of the new covenant.'[125]

This covenantal framework, for Packer, sustains the penal, substitutionary character of Christ's atonement. The covenant of works,[126] broken by the first Adam, impugned the entire human race before God with representative, legal guilt. Packer notes this connection between the first Adam and Christ by stating that 'Scripture directs us to covenantal thinking ... *by the specific parallel between Christ and Adam* that Paul draws (Rom. 5:12–18; 1 Cor. 15:21f., 45–49).'[127]

---

[121] Ibid., 105.

[122] Ibid., 118–119.

[123] Ibid., 89–90.

[124] Ibid., 132.

[125] Ibid., 136.

[126] See Packer, 'On Covenant Theology', 13. He states, 'The original covenantal arrangement, usually called the Covenant of Works, was one whereby God undertook to prolong and augment for all subsequent humanity the happy state in which he had made the first human pair – provided that the man observed, as part of the humble obedience that was then natural to him, one prohibition, specified in the narrative as not eating a forbidden fruit.'

[127] Ibid., 20.

Christ (as the second Adam) uses this connection to offer a redemption that is likewise legal in nature, based on the penal demands of God's broken law.[128] He describes how this covenantal relationship points to the legal nature of Adam's sin, the implications for the human race, and the legal–penal character of Christ's saving work.

> Paul proclaims a solidarity between Christ and his people (believers, Rom. 3:22–5:22; the elect, God's chosen ones, 8:33) whereby the law–keeping, sin–bearing obedience of 'the one man' brings righteousness with God, justification, and life to 'the many,' 'all;' and he sets this within the frame of a prior solidarity, namely that between Adam and his descendants, whereby our entire race was involved in the penal consequences of Adam's transgression. The 1 Corinthians passages confirm that these are indeed covenantal solidarities; God deals with mankind through two representative men, Adam and Christ; all that are in Adam die; all that are in Christ are made alive. This far–reaching parallel is clearly foundational to Paul's understanding of God's ways with our race, and it is a covenantal way of thinking, showing … that covenant theology is indeed biblically basic.[129]

Packer is not unique in locating Christ's redemption within a covenantal frame of reference or in developing the soteriological implications of the relationship and Adam and Christ. Karl Barth also sees salvation against a covenantal backdrop.[130]

Barth and Packer differ, however, in their understandings of how God provides salvation within the covenant. Barth places Jesus Christ at the forefront of the covenant as the One in whom all humanity is elect, thus reconciling all humanity in the atonement. Packer places God's decree of election at the forefront of the covenant, limiting the effect of Christ's atonement to the elect. God's decree then leads the elect to Jesus Christ who occupies a place at a later point in the logic of the covenant. Christ's

---

[128] Ibid., 15–16. Packer claims, 'With him [Christ] as our sponsor and representative, the last Adam, the second "public person" through whom the Father deals with our race, the Covenant of Grace is archetypally and fundamentally made, in order that it may now be established and ratified with us in him.'

[129] Ibid.

[130] See Barth, *Church Dogmatics*, IV.1., 34–35. Barth states, 'Jesus Christ is the atonement. But that means that He is the maintaining and accomplishing and fulfilling of the divine covenant as executed by God Himself. He is the eschatological realisation of the will of God for Israel and therefore for the whole race. And as such He is also the revelation of this divine will and therefore of the covenant.'

death for sin, in Packer's view, applies only to the elect and serves to rectify their guilty legal status before God's law. From God's election proceeds the legal justification that changes the elect person's formal standing with God. Logically following justification is the existential transformation experienced in the sanctifying work of the Holy Spirit. From this limited role of Christ in soteriology, Packer does not have a need for an Incarnation that provides anything more than a sinless sacrifice as forensic satisfaction of God's law, at least until after the formal relationship with God has been established for the elect through their justification. From that point forward in Packer's logic, Christ's humanity has sweeping implications for the experience of sanctification.

Packer's understanding of covenant follows the distinctive path of Federal Calvinism in its assumption that the law of God (that reflects God's character through the demands of God's covenant) functions like modern, western notions of law and guilt in which abstract principles of justice are invoked apart from the context of relationship.[131] This particular use of the concept of covenant then constricts the immediate scope of Christ's impact on humanity through his incarnation by presenting the dominant purpose of

---

[131] See J.B. Torrance, Introduction to *The Nature of the Atonement*, by J. McLeod Campbell, (Edinburgh: Handsel, 1996[2]), 5–7. Torrance accuses federal Calvinism ('developed at the end of the sixteenth and particularly in the seventeenth century in England and Scotland') of going beyond the longstanding notion of one, unified covenant of grace (held by Calvin) and distorting the notion of covenant by confusing it with a legal contract, positing a disjunction between grace and law, and presenting fallen humanity as primarily defined by a guilty relationship to God's through Adam's violation of the law (covenant of works) rather than by the mediation of Christ for all through the Incarnation. These premises, claims Torrance, lead to the conclusion that Christ's work is only on behalf of the elect and focus the attention of individual believers 'less on the indicatives of grace and more on the imperatives of repentance, obedience and faith.' See also N.T. Wright, *What Saint Paul Really Said: Was Paul of Tarsus the Real Founder of Christianity?* (Grand Rapids: Eerdmans, 1997), 129. Wright understands the context of covenant to undergird the New Testament writer's reference to justification. Yet, he argues that the covenant is intrinsically grounded in God's desire for relationship with people. Hence, a person's legal status before God has to do with belonging to God's family. Illustrating from the use of the term 'justification' in the book of Romans, Wright states that '"justification", as seen in 3:24–26, means that those who believe in Jesus Christ are declared to be members of the true covenant family; which of course means that their sins are forgiven, since that was the purpose of the covenant. They are given the status of being "righteous" in the metaphorical law court. When this is cashed out in terms of the underlying covenantal theme, it means that they are declared, in the present, to be what they will be seen to be in the future, namely the true people of God.'

the incarnation as the remedy of the legal guilt incurred by the race through Adam.

Packer presses his point about the purpose of the Incarnation by contending, 'Why do Christians insist that God's forgiveness of sins is only ever possible on the basis of an atoning sacrifice? Ultimately, it is because Jesus saw the making of atonement as the main purpose of his coming ...'[132] He is closely in line with Calvin who claims, 'The sole purpose of Christ's incarnation was our redemption. ... [S]ince all Scripture proclaims that to become our Redeemer he was clothed with flesh, it is too presumptuous to imagine another reason or another end.'[133] Calvin discusses the redemption accomplished by Christ in his incarnation as including victory over death, sin and evil powers.

> It was his task to swallow up death. Who but the Life could do this? It was his task to conquer sin. Who but very Righteousness could do this? It was his task to rout the powers of world and air. Who but a power higher than world and air could do this? Now where does life and righteousness, or lordship and authority of heaven lie but with God alone? Therefore our most merciful God, when he willed that we be redeemed, made himself our Redeemer in the person of his only–begotten Son [cf. Rom. 5:8].[134]

Likewise, Packer includes the effects of Christ's three–fold office under the theme of mediation, but his forensic understanding of the atonement occupies the central role in the work of mediation.[135] Any other purposes he sees in the Incarnation are derivative from and not integrated with the main, forensic purpose of his death.[136]

Certainly, Calvin relates the Incarnation to the forensic element of the atonement.[137] However, his position is somewhat more nuanced than Packer's. While focusing on redemption as the purpose of the Incarnation, he lists the forensic purpose of the Incarnation as 'the second requirement,'

---

[132] J.I. Packer, 'Jesus Christ, the Only Saviour', in *Shorter Writings*, 1.47.

[133] Calvin, *Institutes*, II.xii.4.

[134] Ibid., II.xii.2.

[135] Packer, 'Jesus Christ, the Only Saviour', 102–103.

[136] Ibid., 106.

[137] See Calvin, *Institutes*, II.xii.3. He states, 'The second requirement of our reconciliation with God was this: that man, who by his disobedience had become lost, should by way of remedy counter it with obedience, satisfy God's judgment, and pay the penalties for sin. Accordingly, our Lord came forth as true man and took the person and the name of Adam in order to take Adam's place in obeying the Father, to present our flesh as the price of satisfaction to God's righteous judgment, and, in the same flesh, to pay the penalty that we had deserved.'

after first declaring that 'it was necessary for the Son of God to become for us 'Immanuel, that is, God with us' … and in such a way that his divinity and our human nature might by mutual connection grow together.'[138] To Calvin, the Incarnation is oriented toward the union of God and humanity through Christ, from which purpose emerges its formal and forensic significance on the cross. For Packer, however, the forensic purpose of the Incarnation predominates. The theme of union with Christ takes on a derivative status. In *Concise Theology*, he addresses the Incarnation well before he addresses the relational theme of adoption, treating the relational dimension of salvation under the heading of adoption and the forensic and moral benefits of salvation as ramifications of the Incarnation.[139]

Since the value of Christ's incarnation, in Packer's view, is primarily legal or forensic, he gives passing recognition to the epistemological role of the Incarnation, but never develops it. He affirms, 'Since God is Jesus–like, hearing and watching Jesus gives full knowledge of the divine character.'[140] However, his emphasis on the fundamentally propositional character of God's revelation sets the boundary for the epistemological value of the Incarnation, even though he emphasises the personal character of that revelation. By granting logical priority to written revelation in the knowledge of God he actually limits the epistemological role of the Incarnation to the *content* of what is known about God the Father. In his epistemological *method*, however, he gives priority to Scripture.[141] This limitation in the type of knowledge Jesus alone can provide results from the way Packer relates the Incarnate Word of God to the written Word of God. The doctrine of revelation (including the doctrine of Scripture) appears in his theological schema before the doctrine of reconciliation (including the doctrine of Christ).[142]

Packer sets the stage for the Incarnation to provide knowledge of God when he defines the *Logos* in rationalistic terms. He says of Jesus,

> By His words and works, and by the over–all character of His life and ministry, Jesus Christ perfectly revealed God (Jn. I.18, xiv. 7–11). His personal life was a perfect revelation of the character of God; for the Son is the image of God (2 Cor. iv.4; Col. I.15; Heb. I.3), His *logos* (word,

---

[138] Ibid., II.xii.1.

[139] Packer, *Concise Theology*, 108–110, 167–168.

[140] Packer, 'Jesus Christ, the Only Saviour', 106.

[141] Packer differs from Calvin in the arrangement of his theology by dealing first with what he considers the primary epistemological medium of Scripture, whereas Calvin deals first with the object of knowledge, then moves to the medium of Scripture.

[142] Packer, *Concise Theology*, xi–xiv.

regarded as expressing His mind, Jn. I.1 ff.), in whom as incarnate, all the divine fullness dwelt (Col. I.19, ii. 9).[143]

This would seem to provide him the opportunity to make more of the epistemological value of the Incarnation in light of how the Logos would relate God's mind to the human mind. However, two factors indicate that the Incarnation has a decidedly secondary epistemological function for Packer in providing knowledge of God the Father. First, he places Scripture at the forefront of his theological schema. Second, he combines his view that the mind or reason is a discrete, regulative faculty with a dualistic view of truth that treats as one level of 'truth' that which can be perceived through simple ratiocination and permits a knower to be separate from what is known (notwithstanding his insistence that the Holy Spirit must provide enlightenment).

Packer clearly distinguishes between the roles of the Son and the Spirit in the way each mediates knowledge of the Father. The Spirit provides rational knowledge of the Father through illuminating the message of Scripture through the reason to the will, drawing attention to the Son and enabling the will to exercise saving faith in the Son. The Son provides humans with actual relationship with the Father by putting away forensic guilt on the cross and modelling restored humanity.

Packer connects his understanding of the *imago Dei* with his doctrine of Christ by revisiting the themes of relationship and dominion, finding them restored in Christ. Building on the premise that Christ is present through the Holy Spirit he claims,

[W]e were made for relationships, first with God and then with created persons; that this, indeed, is part of God's image in us, inasmuch as God himself is triune, each divine person existing in constant conscious relationship to the other two; and that through the re–creative effect of God's saving relationship to us through Jesus Christ, our capacity for relationships at the deepest level with other human beings, a capacity which sin has in large measure impaired, is progressively restored to us, so that we find ourselves free in Christ for genuinely human relationships in a way that was never true before.[144]

He then appeals to Jesus' present exercise of 'dominion' over human history to provide assurance of God's love and 'positive meaning' in even the most difficult or confusing circumstances.[145]

---

[143] J.I. Packer, 'Revelation', in *NBD*, 1093.
[144] Packer, 'Jesus Christ the Lord', 35.
[145] Ibid., 36.

The Incarnation of the Son of God completes the *imago Dei* in Packer's thought. Human nature is fulfilled in Jesus Christ as his forensic atonement opens the way for his moral character to be emulated. As the *Logos* of God he embodies God's rationality by communicating God's will and character to humanity.

7.3.2 Kenosis

The question of how Christ's humanity relates to all humanity raises the issue of how Jesus' humanity relates to his deity, specifically, how he possesses full deity within the limitations of his humanity. Packer understands 'kenosis' Christology to claim that 'for the Son to experience human limitations properly he had to abandon some divine powers when becoming man.'[146] Packer rejects this view, holding that Christ's possession of the full powers of divinity was in no way compromised by his humanity. This defence against his understanding of kenotic Christology is aimed at four issues: the reality of Jesus' temptation, Jesus' ability to uphold the universe as the *Logos*, the limits of Jesus' knowledge, and the nature of Jesus' personality and consciousness.

First, he defends Jesus' temptation as involving real pain and struggle but not the ability to sin.

> The Gospels show Jesus experiencing human limitations … and human pain … Hebrews shows that had he not thus experienced human pressures – weakness, temptation, pain – he would not be qualified to help us as we go through these things …[147]
> Jesus, being divine, was impeccable (could not sin), but this does not mean that he could not be tempted.[148]

He insists that Jesus was sinless, referring to him as the 'personally innocent and sinless sacrificial victim.'[149] Furthermore, he makes Jesus' sinlessness dependent on the claim that he possessed full deity[150] and denies

---

[146] Ibid., 38.

[147] Packer, *Concise Theology*, 108.

[148] Ibid., 109–110.

[149] Packer, 'The Uniqueness of Jesus Christ', 77.

[150] Ibid., 78. See also *Concise Theology*, 110. He states, 'Being human, Jesus could not conquer temptation without a struggle, but being divine it was his nature to do his Father's will (John 5:19, 30), and therefore to resist and fight temptation until he had overcome it.'

that Jesus' ability to fully experience humanity means that he shared the fallenness that results from sin.[151]

Second, Packer hesitates to take a bold position regarding *how* Jesus upholds the universe (Colossians 1:17) within the limitations of his humanity. He claims that it is unreasonable to assume that Jesus performs all his acts through his humanity. It is possible that in some sense the *Logos* could engage in that activity outside his humanity. Primarily, though, he feels that it is unnecessary for us to know the particulars of how he sustains creation in his humanity.[152]

---

[151] Ibid. Packer's position seems to follow in the tradition of Augustine who sought to protect Christ's nature from sin by interpreting 2 Cor. 5:20–21 ('God … has made him to be sin for us.') to mean that God made Christ to be 'a sacrifice by which our sins maybe remitted.' *On Original Sin*, 37.250. This seems to mark a decided from from the direction implied by Gregory Nazianzen in his classic statement, 'For that which He has not assumed He has not healed; but that which is united to His Godhead is also saved.' He goes on to ask, 'What then of our flesh? Is that not subject to condemnation? You must therefore either set aside the latter on account of sin, or admit the former [the fallenness of the mind] on account of salvation. If He assumed the worse that He might sanctify it by His incarnation, may he not assume the better that it may be sanctified by His becoming Man?' See *To Cledonius the Priest Against Apollinarius,* in *Select Orations*, C.G. Browne and J.E. Swallow (trs.) in P. Schaff and H. Wace (eds.), *A Select Library of Nicene and Post–Nicene Fathers of the Christian Church* (Grand Rapids: Eerdmans, 1983²), 440.

[152] Packer, 'Jesus Christ the Lord', 40–41. Packer elaborated on this point in an interview with the author (2 July 1999), stating that Christ retained his deity by knowing the Father's will and by willingly obeying the Father, that is, by not calling to mind things he had it in him to call to mind and not doing things he had it in him to do. Packer stated his affirmation of the '*extra Calvinisticum*.' He declares that the Son is one Person within the Godhead, but in a way unimaginable to us. That is, the Son operated in two distinct modes. This is the only possibility in light of the cosmic functions of the Logos. He somehow upheld the universe during his incarnation. It was through the Son that the Father and the Spirit experience humanity, so that we cannot say there is something God does not experience or know. In his unpublished course notes ('Systematic Theology B, Man, Sin, and Grace,' section on 'Christ in Christian Thought', 3) he claims that the *extra Calvinisticum* 'goes back to Athanasius!' See also G.C. Berkouwer, *The Person of Christ*, J. Vriend (tr.), (Grand Rapids: Eerdmans, 1954), 93–94. Berkouwer describes the *extra Calvinisticum* as the belief that 'by the Incarnation the Logos is not included in the flesh but that, as the Catechism has it, "since the Godhead is illimitable and omnipresent, it must follow that it is beyond the bounds of the human nature it has assumed, and yet nonetheless is in this human nature and remains personally united to it."' He also affirms that this belief was common in pre–Reformation theology, stating, 'Athanasius already had it and Augustine gave it specific formulation when he wrote: "Christ added to himself that which he was not; he did not lose what he was"' [*Epistle of Leo*, IV].

When addressing the conundrum of how Jesus could have been omniscient while claiming not to know certain things, he claims that 'omniscience should be defined as power to know all that one wills to know, and the Son's ignorance be explained in terms of the fact that he never willed to know by supernatural means more than he knew that the Father willed him to know.'[153] He rejects *kenosis* Christology for giving up too much ground in its attempt to account for the limitations of Jesus' knowledge. Thus, he attempts to steer a middle ground in reconciling the limits of Jesus' human knowledge with the omniscience of his divine nature.

> A question arises about his knowledge while on earth: though sometimes he knew facts at a distance, and seems always to have been utterly and immediately clear on spiritual issues, there were times when he showed ignorance, and it has been suggested that rather than put this down to play–acting (as the Fathers sometimes did) we should posit some pre– incarnate self–emptying of divine powers – in this case, of the capacity to know whatever he willed to know, the capacity which we call omniscience. This *kenosis*–theory is not, however, easy to make fit the facts (because Jesus knew, not only so little, but also so much); nor is it easy to make sense of in its own terms (because it sounds like a di– or tri– theistic fairy story rather than Trinitarian theology).[154]

Packer's response to *kenosis* Christology seems to focus on the purpose of Jesus' various acts (resembling Calvin's differentiation between Jesus' divine works and his human works) as the reconciliation of human limitations and incommunicable divine attributes within the Chalcedonian commitment to two natures in one person.[155]

---

[153] Ibid., 41.

[154] Packer, 'The Uniqueness of Jesus Christ', 79.

[155] Calvin, *Institutes*, II.xiii.4. Calvin states, 'For even if the Word in his immeasurable essence united with the nature of man into one person, we do not imagine that he was confined therein. Here is something marvelous: the Son of God descended from heaven in such a way that, without leaving heaven, he willed to be borne in the virgin's womb, to go about the earth, and to hang upon the cross; yet he continuously filled the world even as he had done from the beginning!' See also Athanasius, *De Incarnatione*, R.W. Thomson (ed., tr.), (Oxford: Clarendon, 1971), 175. Athanasius sounds much like Calvin when he says, 'He was not enclosed in the body, nor was he in the body but nowhere else. Nor did he move the latter while the universe was deprived of his action and providence. But what is most wonderful is that, being the Word, he was not contained by anyone, but rather himself contained everything. And as he is in all creation, he is in essence outside the universe but in everything by his

He offers a more nuanced answer to the question of whether Jesus could truly have been only one person (as claimed by the Council of Chalcedon) while being conscious of his divine identity and genuine humanity. He attempts to deal with the dilemma in three ways. First, he makes Jesus' humanity adjectival to his divine personhood. Jesus' 'humanity was and is, so to speak, adjectival to the person whose it is, and who lives for ever in the consciousness of his identity as God's Son.'[156] The intent here is to make the limitations of humanity less definitive of Jesus' total experience.

Second, he defines humanity in terms of constituent qualities, not the nature of consciousness, stating, 'Of course, in calling Jesus "a man" we mean only to say that no constituent human quality was lacking to him, without raising the question whether his demonstrable dependence on and submission to the Father reflected a consciousness of creaturehood or not ...'[157] This qualification, like the first, defends the integrity of Jesus' humanity by defining it more in terms of the general phenomena of human experience rather than in terms of individual psychology.

Chalcedonians have usually said that Jesus, the Word made–flesh, was man generically and qualitatively, but not 'a man' in the sense of an individual human being with a creaturely identity, and they have wed the technical terms *hypostatic* union and *enhypostasia* to express the thought that Jesus' manhood exists only as the manhood – that is, the sum of human characteristics – of the divine person who is God's eternal Son. And in voicing this thought they certainly have the backing of the apostle John![158]

At the same time, Packer links the ideas of person and personality by stating, 'The Chalcedonian tradition proclaims him as one person, and that must mean one personality, and that must mean one centre of consciousness, one subject–self, one psychological ego.'[159] Apparently, for Packer, Jesus did indeed possess an individual psychological self that allowed him self–conscious relationship with the Father but that did not

---

power, ordering everything and extending his providence over everything. And giving life to all, separately and together, he contains the universe and is not contained, but in his Father only he is complete in everything. So also being in a human body and giving it life himself, he accordingly gives life to everything, and was both in all and outside all.'

[156] Packer, 'Jesus Christ the Lord', 41.

[157] Ibid., 42–43.

[158] Ibid., 42.

[159] Ibid., 41.

constitute a qualitative boundary between humanity and divinity within his person, such that to be human would by definition exclude divinity.

Third, Packer defends and portrays Jesus' humanity in terms of his ability to share in the experience of embodiment (with the exception of sin). He attempts this by defining

> personhood and personality ... in terms of relatedness to other realities. If Jesus was related to the Father in terms of co–eternity, co–equality and co–creatorship, then he was a divine person. If his experience of relatedness to things and people – experience, that is, of thinking, feeling, choosing, giving, receiving; of being hungry, hurt, excited, tired, disappointed; of being aware of the opposite sex, and so on – corresponded in a fundamental and comprehensive way, not indeed to ours as it is, under sin's taint, but to what ours and Adam's would have been had the Fall not happened, then he was a human person. Both things are true so we speak of him as a divine–human person.[160]

He goes on to comment that

> John's statement that the Word became flesh means more than that he encased himself in a physical body. It means that he took to himself, and entered right into, everything that contributes to a fully human experience. ... By virtue of what he experienced as a healthy first–century Jewish male before his death at thirty–three, he can now enter sympathetically into all human experiences, those of girls and women, sick folk, the aged, and addicts (for instance) no less than those of young males like himself.[161]

Packer's use of Chalcedonian Christology to defend against *kenotic* Christology illustrates his commitment to insulate Jesus' divine nature from the sin nature of fallen humanity. In this schema, the atonement as a penal, forensic act is sufficient to satisfy the formal, legal guilt borne by humans for their sin. Jesus' atonement for sin is efficacious only if his divine nature never actually touches fallen human nature.

Summary

J.I. Packer's theological anthropology begins with an understanding of the *imago Dei* that draws heavily upon the history of rationalistic interpretations (most notably in Augustine), yet incorporates the emphasis

---

[160] Ibid., 43.
[161] Packer, 'A Modern View of Jesus', 71.

on righteousness found in John Calvin and John Owen. The *imago Dei*, for Packer, is relational righteousness fulfilled through rationality. As the standard for piety, this relational righteousness is based on the absolute moral purity of God as expressed in God's Law, communicated inerrantly through Scripture, and embodied in Jesus Christ.

Packer emphasises that the whole person is corrupted by sin, depicting the functionality of the person through the categories of rationalistic faculty psychology. Through these faculties the relational righteousness of the *imago Dei* is fulfilled, primarily as God illumines the mind so that the will is renewed. A conundrum appears in this formula, however, when Packer insists that it is through the will that the mind has been blinded by sin. He makes the human will and human reason subject to the effects of sin in different ways. The will must be liberated in order for the other faculties to be properly re–ordered. Yet, the liberation of the will depends on the illumination of the mind. Ultimately, the faculty of reason occupies a dominant or controlling role in the realisation of the restored *imago Dei*. Packer affirms dignity and eschatological hope for those whose faculties are impaired. However, he constructs an anthropology in which the possibility of present relationship with God depends so heavily on the functioning of the faculties that there are no logical grounds upon which those who with impaired faculties could be considered relationally righteous.

The Incarnation figures further into his anthropology and piety by providing for the restoration of the *imago Dei* primarily through Jesus' penal, forensic, substitutionary atonement for sin as the basis of justification. Jesus also provides the perfect model of relational righteousness as the guide for sanctification. His fully divine and fully human natures allow his incarnation to qualify for the saving effect of the atonement. All humanity is not restored through Jesus' humanity; only those whom God has eternally elected to experience the saving value of his atonement.

This summary of Packer's anthropology raises questions that will have bearing on his understanding of piety, that is, on the Christian experience of restoration into the *imago Dei*. First, do his assumptions about the relationship of the Incarnation, truth and revelation reflect a dualism in which soteriology and epistemology are divided in the purpose of the Incarnation? Asked differently, is the epistemological necessity of the Incarnation equal to that of Scripture? If not, is the Incarnation adequate for soteriology when distinguished from epistemology in this manner? If there is indeed an (even subtle) epistemology/soteriology dualism, can the Incarnation actually model a piety in which God is personally known?

Despite the many merits of his approach, Packer's theological anthropology and piety reflect a decidedly rationalistic and individualistic tone. Even though he points out the corporate implications, his starting points and definitions present a picture that must be constantly qualified in order to avoid the charge of individualistic rationalism. His approach could be improved upon were he not to weave faculty psychology so tightly into his understanding of the *imago Dei* from the outset and compartmentalise the role of the Incarnation in his soteriology.

The effects of theological anthropology on piety for J.I. Packer can be further illuminated by investigating the substructure of his theology, that is, his theological method. Themes that have significantly shaped his theological anthropology and piety are deeply embedded in his methodological commitments. Thus, the fullest understanding of theological anthropology's influence on piety for Packer is only possible by considering the theological method that underlies both.

Chapter 8

Theological Method

While theological anthropology makes a major contribution to J.I. Packer's theology of the Christian life, it does not stand alone in this position of influence. Steven L. Porter observes that 'the doctrine of sanctification is … a complex doctrine in that it is the culmination of conclusions reached in just about every other theological category (e.g. theological anthropology, harmartiology [sic.], soteriology, Christology, pneumatology, ecclesiology, etc.)'[1] However, the role of theological anthropology has perhaps been less obvious in the particular stream of evangelicalism to which Packer belongs. This may be partially attributed to a reaction against those who appealed to anthropology in their move away from the 'fundamentals' of the Christian faith since the Enlightenment. Thus, the question of theological anthropology's formative influence on piety takes on added significance when those who embrace a certain piety are unaware of the contributing influences to that piety. They are left with only crippled means of self–reflection and self–correction.

Piety is not fully understood, however, even when its relationship to theological anthropology (or any other doctrine) has been clarified. The interplay of theological method is an issue, like theological anthropology, to which evangelicals in Packer's tradition have not always given due attention. Yet, theological method both shapes and reflects the assumptions made in theological anthropology and piety.

Packer's theological method reflects his views on four of the key issues that have been considered: the nature of the rationality that God and humanity share, the sense in which that shared rationality relates to the nature of the *imago Dei*, the relationship of creation and redemption as expressed in the Incarnate Son of God as the *imago Dei*, and the nature of humanity's experience of that redemption through Christ.[2]

---

[1] S.L. Porter, 'On the Renewal of Interest in the Doctrine of Sanctification: A Methodological Reminder,', *Journal of the Evangelical Theological Society* 45, no. 3 (2002), 415.

[2] See A.E. McGrath, *A Scientific Theology*, vol. I, *Nature* (Grand Rapids: Eerdmans, 2001), 24–25. McGrath recognizes the significance of defining the nature of what God and humanity share, how that is expressed in the Incarnation, and how it is

Discussion of Packer's theological method has intentionally been reserved for the final phase of this study in order to better illustrate the trialogical relationship between his doctrines of theological anthropology and piety, and his theological method. This means of proceeding follows the model proposed by T.F. Torrance when he observed that the means of knowing an object are conditioned by the object that is to be known. He states, 'In the nature of the case a true and adequate account of theological epistemology cannot be gained apart from substantial exposition of the content of the knowledge of God, and of the knowledge of man and the world as creatures of God. It is scientifically false to begin with epistemology.'[3] That is, in Torrance's view, experience and practice must precede explanation.

Packer appears to agree with Torrance's point when he makes commitment to and experience of the object of one's knowledge prerequisite to the possibility of knowing that object. He argues that this approach preserves the integrity of the relationship between theology and its object. A tension exists, he claims, between 'the educational demand that method be unprejudiced, open–minded and scientific – in a word, *rational* – and the churchly requirement that method be faithful and obedient, confessional and doxological – in a word, *religious*.'[4]

---

experienced in redemption when he observes, 'The Christological dimensions of the doctrine of creation are such that the divine rationality – whether this is conceptualized as *logos* or as *ratio* – must be thought of as being *embedded in creation and embodied in Christ*. The same divine rationality or wisdom which the natural sciences discern within the created order is to be identified within the *logos* incarnate, Jesus Christ. Creation and Christ ultimately bear witness to the same God, and the same divine rationality.'

3   T.F. Torrance, *Theological Science* (London: Oxford University Press, 1969), 10. Torrance applies to theological knowledge the insights gained from developments in the field of quantum physics. He contends that modern theology has assumed, in Newtonian fashion, that the epistemological criteria for knowing God can be established prior to and independent of actually being in submissive, personal relationship to God. Quantum physics has demonstrated that an object of knowledge contains within itself the criteria whereby it can be understood. True knowledge of an object, therefore, demands that the knower be willing to allow the structure and criteria of knowledge to be shaped by the actual experience of the object known. In theology this does not imply that God can or must be approached with no prior information or conceptual framework. Rather, it means that those who seek to know God must allow the *actuality* of God's person and work to have methodological priority and control over the conceptual frameworks and epistemological criteria that serve as the means or *possibility* for knowing God.

4   Packer, 'Method, Theological', *NDT*, 424–425.

Furthermore, he suggests that the tension is resolved by allowing the object of knowledge to control the process of knowing.

> [B]elievers who define 'unprejudiced', 'open–minded' and 'scientific' as meaning 'determined by the object of study itself' rather than 'shaped by the anti–Christian positivism of some natural and historical scientists', and who go on to recognize that the central object of study is in fact the living creator, self–revealed in Scripture as triune personal Subject, have already in principle overcome this tension ...[5]

This statement reflects Packer's understanding of a theocentric theological method. Methodological objectivity is defined not by a detached, neutral stance, but by a commitment to the object being studied.

Knowledge of God, for Packer, is possible because of the rationality that human beings share with God as a result of being created in God's image.[6] The nature of true rationality, that is, rationality that leads to true knowledge of God, appears to rely upon personal relationship with the God from whom that rationality derives. Packer reflects a fideistic strain when he says about the possibility of knowing God, '[T]he proof of the pudding is in the eating, and anyone who is actually following a recognised road will not be too worried if he hears non–travellers telling each other that no such road exists.'[7] He insists that the nature of God, as the object of knowledge, governs the process by which that knowledge is obtained.

However, two features of his theology call into question the consistency of this commitment with his practise. First, in the organisation of his theology he treats the doctrine of Scripture before the doctrine of God, thus placing the means of knowledge before the object of knowledge. Second, in his Christology he acknowledges that Christ provides *content* of the knowledge of God, but acknowledges hardly any role of Jesus Christ for the epistemological *process* of knowing God. This move allows other *a priori* epistemological commitments to dictate the means of knowing God.

Packer prioritises God's self–revelation through Scripture because he believes it is direct, propositional communication from God. The human language through which God's revelation is conveyed bears a close correspondence to the reality revealed. The reality conveyed by language is presented as the mind or thoughts of God, which, as God's words, 'the

---

[5] Ibid., 425.

[6] Packer, 'The Adequacy of Human Language', 27. Packer states, 'God is rational and unchanging, and all men in every generation, being made in God's image, are capable of being addressed by him.'

[7] Packer, *Knowing God*, 15.

Holy Spirit causes ... to be reapplied in our own minds and consciences.'[8]
He asks rhetorically, 'Can human language, specifically the language of the
Bible, be divine language also – God's own verbal utterance, whereby he
gives us factual information about himself? Can words of men really be
words of God, conveying to us the Word – that is, the message – of God?
Historically, the answer has been yes.'[9]

He firmly withstands all attempts to deny the capability of human
language to accurately capture divine realities, including attempts by
Friedrich Schleiermacher, Rudolf Bultmann, Paul Tillich, Ludwig
Wittgenstein, Immanuel Kant, Alfred J. Ayers, Ferdinand de Saussure, and,
more recently, Dennis Nineham.[10]

Theological method, to Packer, deals with both the procedures by which
theology is done and the justification for those procedures.[11] He observes
two general types of theological method. The first gives priority to the text
of the Bible as 'the revealed Word of God' that provides authoritative
guidance as the text is progressively understood through research and the
illumination of the Holy Spirit.[12] The second type gives priority to 'the
historical institutional church' as the guide for 'infallibly identifying and
interpreting the Scriptures.'[13] These alternatives differ primarily with
respect to the locus of interpretive responsibility and capability. From this
basic distinction emerge other distinctions such as differing views on the
nature of Biblical authority and the focus of the Holy Spirit's ministry.
Packer clearly supports and utilises the first of these approaches wherein
the locus of interpretation lies with the individual. He develops this
approach in terms of the hermeneutical and exegetical principles upon
which it relies.

8.1 Development

Consideration of Packer's theological method must begin with his evolving
attitude toward the discipline of hermeneutics. Alister McGrath records
Packer's ambivalence toward hermeneutics, prompted largely by Anthony
Thiselton's address to the National Evangelical Anglican Congress at
Nottingham in 1977. Packer left the congress disappointed that it had not
attempted to generate relevant biblical answers to contemporary questions.

---

[8] Packer, 'The Adequacy of Human Language', 27.
[9] Ibid., 23.
[10] Ibid., 27–29.
[11] Packer, 'Method, Theological', 425.
[12] Ibid.
[13] Ibid.

Rather, in his opinion, it opened further questions.[14] His particular concerns about hermeneutics related to the approach taken by Thiselton. McGrath observes, 'Packer never discounted the importance of hermeneutical questions; however, he felt that the approach adopted by Thiselton risked generating a relativistic mindset, which could pervade every aspect of theology.'[15] Since that time Packer has authored numerous monographs on hermeneutics. In 1983 he interacted with Hans–Georg Gadamer's concept of two hermeneutical horizons by offering an affirming modification within an evangelical framework.[16] Then, ironically, in a 1990 article he commends Thiselton's work, stating that he, 'for one, has contributed masterfully and at length in *The Two Horizons* ... and in many other places' to the discussion of issues raised by 'Schleiermacher, Heidegger, Bultmann, Gadamer, Fuchs, Ebeling, and Derrida.'[17] Though Packer claims not to have changed his theology over the years, his later writings make it evident that he has grown in his appreciation for the challenges and the necessity of hermeneutics. He has sought to offer critical analysis of a range of questions that have been developed within the broader theological community.[18]

Those who have influenced Packer's theological method are the same persons he credits for influencing the content of his theology, particularly his conclusions regarding anthropology and piety. He is very much aware of the relationship between his method and his theology, stating, 'If you ask me for models of my kind of Bible–based theologising, I would name John Calvin and the Puritan, John Owen.'[19] He elaborates on the contributions made by Calvin and Owen, and expands his list of contributors by describing those who

> mean by interpretation applying to ourselves the doctrinal and moral instruction of the Bible, read as an historically structured, self–authenticating and self–interpreting organism of revealed truth. Patristic expositor–theologians like Chrysostom and Augustine, and Protestant expositor–theologians like John Calvin, John Owen, Matthew Henry,

---

[14] McGrath, *To Know and Serve God*, 213–218.

[15] Ibid., 218.

[16] Packer, 'Infallible Scripture and the Role of Hermeneutics', 346.

[17] J.I. Packer, 'Understanding the Bible: Evangelical Hermeneutics', in *Shorter Writings*, 3.158.

[18] For example, see his three published addresses to the Conference on Biblical Inerrancy, entitled 'The Challenge of Biblical Interpretation: Creation', 'The Challenge of Biblical Interpretation: Women', and 'The Challenge of Biblical Interpretation: Eschatology', in *Shorter Writings*, 3.171–212.

[19] J.I. Packer, 'In Quest of Canonical Interpretation', in *Shorter Writings*, 3.221.

Charles Hodge, William Hendriksen, and the great if strange Karl Barth, have gone this way. It is essentially the approach which [Brevard] Childs calls 'canonical' and defends as such.[20]

The influences that have shaped Packer's theological method appear somewhat more diverse as they are traced further back, however.

Augustine is clearly the patristic theologian who has most profoundly influenced Packer. Justo L. Gonzalez suggests that the patristic stream represented by Tertullian was predominantly concerned with the notion of law in theology, whereas that represented by Origen focused on the theme of truth.[21] He goes on to argue that Augustine was the premier representative of the Western tradition that drew from and blended these two emphases 'to develop its own brand of orthodoxy.' [22] Gonzalez's paradigm would indicate that Packer's theological method reflects this Augustinian synthesis as it was further shaped by Augustine's Neoplatonic perspectives on the nature of the soul. [23]

The specific influence of the Puritans on Packer's theological method is seen in his hermeneutical use of 'justification by faith' as the definitive theological motif in Scripture. He credits the Puritans with drawing upon the work of the Reformers to correctly identify justification by faith as a primary hermeneutical principle. He states, 'Built into the Puritan hermeneutic was the belief, argued so successfully by the Reformers that their English successors could in practice take it for granted, that justification by faith through Christ by grace is a God–given grid or prism through which all Scripture should be passed in order fully to see what light and truth it has for us.'[24] For the Puritans, he claims,

> The key is justification by faith, and the door (as we should expect) is the Epistle to the Romans. ... These principles of exegesis were handed on to the Puritan brotherhood by Perkins, who laid it down that if one began one's study with Romans, and followed it with John's Gospel, one had

---

[20] Packer, *Truth and Power*, 91.

[21] J.L. Gonzalez, *Christian Thought Revisited: Three Types of Theology* (Nashville: Abingdon, 1989), 27.

[22] Ibid., 101.

[23] Ibid., 102. See also Grenz, *The Social God and the Relational Self*, 84. Grenz suggests that Augustine's Neoplatonism extends its influence through John Locke's empiricism and the Puritans' emphasis on experimental religion and assurance of salvation.

[24] Packer, *Among God's Giants*, 86–87.

the key to the entire Bible; analysis shows that these principles have virtually axiomatic status in all Puritan exegesis.[25]

The Puritans' limited awareness of other worldviews and cultures may partially account for their exclusive adoption of a Western, forensic view of relationship and reconciliation with God. Yet, in light of recent scholarship, it is not clear what criteria Packer uses for determining that justification by faith is the dominant motif of the book of Romans.[26] This choice can be questioned in light of work such as that by N.T. Wright, who argues that justification by faith must be understood as denoting membership among God's people rather than as the Western, forensic concept of legal exoneration.[27]

Packer places great emphasis on the task of application in the hermeneutical enterprise. Nowhere is the importance of application or response more pronounced in Packer's thought than in his philosophy of preaching. When he speaks of those who have shaped his philosophy of preaching, he reflects his belief (following the Puritans) that pastoral intentions must propel theology. The primary influences on his preaching were

John Chrysostom, Augustine, Martin Luther, Hugh Latimer, John Knox, Richard Baxter, John Bunyan, George Whitefield, John Wesley, Jonathan Edwards, Charles Simeon, Robert Murray McCheyne, Charles Spurgeon, John Charles Ryle, Martyn Lloyd–Jones, and Billy Graham [because] … their goal in preaching was to become the means of God's encounter with their hearers, and second, that it was by focusing God's teaching in Scripture that they sought to achieve this purpose.

Preaching, to them, was God–taught information set forth with God–given freedom and forthrightness in a God–prompted application; and they were sure that, as in apostolic days, so in their own and every

---

[25] Ibid., 67.

[26] See also Calvin, *Institutes*, III.xi.4. Calvin assigns the same theological value to 'justification by faith,' both overall and in respect to Paul's thought. He says that Paul 'teaches that the sum of the gospel embassy is to reconcile us to God, since God is willing to receive us into grace through Christ, not counting our sins against us (II Cor. 5:18–20). … Doubtless, he means by the word "reconciled" nothing but "justified."'

[27] Wright, *What St. Paul Really Said*, 125–126. Wright contends that the heart of the Paul's gospel is not the concept of justification by faith, but the claim that 'Jesus Christ is Lord.'

subsequent era, preaching the Bible in this way was, remained, and ever would be basic for the health of the church. That is my belief, too ...[28]

Though his theology differs markedly at points from some individuals on this list (e.g. John Wesley and Billy Graham), they shaped his approach to theology by shaping the way he understands Scripture to function as the source of preaching and of theology.

D. Martyn–Lloyd Jones had perhaps the most powerful contemporary influence on Packer's theological method by way of the preaching ministry. Though Packer claims that Lloyd–Jones had no influence on his theology,[29] Lloyd–Jones made an obvious impact on Packer's theological process through the ministry of preaching.

> The definition [of preaching] I offer – the definition with which I live, which commands my conscience and guides me in preparing specific messages – is theological (that is, Trinitarian and theocentric) and functional (that is, centering on intention and effect). This definition, or concept, was given me in embryo during the winter of 1948–49, when I was privileged on Sunday evenings to sit under the preaching of the late D. Martyn Lloyd–Jones at Westminster Chapel in London, England. ... Since then I have lived, worshiped, and preached under an ineffable sense of the authority of what Dr. Lloyd–Jones was doing.[30]

As Packer indicates, Lloyd–Jones's contribution to his ministry goes far beyond mere homiletical technique. It is consonant with Packer's more explicitly stated methodological views about the hermeneutical importance of a theocentric and applicational approach to biblical interpretation. He states, '[T]heology is essentially a practical matter, and is best studied with a practical end directly – existentially, we might say – in view.'[31] He holds to this practical orientation even when discussing the purpose of knowing God, stating, 'The purpose of knowledge is that we might apply it to life. This is nowhere truer than in Christianity, where true knowledge (knowledge of the true God) is precisely knowledge about God–applied.'[32] In his practical, pastoral orientation to theology he strives to integrate knowledge and application. However, he must make this effort because he assumes a hermeneutical starting point where knowledge and response are

---

[28] Packer, *Truth and Power*, 159.
[29] Packer interview, (2 July 1999).
[30] Packer, *Truth and Power*, 161.
[31] Packer, *Among God's Giants*, 84.
[32] Packer, *Growing in Christ*, 18. See also *Knowing God*, 17–18.

conceived separately. The implications of this knowledge/application split and the two–step hermeneutical process it demands will be taken up later.

Finally, and perhaps most curiously, Packer acknowledges a measure of value in Karl Barth's theological method, despite the fact that he vigorously disagrees with Barth on many points. Of all the significant theological figures that Packer addresses, he expresses the greatest ambivalence about Barth's work. On one hand, the importance of hermeneutics for evangelicals (according to Packer), derives from the same concern that Barth had, i.e. that the Word of God be able to speak meaningfully across the ages and not have its message trapped in time.[33] He commends Barth for challenging the trend among some Protestants to find their theological bearings in the ever–changing moods and values of the surrounding culture. Packer commends Barth's emphasis on the priority of God's self–revelation, the Christological orientation of that revelation in Scripture, and the Christological character of reconciliation. He comments, 'Barth sought to reverse this [trend] by setting forth the self–authenticating witness of a self–authenticating Bible to the self–authenticating risen Christ. This Christ, Barth argued, is present with us through the Spirit as one who by his death and resurrection has already reconciled our sinful race to our Maker. … so far so good, one might think.'[34]

On the other hand, Packer attempts to show where he thinks Barth erred, thus setting in relief his own view that legitimate biblical interpretation depends upon commitments to biblical inspiration and authority, the definitive role of law for gospel, and a restricted view of election and atonement.

> [I]n Barth's working out of his agenda, in which everything depended on how convincingly he handled the Bible, two major problems emerged. First, Barth would not affirm the God–givenness of the biblical text as a divine–human product – God's instructional witness to himself in the form of celebratory and didactic human witness to him.[35]
>
> Second, the attempt to support Barthian distinctives by straightforward biblical exposition repeatedly fails. Barth's negating of general revelation

---

[33] K. Barth, *Church Dogmatics*, I.1., *The Doctrine of the Word of God*, 124,132–133. Barth views the transhistorical and transcultural character of the Word of God as located in God's revelation, which lies behind and is expressed through Scripture (as well as preaching). He speaks of the Bible as the Word of God in a derivative but not an essential sense, stating, 'Thus when it is revelation we are looking at or starting from, we must say of proclamation and the Bible, that they are God's Word, by from time to time becoming God's Word' (132–133).

[34] Packer, *Truth and Power*, 115–116.

[35] Ibid., 116.

as a basis for natural theology; his insistence on the priority of Christ to Adam and of gospel to law (with the supralapsarianism, that is, the view that God directly willed the fall, that this involves); and his universalistic claim that all mankind, having been rejected in Christ's death, was then elected in Christ's resurrection (a claim that makes the non–salvation of anyone at all an apparent impossibility, as Barth acknowledged) – none of these can be made good by any ordinary form of exegesis.[36]

Packer's criticism of Barth provides illumination into a number of his own methodological values. He states, 'Barth's theological exegesis of the most general of biblical imperatives yields only indicatives, not imperatives, because his method requires him to treat the texts as human testimony to what God once said rather than as God's direct indication to all readers concerning his moral will.'[37] Rather, in Packer's view, God's self–revelation takes the form of the law to communicate the nature of God's character. Naturally, then, Packer would emphasise a type of biblical authority that issues directly from God's mind and would take issue with Barth's prioritisation of gospel over law.

Overall, Packer's treatment of Barth shows significant affinity with the overarching theological concerns that drove Barth, but equally significant hesitation about the methodology by which Barth attempted to address these concerns. Packer's specific criticisms reflect and clarify the load that he expects his contrasting positions to bear in his theological system. This prepares the way for a fuller examination of Packer's own theological method.

8.2 Characteristics

8.2.1 Assumptions

8.2.1.1 THE AUTHORITY AND INERRANCY OF THE BIBLE

Biblical inerrancy is a pivotal concept for piety for Packer on the basis of his rationalistic anthropology. God's mind must be flawlessly communicated to the human mind in order for the will to be renewed and the *imago Dei* restored. The implications of that stance are extensive. A commitment to inerrancy constitutes the cornerstone assumption of his

---

[36] Ibid., 117.
[37] Ibid.

theological method.[38] Inerrancy is, he states, 'a methodological commitment that is perceived as part of a Christian's discipleship.'[39] Inerrancy is linked with discipleship, for Packer, because it represents a commitment to allowing Scripture to dictate one's faith and obedience, 'exegeting Scripture in a harmonious way,' and treating Scripture as God's instruction.[40]

Packer defines 'inerrant' as 'only a negative way of saying 'totally true and entirely trustworthy.'[41] He elaborates the word's negative and positive connotations.

> Belief in inerrancy does not commit me to belief in the inerrancy of any particular interpreter, not even myself. Nor does it commit me to disregarding any aspect of the humanness of Scripture. Acceptance of inerrancy does not commit a person to arbitrary and evasive oscillations between literal and non–literal interpretation, either.
>
> On the positive side, asserting inerrancy does commit one to a radical and rigorous *a posteriori* procedure whereby great pains are taken not to read into the text anything that cannot certainly be read out of it. Further, one is committed to robustly embracing all that the Scripture affirms when grammatically and historically exegeted.[42]

Though he denies that inerrancy involves any 'exegetical *a priori*,'[43] it most certainly involves a philosophical *a priori*.

The concept of inerrancy reflects the close correspondence that he sees between the structural and material aspects of God's revelation through Scripture. Following B.B. Warfield, Packer refers to 'two classes' of biblical passages. 'In one of these classes of passages the Scriptures are

---

[38] J.I. Packer, 'Upholding the Unity of Scripture Today', in *Shorter Writings*, 3.141. Packer's insistence that inerrancy is a fact and a logical necessity must be qualified by his admission that 'inerrancy ought always to be held as an article of faith not capable of demonstrative proof but entailed by dominical and apostolic teaching about the nature of Scripture.' However, he believes that the unity of Scripture is now a demonstrable possibility. He claims that 'we have now reached a point in technical evangelical scholarship at which the possibility of an entirely harmonious exegesis of the whole Bible has been shown in such conclusive detail that the century–old liberal assertion that this position cannot be held with intellectual integrity may safely be dismissed as refuted.' However, he does not identify those whose scholarship has demonstrated this conclusion.

[39] Packer, 'Inerrancy and the Divinity and Humanity of the Bible', 164.

[40] Ibid.

[41] Ibid.

[42] Ibid., 164–165.

[43] Ibid., 164.

spoken of as if they were God; in the other, God is spoken of as if he were the Scriptures: in the two together, God and the Scriptures are brought into such conjunction as to show that in point of directness of authority no distinction was made between them.'[44] He claims that together these types of passages 'make an irresistible impression of the absolute identification by their writers of the Scriptures in their hands with the living voice of God.'[45]

While Packer would not go so far as to say that the Scriptures themselves *are* God in an ontological sense, he believes that humans connect with the person of God through understanding the rational content of the mind of God. Scripture is so closely allied with God's mind that to know God personally is impossible apart from the rational content of the Scriptures. Furthermore, he contends that Scripture is not sterile, impersonal information, but the means through which God relates to humanity personally.[46]

Packer's emphasis on the inerrant character of Scripture as the prerequisite for personal knowledge of God appears to reflect the same dualistic epistemological tendencies Dewey J. Hoitenga, Jr. points out in Augustine. Hoitenga points out that Augustine elevates the power of the mind and reason in a manner reminiscent of Plato by separating true knowledge of an object from rational apprehension based either on testimony or sense perception.[47] Augustine, Hoitenga claims, associated true knowledge with vision and belief with propositions. Belief in propositions is thus the prerequisite for knowledge.[48]

Packer uses these Augustinian epistemological assumptions to advance the agenda set forth by the Princeton theologians in their defence of biblical inerrancy. He entered this battle early in his theological career and has continued to participate in it. This method of engagement prioritises Scripture over the Incarnation in epistemological questions because rational knowledge is seen as more verifiable than personal knowledge and is taken to logically precede and convey personal knowledge. Hence, in Packer and the Princetonians, the Incarnation is not offered for epistemological purposes to the same extent as Scripture.

Packer appeals to the notion that Scripture contains one coherent, clear message that transcends historical, geographical, cultural, or other

---

[44] Packer, *'Fundamentalism' and the Word of God*, 86.
[45] Ibid.
[46] Packer, 'Infallible Scripture and the Role of Hermeneutics', 334–335.
[47] Hoitenga, *Faith and Reason from Plato to Plantinga*, 63.
[48] Ibid., 95. Hoitenga asserts that for Augustine, 'The skeptic who believes these propositions has taken the first great step toward *knowing* the objects they represent, whether in the corporeal or incorporeal world.'

phenomena of human experience with relevance and binding authority.[49] Inerrancy guarantees to Packer that the integrity of Scripture's message can be maintained as it reaches across cultural and historical distances. In this way Scripture can teach comprehensible, universally valid truth. The importance of hermeneutics arises from the recognition of this cultural, historical gap. Inerrancy is the premise underlying the possibility meaningful hermeneutical work.

Biblical inerrancy or infallibility (he uses the words interchangeably,[50] though he prefers the term 'inerrancy' for clarity and force of meaning[51]), for Packer, is coextensive with the notion of biblical authority. He asks, '[W]hy does biblical trustworthiness, whether we call it infallibility or inerrancy matter?' His answer is, 'Biblical *veracity* and biblical *authority* are bound up together.' [52] He concludes, '[I]t is important to maintain inerrancy and counter denials of it; for only so can we keep open the path of consistent submission to biblical authority and consistently concentrate on the true problem, that of gaining understanding without being entangled in the false question of how much of Scripture should we disbelieve.'[53]

This commitment to biblical inerrancy as biblical authority serves to direct his theological method. He sees 'biblical authority as methodologically the most basic of theological issues.'[54] Inerrancy appears to play the same role.

[T]he assertion of inerrancy bears directly on our theological method. What it says is that in formulating my theology I shall not consciously deny, disregard, or arbitrarily relativize anything that I find Bible writers teaching, nor cut the knot of any problem of Bible harmony, factual or theological, by assuming that the writers were not consistent with themselves or with each other.[55]

The harmony of Scripture results from the unified mind of God from which Scripture emerges.[56] Thus Packer is able to insist on a tight link

---

[49] Packer, 'Infallible Scripture and the Role of Hermeneutics', 328–332.

[50] Ibid., 349f.. See also *Truth and Power*, 134f. and *'Fundamentalism' and the Word of God*, 94f.

[51] J.I. Packer, 'Encountering Present–Day Views of Scripture', in *Shorter Writings*, 3.21–22.

[52] Packer, *Truth and Power*. 134.

[53] Ibid., 136.

[54] Ibid., 98.

[55] Ibid., 52.

[56] Packer, 'Infallible Scripture and the Role of Hermeneutics', 350. He claims that 'the Scriptures are the products of a single divine mind.' See also 'Upholding the Unity of

between inerrancy, inspiration, and authority as the expression of the link between the structural and material aspects of God's self–revelation in Scripture. However, this link only provides for the *possibility* of accurate and meaningful apprehension of God's mind. It does not necessarily lead to hermeneutical conclusions.[57]

Inerrancy forms the basis, not only for the possibility of absolutely accurate transmission of information from God's mind to the human mind, but also for the possibility of meaningful obedience to God.[58] Thus, Packer's theological method has implications for piety by way of his belief in inerrancy because he believes that the possibility of acceptable obedience to God depends on the possibility of accurate transmission and understanding of God's revelation and expectations for humanity.

Significant implications arise from Packer's particular manner of emphasising the necessity of biblical inerrancy. For instance, his admission that inerrancy is based more on philosophical than on exegetical presuppositions is noteworthy, especially when he connects inerrancy so tightly to the authority and function of God's revelation that obedient discipleship is logically possible only if Scripture functions in the manner that he describes. This would seem to indicate that certain philosophical commitments are more foundational to the Christian life than the Bible itself. It is difficult to overstate the importance of Scripture in Packer's theology of the Christian life. As Packer's understanding of Scripture's role

---

Scripture Today', 138. Here Packer affirms the traditional view of the 'internal coherence' of Scripture, stating, 'As law codes are to be presumed consistent, so all the contents of Scripture, originating as they were held to do from God's mind as their single source, were to be treated as harmonious and were to be interpreted in terms of the principle that the Reformers called the analogy of Scripture or the analogy of the faith (*analogia fidei*).'

[57] Packer, *'Fundamentalism' and the Word of God*, 96. He states, 'The infallibility and inerrancy of biblical teaching does not, however, guarantee the infallibility and inerrancy of any interpretation, or interpreter, of that teaching; nor does the recognition of its qualities as the Word of God in any way prejudge the issue as to what Scripture does, in fact, assert.'

[58] Packer, 'Infallible Scripture and the Role of Hermeneutics', 351–352. He states, 'They [the words "inerrancy" and "infallibility"] are in fact control words, with a self–inviting logic: by affirming biblical infallibility and inerrancy, one commits oneself in advance to receive as God's instruction and obey as God's command whatever Scripture is already known to teach and may in the future be shown to teach. They entail no a priori commitments to specific views, whether of the nature of knowledge or of the correct exegesis of biblical passages that touch on natural events. They indicate only a commitment to the three interpretative principles set out above [interpreting Scripture by Scripture, not pitting one Scripture against another, and interpreting the secondary in light of the primary].'

is unfolded, however, it is discovered that certain philosophical assumptions may be as important to the Christian life as Scripture itself.

8.2.1.2 THE ANALOGY OF FAITH AS RATIONAL COHERENCE

Packer's theological method begins with the philosophical assumption of an inerrant Bible in which God's thoughts are flawlessly communicated to, and are conceptually accessible to human rationality, even with the existence of what he calls 'textual corruptions.'[59] He is clear, however, that belief in inerrancy does not settle actual interpretive questions. He states, 'Faultless formulas about biblical inspiration and authority do us no good while we misunderstand the Bible for whose supremacy we fight.'[60]

The process of biblical interpretation depends upon a methodological commitment to the 'analogy of Scripture' which, for Packer, depicts the internal harmony or rational coherence demanded by a commitment to inerrancy. He observes,

> [W]hat appears to be secondary, incidental, and obscure in Scripture should be viewed in the light of what appears to be primary, central, and plain. This principle requires us to echo the main emphases of the New Testament and to develop a christocentric, covenantal, kerygmatic exegesis of both Testaments ... These three principles together [interpreting Scripture by Scripture, not pitting one Scripture against another, and interpreting the secondary in light of the primary] constitute what the Reformers called *analogia Scripturae*, and the analogy of Scripture, which for clarity's sake I have called the principle of harmony.[61]

He makes this principle synonymous with the 'analogy of faith' as an expression of inerrancy, stating, 'It [inerrancy] prescribes the expository approach that seeks to see how one biblical passage fits with another – the

---

[59] Packer, *'Fundamentalism' and the Word of God*, 90–91. He dismisses the idea that textual corruptions invalidate the possibility of inerrancy, stating, 'It is, of course, true that textual corruptions are no part of the authentic Scriptures, and that no text is free from such slips. But faith in the consistency of God warrants an attitude of confidence that the text is sufficiently trustworthy not to lead us astray. ... This is not to say that textual criticism is needless and unprofitable; but it is to say that, while the work of recovering the original text is not yet finished, and no doubt never will be finished in every minute particular, we should not hesitate to believe that the text as we have it is substantially correct, and may safely be trusted as conveying to us the Word of God with sufficient accuracy for all practical purposes.'

[60] Packer, *Truth and Power*, 138.

[61] Packer, 'Infallible Scripture and the Role of Hermeneutics', 350.

approach that has been called *the analogy of Scripture,* and *the analogy of faith.* It forbids all modes of opposing Scripture to Scripture, of positing real discrepancy and self–contradiction within Scripture ...' [62]

Interestingly, Packer does not use the 'analogy of faith' in reference to historical, patristic interpretation or as synonymous with the 'rule of faith.'[63] As synonymous to the 'analogy of Scripture,' it is oriented only toward the internal harmonization of texts.

8.2.1.3 THE COVENANTAL FRAMEWORK OF THE BIBLE

Packer makes a specific application of the 'analogy of faith' or 'analogy of Scripture' principle when he treats the doctrine of covenants. 'What is covenant theology?' he asks, 'The straightforward, if provocative answer to that question is that it is what is nowadays called a hermeneutic – that is, a way of reading the whole Bible that is itself part of the overall interpretation of the Bible that it undergirds.'[64] The covenants by which God has related to humanity throughout history are reflected in and define the internal coherence of God's revelation in Scripture. Packer claims that neither the gospel, the Word of God as a whole, or the reality of God can be 'properly understood' unless 'viewed within a covenantal frame.'[65]

In the actual operation of Packer's covenantal hermeneutic certain New Testament writings serve as the interpretative grid for the Old Testament. He clarifies this position by stating,

> I see the Old Testament in its totality laying a permanent foundation for faith by its disclosure of God's moral character, sovereign rule, redemptive purpose, and covenant faithfulness and by its exhibiting of the positive dispositions of faith, praise, and obedience contrasted with the negative dispositions of mistrust and rebellion. But on this foundation it sets a temporary superstructure of cultic apparatus for mediating covenant communion with God; and this apparatus the New Testament replaces with the new and better covenant (that is, the better version of God's one gracious covenant) which is founded on better promises and maintained by the sacrifice and intercession of Jesus Christ, the better and greater high priest. This amounts to saying that I think the Old Testament should

---

[62] Packer, *Truth and Power*, 103.

[63] See B.A. Demarest, 'Analogy of Faith', in *EDT*, 44. Demarest points out that Augustine used the principle of 'analogy of faith' in reference to the Apostles' Creed as a hermeneutical safeguard. In *Truth and Power*, 243, Packer claims, 'The phrase *analogy of faith* stands for the principle of interpreting Scripture harmoniously, letting what is basic and clear illuminate what is peripheral and obscure.'

[64] Packer, 'On Covenant Theology', 9.

[65] Ibid., 12,13,15.

be read through the hermeneutical spectacles that Paul (Romans and Galatians), Luke (Gospel and Acts), Matthew, and the writer to the Hebrews provide.[66]

Thus, in Packer's covenantal framework the cultic themes of the Old Testament are interpreted in light of the New Testament writings that most clearly develop the theme of a new covenant. The covenants, then, serve as the regulating hermeneutical principle for the 'analogy of faith.'

It must be noted that Packer considers the Westminster Confession as the definitive expression of covenant theology, claiming that after the contributions of, e.g. 'Huldreich Zwingli, Henry Bullinger, John Calvin, Zacharias Ursinus, Caspar Olevianus, Robert Rollock, John Preston, and John Ball ... the Westminster Confession and Catechisms gave it confessional status.'[67] Though Packer thinks covenant theology is best expressed in the Federal Calvinism articulated at Westminster, he also recognises the possibility that later developments in Calvinism may have departed from Calvin's intentions. For example, he refers to Theodore Beza who

> removed predestination back from where Calvin put it in his final (1559) revision of the *Institutes* – in book III, after the gospel and the Christian life, so that it appears as undergirding a known salvation, as in Romans 8:29–38 – and subsumed it once more under the doctrine of God and providence, as the medievals had done: which was an invitation to study the gospel promises in the light of predestination, rather than vice versa (an invitation also given – regrettably, it may be thought – by the Westminster Confession).[68]

Consistent with that sentiment, he applauds Calvin for his treatment of predestination.

> The way you dealt with predestination, in particular, strikes me as an all–time brilliancy. Like Paul in Romans, you separated it from the doctrine of providence and postponed it till you had spelled out the gospel, with its *bona–fide*, whosoever–will promises; then you brought in the truth of election and reprobation, just as in Romans 8 and 9, not to frighten anyone, but to give believers reassurance, hope, and strength.[69]

---

[66] Packer, 'In Quest of Canonical Interpretation', 217.
[67] Packer, 'On Covenant Theology', 21.
[68] Packer, 'Arminianisms', in *Shorter Writings*, 4.305.
[69] J.I. Packer, 'Fan Mail to Calvin', *CT*, (14 January 1991), 11.

A tension appears in Packer's theology, however, when he equivocates about the theological priorities expressed in the organization of the Westminster Confession while at the same time treating its theological formulae as soteriologically definitive when he addresses predestination and atonement in his own work. In *Concise Theology*, he resembles the procedure of the Westminster Confession (which he questions) and seems to ignore the procedure of Calvin (which he extols) by placing predestination under the doctrine of God and treating it before the Gospel.[70]

8.2.1.4 THE CANONICAL CHARACTER OF THE BIBLE

In one sense, Packer's commitment to a canonical approach to Scripture is merely an affirmation of the historic, Protestant acceptance of the sixty–six books of the Old and New Testaments as inspired by God.[71] However, he also uses 'canonical' to denote the nature of the theological task as it articulates God's message throughout the ages so as to evoke obedient response. Packer follows a conventional hermeneutical distinction between interpretation and application.[72] A canonical approach to Scripture enables the applicational aspect of hermeneutics.

---

[70] Packer, *Concise Theology*, table of contents. Packer begins his theological structure with the doctrine of Scripture then addresses 'Interpretation,' and 'General Revelation.' He includes more categories than the Confession but follows the order of 'Creation,' 'Sovereignty,' 'Predestination,' and 'Trinity' (with various related themes interspersed). See also *The Westminster Confession of Faith: An Authentic Modern Version*, v. The order of the Confession begins with 'Holy Scripture,' 'God and the Holy Trinity,' 'God's Eternal Decrees,' 'Creation,' and 'Providence.'

[71] Packer, 'In Quest of Canonical Interpretation', 214–215. He states, 'The first thing to say is that I perceive the sixty–six books of the Protestant canon to be the Word of God given in and through human words. Canonical Scripture is divine testimony and instruction in the form of human testimony and instruction.' Interestingly, Packer appears to send mixed signals about the value of experience in validating and interpreting the text of Scripture. He contends that the cumulative experience of the church is a source of validation for the canon. 'Then, theologically, I see the attestation of the Protestant canon by the Holy Spirit growing stronger year by year as more and more Bible readers have the sixty–six books authenticated to them in actual experience' (216). Yet, in the same article he disallows experience as a criterion for interpretation, stating, 'The truth of theological assertions should be decided by asking whether they faithfully echo Scripture, not whether God has blessed folk who have held them' (214). At best, this presents an unclear picture of exactly what experience can and cannot accomplish in regard to Scripture.

[72] This methodological distinction can be found in numerous hermeneutics texts that have been the mainstay of evangelical hermeneutics. See, for example, A. Berkeley Mickelsen, *Interpreting the Bible* (Grand Rapids: Eerdmans, 1963), 356–357; Bernard Ramm, *Protestant Biblical Interpretation* (Grand Rapids: Baker, 1970³),

He reflects on the task of systematic theology from the perspective of a canonical approach, equating it to the applicational task of hermeneutics.

[O]ne purpose of systematic theology is to achieve what I call a 'canonical interpretation' of Scripture. I mean by that a theological exegesis showing what each part of canonical Scripture means for us today; in other words, seeing what word to us from the Lord is breaking forth from what is rightly called 'God's Word written' (Anglican Article 20); or, to use old–fashioned language, telling us how what we read in the Bible applies to us; or, to put it in modern terms, grasping what God is communicating to us, here and now, in and through the inspired text.[73]

A canonical approach to Scripture, for Packer, like a covenantal framework, assumes the inner coherence of Scripture. It moves a step further toward fulfilling the purpose of God's revelation by making that coherence evident. Packer reflects on his theological work by saying,

[I]f I know myself I am first and foremost a theological exegete. My constant purpose was and is to adumbrate on every subject I handle a genuinely canonical interpretation of Scripture – a view that in its coherence embraces and expresses the thrust of all the biblical passage and units of thought that bear on my theme – a total, integrated view built out of biblical material in such a way that, if the writers of the various books knew what I had made of what they taught, they would nod their heads and say that I had got them right.[74]

Both theological and canonical interpretation are aimed at developing the implications of Scripture in a manner that is congruent with the author's original intent.

Packer equates canonical exegesis with theological exegesis, affirming Brevard S. Childs's emphasis on the former and Karl Barth's emphasis on the latter. This type of exegesis, he claims, is '"churchly" (as opposed to 'worldly') in that it (1) reads all Scripture as witness to the living God and (2) reads each book of Scripture as part of the total canon that bears this

---

112–113; Grant R. Osborne, *The Hermeneutical Spiral: A Comprehensive Introduction to Biblical Interpretation* (Downers Grove: InterVarsity, 1991), 14; and, more recently, W.W. Klein, C.L. Blomberg, and R.L. Hubbard, Jr., *Introduction to Biblical Interpretation* (Nashville: Thomas Nelson, 2002[2]), 401ff.

[73] J. I. Packer, 'Understanding the Differences', in Alvera Mickelsen (ed.), *Women, Authority and the Bible* (Downers Grove: InterVarsity, 1986), 296.

[74] Packer, 'In Quest of Canonical Interpretation', 223.

witness.'[75] By focusing on Scripture's relationship to the living God as a witness, Packer reflects his belief that Scripture is relevant across time and culture because it is the eternal Word of the living God. Interpreted canonically, Scripture's identification with the Word of God becomes evident as it is applied to the lives of people in all places and times.

8.2.1.5 THE CHRISTOLOGICAL FOCUS OF THE BIBLE

The internal coherence of Scripture, upon which Packer's theological method depends, is reflected in his commitments to the inerrancy, covenantal framework, and canonical character of Scripture. All of these features culminate in Jesus Christ, who is the innermost principle of Scripture's internal coherence.[76] Christology sustains the commitment to inerrancy in three ways for Packer. First, it demonstrates the credibility of belief in inerrancy. Second, it demonstrates the essential relationship between inerrancy and authority. Third, it provides an essential hermeneutical criterion.

Packer defends the plausibility of an inerrant written Scripture on the basis of the affirmation that Jesus was both fully divine and fully (though sinlessly) human. Jesus' moral perfection is sustained by the dominance or definitive role of his divinity in the relationship between his divine and human natures. Likewise, Packer argues for the perfection (inerrancy) of the biblical text because its divine origin defines the nature of its divine–human character. He states,

> Conservationist [Packer's descriptor for those who reject the anti–supernatural assumptions of liberalism and 'hold to the old paths'] reflection on both the divine–human person of Jesus Christ and the divine–human text of Holy Scripture starts by affirming the reality of the divinity and then celebrates the exaltation of the humanity in union with it, whereas liberal reflection on both starts by emphasizing the limits of the humanity and ends up scaling the divinity down.[77]

---

[75] Packer, 'Infallible Scripture and the Role of Hermeneutics', 345.

[76] Packer, 'Upholding the Unity of Scripture Today', 137. Packer applauds the efforts of Karl Barth and T. F. Torrance in attempting to counter 'the liberal idea of an ultimate evolutionary pluralism in Scripture' with a 'theologically unitive hermeneutics based on Chalcedonian Christology.'

[77] Packer, *Truth and Power*, 121. It could be asked whether it is fair to polarise the positions in this manner. Is it logically necessary that taking Jesus Christ's humanity as a starting point for understanding his nature results in compromising the nature of his divinity?

This view assumes that the divine nature of Scripture is bound up with a particular transmission process.[78] Without overriding the uniqueness of each writer's personality, style, and circumstances God directly communicated thoughts to and through the human writers of the text.[79]

This direct link with the mind of God implies for Packer that the error–free character of the text[80] and the authority of its message are correlative. Inerrancy and authority, while deriving ultimately from the mind of God, are expressed in and validated by the divine–human nature of Jesus Christ. He rejects the argument for biblical errancy that is based on the comparison between the divine–human character of the Bible and Jesus' divine–human nature. Instead, he reverses the comparison and argues for an inerrant Bible based on the possibility that Jesus was sinless while being fully divine and fully human. He suggests that 'we take it as indicating something about the reality of the union between the divine and the human …'[81]

The person of Jesus Christ constitutes not only the plausibility of inerrancy, but the consummate content of what is inerrantly communicated. He is the supreme expression of God's verbal or propositional revelation. Packer takes up this point by stating, 'Now the basic form of God's self–disclosure, as reported in Scripture, was His direct speech: speech to and through patriarchs and prophets (including apostles), who were no strangers

---

[78] Packer, *'Fundamentalism' and the Word of God*, 77. Packer follows B.B. Warfield's exegesis of 2 Tim. 3:16 and the view that inspiration 'teaches the divine origin of "all Scripture."'

[79] Ibid., 78. 'Inspiration did not necessarily involve an abnormal state of mind on the writer's part, such as a trance, or vision, or hearing a voice. Not did it involve any obliterating or overriding of his personality. Scripture indicates that God in His providence was from the first preparing the human vehicles of inspiration for their predestined task, and that He caused them in many cases, perhaps in most, to perform that task through the normal exercise of the abilities which He had given them.' Packer goes on to deny what he calls the '"dictation" or "typewriter" theory of inspiration' as it would imply a certain *process* by which Scripture was conveyed to human authors. Though dictation would describe what Packer believes about the actual *product* of inspiration, he prefers the term '*accommodation*,' to describe the process. This word indicates 'that God completely adapted His inspiring activity to the cast of mind, outlook, temperament, interests, literary habits and stylistic idiosyncrasies of each writer' (p. 79).

[80] Ibid., 98. Packer adds the qualification that 'the infallibility and inerrancy of Scripture are relative to the intended scope of the Word of God. Scripture provides instruction that is true and trustworthy, not on every conceivable subject, but simply on those subjects with which it claims to deal.'

[81] Packer, *'Fundamentalism' and the Word of God*, 82–84. See also G.C. Berkouwer, *Holy Scripture*, J.B. Rogers (tr.), (Grand Rapids: Eerdmans, 1975), 202. Berkouwer also takes note of this issue and of Packer's response to it.

to the prophetic experience of God's direct speech, and supremely from the lips of His incarnate Son.'[82] Jesus' teachings constitute the ultimate form of God's self–revelation. Inerrancy and authority necessarily go together because of the parallel between Jesus as direct, divine–human revelation from God and Scripture as direct, divine–human revelation from God. Thus, Packer understands the revelatory function of even the Incarnation in a linguistic and rationalistic manner. The Incarnation directs Packer's attention back to the technical precision and rational accessibility of the Scriptural text for epistemological access to God's revelation.

It is at the question of Christ's relationship to Scripture that Packer parts company with some in the Dutch Reformed tradition. For example, he responds to (his perception of) G.C. Berkouwer's argument that 'inerrancy keeps Christians from concentrating on Christ and salvation, which is Scripture's central theme,' by stating, 'I agree with Berkouwer, as all Christians must, that the historical, space–time Christ is the goal and reference point (*scopus*) of all Scripture, but I see no incompatibility between acknowledging this and highlighting the truthfulness of Scripture in its presentation of the historical, space–time events by which this Christ came, and comes, to be known.'[83]

Packer bases his criticism of Berkouwer on the assumption that Christ cannot stand as the interpretive lens for Scripture unless Christ is first known through Scripture. Scripture must be inerrant in order to give adequate witness to Christ. Thus, for Packer, Scripture is the interpretive lens for Christ before Christ is the interpretive lens for Scripture.

However, Packer clearly attempts to emphasise Jesus Christ as the focal point and, in some sense, the interpretive criterion for Scripture. He observes, 'The person and place of the Christ of space–time history is the interpretative key to all Scripture; the Old Testament is to be read in the light of its New Testament fulfillment in and by him, just as the New Testament is to be read in the light of its Old Testament foundations on which that fulfillment rested.'[84] The salient feature of Packer's methodology at this point is that the validity and epistemological reliability of Jesus Christ presupposes an inerrant Bible.

Christology also influences Packer's thought about the task of identifying the contemporary and personal implications or applications of Scripture. The legitimacy of application depends upon the Incarnation as the bridge between the universal and the particular. He claims, 'The particular reality of Jesus Christ – his person, his work, his ministry, his

---

[82] Packer, 'Infallible Scripture and the Role of Hermeneutics', 335.
[83] Packer, *Beyond the Battle for the Bible*, 54.
[84] Packer, *Truth and Power*, 192.

mediation – has got to be applied and made relevant by Christ's messengers to the whole life of all men, everywhere, in every age. The application universalises the particular, so that the particular reality is in truth a reality for everybody.'[85]

The function of Christology in application is dramatically reflected in Packer's view of preaching. He states,

> [A]s one charged, like Paul, to declare 'the whole counsel of God' (Acts 20:26–27) – that is, all that God does for mankind and all that he requires in response – the evangelical preacher will relate the specific content of all his messages to Christ, his mediation, his cross and resurrection, and his gift of new life to those who trust him. In that sense, the preacher will imitate Paul, who when he visited Corinth … 'resolved to know nothing … except Jesus Christ and him crucified' (1 Cor. 2:2). That does not mean, of course, that the evangelical preacher will harp all the time on the bare fact of the crucifixion. It means, rather, that he will use all lines of biblical thought to illuminate the meaning of that fact; and he will never let his exposition of anything in Scripture get detached from, and so appear unrelated to, Calvary's cross and the redemption that was wrought there; and in this way he will sustain a Christ–centred, cross–oriented preaching ministry year in and year out, with an evangelistic as well as pastoral thrust.[86]

Thus, Packer attempts to present Jesus Christ as the comprehensive criterion for both interpreting and applying Scripture. Yet, as he further develops the actual procedures for these tasks, the Christological criterion rarely comes into view with regard to exegesis and interpretation of authorial intent in the text. It must be asked whether a truly Christological destination can realised (through application) if Christology does not just as obviously shape the procedure from the outset (through exegesis and interpretation).[87]

---

[85] J.I. Packer, 'Aspects of Authority', in *Orthos* (papers from Fellowship of the Word and Spirit, no. 9, n.d.), 16.

[86] J.I. Packer, 'Why Preach?' in *Shorter Writings*, 3.252–253.

[87] See John Webster, 'Hermeneutics in Modern Theology: Some Doctrinal Reflections', *SJT* 51, no. 3 (1998), 309–312. Webster seeks to demonstrate that Western theology reflects a trend to do theology apart from explicitly doctrinal considerations. He states, 'Strict governance by Christian doctrine is largely absent from most contemporary Christian writing in hermeneutics.' He goes on to contend that '[t]he invocation of theological categories is not seen as furnishing the primary, irreducible language of Christian depiction of the interpretative process, but at best as providing a kind of backcloth or context for the undisturbed use of non–theological theory.'

An inconsistent, or at least puzzling feature of Packer's use of Christology in his theological method is that he places Christology at the centre of theology, while only citing theism in general as the framework for Christian theology. He observes, '[T]houghts of God can never be right unless they operate within a theistic frame. For theism, as defined, is the *paradigm* of Christian theology – that is, the basic conceptual structure in terms of which all particular views of doctrine should be formed and focused. Views that reflect a different paradigm may be interesting, but they cannot be fully Christian.'[88]

This reference to theism as the paradigm for Christian theology is curious because, as previously shown, Packer seeks to make Christology the defining paradigm for the task of applying Scripture to life and even for the overall thrust of Scripture. He seems to see the same hermeneutical effects for a Christological approach to Scripture as for a canonical approach to Scripture. When he then equates a canonical approach with the theological task itself and appeals more broadly to 'theism' as the framework for theology he appears vague about the specific way in which Christology would define a theistic framework for theology. Stephen Neill argues that in *Knowing God*, Packer is not sufficiently 'Christo–centric in his approach.' He continues that, 'To be fair to Dr. Packer, Jesus Christ always does come in somewhere in his presentation of each theme, but sometimes at the end of an argument, where we would bring him in at the

---

Furthermore, he traces this tendency in conservative Protestantism, despite its self–conscious efforts to the contrary. Packer's own theological roots are evident in Webster's claim that '[c]onservative Protestantism has produced an entire armory of materials on just this point – though their relative lack of sophistication, their entanglement in polemics and apologetics, their reliance on scholastic or nineteenth century construals of the nature of the Bible and their generally rationalistic understanding of theological method, have all contributed to the marginalisation of this strand of Christian thought.' Webster finds in Spinoza (312) a model of a highly rationalistic approach to sacred literature to which Packer's methodological assumptions bear remarkable resemblance. 'The fundamental axiom' of this approach 'is that of the aseity and transcendence of the interpretive act.' The theological ramification of this approach, Webster points out, is that '[t]he integration of the doctrines of Trinity and revelation is always threatened when revelation, isolated from consideration of the being of God, becomes a theological epistemology and is developed in such a way as to furnish a non–dogmatic prologue to dogmatics proper' (323).

[88] J.I. Packer, 'Taking Stock in Theology', in J.C. King (ed.), *Evangelicals Today* (Guildford and London: Lutterworth, 1973), 25.

beginning.'[89] This feature raises a question concerning whether Packer's theological method is truly as Christological as he claims.[90]

At this point Packer appears to provide an intriguing combination of values in his theological method. On one hand, he emphasises that Scripture has not accomplished its purpose until it is has been obeyed. On the other hand, the actual hermeneutical methodology he teaches makes it appear that the meaning of Scripture can, at least in theory, be discerned apart from obedience to that text. This division between meaning and response is possible because he operates with a predominantly descriptive understanding of the nature of language.[91] This limitation on the way Christology actually functions in his hermeneutic results from the particular manner in which he differentiates between the acts of interpretation and application in hermeneutics.[92]

---

[89] Neill, Review of *Knowing God*, 77.

[90] See E.A. Dowey, Jr. *The Knowledge of God in Calvin's Theology* (New York: Columbia University Press, 1952), 246–247. Packer's attempt to be Christological appears to resemble Dowey's description of Calvin's Christocentrism. Dowey states, 'The center of Calvin's thought, around which all else moves, is the divine provision for and the divine accomplishment of the salvation of sinful humanity through Jesus Christ to the glory of God alone. That is to say, Calvin's thought has a *soteriological center* which dominates all his theology, but not all elements equally. Although Calvin's soteriology proper is profoundly Christocentric, it is not strictly accurate to say that his thought or theology as a whole is Christocentric. This is true because there is an inherent dialectic within his soteriology by which it is related to and is set within non–soteriological elements upon which it depends for its meaning.'

[91] See A.C. Thiselton, *New Horizons in Hermeneutics* (Grand Rapids: Zondervan, 1992), 16. Thiselton draws attention to the work of Ernst Fuchs and J.L. Austin in which 'they rightly focussed n the capacity of language *to perform acts*: in the case of some parables, to *make pledges or offers*, to *effect acts of forgiveness*, to *subvert* institutional assumptions, and so forth.' Packer apparently ascribes to Scripture a more descriptive than performative character. See also S.C. Barton, 'New Testament Interpretation as Performance', *SJT* 52, no. 2 (1999), 179. Barton suggests that the 'performance metaphor has significant potential for the revitalization of NT interpretation.'

[92] A sharp distinction between interpretation and application is not uniformly upheld, even by evangelical theologians. As previously cited, H.M. Conn (*Eternal Word and Changing Worlds*, 220) contends that understanding the original meaning of a text is impossible apart from personal response to it. Conn, a Reformed missiologist, challenges the history of theological method characteristic of his own tradition, claiming that it has departed from Calvin's theological method. Conn claims that Calvin confronted the abstractionist or essentialist tendency of scholastic theology of his day by practising contextualized, pastoral theology. However, according to Conn, many in the Reformed tradition that developed since Calvin have exhibited the same essentialist, abstractionist tendencies that Calvin rejected (218–219). He contrasts the

8.2.2 *The Nature of Hermeneutics*

Packer's attitude toward the value of hermeneutics seems to have changed over the years. Despite his earlier hesitations about hermeneutics, he later admits and affirms the importance of hermeneutics for piety, stating that 'a life transformed by Scripture from an ego–trip into an intoxication with Jesus Christ is evidence of understanding at the deepest and truest level. Thus, it appears at last that evangelical hermeneutics belong to the discipline of Christian discipleship ...'[93] Hermeneutics now occupies a place of value in his theology inasmuch as it is prerequisite for the rational apprehension of Scripture upon which piety depends. He now appears to see hermeneutics less as a uniformly deconstructive effort destined for relativism and more as synonymous with the process of doing theology.[94]

8.2.2.1 THE RELATIONSHIP OF INTERPRETATION AND APPLICATION

One highly salient feature of Packer's approach to hermeneutics is his adherence to the assumption that the original, intended meaning of the Scriptural text (authorial intent) is at least theoretically ascertainable through an abstract or objective process of exegesis that precedes contemporary, personal response to (application of) the text. He describes this sequential methodology as follows.

> [E]vangelical biblical interpretation proceeds by the following three stages: exegesis, synthesis, and application.

---

work of Louis Berkhof, as a model of essentialist, Reformed theology, (and whom Packer admits to following) with G.C. Berkouwer, whose theological work grew from applicatory or pastoral concerns. In similar fashion R.S. Anderson presents a case for 'Christopraxis as a hermeneutical criterion.' See R.S. Anderson, 'The Resurrection of Jesus as Hermeneutical Criterion', pt. I *TSF Bulletin* 9 (January–February 1986), 11. In Anderson's model, to use a Christological hermeneutic means that the message of Scripture is interpreted in light of what is congruent with the life giving, restoring work of God that is validated, defined, and carried out by the Risen Christ. This type of Christological hermeneutic differs from Packer's Christological hermeneutic by allowing experiential exigency to provide the starting point for theological reflection on the text of Scripture. Experience is not the final determinant of the text's meaning, but is the context for which the meaning of Scripture is to discerned as it gives guidance on the appropriate response to the work of the Risen Christ in that situation. Packer's model, in contrast, moves in the other direction from the text of Scripture to personal exigency.

93 Packer, 'Understanding the Bible: Evangelical Hermeneutics', 159.

94 Packer, 'Infallible Scripture and the Role of Hermeneutics', 334. Though careful to emphasise the necessity of contextual exegesis he claims that, 'in idea theology is neither more nor less than an analytical and applicatory echo of the given Word of God.'

Exegesis means bringing out of the text all that it contains of the thoughts, attitudes, assumptions, and so forth – in short, the whole expressed mind – of the human writer.

Synthesis here means the process of gathering up and surveying in historically integrated form the fruits of exegesis – a process that is sometimes, from one standpoint and at one level, called 'biblical theology' in the classroom and at other times, from another standpoint and at another level, called 'exposition' in the pulpit.

Application means seeking answers to these questions: If God said and did in the circumstances recorded what the text tells us He said and did, what does He say and what is He doing and what will He do to us in our circumstances?[95]

Insisting that, '[e]vangelical interpretation is inductive from first to last,'[96] he points out the need follow the Renaissance and Reformation principle 'that all ancient documents, biblical texts among them, should be understood *literally* as opposed to *allegorically*.'[97]

In the starting point of this process, Packer makes the possibility of application contingent on the prior work of discerning the essential meaning of the text, though he is clear that the work of interpretation is not complete apart from application.[98] This distinction between interpretation and application is not absolute for Packer. He adds nuance to it through his commendation of Gadamer's two–horizons approach, in which the situation of the original text and the situation of the interpreter inform each other as the twin foci of an elliptical process.

The insight is that at the heart of the hermeneutical process there is between the text and the interpreter a kind of interaction in which their

---

[95] Ibid., 345.

[96] Packer, 'Understanding the Bible: Evangelical Hermeneutics', 153.

[97] Ibid., He goes on to develop three additional principles. 'The second principle is: the *coherence, harmony, and veracity* of all biblical teaching must be taken as our working hypothesis in interpretation. What this means is that Scripture must be expounded in accordance with Scripture' (155). 'The third principle is: interpretation involves *synthesizing* what the various biblical passages teach, so that each item taught finds its proper place and significance in the *organism* of revelation as a whole' (155). 'The fourth principle is: *the response for which the text calls* must be made explicit. All the biblical books were written to build up their readers in faith, obedience, and worship, and interpretation is neither complete nor correct until the material exegeted and synthesized has been so angled in presentation as to further this, its original purpose' (157).

[98] Packer, 'The Adequacy of Human Language', 27.

respective panoramic views of things, angled and limited as these are, 'engage' or 'intersect' – in other words, appear as challenging each other in some way. ... Every interpreter needs to realize that he himself stands in a given historical context and tradition, just as his text does, and that only as he becomes aware of this can he avoid reading into the text assumptions from his own background that would deafen him to what the text itself has to say to him.[99]

Though he admits in this statement that a valid interpretation of a text depends on interplay between the contemporary interpreter's situation and the original writer's intent, he limits the effect of this interplay to the mitigation of cultural, historical myopia that can misdirect the interpretive process. The individual interpreter's personal experience does not register as a valid interpretive factor.

Interestingly, however, Packer considers his approach to be an integrated view of biblical hermeneutics, insisting that 'understanding is never abstract and theoretical; it is always understanding of the work and will of the living God who constantly demands to change us.'[100] He readily admits the effect of 'what sociologists call *cultural prejudice*' and that as a result, 'we shall always be men and women of our time, nurtured by our cultural milieu and also narrowed by it.'[101] This integrated process is depicted as a hermeneutical spiral in which the activities of exegesis, synthesis, and application produce a theology that then determines the integrity of those activities.

I use the phrase 'hermeneutical circle' to express the truth ... that our exegesis, synthesis, and application is determined by a hermeneutic – that is, a view of the interpretative process – that is determined by an overall theology, a theology that in its turn rests on and supports itself by exegesis, synthesis, and application. Thus defined, the circle is not logically vicious; it is not the circle of presupposing what you ought to prove, but the circle of successive approximation, a basic method in every science. From this standpoint it might be better to speak of the

---

[99] Packer, 'Infallible Scripture and the Role of Hermeneutics', 338–339.

[100] Packer, *Truth and Power*, 147. While here Packer subsumes the act of exegesis under the heading of hermeneutics, he elsewhere relates the two terms in the opposite manner, placing hermeneutics as a discipline within the activity of exegesis. See also J.I. Packer, 'Maintaining Evangelical Theology', in J.G. Stackhouse, Jr. (ed.), *Evangelical Futures: A Conversation on Theological Method* (Grand Rapids: Baker, 2000), 185.

[101] Ibid., 145–146.

hermeneutical *spiral*, whereby we rise from a less exact and well–tested understanding to one that is more so.[102]

Nevertheless, Packer treats the process of ascertaining the original meaning of the text as a first step to which he gives less emphasis to the Holy Spirit's role than with the subsequent steps. Thus, he states, 'the first task is always to get into the writer's mind by grammatico–historical exegesis of the most thoroughgoing and disciplined kind, using all the tools provided by linguistic, historical, logical, and semantic study for the purpose.'[103] He enjoins 'empathy' as the prerequisite for this initial phase. That is, the interpreter must avoid the myth of a 'cultivated detachment that became a cramping convention in academic Bible work, even that of the Reformers' most faithful heirs, about a century and a half ago.'[104] Still, he differentiates between the approaches needed for the interpreter to discern what the text *meant* and what it *means*.

> Understanding of what Scripture means when applied to us – that is, of what God in Scripture is saying to and about us – comes only through the work of the sovereign Holy Spirit, who alone enables us to apprehend what God is and see what we are in His eyes. (This is a different point from that made above: the empathy of which I spoke enables us to grasp what Scripture *meant*, but it takes the Spirit's enlightenment to show us what it *means*.)[105]

In this schema the overall hermeneutical act is incomplete without personal application of the text. However, by dividing the process into two parts – one that depends on the unassisted rational process and the other that depends on the Holy Spirit's illumination, Packer appears to introduce into hermeneutics a distinction that makes the full apprehension of the Word of God less than fully dependent on God. His advocacy of a 'hermeneutical spiral' is thus more uni–directional than it appears.

This epistemological distinction between the interpretation or exegesis of Scripture's original meaning and its meaning for contemporary audiences is nowhere better illustrated than in his claim that '[t]he truth of theological assertions should be decided by asking whether they faithfully echo

---

[102] Packer, 'Infallible Scripture and the Role of Hermeneutics', 348. Interestingly, Packer's use of the phrase 'hermeneutical spiral' in this 1983 publication predates Grant Osborne's use of the same phrase as the title of his 1991 book.

[103] Ibid., 350.

[104] Ibid., 335–336.

[105] Ibid., 337.

Scripture, not whether God has blessed folk who have held them.'[106] That is to say, the experience of individuals with the text of Scripture has little or no ultimate hermeneutical power in discerning the meaning of the text.[107]

His approach to the *analogy of Scripture* assumes that no factors external to the text have significant bearing on the interpretation of the text. This, again, reflects Packer's understanding of the nature of language as it functions in God's self–revelation. The scriptural revelation functions primarily in a descriptive, not a performative capacity. The performative character comes from the work of the Holy Spirit through the written Word of God.[108] This methodological cleavage between the original meaning of God's Word and the contemporary power of God's Word would seem, logically, to imply a dilemma in which the text's original meaning is somewhat less than direct, timeless self–revelation from God until it passes

---

[106] Packer, 'In Quest of Canonical Interpretation', 214.

[107] See F. Watson, *Text, Church and World: Biblical Interpretation in Theological Perspective* (Grand Rapids: Eerdmans, 1994), 231–236. Watson points out that though the text of Scripture can indeed be read by those outside any commitment or submission to the text, there are theological principles involved in the exegesis of the text. He offers Luther's interpretative struggle with the law–gospel dilemma as an example of how difficult it can be to discern the intent of a particular text (i.e. whether the words are indeed speaking gospel or being misused by Satan to speak law and oppress). Merely reading the words will not answer the question of the text's meaning. One must have a growing acquaintance with the nature of the Gospel in order to interact with the question. From whence then does one obtain this sense of the Gospel but from first reading the text? The dialectic (hermeneutical circle or spiral) is necessary. Certainly, this seems consistent with Packer's view. However, Packer's appeal to a rationalistic exegetical process assumes a conceptual distinction between the canons of exegesis and the canons of application. Watson states, 'Hermeneutics, theology and exegesis flow into and out of each other with no fixed dividing–lines; on occasion they may be practised simultaneously' (241).

[108] Packer, 'The Adequacy of Human Language', 34–35. It must be noted that for Packer the Bible, along with imperative, contains illuminative, and celebratory language. Performative language, to Packer, is used by God when, by making covenants (e.g., with Abram in Genesis 17:2–4), God 'causes the state of affairs spoken of to exist.' This usage within Scripture is not the same, however, as Scripture itself functioning as a performative act with the reader. Rather, in Packer's schema Scripture serves as descriptive language to report on or describe God's use of performative language. By contrast, K.J. Vanhoozer, an evangelical theologian who recognises a propositional character to Scripture, claims that 'the Scripture principle – the way in which one identifies the Bible as the Word of God – should be formulated in terms of divine communicative action.' See K.J. Vanhoozer, 'The Voice and the Actor: A Dramatic Proposal about the Ministry and Minstrelsy of Theology', in J.G. Stackhouse, Jr. (ed.), *Evangelical Futures: A Conversation on Theological Method* (Grand Rapids: Baker, 2000), 101.

through the second stage of the process (i.e. application). In this sense, the actual functioning of Packer's methodology would not be far from Barth's claim that Scripture 'becomes' the Word of God.[109]

A highly rationalist anthropology either precedes or follows from this view of God's self–revelation and the hermeneutics that are used in approaching it. The piety in which the restoration of God's image is personally experienced depends most heavily, then, on the faculty of reason to discern the meaning of God's Word so that it can then be applied in context as illumined by the Holy Spirit.

Packer is intent on beginning the hermeneutical spiral with the static, crystallized meaning of the text in the mind of the original author. The meaning inherent in the text may or may not be fully grasped by any particular interpreter, but the assumption of its existence and accessibility to the canons of reason undergirds the applicational enterprise. Though he attempts to avoid a hermeneutical tension by insisting that these aspects of the hermeneutical process must go together, an innate tension seems operative in his classification of the exegetical process as a merely rational exercise and his assignment of the Holy Spirit's work to the applicational aspect. He points to the '*clarity* and *perspicuity* of the entire collection [the canon], as a body of intrinsically intelligible writings that demonstrably belong together and constantly illuminate each other.'[110] He does not link this 'intrinsic intelligibility' to any direct involvement of the Holy Spirit in the act of interpretation.

This tension is evident in Packer's advocacy of the well–known hermeneutical maxim that interpretation is one, but application is many. His criticism of Karl Barth's hermeneutic illustrates this point.

> Applications vary with situations, but … the core truths about God's work, will, and ways that each biblical book teaches, and that God Himself thereby teaches, remain both constant in themselves (for God does not change!) and permanently accessible to the careful exegete. …
> But Barth's approach to exegesis, which appears to build on God's freedom to 'say' different things to different people at different times out of the same words of human witness to Him, has naturally and inevitably led to what Kelsey calls 'the unprecedented theological pluralism marking the neo–orthodox era [David H. Kelsey, *The Uses of Scripture* (Philadelphia: Fortress, 1975)].' This pluralism is something that, if I am right, future generations will see as the direct result of the hermeneutical Achilles' heel in Barth's epoch–making and formally correct reassertion

---

[109] See Barth, *Church Dogmatics*, I.1., (trans. Thomson), 124,132–133.
[110] Packer, 'Understanding the Bible: Evangelical Hermeneutics', 150.

of the authority of the Bible as God's channel of communication to sinful men.[111]

Herein Packer assumes that the objective dimension of God's Word is the human authorial intent behind the text itself, i.e. that God's intent in the Word is identical with the human authorial intent.

The identification of God's intent with authorial intent shows in Packer's description of a hermeneutical process in which original meanings can be detached from their original settings before being reapplied to other settings. He states,

> So, just as it is possible to identify in all the books of Scripture universal and abiding truths about the will, work, and ways of God, it is equally possible to find in every one of them universal and abiding principles of loyalty and devotion to the holy, gracious Creator; and then to detach these from the particular situations to which, and the cultural frames within which, the books apply them, and to reapply them to ourselves in the places, circumstances, and conditions of our own lives today. Rational application of this kind, acknowledging but transcending cultural differences between the Bible worlds and ours, is the stock–in–trade of the evangelical pulpit and the recognized goal of the evangelical discipline of personal meditation on the written text ...[112]

Universal principles that can and must be extracted from the textual material then fitted to other situations seem to serve as the axis of the hermeneutical process.

A second evidence of tension in Packer's hermeneutic is his suggestion that application is the hermeneutical component that completes the Word of God. Despite his advocacy of a hermeneutical spiral, he depicts application as the final phase in a sequence.

> Only the evangelical theory of application remains rationally intelligible to the very end. On that theory, application is the last stage in the temporal process whereby God speaks to each generation and to individuals within each generation: God who gave His Word in the form of the rational narration, exposition, reflection, and devotion that Holy Scripture is, now prompts the making and receiving of rational application of it. This application is the Word of God to you and to me.[113]

---

[111] Ibid., 330.

[112] Packer, 'Understanding the Bible: Evangelical Hermeneutics', 157.

[113] Packer, 'Infallible Scripture and the Role of Hermeneutics', 347.

Indeed, this focus on personal response as innate to the Word of God avoids the deadening risk of a historically encrusted Word that fails to speak contemporaneously. However, by suggesting that the task of application is discrete from and subsequent to the task of exegesis, he seems to permit the preliminary interpretive tasks to be undertaken in historical and rational abstraction from the God whose Word is being interpreted. Moreover, his repeated claim that the text itself is the Word of God because of its source and divinely rational character would be undermined by detaching the ministry of the Holy Spirit from the very first step in apprehending that Word. Logically, this would imply that the text itself is not fully the Word of *God*.

This risk of dead abstraction is further illustrated in Packer's suggestion that the Scripture can be legitimately used in a manner that does not necessarily involve the important work of application. He comments,

> To pass on biblical content, unapplied, is only to teach, not to preach. A lecture, as such, is not a sermon. Preaching is teaching plus – plus what? Plus application of truth to life. One's adequacy as a preacher, interpreting God's Word to God's people, is finally determined not by erudition of one's exegesis but by the depth and power of one's application.[114]

This concession indicates that, to Packer, the original meaning of the Scriptural text is prerequisite to the existential impact of the text and can be detached from the impact of that text. Furthermore, the ministry of teaching the Scripture would seem to be possible apart from the Spirit–guided, applicational purposes of the Scripture, thus creating a sort of functional chasm between the *content* and the *intent* of God's Word.

Despite this methodological tension in his hermeneutic, Packer's pastoral orientation and concern for piety shows through in his methodology when he insists that the work of hermeneutics is not complete without application.

> The heart of the hermeneutical problem does not lie in the determining of the historical meaning of each passage … it lies, rather, in seeing how it applies to you, me, and us at the point in history and personal life where we are now. … My only point against Ebeling – which would certainly have been Luther's too, had Luther foreseen him – is that it is the present utterance of the living God, and nothing less, that is being applied; this

---

[114] Packer, *Truth and Power*, 165.

means (putting it the other way around) that the applied teaching of Holy Scripture is in truth the message and instruction of God our Maker.[115]

Full understanding of Scripture, for Packer, demands a synthesis of interpretation (i.e. the exegetical attempt to recover the original, historical meaning of the text) and application.

He offers a four–fold description of the applicational task that reflects a sequential, rationalistic approach to what would otherwise appear to be the least rationalistic aspect of his hermeneutic. This description aligns with his use of faculty psychology in his anthropology and shows how he understands Scripture to function in the restoration of the person.

> There is, first, *application to our mind*, where the logical form is this: the truth presented shows us that we ought not to think thus–and–so (and if we have thought it up to now, we must stop thinking it); instead, we should think such–and–such. Second, there is *application to our will*, where the logical form is that the truth presented shows us we ought not to behave thus–and–so (and if we have started, we must stop at once); instead, we ought to do such–and–such. Third, there is *application to our motivating drives*, where the logical form is this: the truth presented shows us that if we are living as we should and want to, we have very good reason and every encouragement to carry on, and if we are not living so, we have very good reason and every encouragement to change our ways. Fourth, there is *application to our condition*, where the logical form is found in the question: How do we stand in relation to the truth presented? Have we faced it, taken it to heart, measured and judged ourselves by it? How do we stand in relation to the God who speaks it to us?[116]

The relationship of interpretation and application in Packer's hermeneutic corresponds to the relationship of mind and will in his anthropology. As argued previously, God's Word addresses the sinful, alienated condition of humanity at the fundamental level of the will but does so through the medium of the mind or reason. Packer's concern for piety is evident throughout his exposition of the hermeneutical process, even with the distinction noted. This concern is particularly obvious in his understanding of the Holy Spirit's role in hermeneutics.

---

[115] Packer, 'Infallible Scripture and the Role of Hermeneutics', 346.

[116] Packer, *Truth and Power*, 168–169.

8.2.2.2 THE ROLE OF THE HOLY SPIRIT

Packer attempts to correct what he feels is a deficiency of emphasis on the Holy Spirit by pointing to the Spirit's progressive enabling of the church's interpretive process throughout history.

> [I]n the task of interpreting Scripture theologically cognizance of, and encounter with, the historic Christian interpretative tradition, uniform or pluriform as at each point it may be, is of major methodological importance. Since Pentecost the Holy Spirit has been present and active in the church, and part of His ministry has been to teach God's people to understand the Scriptures and the message they contain ... The only course that the doctrine of the Holy Spirit in the church will sanction is to approach Scripture in the light of historic Christian study of it. Church tradition, in the sense of *traditio tradita*, that which is handed on, should be valued as a venture in biblical understanding by those who went before us, whom the Spirit helped as He helps us.[117]

He speaks here of the Spirit's role in interpretation in a general sense, as if each facet of the process were equally dependent on the Spirit. Certainly, he does not entirely eliminate the Holy Spirit's role from the interpretation of the authorial intent or original meaning of the text nor relegate it solely to the task of application. He denies the possibility of pure, unassisted, epistemological neutrality, insisting that the Spirit must witness to the divine authority of the text and illuminate the 'theological contents of Scripture.'[118]

In part, his emphasis on the Holy Spirit's role in hermeneutics is an apologetic against the accusation that evangelical hermeneutics are overly rationalistic.

> Evangelical theology affirms a correlation between the rational process whereby principles, having been established from biblical particulars, are applied to cases and persons, and the teaching ministry of the Holy Spirit, who enables our sin–darkened minds to draw and accept these correct conclusions as from God. Because correct application is a strictly rational process, most evangelical textbooks on interpreting Scripture say little or nothing about the Holy Spirit, Scripture's ultimate author, as the great

---

[117] Packer, 'Infallible Scripture and the Role of Hermeneutics', 352.

[118] Packer, 'Maintaining Evangelical Theology', 187. As mentioned previously, Packer personally stated to the author his disagreement with the Princeton theology's assumption that truth could be attained from an utterly neutral epistemological posture. He questions the epistemology of Common Sense Realism in favour of the Holy Spirit's ministry in epistemology.

hermeneut who by leading and enlightening us in the work of exegesis, synthesis, and application, actually interprets that Word in our minds and to our hearts. The omission unhappily allows evangelical rationality in interpretation to look like a viciously self–reliant rationalism, while by contrast the regular neoorthodox appeal to the Spirit as interpreter ... looks like proper humility ...[119]

Again, Packer strives to present a hermeneutical process that is thoroughly integrated in its dependence on the Holy Spirit. The process depends on a prior commitment to obedience and must be directed by the Spirit throughout.

It is a recurring reality of Christian experience that those who explore the Bible with a purpose of humble obedience to all the Spirit shows them in the text find that the fruit of their exploring is more than factual knowledge of God's work and will; it is in truth fellowship with their Lord in person. Conviction of truth, consecration of heart, communion with Christ, and confidence in his love, become aspects of a single ball of wax ... when Christians open themselves to what the Westminster Confession I.x calls 'the Holy Spirit speaking in the Scripture.'[120]

However, in general his writings reflect an inconsistent pattern of emphasis regarding the points at which the Spirit's assistance is needed. For example, elsewhere he notes that the Spirit's primary function relates to the work of application. He states, 'It is in application specifically that we need divine help. Bible commentaries, Bible classes, Bible lectures and courses, plus the church's regular expository ministry, can give us fair certainty as to what Scripture meant ... but only through the Spirit's illumination shall we be able to see how the teaching applies to our own situation.'[121]

This apparent discrepancy of emphasis is never addressed or reconciled in his writings. His tendency, however, is to emphasise the Spirit's role in the applicational phase of hermeneutics such that, methodologically, he gives the impression that the Spirit's role is not necessary (or at least *as* necessary) prior to that phase.

The intrinsic, irreducible rationality of the hermeneutical process, to Packer, indicates a structural correspondence between uniformity of meaning in the text and the human rational structure by which that meaning is apprehended.

---

[119] Packer, 'Infallible Scripture and the Role of Hermeneutics', 347.

[120] Packer, *Truth and Power*, 193–194.

[121] Ibid., 149.

[T]his Spirit–given understanding *comes by* a rational process that can be stated, analyzed, and tested at each point. Therefore unanimity is always in principle possible, and in any age plurality of theological views, however inescapable and indeed stimulating in practice, must be seen as a sign of intellectual and/or spiritual deficiency in some if not all of God's learning people [emphasis added].[122]

Here Packer argues that the criteria for evaluating biblical interpretation are related to the rational structure through which the Spirit works. The criteria do not emerge from, nor are they directly related to the Spirit's work in and through the text.[123] This paradigm does not afford, however, any criteria for recognising or evaluating whether the Spirit is active in interpretation. The work of application, to which he most consistently and directly attaches the Spirit's role, depends on prior exegetical work. Ironically, the experiential character of application is the object of Packer's greatest suspicion. On one hand, his 'spiral' allows the hermeneutical process to be theoretically self–correcting. Yet, his caveats about the subjectivity of experience undermine the formative influence that application or experience could have in exegetical interpretation.[124]

---

[122] Packer, 'Infallible Scripture and the Role of Hermeneutics', 337.

[123] R.S. Anderson, '"Real Presence" Hermeneutics: Reflections on Wainwright, Thielicke, and Torrance', *TSF Bulletin* 6 (November–December 1982), 6. For Anderson, the 'epistemological relevance of the Holy Spirit' refers more immediately to the personal knowledge of God provided through Jesus Christ. Anderson states, 'The presence of the Spirit opens up the human self to a fully rational and spiritual correspondence to the self–knowledge of God, anchored on the human side through the indissoluble relation of divine and human in Jesus Christ (*homoousion*). ... Propositions, as logical forms of thought, are not thereby excluded from theological statements. For that knowledge which God reveals through Word and Spirit, indissolubly united with his own being, also entails true knowledge as against that which is false.' Anderson presents a scenario in which the propositional message of Scripture is involved in the hermeneutical process, but not as a step on the way to the knowledge of God. Rather, he suggests, the Holy Spirit more directly mediates the personal knowledge of God through Jesus Christ. Scripture expresses this revelation in logical form, but the logic is derived from the Person revealed. In Packer's scenario, the logic of Scripture seems to precede, stand apart from, and control the knowledge of the Person revealed.

[124] Packer appears to understand rationality as more abstract and conceptual than intuitive and experiential in nature. This would account for his distinction between conceptual knowledge and experiential knowledge. T.A. Noble argues that Calvin saw conceptual knowledge and intuitive knowledge as equal aspects of rationality because Calvin saw the Incarnate Word of God and the written Word of God in a more integrated, interdependent manner. Since they 'cannot be separated,' Noble

Inasmuch as he sees the Spirit's role most dominant in this experiential aspect of hermeneutics, it may be questioned whether he indeed acknowledges the Spirit's role in hermeneutics as he much as he wants to do or thinks that he does. The distinction Packer makes between the Spirit's role in interpretation and the Spirit's role in application suggests that Scriptural revelation can be understood at a rational level before it is embraced at an experiential level.[125]

The subject of the Holy Spirit's role in hermeneutics provides an important case study for assessing whether Packer's approach to both theology and piety is anthropocentric. He contends that the Spirit certainly validates the divine origin and authority of Scripture in the believer's experience. Moreover, the Spirit guides the submissive believer to the meaning/application of the text that is consistent with God's will. In these claims Packer attempts to avoid the danger of a rationalism that makes the meaning of the text accessible apart from the God of the text. Yet, his separation of the hermeneutical process into phases of which the Spirit's role is more prominent in application than in exegesis indicates the presence and influence of an anthropocentric rationalism. Thus, tension appears in Packer's theological method even in his treatment of the Holy Spirit, the theological theme to which he appeals most vigorously in order to avoid anthropocentric rationalism.

8.2.3 The Nature of Theology

Theology, for Packer, must be propelled and guided by pastoral intentions. He states, '[I]t is vital to realize that truth is for people, and therefore, the pastoral function of theology is ultimately primary.'[126] Theology is the premier expression and means of the applicational intent and pietistic trajectory of Scripture. It is an activity as much as a deposit. 'The supreme skill,' Packer claims, 'in the art and craft of theology is to link the theoretical and cognitive aspects of God's revealed truth with its practical and transformative aspects in an unbreakable bond.'[127]

---

contends, 'our experience of God in Christ is rational through and through. It is rational first in that it is direct, first–hand *notitia intuitive*, and that intuitive knowledge of all real objects of experience is not only rational but the basis of all rational knowledge.' See T.A. Noble, 'Scripture and Experience', *Themelios* 23, no. 1 (1997), 34.

[125] The implications of this position can be more fully seen when contrasted with Karl Barths's contention that revelation depends upon and follows reconciliation. See Barth, *Church Dogmatics*, IV.1., 34.

[126] Packer, 'Maintaining Evangelical Theology', 184.

[127] Ibid., 185.

The pastoral and pietistic intentions of Scripture and theology can be summarised, he claims, in the biblical notion of wisdom. He argues that 'true theology is essentially identical with God's gift of wisdom.'[128] He elucidates this link between theology and wisdom in terms of the Holy Spirit's activity in sanctification, stating, 'So *theologia* is really an aspect of the reality of sanctification; it is a pointer to, and a benchmark of, the way the Holy Spirit uses the word of God to change people, making them like Christ.'[129] This claim would suggest that piety is impossible apart from an objective framework of truth that theology can provide.

On a general level, Packer suggests 'five principles that should guide our practice of theology in the twenty–first century.'[130] The first principle is to 'maintain the trajectories,' i.e. keep the pietistic concerns of godliness at the centre of focus. Second, he recommends resisting the tendency of specialisation to fragment the work of theology and thus create unbalanced spirituality. Third, theology must remain anchored in the Bible as God's divine Word. Fourth, it must stay in dialogue with the culture for the sake of meaningful, persuasive encounter. Finally, he encourages continual dialogue with non–evangelical traditions in order to learn from all who claim to belong to Jesus Christ.[131]

The specific work of theology is related to the work of hermeneutics for Packer. He uses the analogy of a rising spiral to describe theology in the same way he described hermeneutics.[132] Theology and hermeneutics are related, though not identical, and function in much the same manner by utilising a mutually informing dialectic. Theology and hermeneutics are distinct, however, in that theology encompasses the work of hermeneutics, extending the fruit of hermeneutics into the comprehensive mission of the church.

---

[128] J.I. Packer, 'Theology and Wisdom', in J.I. Packer and S.K. Soderlund (eds.), *The Way of Wisdom: Essays in Honor of Bruce K. Waltke* (Grand Rapids: Zondervan, 2000), 1.

[129] Ibid., 11.

[130] Packer, 'Maintaining Evangelical Theology', 186.

[131] Ibid., 186–188.

[132] See J.I. Packer, 'Theology and Bible Reading', in Elmer Dyck (ed.), *The Act of Bible Reading* (Downers Grove: InterVarsity, 1996), 67. He states, 'Theology, with its network of internal linkages, has sometimes been described as a circle or (better) a rising spiral, the thought being that until you have toured the whole of which each item is a part, your understanding of that item is certainly deficient. But when you come back to it after making the tour, you understand it at least a little better than you did before.' See again his description of the hermeneutical act as that of a rising spiral in 'Infallible Scripture and the Role of Hermeneutics', 338.

Packer distinguishes ten disciplines, related in linear fashion within the overall scope of theology: exegesis, biblical theology, historical theology, systematic theology, apologetics, ethics, missiology, spirituality, liturgy, and practical theology.[133] Systematic theology constitutes the functional core of this sequence, building on the work what precedes it, then extending and determining the work of what follows. Packer's depiction of both the hermeneutical process and the work of theology as a rising spiral appears to conflict with the linear picture he offers in this outline. Systematic theology functions much like a prism for the other disciplines before and after it on this linear continuum. It is, he describes, 'a stockpiling discipline that gathers and combines all the resources of knowledge about God. The six following disciplines draw upon it, interact with and put to work its findings.'[134]

The priority of rationality in Packer's theology and theological method reflects his anthropological assumptions about the fundamentally rational nature shared by God and humanity.[135] Though he describes the heart of the

---

[133] Ibid., 68–71.

[134] Ibid., 69–70. He states, 'Systematic Theology gathers to itself the findings of exegesis, biblical theology and historical theology in a watershed discipline. It is what we have been coming up to in all that we have discussed this far, and all the disciplines still to be mentioned will draw down from it. Systematic theology thinks through the material that biblical and historical theology present in order to find a way of stating the whole faith today, topic by topic and in all its fullness, that will show its coherence and cogency in relation to current interests, assumptions, questions, doubts and challenges, both outside and inside the churches. Some have chosen to call the discipline dogmatic theology on the grounds that it deals with the defined faith (the dogmas) of the church, but "systematic" says more about its scope and is therefore preferable. ... When properly managed, it appears as a discipline of declaratory and applicatory biblical interpretation which merits the description 'systematic' not because it imposes a speculative system (it does not) but because it thinks biblical themes together in the way that Scripture itself does and sets forth each as part of a God–centered, thought–out, self–consistent whole. Good systematic theology always commends itself as a testimony to the God of the gospel, the triune Creator–Redeemer, and as a transcript of this God's self–disclosure and of the revelation of his mind as set forth in the Bible.'

[135] Grenz, *The Social God and the Relational Self,* 67–86. Grenz attributes this priority on revelation to the methodological tendency to see rationalism as the common denominator between divine and human personhood. He traces one stream of this epistemological priority on the individual, rational self from Augustine through Boethius, Calvin, and the Puritan and Pietist movements. He finds another stream in Descartes, Locke, and Kant. Though there are considerable differences in the conclusions drawn by individuals in these chains, the common thread is the belief in a universal, rational self that is possessed by each individual. Grenz claims, 'Kant

imago Dei as relational righteousness, both relationship and righteousness are dependent on rationality. He portrays this contingency when he states that 'theology pursues revealed truth about the Creator in order to know him relationally in a life of worship and obedience, thus using truth for his glory and for the correcting and directing of our thoughts and ways in his service.'[136] Relationship and righteousness (the essence of the *imago Dei*), then, depend on rationality through the act of theology.

Interestingly, Packer seeks to avoid an anthropocentric orientation to the Bible by appealing to its 'God–centeredness' that theology is intended to safeguard.[137] Theology protects the theocentrism of the Bible by preserving the message of God's rational, propositional self–revelation.[138] It is not clear, however, *how* theology does this when it depends upon an exegetical process that is highly rationalistic. He presents Christ as the lens and the ultimate object of focus for all biblical revelation but stops short of showing how this is works, especially in his own exegesis. The method he actually demonstrates could easily lead to the very anthropocentism he strives to avoid.[139]

---

provided the final intellectual foundation for the shift to radical individualism that Augustine initiated and Enlightenment thinkers such as Descartes and Locke augmented.' By locating the self in a 'world of its own knowledge ... Kant established the individual, autonomous self as the locus of reason and by implication as the focal point of the scrutiny of rationality itself. By attempting a thorough critique of the nature and limitations of reason, he launched a new era, characterized by a focus on intense self–reflection' (76). In the religious realm, Calvin adopted this assumption in his emphasis on self–mastery, the Puritans by their emphasis on introspection as the means to assurance of salvation, and the Pietists by their elevation of regeneration and conversion as the high points of salvation. See also Jones, *Revelation and Reason in the Theology of Carl F.H. Henry, J.I. Packer, and Ronald H. Nash*, 119. Jones contends that Packer bases the possibility of revelation on 'the linguistic capability intrinsic to humanity as created in the image of God.'

[136] Packer, 'Theology and Bible Reading', 67.

[137] Ibid., 84. He states, 'Without the ministrations of theology challenging us again and again not to force what we read into an anthropocentric, egocentric mold, we are in danger of missing the life–changing impact of this emphasis and ending up among those whose reading of the Bible never brings them to embrace the Bible's point of view.'

[138] Ibid., 85.

[139] T.F. Torrance, *The Christian Doctrine of God, One Being Three Persons* (Edinburgh: T & T Clark, 1996), 106. Torrance criticises anthropocentric approaches to theology but suggests an alternative that allows a legitimate 'anthropomorphic' aspect to theological epistemology. This aspect is derived from the *imago Dei* but reverses the order evident in Packer's thought. In Torrance's order, the relational aspect of the image provides the space into which God's self–revealing initiative finds resonance

A theological method driven by the anthropological assumption of a rational self as the ontological commonality between God and humanity leads, furthermore, to the notion that theology is reliable because it is static in nature. Theology is a repository of truth about God that never changes (though human comprehension of that truth may grow) because God never changes. Theological method, then, is a process for identifying, collecting, and organising the various aspects of that Truth in the manner that most accurately reflects the nature of the Truth. Packer affirms Thomas Oden's return from liberalism to historic orthodoxy, extolling the virtue of those who stay 'at home' and build defences against assaults by honouring the time–tested perspectives of historical theology. This he calls the 'evangelical method.'[140] He is fond of comparing his theological vocation to that of a 'sewage man' whose 'goal in dogmatics is to find pure streams and to strain out sewage.'[141] This image connotes a discomfort with all interpretations of biblical phenomena that do not immediately display the inner harmony of biblical revelation.

Packer's view of theology as a static repository of divine truth is reflected in his treatment of theological paradox. He defines paradox as 'the unexpected and seemingly irrational or impossible.'[142] He acknowledges the existence of verbal and logical paradoxes, but expresses the greatest interest in what he calls 'ontological paradox,' which 'is the seeming incompatibility of statements describing reality, or inferences drawn from those statements.'[143] As examples of this type of paradox he cites 'faith as man's act and equally God's gift; God ordaining and overruling all human action without destroying human liberty and answerability, or becoming the author of sin in a morally blameworthy sense ... God determining the words of prophets, apostles, and biblical writers without impeding their freedom and spontaneity in self–expression.'[144] This list of examples corresponds to the theological issues to which Packer has given the greatest apologetic attention in his theological career: the nature of faith, the sovereignty of God, and the inerrancy of Scripture.

Commending 'neo–orthodox' theologians for dealing with paradox in a manner that recognises the immeasurable distance between Creator and

---

in the secondary aspect of human knowing. Theomorphism, however, precedes and sustains any anthropomorphic dimension of the knowledge of God.

[140] J.I. Packer, foreword to *After Modernity ... What? Agenda for Theology*, by T. Oden (Grand Rapids: Zondervan, 1990), 10.

[141] Packer, *Truth and Power*, 98. See also J.I. Packer, 'God's Plumber and Sewage Man', *CT*, (6 April 1992), 15.

[142] J.I. Packer, 'Paradox in Theology', in *NDT*, 491.

[143] Ibid.

[144] Ibid.

creature, he nevertheless finds fault with their approach for their 'unwillingness to be bound by the consistent rationality of Scripture.'[145] His understanding of 'consistent rationality' involves a consistency that is measured by the degree of logical coherence between all the claims and perspectives found in Scripture. These claims serve as mutual points of reference for each other.[146] This type of rational consistency appears to provide its own criteria for hermeneutical legitimacy, leaving it open to the charge of predetermining the range of conclusions that can be reached. Moreover, such a procedure appears to reflect the very anthropocentric rationalism that Packer otherwise seeks to avoid.[147]

If the authority of the Bible as God's Word is bound up in the strictly internal logical relationship of each assertion to every other assertion, there is no external point of reference by which it can be discerned whether the self–interpreting character of Scripture yields substantive progress in apprehending God's self–revelation, as Packer claims to do with his rising spiral. In fact, this paradigm would seem to contradict or fail to support Packer's otherwise 'world–affirming' anthropology and piety by creating a functionally docetic hermeneutic in which the understanding of Scripture is detached from and unaccountable to the redemptive effect of its message in life.

First, the meaning of the Scriptural text is at the mercy of the predetermined rational criteria of the interpreter. Second, the meaning of the text as the Word of God is considered separable into two aspects: the original meaning of the text (the authorial intent), which can be determined objectively or clinically, and the experiential or applicational response to the text, which requires the Holy Spirit's ministry of illumination. This approach poses a hermeneutical dualism in which the Word of God is

---

[145] Ibid., 492.

[146] See T.F. Torrance, *The Ground and Grammar of Theology* (Belfast: Christian Journals, 1980), 36. Torrance suggests, in contrast, a coherence or harmony that is determined by the relationship of Scriptural claims to the common object of their witness. He warns of a dangerous dualism when 'theological statements may be treated as logical propositions to be analyzed and interpreted in their syntactical and coherent interrelations: which may lead in a fundamentalist direction, in which people are concerned mainly with the relation of statement to statement in a formalistic elision of the truth of being with the truth of statement ...'

[147] See T.F. Torrance, *God and Rationality* (London: Oxford University Press, 1971), 101–103. Torrance concludes that this method of theology utilises a Newtonian approach that determines *a priori* what conclusions can be reached by establishing pre–set categories that control what can be observed. This method, Torrance contends, demands that the knower, rather than that which is to be known, serve as the primary epistemological resource.

theoretically divisible from the effect that seems inherent to its nature as Word of God (e.g. Isaiah 55:10–11).[148]

Packer's portrayal of theology as static does not, however, imply a complete ontological correspondence between theology and the truth that it signifies. In order to describe the distinction he draws upon Aquinas's doctrine of analogy.[149] The integrity of this theological model, however, is determined directly (even if analogically) by the extent to which theological assertions correspond to the original or authorial intent of the Scriptural text. Exegesis, hermeneutics, and theology converge to approximate the

---

[148] See Torrance, *The Ground and Grammar of Theology*, 28. Torrance traces Kant's influence in the hermeneutical dualism that separates the form of God's Word from the content of God's Word and allows the interpreter the dubious notion that the phenomenon of the Word can then be separated from the material reality of the Word and engaged from a posture of neutrality. He states, 'The dualism at work behind this approach cuts off the word of the Scriptures from the objective Word of God ...' (30). See also C. Westermann, *Isaiah 40–66: A Commentary* (Philadelphia: Westminster, 1969), 289. Westermann sees a unity between the meaning and effect of God's Word. He states, 'For our prophet the word is not primarily something with a content, but the instrument by means of which something is effected. God's word is a word that does things. When God speaks, something comes about.' In comparison, Packer seems to follow the line of commentators such as E.J. Young who locate the source of efficacy for God's Word in the propositional truthfulness that is itself derived from God's mind. Young moves in the direction of dualism between word and effect when he observes that 'the word of God which comes from His mouth is made known to man by means of the media of revelation. ... The reference is to propositional revelation, and the origin of this propositional revelation (as also in 2 Tim. 3:16) is God Himself. The word originates in the mind of God, goes out from His mouth, and comes to man either in spoken or written form through the divinely appointed media of revelation. There is no magical power in this word, nor is it charged with a power akin to mana. The reason why it unfailingly accomplishes the purpose for which it is sent forth is that it is divine. It is the very expression of the truth itself and hence cannot fail.' See E.J. Young, *The Book of Isaiah* (Grand Rapids: Eerdmans, 1972), III.384.

[149] Packer, 'What Did the Cross Achieve?' 92–93. He states, 'ordinary language is used to speak intelligibly of a God who is partly like us (because we bear his image) and partly unlike us (because he is the infinite Creator while we are finite creatures). All theological models, like the non–descriptive models of the physical sciences, have an analogical character; they are, we might say, analogies with a purpose.' See also J.I. Packer, 'God', in *NDT*, 274–277. Here he admits that as Christian thought progressed it made use of Greek philosophical categories, particularly those found in Plato, Aristotle, and the Stoics. He questions whether those categories were the best fit for the biblical ideas in view, but insists that 'those who used them from the 2nd to the 20th century have never let them obscure the fact that God is personal, active and very much alive' (276).

ontological Word of God contained in authorial intent. Though theology may be, to Packer, analogical in character, it nonetheless serves as the epistemological means of access to the ontological structure of God's revelation in Scripture.

The static character of Scripture's ontological structure constitutes the material with which theology works as an activity to produce the foundation of orthodoxy that he also labels as the repository of truth. As an activity, theology involves four tasks: receptive, critical, applicatory, and communicative.[150] The repository nature of theology stands alongside and complements the functional tasks of theology.

> There is another way of looking at theology that is complementary to the functional account ... This is to see it as the repository (or better still, the deposit itself) of all the truth and wisdom that over the centuries have been found in Scripture, analyzed for coherence, vindicated against skepticism and successfully upheld against alternative understandings. 'Orthodoxy' ('right opinion') is the standard label for this material.[151]

In his description of orthodoxy and its relationship to theology, Packer illuminates his understanding of the nature of doctrine as well. He calls orthodoxy 'the content of 'doctrine,' the theological belief that the church professes and teaches,' which is 'the common core of belief that the church has maintained consistently since apostolic days.'[152] For Packer, the Apostle's Creed summarizes this belief.[153]

The functional nature of theology depends upon the static nature of theology (orthodoxy). Packer describes this relationship as follows. 'Christian theological activity (theologizing) ... is essentially a working over of the deposit of theology ... To study theology is to involve oneself in the task of appropriating, analyzing, evaluating, servicing, and where there is need, reconditioning this heritage of orthodoxy in its application to life.'[154]

Packer appears to believe that the process leading to the creedal conclusions of orthodoxy was the same upward spiral of activities involved in exegesis, hermeneutics, and theology. God's revelation in Scripture is the initiating factor in this spiral, though the spiral is interrupted by a decisive convergence in the creeds that then provides parameters for the spiral from

---

[150] Packer, 'Theology and Bible Reading', 75.
[151] Ibid., 76.
[152] Ibid.
[153] Ibid.
[154] Ibid., 77.

that point.[155] Packer appeals to the repository of orthodoxy as the guardian of the functional aspect of theology. He states, 'At the present juncture in Christian history, what is needed is not novelty, but a renewal of this heritage through a return to its biblical roots.'[156] Thus, as reflected in his previously cited commendation of Thomas Oden, he is clearly suspicious of creativity and innovation in the work of theology.

Summary

J.I. Packer's theological method reflects an unwavering commitment to the controlling principle of biblical inerrancy and authority. Further commitments to a covenantal, canonical, and Christological orientation reflect his desire for a theocentric method that is ultimately governed by God's self–revelation rather than by the canons of human reason.

When the intrinsic logic and functionality of Packer's method is closely examined, however, it may not be as theocentric as he claims and wishes it to be. Obvious parallels can be seen between his theological method and his theological anthropology. Human reason appears to occupy a place of functional priority in discerning the data of God's revelation through conventional means of literary and linguistic interpretation. This phase is prior to the phase when the Holy Spirit's illumination is most emphasised for the work of applying the message in a personal sense. The prospect of growth in godliness is possible only as the outcome of this rationalistic process. Implicitly, then, Packer's theological method appears to rest on rather anthropocentric assumptions.

---

[155] Packer admires the theological method of Scottish theologian J. Orr, using Orr's theological work as a model for challenging cultural drifts in which authoritative revelation from God is ignored. Packer specifically makes use of Orr's appeal to doctrine and dogma as, respectively, the coherent strands of God's revelation and the conclusions developed in response to that organic revelation. See J.I. Packer, 'On From Orr: the cultural crisis, rational realism, and incarnational ontology', *Crux* 32 (September, 1996), 12–26. Orr identifies the starting point of the theological process as a law or principle inherent in God's revelation. This principle provides the integrity or substance with which theology works and on which it reflects. Otherwise, Orr's definitions of doctrine, theology, and dogma are quite consistent with Packer's. Doctrine, for Orr, is the substance of the Christian message. Theology is the set of labours working with the material of doctrine and generating conclusions for the Christian life. Dogma is the result of theology that becomes definitive, sustainable, and sustaining for the church's integrity. See J. Orr, *The Progress of Dogma* (London: Hodder and Stoughton, 1901), 31.

[156] Packer, *Truth and Power*, 110.

Chapter 9

Conclusion

J.I. Packer has wielded an unusual level of influence on the character of twentieth–century, English–speaking evangelicalism. This influence is noteworthy not only because of its breadth across denominational lines, but also because of Packer's identity as a British Anglican. For at least thirty years his greatest imprint has been outside his native land and his own denomination.

In a lengthy career as a theologian of international reputation Packer has written prolifically. In numerous lesser–known writings he has sought to engage issues debated primarily within ecclesiastical or academic circles. Yet his reputation has been secured largely through writings aimed at educated lay readers. His favourite themes have been soteriology, Scripture, and piety. As a self–styled, modern–day Puritan, his theological agenda has been a thoroughgoing attempt to recapture the theological values of Calvinism as it was articulated and lived out among key seventeenth–century English Puritans and perpetuated in more modern times by the Princeton tradition. From these historical and theological roots he has attempted to cultivate a theology of the Christian life that reflects a rich Puritan ethos and speaks prophetically to the influences affecting the current condition of Christianity. Most noteworthy among these influences are forms of piety that he considers to be unhealthy and unbiblical due to passivistic or perfectionistic tendencies. His earliest personal experiences in the Christian faith season his theological agenda with pathos.

The theology of piety that Packer develops is marked by several important features: an Augustinian concept of original sin as prideful rebellion, a constant emphasis on the power of indwelling sin in the life of the Christian, the role of predestination and election to provide a theocentric focus to piety and to resolve the tension between his monergistic view of justification and his synergistic view of sanctification, an individualistic and introspective approach to assurance of salvation, the necessity of mortification and vivification as disciplines for growth in grace, and the offer of hope to sustain the vigorous struggle with sin to which all Christians are called.

Packer's theological anthropology undergirds his theology of piety with a view of the *imago Dei* that functionally prioritises the rational faculties, particularly the faculty of reason, for the restoration and realisation of the relational righteousness that he believes constitutes the material aspect of the *imago*. The Incarnation of the Son of God plays a significant role in Packer's anthropology and piety, but primarily as a means to the end of a perfect and therefore efficacious forensic atonement. Thereafter the Incarnation provides a model for godly living. In Packer's forensic soteriology the Incarnation does not function so as to allow the Son of God to touch the fallen human experience directly. The forensic atonement leads then to the existential aspects of union with Christ and sanctification because these aspects of soteriology cohere by means of God's sovereign election.

Theological method is tightly interwoven with theological anthropology and piety in Packer's thought. In fact, it could be said that anthropology and piety *are* his methodology. The piety that emerges from this schema predictably emphasises the priority of a rational approach to relationship with God through precise comprehension of and response to the message of an inerrant Bible. The hermeneutical methodology he suggests reflects a subtle but influential inclination toward rationalism by frequently eliminating or minimizing the need for the Holy Spirit in the exegetical phase and operating with a rather artificial distinction between interpretation and application. Certainly, an emphasis on the priority of Scripture in the Christian life is not unique to Packer. The distinctive mark of his theology of the Christian life is the proportion and character of his emphases.

Rational interaction with Scripture is the starting point and, thus, exercises more control over his entire system of piety than is obvious at first glance. Though he sends mixed signals about the necessity of the Holy Spirit's role in every phase of biblical interpretation, rationalistic exegesis is frequently presented as an objective process that depends merely on the rational faculties shared by all humanity.

The result of this convergence of theological anthropology, theological method and doctrine of sanctification is a piety that goes far toward being 'world–affirming,' that is, integrating all aspects of the embodied human experience into hearty response to God as the fulfilment of the *imago Dei*. Packer is to be commended and thanked for his articulation of a realistic, well–grounded approach to piety and for combating versions of piety that fail to integrate the entirety of the human experience in responsive obedience to God. Likewise, he attempts to anchor piety solidly in theological anthropology rather than in the ever–shifting, narcissistic moods of secular culture. His defence of Scripture as the authoritative Word of God issues a relevant and much–needed prophetic call to a world that tends to deny, reject or dilute the notion of divine revelation and authority.

The Puritan/Princeton tradition that Packer represents and which has informed the corporate ethos of American evangelicalism has many virtues. At best, however, this approach to theology does not address epistemological issues that have been raised in the postmodern world. Furthermore, this approach may not even be equipped to do so with its epistemological apparatus. The effect of this approach is to place piety in relationship to anthropology and method in a highly individualistic and rationalistic manner. In practical terms, this can have the opposite effect of what Packer intends, namely, isolation and doubt. Packer and his tradition may not be well equipped to foster growth in Christian maturity for those whose epistemological constructs eschew individual rationalism and propositions as the prerequisite to relationship.

Only with the passage of time will it be known whether Packer's theology the Christian life will gain and retain a hearing in a world of epistemological diversity. At this point, it appears that while he has contributed significantly toward the sanity and health of evangelical piety, a more consistently Christocentric and corporate understanding of theological anthropology and theological method will be needed in order to sustain a piety in which God's redemptive work can be received and recognised in every facet of human experience. Whether or not his theological anthropology and theological method are capable of consistently supporting such a piety, there is no doubt that this vision of healthy Christian living compels J.I. Packer. The Church is indebted to him for his long and significant contribution toward the realisation of this vision.

Bibliography

Primary Sources

Packer, J.I., 'Abolish' in C. Brown (ed.), *New International Dictionary of New Testament Theology* (Grand Rapids: Zondervan, 1975), I.73–74

– 'An Accidental Author', *Christianity Today* (15 May 1987), 11

– 'Accuse', in C. Brown (ed.), *New International Dictionary of New Testament Theology* (Grand Rapids: Zondervan, 1975), I.84

– 'Acquitted', *Span*, 1 (1973), 10–11

– 'The Adequacy of Human Language', in N. Geisler (ed.), *Inerrancy* (Grand Rapids: Zondervan, 1980), 197–226

– Foreword to T. Oden, *After Modernity ... What? Agenda for Theology* (Grand Rapids: Zondervan, 1990)

– 'Aitken, Robert', in D.M. Lewis (ed.), *The Blackwell Dictionary of Evangelical Biography: 1730–1860* (Oxford: Blackwell, 1995), I.6

– 'All Men Will Not Be Saved', *Banner of Truth* (March/April 1966), 3–6

– 'Anglican Theology', unpublished course notes (Vancouver: Regent College, 1998)

– *Among God's Giants: The Puritan Vision of the Christian Life* (Eastbourne: Kingsway, 1991)

– 'Anglican–Methodist: Which Way Now?', in J.I. Packer (ed.), *Fellowship in the Gospel* (Appleford: Marcham Manor, 1968), 9–38

– *An Anglican to Remember: William Perkins: Puritan Popularizer* (London: St. Antholin's Lectureship Charity, 1996)

– 'Anglicanism Today: The Path to Renewal', in G. Egerton (ed.), *Anglican Essentials* (Toronto: Anglican Book Centre, 1995), 53–63

– *The Apostles' Creed* (Berkshire: Marcham Books, n.d)

– Foreword to S. Leuenberger, *Archbishop Cranmer's Immortal Bequest: The Book of Common Prayer of the Church of England: An Evangelistic Liturgy,* trans. S. Leuenberger and L. J. Gorin, Jr. (Grand Rapids: Eerdmans, 1990)

– 'Are Non–Christian Faiths Ways of Salvation?', *Bibliotheca Sacra* 130 (April–June 1973), 110–116

– 'Are Pain and Suffering Direct Results of Evil?', in F. Colquhoun (ed.), *Moral Questions* (London: Church Pastoral Aid Society, 1977), 26–29

– 'Arminianisms', in *The Manifold Grace of God* (London: The Puritan and Reformed Studies Conference, 1968), 22–34

– 'Aspects of Authority', in *Orthos* 9 (Fellowship of the Word and Spirit, n.d)

- 'Assessing the Anglican–Roman Catholic Divide: An Anglican Perspective', *Crux* 33 (June 1997), 10–16
- 'Atonement', in D. Atkinson and D. Field (eds.), *New Dictionary of Christian Ethics and Pastoral Theology* (Leicester: Inter–Varsity, 1995), 174–177
- *Augustinian and Wesleyan Views about Holiness*, audio cassette (Edinburgh: Rutherford House, n.d.)
- 'Authority in Preaching', in M.Eden and D.F. Wells (eds.), *The Gospel in the Modern World: A Tribute to John Stott* (Leicester: Inter–Varsity, 1991), 199–212
- 'Baptism: A Sacrament of the Covenant of Grace', *Churchman* 49 (1955), 2:76–84
- 'Battling for the Bible', *Regent College Bulletin* 9 (1979), 4:no page
- Introduction to P. Fromer (ed.), *The Best in Theology*, vol. I (Carol Stream, Ill.: Christianity Today, 1986)
- Introduction to P. Fromer (ed.), *The Best in Theology*, vol. II (Carol Stream, Ill.: Christianity Today, 1988)
- Introduction to H. Smith (ed.), *The Best in Theology*, vol. III (Carol Stream, Ill.: Christianity Today, 1989)
- Introduction to J.I. Yamamoto (ed.), *The Best in Theology*, vol. IV (Carol Stream, Ill.: Christianity Today, 1990)
- *Beyond the Battle for the Bible* (Westchester, Ill.: Cornerstone, 1980)
- 'The Bible and the Authority of Reason', *Churchman* 75 (October–December 1961), 207–219
- 'The Bible in Modern Theology', *Bible League Quarterly* (January–March 1960), 129–133
- 'Biblical Authority, Hermeneutics, and Inerrancy', in E.R. Geehan (ed.), *Jerusalem and Athens: Critical Discussions on the Theology and Apologetics of Cornelius Van Til* (Nutley, N.J.: Presbyterian and Reformed, 1971), 141–153
- 'Bringing the Bible to Your Life', *Charisma* (January 1987), 43–46
- 'Bringing the Double Mind to Singleness Of Faith', *Eternity* (November 1988), 59
- 'A Broad Church Reformation?', *The London Quarterly and Holborn Review* 189 (October 1964), 270–275
- 'Call, Called, Calling', in E.F. Harrison (ed.), *Baker's Dictionary of Theology* (Grand Rapids: Baker, 1978), 108–109
- 'Calvin and the Calvinist Tradition', unpublished course notes (Vancouver: Regent College, n.d)
- 'Calvin: A Servant of the Word', in *Able Ministers of the New Testament* (London: The Puritan and Reformed Studies Conference, 1964), 36–55

- 'Calvin the Theologian', in G.E. Duffield (ed.), *John Calvin*, Courtenay Studies in Reformation Theology, vol. I (Appleford: Sutton Courtenay, 1966), 149–175
- 'Calvinism in Britain: Its Status and Prospects', *Torch and Trumpet* (December 1959), 21–22
- 'A Calvinist – and an Evangelist!', *The Hour International* (August 1966), 25–27
- 'Calvin's View of Scripture', in J.W. Montgomery (ed.), *God's Inerrant Word: An International Symposium on the Trustworthiness of Scripture* (Minneapolis: Bethany Fellowship, 1974), 95–114
- 'Can the Dead Be Converted?', *Christianity Today* (11 January 1999), 82
- 'Carpenter', in C. Brown (ed.), *New International Dictionary of New Testament Theology* (Grand Rapids: Zondervan, 1975), I.279
- *Charismatic Christianity and Biblical Theology*, audio cassette (Edinburgh: Rutherford House, n.d.)
- 'Charismatic Renewal: Pointing to a Person and a Power', *Christianity Today* (7 March 1980), 16–20
- 'Children of a Larger God: How Good Theology Expands the Soul', *Leadership* (Summer 1998), 108–113
- Foreword to E.W. Lutzer, *Christ among Other Gods: A Defense of Christ in an Age of Tolerance* (Chicago: Moody, 1994)
- 'Christ Supreme: The Theology of the Letter to the Colossians', unpublished course notes (Vancouver: Regent College, 1994)
- Introduction to R. Baxter, *A Christian Directory*, in *The Practical Works of Richard Baxter*. vol. I. (Morgan, Pa.: Soli Deo Gloria, 2000)
- 'The Christian and God's World', in J.M. Boice (ed.), *Transforming our World: A Call to Action* (Portland: Multnomah, 1988), 81–97
- 'Christian Gravitas in a Narcissistic Age', *Eternity* (July 1988), 46–
- 'Christianity and Non–Christian Religions', *Christianity Today* (21 December 1959), 3–5
- 'The Christian's Purpose in Business', in R.C. Chewning, *Biblical Principles and Business: The Practice*, Christians in the Marketplace Series, vol. 3 (Colorado Springs: NavPress, 1990), 16–25
- 'Church of South India and Reunion in England', *Churchman* 82 (1968), 4:249–261
- *The Collected Shorter Writings of J.I. Packer: Celebrating the Saving Work of God*, vol. 1 (Carlisle: Paternoster, 1998)
- *The Collected Shorter Writings of J.I. Packer: Serving the People of God*, vol. 2 (Carlisle: Paternoster, 1998)
- *The Collected Shorter Writings of J.I. Packer: Honouring the Written Word of God*, vol. 3 (Carlisle: Paternoster, 1999)
- *The Collected Shorter Writings of J.I. Packer: Honouring the People of God*, vol. 4 (Carlisle: Paternoster, 1999)

– 'The Comfort of Conservatism', in M.S. Horton (ed.), *Power Religion: the Selling Out of the Evangelical Church?* (Chicago: Moody, 1992), 283–299
– *Concise Theology: A Guide to Historic Christian Beliefs* (Wheaton: Tyndale House, 1993)
– 'Conscience, Choice and Character', in B. Kaye and G. Wenham (eds.), *Law, Morality and the Bible* (Downers Grove: InterVarsity, 1978), 168–192
– Review of J.R.W. Stott, *The Contemporary Christian: Applying God's Word to Today's World*, in *Christianity Today* (7 February 1994), 59
– 'Contemporary Views of Revelation', in C.F.H. Henry (ed.), *Revelation and the Bible: Contemporary Evangelical Thought* (Grand Rapids: Baker, 1958), 89–104
– 'Counterpoint: A Protestant Assessment', *Eternity* (October 1986), 25
– 'Crises of Faith Are Yardsticks for Growth', *Eternity* (January 1989), 45
– Review of J.R.W. Stott, *The Cross of Christ*, in *Christianity Today* (4 September 1987), 35–36
– 'Crosscurrents among Evangelicals', in C. Colson and R. Neuhaus (eds.), *Evangelicals and Catholics Together: Toward a Common Mission* (London: Hodder and Stoughton, 1996), 147–174
– David Martyn Lloyd–Jones', in A. Spangler and C. Turner, (eds.), *Heroes* (Ann Arbor: Servant, 1985)
– Introduction to J. Owen, *The Death of Death in the Death of Christ* (Carlisle, Pa.: Banner of Truth, 1959), 1–25
– 'Death: Life's One and Only Certainty', *Eternity* (March 1965), 22–26
– 'Defile', in C. Brown (ed.), *New International Dictionary of New Testament Theology* (Grand Rapids: Zondervan, 1975), I.447–449
– 'Despise', in C. Brown (ed.), *New International Dictionary of New Testament Theology* (Grand Rapids: Zondervan, 1975), I.461–462
– 'Destroy', in C. Brown (ed.), *New International Dictionary of New Testament Theology* (Grand Rapids: Zondervan, 1975), I.471
– 'Determine', in C. Brown (ed.), *New International Dictionary of New Testament Theology* (Grand Rapids: Zondervan, 1975), I.476–478
– 'The Devil's Dossier: Before Christians Engage in Spiritual Warfare, They Should Know Something about the Enemy', *Christianity Today* 21 (June 1993), 24
– 'Dirt', in C. Brown (ed.), *New International Dictionary of New Testament Theology* (Grand Rapids: Zondervan, 1975), I.479–480
– 'The Doctrine of Justification in Development and Decline among the Puritans', in *By Schisms Rent Asunder* (London: The Puritan and Reformed Studies Conference, 1969), 18–30
– Review of N. Micklem, *The Doctrine of Our Redemption* in *Churchman* 75 (March 1961), 60–61
– Foreword to J.M. Boice, *Does Inerrancy Matter?* (Oakland: International Council on Biblical Inerrancy, 1979)

- 'Does It Really Matter?', *Eternity* (January 1987), 30
- 'Doing It My Way: Are We Born Rebels?', in J.N. Akers, J.H. Armstrong, and J.D. Woodbridge (eds.), *This We Believe: The Good News of Jesus Christ for the World* (Grand Rapids: Zondervan, 2000), 43–58
- 'Dying Well is the Final Test', *Eternity* (April 1987), 46
- 'Election', in J.D. Douglas (ed.), *The New Bible Dictionary* (London: Inter–Varsity, 1961), 357–361
- Preface to Peter Toon, *The Emergence of Hyper–Calvinism in English Nonconformity 1689–1765* (London: The Olive Tree, 1967)
- 'The Empowered Christian Life', in G.S. Grieg and K.N. Springer (eds.), *The Kingdom and the Power: Are Healing and the Spiritual Gifts Used By Jesus and the Early Church Meant for the Church Today?: A Biblical Look At How to Bring the Gospel to the World Today* (Ventura, Calif.: Regal, 1993), 207–215
- 'Encountering Present–Day Views of Scripture', in J.M. Boice (ed.), *Foundations of Biblical Authority* (Grand Rapids: Zondervan, 1978), 61– 82
- 'Episcopal Idol – A Consideration of *Honest to God*', *The Evangelical Christian* (October 1963), 4–5; 32–35
- *The Evangelical Anglican Identity Problem: An Analysis*, Latimer Studies, no. 1 (Oxford: Latimer House, 1978)
- 'An Evangelical View of Progressive Revelation', in K.S. Kantzer (ed.), *Evangelical Roots: A Tribute to Wilbur M. Smith* (Nashville: Thomas Nelson, 1978), 143–158
- 'Evangelicals and the Way of Salvation: New Challenges to the Gospel– Universalism, and Justification by Faith', in K.S. Kantzer and C.F.H. Henry (eds.), *Evangelical Affirmations* (Grand Rapids: Zondervan, 1990), 107–136
- *Evangelism and the Sovereignty of God* (Downers Grove: InterVarsity, 1961)
- Introduction to J. Burroughs, *An Exposition of the Prophecy of Hosea*, J. Sherman (rev.), reprint of the 1865 ed., (Beaver Falls, Pa.: Soli Deo Gloria, 1989)
- 'Expository Preaching: Charles Simeon and Ourselves', *Churchman* 74 (April–June 1960), 94–100
- *Facing Holiness*, audio cassette (Edinburgh: Rutherford House, n.d.)
- 'Faith', in E.F. Harrison (ed.), *Baker's Dictionary of Theology* (Grand Rapids: Baker, 1978), 208–211
- 'Faith', in W.A. Elwell (ed.), *Evangelical Dictionary of Theology* (Grand Rapids: Baker, 1984), 399–402
- 'The Faith of the Protestants', in T. Dowley (ed.), *Eerdman's Handbook to the History of Christianity* (Grand Rapids: Eerdmans, 1978[2]), 374–375
- *Faithfulness and Holiness: The Witness of J. C. Ryle* (Wheaton: Crossway, 2002)
- 'Fan Mail to Calvin', *Christianity Today* (14 January 1991), 11

- 'Fear of Looking Forward', *Christianity Today* (12 December 1994), 13
- 'Feet in the Clouds', *Regent College Bulletin* 4 (1984), 1.no page
- 'Fellowship: The Theological Basis', *Christian Graduate* (September 1963), 7–11
- 'Firm', in C. Brown (ed.), *New International Dictionary of New Testament Theology* (Grand Rapids: Zondervan, 1975), I.664
- *For Man's Sake* (Exeter: Paternoster, 1978)
- 'Freedom, Free Will', in E.F. Harrison (ed.), *Baker's Dictionary of Theology* (Grand Rapids: Baker, 1978), 229–230
- 'From the Scriptures to the Sermon', *Ashland Theological Journal* 22 (1990), 42–64
- 'Fundamentalism and the British Scene', *Christianity Today* 29 (September 1958), 3–6
- 'The Fundamentalism Controversy: Retrospect and Prospect', *Faith and Thought* (Spring 1958), 35–45
- *'Fundamentalism' and the Word of God: Some Evangelical Principles* (London: Inter–Varsity, 1958)
- 'Gain and Loss', in R.T. Beckwith (ed.), *Towards a Modern Prayer Book* (Appleford: Marcham Manor, 1966), 74–90
- 'George Whitefield: Man Alive', *Crux* 16 (December 1980), 23–26
- 'George Whitefield: The Startling Puritan', *Christian History* 12 (May 1993), 38–40
- 'God', in S.B. Ferguson, D.F. Wright, and J.I. Packer (eds.), *New Dictionary of Theology* 274–277. (Leicester: Inter–Varsity, 1988), 274– 277
- *God Has Spoken: Revelation and the Bible* (London: Hodder and Stoughton, 1964)
- 'God: From the Fathers to the Moderns', in J.I. Packer, G.R. Osborne, C. Brown, *et al* (eds.), *Exploring the Christian Faith: A Contemporary Handbook of What Christians Believe and Why*, Nelson's Christian Cornerstone Series (Nashville: Thomas Nelson, 1996), 96–101
- 'God the Image–Maker', in M.A. Noll and D.F. Wells (eds.), *Christian Faith and Practice* (Grand Rapids: Eerdmans, 1988), 27–50
- *God in Our Midst: Seeking and Receiving Ongoing Revival* (Ann Arbor, Mich.: Servant, 1987)
- 'God Is', in J.I. Packer, G.R. Osborne, C. Brown, *et al* (eds.), *Exploring the Christian Faith: A Contemporary Handbook of What Christians Believe and Why*, Nelson's Christian Cornerstone Series (Nashville: Thomas Nelson, 1996), 86–101
- *God Speaks to Man: Revelation and the Bible* (Philadelphia: Westminster, 1965)
- 'Godliness', in D. Atkinson and D. Field (eds.), *New Dictionary of Christian Ethics and Pastoral Theology* (Leister: Inter–Varsity, 1995), 410–411
- 'Godliness in Ephesians', *Crux* 25 (March 1989), 8–16

– *God's Plans for You* (Wheaton: Crossway, 2001)
– 'God's Plumber and Sewage Man', *Christianity Today* (6 April 1992), 15
– *God's Words: Studies of Key Bible Themes* (London: Inter–Varsity, 1981)
– 'Good', in J.D. Douglas (ed.), *The New Bible Dictionary* (London: Inter–Varsity, 1961), 483
– 'The Good Confession', in J.I. Packer (ed.), *Guidelines: Anglican Evangelicals Face the Future* (London: The Church Pastoral–Aid Society, 196), 13–38
– 'Good Pagans and God's Kingdom', *Christianity Today* (17 January 1986), 22–25
– Foreword to J. MacArthur, *The Gospel According to Jesus: What Does Jesus Mean When He Says, "Follow Me"?* (Grand Rapids: Zondervan, 1988)
– 'The Gospel Bassoon', *Christianity Today* (28 October 1996), 24
– 'The Gospel: Its Content and Communication: A Theological Perspective', in R. Coote and J.R.W. Stott (eds.), *Down to Earth: Studies in Christianity and Culture* (Grand Rapids: Eerdmans, 1980), 97–114
– 'The Gospel and the Lord's Supper', *Mission and Ministry* (Summer 1990), 18–24
– *The Gospel in the Prayer Book* (Abingdon: Marcham, 1966)
– *Great Grace: A 31–Day Devotional*, B. Feia (comp.) (Ann Arbor, Mich.: Servant, 1997)
– *A Grief Sanctified: Passing through Grief to Peace and Joy* (Ann Arbor, Mich.: Servant, 1997)
– *Growing in Christ* (Wheaton: Crossway, 1994)
– Preface to D. Field (ed.), *Here We Stand: Justification by Faith Today* (London: Hodder and Stoughton, 1986)
– Preface to *Guidelines: Anglican Evangelicals Face the Future* (London: The Church Pastoral–Aid Society, 1967)
– 'Hermeneutics and Biblical Authority', *Churchman* 81 (Spring 1967), 7–21
– 'History Repeats Itself', *Christianity Today* (22 September 1989), 22
– Preface to J.C. Ryle, *Holiness: Its Nature, Hindrances, Difficulties, and Roots*, centenary ed. (Welwyn: Evangelical Press, 1979)
– 'Holiness Movement', in S.B. Ferguson, D.F. Wright, and J.I. Packer (eds.), *New Dictionary of Theology* (Leicester: Inter–Varsity, 1988), 314–415
– 'Holiness: What It Is, Why It Matters', *Faith and Renewal* (March/April 1993), 3–11
– 'Holy Spirit', in S.B. Ferguson, D.F. Wright, and J.I. Packer (eds.), *New Dictionary of Theology* (Leicester: Inter–Varsity, 1988), 316–319
– 'The Holy Spirit–And Authority', *The Almond Branch* (1962), 9–12
– 'The Holy Spirit and His Work', *Crux* 23 (June 1987), 2–17
– 'The Holy Spirit in the Book of Common Prayer', in S. Harris (ed.) *The Holy Spirit* (Charlotteville: St. Peter, 1993)

- 'Holy Spirit and the Local Congregation', *Churchman* 78 (June 1964), 98–108
- 'The Holy Spirit and Ourselves', unpublished course notes (Vancouver: Regent College, n.d.)
- *Hot Tub Religion* (Wheaton: Tyndale House, 1987)
- 'How Christians Should Understand Themselves', *Eternity* (July 1986), 36
- 'How to Recognize a Christian Citizen', *Christianity Today* (19 April 1985), 4–8
- 'I Believe in the Resurrection of the Body', *HIS* (April 1985), 16–17
- 'Ignatius of Loyola', in T. Dowley (ed.), *Eerdman's Handbook to the History of Christianity* (Grand Rapids: Eerdmans, 1978²), 411
- 'Ignorance', in E.F. Harrison (ed.), *Baker's Dictionary of Theology* (Grand Rapids: Baker, 1978), 276–277
- 'Implications of Biblical Inerrancy for the Christian Mission', in J. Gregory (ed.), *The Proceedings of the Conference on Biblical Inerrancy* (Nashville: Broadman, 1987), 245–250
- 'In Quest of Canonical Interpretation', in R.K. Johnston (ed.), *The Use of the Bible in Theology: Evangelical Options* (Atlanta: John Knox, 1985), 35–55
- 'Inerrancy and the Divinity and Humanity of the Bible',"in J. Gregory (ed.), *The Proceedings of the Conference on Biblical Inerrancy* (Nashville: Broadman, 1987), 135–142
- 'Infallible Scripture and the Role of Hermeneutics', in J.D. Woodbridge and D.A. Carson (eds.), *Scripture and Truth* (Grand Rapids: Zondervan, 1983), 325–358
- 'Inner Man', in J.D. Douglas (ed.), *The New Bible Dictionary* (London: Inter–Varsity, 1961), 563–564
- 'Inspiration', in J.D. Douglas (ed.), *The New Bible Dictionary* (London: Inter–Varsity, 1961), 564–566. Reprint, 'The Inspiration of the Bible', in P.W. Comfort (ed.), *The Origin of the Bible* (Wheaton: Tyndale House, 1992), 29–36
- 'The Inspiration and Infallibility of Holy Scripture', *Symposium of Articles from the TSF Bulletin* (no date), 16–18
- 'Interview with J. I. Packer', *Discipleship Journal* (July 1982), 41–44
- *Introduction to the Bible*, (London: Scripture Union, 1978)
- 'Introduction: on Covenant Theology', in H. Witsius, *The Economy of the Covenants Between God and Man: Comprehending a Complete Body of ivinity*, W. Crookshank (tr., rev.), (London: Printed for R. Baynes, 1822); reprint, (Escondido, Calif.: Den Dulk Christian Foundation; Phillipsburg, N.J., Presbyterian and Reformed, 1990)
- *Introduction: Lambeth, 1958.* In *Eucharistic Sacrifice: The Addresses Given at the Oxford Conference of Evangelical Churchmen, September, 1961* (London: Church Book Room Press, 1962)

- Foreword to E. Hindson (ed.), *An Introduction to Puritan Theology: A Reader* (Grand Rapids: Baker, 1976)
- 'An Introduction to Systematic Spirituality', *Crux* 11 (March 1990), 2–8
- 'Is Hell out of Vogue in This Modern Era', *United Evangelical Action* (September 1989), 10–11
- 'Is Systematic Theology a Mirage', in J.D. Woodbridge and T.E. McComiskey (eds.), *Doing Theology in Today's World: Essays in Honor of Kenneth S. Kantzer* (Grand Rapids: Zondervan, 1991), 17–37
- *The J. I. Packer Collection*, (Downers Grove: InterVarsity, 1999)
- 'Jesus Christ the Lord', in J.R.W. Stott (ed.), *Obeying Christ in a Changing World* (London: Harper Collins, 1977), I.32–60
- 'Jesus Christ, the Only Saviour', in G. Egerton (ed.), *Anglican Essentials: Reclaiming Faith within the Anglican Church of Canada* (Toronto: Anglican Book Centre, 1995), 98–110
- 'Jewish Evangelism and the Word of God', *CWI Herald* (June–August 1988), 15–18
- 'John Calvin and the Inerrancy of Holy Scripture', in J.D. Hannah (ed.), *Inerrancy and the Church* (Chicago: Moody, 1984), 143–188
- 'John Owen on Communication from God', in *One Steadfast High Intent* (London: The Puritan and Reformed Studies Conference, 1966), 17–29
- 'Jonathan Edwards and the Theology of Revival', in *Increasing in the Knowledge of God* (London: The Puritan and Reformed Studies Conference, 1960), 13–28
- 'Just, Justify, Justification', in E.F. Harrison (ed.), *Baker's Dictionary of Theology* (Grand Rapids: Baker, 1978), 303–308
- 'Justification', in W.A. Elwell (ed.), *Evangelical Dictionary of Theology* (Grand Rapids: Baker, 1984), 593–597
- 'Justification in Protestant Theology', in J.I. Packer, M. Butterworth, S. Motyer, J. Atkinson, G.L. Bray, and D.H. Wheaton (eds.), *Here We Stand: Justfication by Faith Today* (London: Hodder and Stoughton, 1986), 84–102
- *Keep Yourselves from Idols* (Grand Rapids: Eerdmans, 1963)
- 'Keeping Your Balance: A Christian's Challenge', *Eternity* (January 1988), 18
- '"Keswick" and the Reformed Doctrine of Sanctification', *The Evangelical Quarterly* 27 (1955), 153–167
- *Keep in Step with the Spirit* (Old Tappan, N.J.: Revell, 1984)
- *A Kind of Noah's Ark?: The Anglican Commitment to Comprehensiveness*, Latimer Studies, no. 10 (Oxford: Latimer House, 1981)
- 'A Kind of Puritan', in C. Catherwood (ed.), *Martyn Lloyd–Jones: Chosen By God* (Crowborough: Highland, 1986), 33–57
- Foreword to B. Milne, *Know the Truth: A Handbook of Christian Belief* (Leicester: Inter–Varsity, 1982)

- Foreword to S.B. Ferguson, *Know Your Christian Life* (Downers Grove: InterVarsity, 1981)
- *Knowing Christianity* (Wheaton: Harold Shaw, 1995)
- *Knowing and Doing the Will of God* (Ann Arbor, Mich: Servant, 1995)
- *Knowing God* (London: Hodder and Stoughton, 1973)
- 'Knowing Notions or Knowing God?', *Pastoral Renewal* (March 1982), 65–68
- 'A Lamp in a Dark Place: 2 Peter 1:19–21', in E.D. Radmacher (ed.), *Can We Trust the Bible?* (Wheaton: Tyndale House, 1979), 15–30
- Preface to B. Kaye and G. Wenham (eds.), *Law, Morality and the Bible* (Downers Grove: InterVarsity, 1978)
- 'Leisure and Life–Style: Leisure, Pleasure, and Treasure', in D.A. Carson and J.D. Woodbridge (eds.), *God and Culture: Essays in Honor of Carl F. H. Henry* (Grand Rapids: Eerdmans, 1993), 356–368
- 'Let's Stop Making Women Presbyters', *Christianity Today* (11 February 1991), 18–21
- 'The Letter to the Ephesians (and others): An Analysis', unpublished course notes (Vancouver: Regent College, n.d.)
- 'Liberty', in J.D. Douglas (ed.), *The New Bible Dictionary* (London: Inter–Varsity, 1961), 732–734
- *Life in the Spirit: A 30–Day Devotional* (Wheaton: Crossway, 1996)
- Foreword to K.E. Bockmuehl, *Living by the Gospel: Christian Roots of Confidence and Purpose* (Colorado Springs: Helmers and Howard, 1986)
- 'The Lord of Glory', unpublished course notes (Vancouver: Regent College, n.d.)
- 'The Love of God: Universal and Particular', in T.R. Schreiner and B.A. Ware (eds.), *The Grace of God, the Bondage of the Will* (Grand Rapids: Baker, 1995), 413–428
- 'Luther', in *Approaches to Reformation of the Church* (London: The Puritan and Reformed Studies Conference, 1965), 25–33
- 'Luther Against Erasmus', *Concordia Theological Monthly* 37 (April 1966), 207–221
- 'Maintaining Evangelical Theology', in J.G. Stackhouse, Jr. (ed.), *Evangelical Futures: A Conversation on Theological Method* (Grand Rapids: Baker, 2000), 181–189
- Introduction to J. Tolhurst (ed.), *Man, Woman and Priesthood* (Leominster: Gracewing, 1989)
- 'The Means of Conversion', *Crux* 25 (December 1989), 14–22
- 'Meeting God: Some Thoughts on Isaiah 6', *SCP Journal* 6, no. 1 (1984), 75–79
- 'The Message is Unchanged', *Alliance* Witness (23 June 1982), 10–14
- 'Method, Theological', in S.B. Ferguson, D.F. Wright, and J.I. Packer (eds.), *New Dictionary of Theology* (Leicester: Inter–Varsity, 1988), 424–426

- 'Ministry of the Word Today', *The Presbyterian Guardian* (July–August 1965), 87–90
- 'Mistaking Rome for Heaven', *Christianity Today* (12 September 1989), 15
- 'The Montreal Declaration of Anglican Essentials', *Churchman* 109, no. 3 (1995), 219–225
- Review of W.D. Spencer, *Mysterium and Mystery: The Clerical Crime Novel* in *Christianity Today* (21 April 1989), 51
- 'The Mystery of the Incarnation', *HIS* (December 1982), 19–22
- 'The Nature of the Church', *Christianity Today* (8 June 1962), 22–23
- 'New Lease on Life: A Preface to *The Principles of Theology* by W. H. Griffith Thomas', *Churchman* 92, no.1 (1978), 44–52
- *The New Man* (London: Scripture Union, 1978)
- 'Obedience', in J.D. Douglas (ed.), *The New Bible Dictionary* (London: Inter–Varsity, 1961), 904–905
- 'On Being Serious about the Holy Spirit', in D. Wells (ed.), *God the Evangelist: How the Holy Spirit Works to Bring Men and Women to Faith* (Grand Rapids: Eerdmans, 1987), xii–xvii
- 'On from Orr: The Cultural Crisis, Rational Realism, and Incarnational Ontology', *Crux* 32 (September 1996), 12–26
- 'On Knowing God', in J.M. Boice (ed.), *Our Sovereign God: Addresses Presented to the Philadelphia Conference on Reformed Theology* (Grand Rapids: Baker, 1977), 61–75
- 'One Body in Christ: The Doctrine and Expression of Christian Unity', *Churchman* 80 (March 1966), 16–26
- Review of E.L. Mascall, *The Openness of Being: Natural Theology Today* *Churchman* 88 (January–March 1974), 58–59
- 'The Origin and History of Fundamentalism', in *The Word of God and Fundamentalism: The Addresses Given at the Oxford Conference of Evangelical Churchmen, 19th to 21st September, 1960* (London: Church Book Room Press, 1961), 100–127
- 'Orthodoxy', in E.F. Harrison (ed.), *Baker's Dictionary of Theology* (Grand Rapids: Baker, 1978), 389–390
- Review of D. McCasland, *Oswald Chambers: Abandoned to God* *Christianity Today* (4 October 1993), 36
- 'Our Lifeline: The Bible Is the Rope God Throws Us While the Rescue Is in Progress', *Christianity Today* (28 October 1996), 22–25
- 'Our Lord and the Old Testament', *Bible League Quarterly* (January– March 1963), 70–74
- *Our Lord's Understanding of the Law of God*, Dr. G. Campbell Morgan Memorial Lecture, no. 14 (Glasgow: Pickering and Inglis, 1962)
- 'The Oxford Evangelicals in Theology', in J.S. Reynolds, *The Evangelicals at Oxford 1735–1871: A Record of an Unchronicled Movement with the Record Extended to 1905* (Appleford: Marcham Manor, 1975), 82–94

- 'Packer the Picketed Pariah', *Christianity Today* (11 January 1993), 11
- 'Paradox in Theology', in S.B. Ferguson, D.F. Wright and J.I. Packer (eds.), *New Dictionary of Theology* (Leicester: Inter–Varsity, 1988), 491–492
- *A Passion for Faithfulness: Wisdom from the Book of Nehemiah*, Living Insights Bible Study Series (Wheaton: Crossway, 1995)
- *A Passion for Holiness* (Nottingham: Crossway, 1992)
- 'Paths of Righteousness', *Eternity* (May 1986), 32–37
- 'Pentecostalism 'Reinvented': The Charismatic Renewal', in H.B. Smith (ed.), *Pentecostals from the Inside Out* (Wheaton: Victor, 1990), 145–149
- 'People Matter More Than Structures', *Crusade* (April 1978), 24–25
- Review of D.F. Wells, *The Person of Christ* in *Evangelical Review of Theology* 10 (January 1986), 85–86
- 'Piety', in J.D. Douglas (ed.), *New Bible Dictionary* (London: Inter– Varsity, 1961), 995–996
- 'Piety on Fire', *Christianity Today* (12 May 1989), 18–23
- *The Pilgrim's Principles: John Bunyan Revisited* (London: St.Antholin's Lectureship Charity, 1999)
- *The Plan of God* (London: Evangelical Press, 1962)
- 'The Pleasure Principles: Why the Christian Mission on Earth Is Not Unrelieved Heroic Misery', *Christianity Today* (22 November 1993), 24– 26
- 'Pondering Anglican Woes: An Interview with J. I. Packer', *Touchstone* (December 2002), 42–44
- 'Poor Health May Be the Best Remedy: But If You've Got a Headache, Thank God for Aspirin', *Christianity Today* (21 May 1982), 14–16
- 'Postscript: I Believe in Women's Ministry', in M. Bruce and G.E. Duffield (eds.), R.T. Beckwith (rev.), *Why Not: Priesthood and the Ministry* (Abingdon: Marcham Manor, 1976), 160–174
- 'Power for a Purpose', *Discipleship Journal* (January 1994), 18–23
- Foreword to and editor of J.C. Ryle, *Practical Religion: Being Plain Papers on the Daily Duties, Experience, Dangers, and Privileges of Professing Christians* (London: James Clarke and Co., 1964)
- Introduction to the 19th century reprint edition of R. Baxter, *The Practical Works of Richard Baxter*, vol. 4 (London: George Virtue. Reprint, Ligonier, Pa.: Soli Deo Gloria, 1991)
- 'Prayer 101: Talking to God', *HIS* (November 1985), 28–29
- 'The Preacher as Theologian: Preaching and Systematic Theology', in D. Jackman and C. Green (eds.), *When God's Voice is Heard* (Leicester: Inter–Varsity, 1995), 79–95
- 'Preaching as Biblical Interpretation', in R.R. Nicole and J.R. Michaels (eds.), *Inerrancy and Common Sense* (Grand Rapids: Baker, 1980), 187–203
- 'Predestination', in J.D. Douglas (ed.), *The New Bible Dictionary* (London: Inter–Varsity, 1961), 1026

- 'Problem Areas Related to Biblical Inerrancy', in J. Gregory (ed.), *The Proceedings of the Conference on Biblical Inerrancy* (Nashville: Broadman, 1987), 205–213
- 'The Problem of Eternal Punishment', *Crux* 26 (September 1990), 18–25
- 'The Problem of Universalism Today', *Theology Review* 5 (November 1969), 16–24
- 'The Problems of Universalism', *Bibliotheca Sacra* 130 (January–March 1973), 3–11
- 'The Puritan Conscience', in *Faith and a Good Conscience* (London: The Puritan and Reformed Studies Conference, 1962), 18–31
- 'Puritan Evangelism', *The Banner of Truth* (February 1957), 4–13
- 'The Puritan Idea of Communion with God', in *Press Toward the Mark* (London: The Puritan and Reformed Studies Conference, 1961), 5–15
- 'Puritan Preaching', *The Evangelical Christian* (October 1960), 18–21
- 'Puritan, Puritanism', in E.F. Harrison (ed.), *Baker's Dictionary of Theology* (Grand Rapids: Baker, 1978), 431
- 'The Puritan Approach to Worship', in *Diversity in Unity* (London: The Puritan and Reformed Studies Conference, 1963), 3–14
- 'The Puritan Conscience', in *Faith and a Good Conscience* (London: The Puritan and Reformed Studies Conference, 1962), 18–31
- 'Puritan Theology for Today', unpublished course notes (Vancouver: Regent College, 1992)
- 'The Puritan Treatment of Justification by Faith', *Evangelical Quarterly* 24, no. 3 (1952), 131–143
- 'The Puritan View of Preaching the Gospel', in *How Shall They Hear?* (London: The Puritan and Reformed Studies Conference, 1959), 11–21
- 'Puritanism as a Movement of Revival', *Evangelical Quarterly* 52, no 1 (1980), 2–16
- 'The Puritans', in J.I. Packer, *et al* (eds.), *Exploring the Christian Faith: A Contemporary Handbook of What Christians Believe and Why*, Nelson's Christian Cornerstone series (Nashville: Thomas Nelson, 1996), 313–315
- 'The Puritans as Interpreters of Scripture', in *A Goodly Heritage* (London: The Puritan and Reformed Studies Conference, 1958), 18–26
- 'The Puritans and the Lord's Day', in *Servants of the Word* (London: The Puritan and Reformed Studies Conference, 1957), 1–9
- 'The Puritans and Spiritual Gifts', in *Profitable for Doctrine and Reproof* (London: The Puritan and Reformed Studies Conference, 1967), 15–27
- 'Put Holiness First', *Christian Life* (May 1985), 46–47
- 'Questions About IVF', *Breakthrough* (May 1962), 15
- 'The Reality Cure',' *Christianity Today* (14 September 1992), 34–35
- 'A Reasonable Faith', *Decision* (December 1993), 13–14, 38
- 'The Reconstitution of Authority', *Crux* 18 (December 1982), 2–12

- 'The Redemption and Restoration of Man in the Thought of Richard Baxter', DPhil thesis (University of Oxford, 1954)
- Foreword to R.W. Ruegsegger (ed.), *Reflections on Francis Schaeffer* (Grand Rapids: Zondervan, 1986)
- 'Regeneration', in W.A. Elwell (ed.), *Evangelical Dictionary of Theology* (Grand Rapids: Baker, 1984), 924–926
- Introduction to J. Gwyn–Thomas, *Rejoice ... Always!* (Edinburgh: Banner of Truth, 1989)
- 'Renewal and Revival', *Channels* (Spring 1984), 7–9
- 'Representative Priesthood?', *Churchman* 86 (Summer 1972), 86–88
- 'Representative Priesthood and the Ordination of Women', in G.E. Duffield and M. Bruce (eds.), *Why Not?* (Abingdon: Marcham, 1972), 78–80
- 'Reservation', in J.A. Motyer and J.I. Packer (eds.), *Reservation: The Addresses Given at Church Society Annual Meeting, 14th June, 1960* (London: Church Book Room Press, 1960), 1523
- 'Reservation: Theological Issues', in C.O. Buchanan (ed.), *Reservation and Communion of the Sick* (Bramcote: Grove Books, 1972), 15–21
- 'Retooling the Clergy Factories', *Churchman* 82 (Summer 1968), 120–124
- 'Revelation and Inspiration', in E.F. Kevan, A.M. Stibbs, and F. Davidson (eds.), *New Bible Commentary* (London: Inter–Varsity, 1954), 12–18
- 'The Revised Catechism', *Churchman* 75 (April–June 1961), 107–118
- 'Revival'," *Christian Graduate* (December 1971), 97–100
- 'Richard Baxter', *Theology* 56 (May 1953), 174–178
- 'Rome's New Look', *Frontier* (Summer 1963), 138–140
- 'Rome's Persistent Renewal', *Christianity Today* (22 June 1992), 19
- 'Sacrifice and Satisfaction', in J.M. Boice (ed.), *Our Savior God: Man, Christ, and the Atonement: Addresses Presented to the Philadelphia Conference on Reformed Theology, 1977–1979* (Grand Rapids: Baker, 1980), 125–137
- 'Sanctification–Puritan Teaching', *The Christian Graduate* (December 1952), 125–128
- 'Scripture, Inerrancy and the Church', *Touchstone* (Fall 1991), 3–4
- 'A Secular Way to Go', *Third Way* (April 1977), 3–5
- 'Seeing God in the Dark', *Discipleship Journal* (May 1992), 10–12
- 'Shepherds after God's Own Heart', *Faith and Renewal* (November/December 1990), 12–17
- 'Shy Sovereign', *Tabletalk* (June 1988), 4
- Introduction to J. Owen, *Sin and Temptation: The Challenge to Personal Godliness*, J.M. Houston (ed.) (Portland: Multnomah, 1983), xvii–xxix
- 'Situations and Principles', in B. Kaye and G. Wenham (eds.), *Law, Morality and the Bible* (Downers Grove: InterVarsity, 1978), 151–167

– 'Sola Fide: The Reformed Doctrine of Justification', in R.C. Sproul (ed.), *Soli Deo Gloria: Essays in Reformed Theology: Festschrift for John H. Gerstner* (Philadelphia: Presbyterian and Reformed, 1976), 11–25
– '"Sola Scriptura" in History and Today', in J.W. Montgomery (ed.), *God's Inerrant Word: An International Symposium on the Trustworthiness of Scripture* (Minneapolis: Bethany Fellowship, 1974), 43–62
– 'Soldier, Son, Pilgrim: Christian, Know Thyself', *Eternity* (April 1988), 33
– 'Some Thoughts on General Revelation', *Christian Graduate* (September 1956), 114–121
– 'The Spirit with the Word: The Reformational Revivalism of George Whitefield', in W.P. Stephens (ed.), *The Bible, the Reformation and the Church: Essays in Honour of James Atkinson* (Sheffield: Sheffield Academic Press, 1995), 166–189
– 'The Status of the Articles', in H.E.W. Turner (ed.), *The Thirty–Nine Articles of the Church of England* (Oxford: Mowbray, 1964), 25–57
– 'Steps to the Renewal of the Christian People', *Crux* 22 (March 1986), 2–11; reprint in P. Williamson and K. Perotta (eds.), *Summons to Faith and Renewal* (Ann Arbor: Servant, 1983)
– 'Still Surprised by Lewis', *Christianity Today* (7 September 1998), 54–60
– 'The Study of God', *Moody Monthly* (April 1977), 36–39
– 'A Stunted Ecclesiology? The Theory and Practice of Evangelical Churches', *Touchstone* (December 2002), 37–41
– 'The Substance of Truth in the Present Age', *Crux* 33 (December 1997), 3–11
– 'Systematic Theology A, God: Communication and Communion', unpublished course notes (Vancouver: Regent College, 1996)
– 'Systematic Theology B, Man, Sin and Grace', unpublished course notes (Vancouver: Regent College, 1997)
– 'Systematic Theology Overview', unpublished course notes (Vancouver: Regent College, 1989)
– 'Taking Stock in Theology', in J.C. King (ed.), *Evangelicals Today* (Guildford and London: Lutterworth. 1973), 15–30
– *The Ten Commandments* (Basingstoke/Abingdon: Chandos Press/Marcham, 1977)
– 'Thank God for Our Bibles', *Christianity Today* (27 October 1997), 30–31
– 'Theism for Our Time', in P.T. O'Brien and D.G. Peterson (eds.), *God Who is Rich in Mercy: Essays Presented to Dr. D. B. Knox* (Grand Rapids: Baker, 1986), 1–23
– 'Theological Reflections on the Charismatic Movement', *Churchman* 94, no. 1 (1980), 7–25; no. 2 (1980), 108–125
– 'Theology and Bible Reading', in E. Dyck (ed.), *The Act of Bible Reading* (Downers Grove: InterVarsity, 1996), 65–87
– 'Theology on Fire', *Christian History* 13, no. 1 (1994), 32–35

- 'Theology and Wisdom', in S.K. Soderlund and J.I. Packer (eds.), *The Way of Wisdom: Essays in Honor of Bruce K Waltke* (Grand Rapids: Zondervan, 2000), 1–14
- 'Thinking Straight about God', unpublished course notes (Vancouver: Regent College, 1988)
- *The Thirty–Nine Articles: Their Place and Use Today* (Oxford: Latimer House, 1984)
- 'Thirty Years' War: The Doctrine of Holy Scripture', in H.M. Conn (ed.), *Practical Theology and the Ministry of the Church: 1952–1984: Essays in Honor of Edmund P. Clowney* (Phillipsburg, N.J.: Presbyterian and Reformed, 1990), 25–44
- 'Thoughts on the Role and Function of Women in the Church', in C. Craston (ed.), *Evangelicals and the Ordination of Women* (Bramcote: Grove Books, 1973), 22–26
- 'To All Who Will Come', in J.M. Boice (ed.), *Our Savior God: Man Christ, and the Atonement: Addresses Presented to the Philadelphia Conference on Reformed Theology, 1977–1979* (Grand Rapids: Baker, 1980), 179–189
- 'To Make Our Theology Serve Our Godliness', *Leadership* (Spring 1987), 1–2
- *Tomorrow's Worship*, Prayer Book Reform series (London: Church Book Room Press, 1966)
- 'Toward a Confession for Tomorrow's Church.', *Churchman* 87 (Winter 1973), 246–262
- 'Towards a Corporate Presbyterate', in R.P.P. Johnston (ed.), *Ministry in the Local Church: Problems and Pathways* (Bramcote: Grove Books, 1972), 14–20
- 'Training for Christian Service', *The Evangelical Christian* (September 1961), 10–11
- 'Training for the Ministry', in C. Porthouse (ed.), *Ministry in the Seventies* (London: Falcon, 1970), 156–167
- 'The Trinity and the Gospel', in R.A. Bodey (ed.), *Good News for All Seasons: 26 Sermons for Special Days* (Grand Rapids: Baker, 1987), 91–98
- 'True Guidance', *Eternity* (June 1986), 36–39
- *Truth and Power: The Place of Scripture in the Christian Life* (Wheaton: Harold Shaw, 1996)
- 'Understanding the Bible: Evangelical Hermeneutics', in M. Tinker (ed.), *Restoring the Vision* (Eastbourne: MARC, 1990), 39–58
- 'Understanding the Differences', in A. Mickelsen (ed.), *Women, Authority and the Bible* (Downers Grove: InterVarsity, 1986), 295–299
- 'Understanding the Lordship Controversy', *Table Talk* (May 1991), 7
- 'Uniqueness of Jesus Christ: Some Evangelical Reflections', *Churchman* 92, no. 2 (1978), 101–111
- 'The Unspectacular Packers', *Christianity Today* (16 May 1996), 12

- 'Upholding the Unity of Scripture Today', *Journal of the Evangelical Theological Society* 25 (December 1982), 409–414
- 'Walking to Emmaus with the Great Physician', *Christianity Today* 10 (April 1981), 20–23
- 'Wanted: A Pattern for Union', in J.I. Packer (ed.), *All in Each Place: Towards Reunion in England* (Appleford: Marcham Manor, 1965), 17–40
- 'The Way of Salvation', *Bibliotheca Sacra* 129 (July–September 1972), 105–125
- Review of M. Ingham, *Mansions of the Spirit, Crux* 33 (December 1997), 28–38
- 'The Whale and the Elephant', *Christianity Today* (4 October 1993), 11
- 'What Did the Cross Achieve?: The Logic of Penal Substitution', *Tyndale Bulletin* 25 (1974), 3–45
- 'What Do You Mean When You Say God?', *Christianity Today* (19 September 1986), 27–31
- 'What is Evangelism?', in H. Conn (ed.), *Theological Perspectives on Church Growth* 91–105. (Nutley, N.J.: Presbyterian and Reformed, 1976), 91–105
- 'What is Faith?', *Bibliotheca Sacra* 129 (October–December 1972), 291–306
- 'What is Ordination?', in J.I. Packer (ed.), *All in Each Place: Towards Reunion in England* (Abingdon: Marcham Manor, 1965), 181–188
- 'What is Revival?', *Prairie Overcomer* (January 1985), 6–8
- 'What Is at Stake?', *Christianity Today* (5 April 1993), 64–65
- 'What Lewis Was and Wasn't', *Christianity Today* (15 January 1988), 11
- Foreword to J. Blanchard, *Whatever Happened to Hell?* (Durham: (Darlington, Co., Evangelical Press), 1993
- 'Who is God?', in D. Alexander (ed.), *Simple Faith?: An Exploration of Basic Christian Belief* (Berkhamsted: Lion, 1978), 6–8
- 'Why is Authority a Dirty Word?', *Spectrum* (May 1977), 4–6
- 'Why I Left', *Christianity Today* (5 April 1993), 33–35
- 'Why I Signed It', *Christianity Today* (12 December 1994), 34–37
- 'Why I Walked', *Christianity Today* (January 2003), 46–50
- 'Why Preach?', in S.T. Logan, Jr. (ed.), *The Preacher and Preaching: Reviving the Art in the Twentieth Century* (Phillipsburg, N.J.: Presbyterian and Reformed, 1986), 1–29
- 'Why We Need the Puritans', in L. Ryken (ed.), *Worldly Saints: The Puritans as They Really Were* (Grand Rapids: Zondervan, 1986), ix–xv
- 'Wisdom Along the Way', *Eternity* (April 1986), 19–23
- 'With All Thy Mind', *Inter–Varsity* (Autumn 1957), 4–8
- 'The Witness of the Spirit: The Puritan Teaching', in *The Wisdom of Our Fathers* (London: The Puritan and Reformed Studies Conference, 1956), 11–19

- 'The 'Wretched Man' Revisited: Another Look at Romans 7:14–25', in S.K. Soderlund and N.T. Wright (eds.), *Romans and the People of God: Essays in Honor of Gordon D. Fee on the Occasion of His 65th Birthday* (Grand Rapids: Eerdmans, 1999), 70–81
- *Your Father Loves You: Daily Insights for Knowing God* (Wheaton: Harold Shaw, 1986)
- (ed.), *All in Each Place: Toward Reunion in England* (Appleford: Marcham Manor, 1965)
- (ed.), *The Church of England and the Methodist Church: A Consideration of the Report, Conversations between the Church of England and the Methodist Church* (Marcham: Marcham Manor, 1963)
- Personal Curriculum Vitae sent to D.J. Payne (15 February 1995)
- Interview by D.J. Payne (2 July 1999) at Vancouver, British Columbia: Regent College
- Letter to D.J. Payne (11 April 1999)
- Letter to D.J. Payne (17 July 2000)
Packer, J.I., R.T. Beckwith, and G.E. Duffield, *Across the Divide* (Appleford: Marcham, 1977)
Packer, J.I. and L. Wilkinson (eds.), *Alive to God: Studies in Spirituality Presented to James Houston* (Downers Grove: InterVarsity, 1992)
Packer, J.I. and O. Johnston, Introduction to M. Luther, *The Bondage of the Will* (London: James Clarke and Co., 1957), reprint (Grand Rapids: Revell, 1999)
Packer, J.I. and T. Howard, *Christianity: The True Humanism* (Berkhamsted: Word, 1985)
Packer, J.I. and T. Beougher, 'Go Fetch Baxter: This Fiesty Puritan Spent His Life Quieting the Controversy He Started', *Christianity Today* (16 December 1991), 26–28
Packer, J.I., *et al*, *Growing into Union: Proposals for Forming a United Church in England* (London: SPCK, 1970)
Packer, J.I. and W.M. Zoba, *J. I. Packer Answers Questions for Today* (Wheaton: Tyndale House, 2001)
Packer, J.I. and C. Nystrom, *Never Beyond Hope: How God Touches and Uses Imperfect People* (Downers Grove: InterVarsity, 2000)
Packer, J.I. and R. Spittler, 'The Holy Spirit: God at Work', *Christianity Today* (19 March 1990), 27–35
Packer, J.I. and A.M. Stibbs, *The Spirit Within You: The Church's Neglected Possession*, vol. 18, Christian Foundations series, (London: Hodder and Stoughton, 1967)

Secondary Sources

Ahlstrom, S.E., 'From Puritanism to Evangelicalism: A Critical Perspective', in D.F. Wells and J.D. Woodbridge (eds.), *The Evangelicals: What They Believe, Who They Are, Where They Are Changing* (Nashville: Abingdon, 1975), 269–288

Anderson, R.S., 'Anthropology, Christian', in A. McGrath (ed.), *The Blackwell Encyclopedia of Modern Christian Thought* (Oxford: Blackwell, 1993), 5–9

– 'Evangelical Theology', in D.F. Ford (ed.), *The Modern Theologians: An Introduction to Christian Theology in the Twentieth Century* (Oxford: Blackwell, 1997²), 480–495

– 'Imago Dei', in R.J. Hunter (ed.), *Dictionary of Pastoral Care and Counseling* (Nashville: Abingdon, 1990), 571–572

– 'On Being Human: The Spiritual Saga of a Creaturely Soul', in W.S. Brown, N. Murphey, and H.N. Maloney (eds.), *Whatever Happened to the Soul?* (Minneapolis: Augsburg Fortress, 1998), 175–194

– *On Being Human: Essays in Theological Anthropology* (Pasadena: Fuller Seminary, 1982)

– ''Real Presence' Hermeneutics: Reflections on Wainwright, Thielicke, and Torrance', *TSF Bulletin* 6 (November–December 1982), 5–7

– 'The Resurrection of Jesus as Hermeneutical Criterion (Part I)', *TSF Bulletin* 9 (January–February 1986), 9–15

Anselm, *Cur Deus Homo*, in *Basic Writings*, S.N. Deane (tr.) (LaSalle, Ill.: Open Court, 1962²), 171–288

– *Anselm of Canterbury*, J. Hopkins and H. Richardson (eds., trs.) (Toronto: Edwin Mellen, 1976)

Aquinas, T., *The Summa Theologiae*, Fathers of the English Dominican Province (eds.), I.93.9 (London: Burns, Oates and Washburne, 1938³)

Armstrong, B.C., *Calvinism and the Amyraut Heresy: Protestant Scholasticism and Humanism in Seventeenth–Century France* (Madison: University of Wisconsin Press, 1969)

Athanasius, *Against the Heathen* and *On the Incarnation of the Word*, in P. Schaff and H. Wace (eds.), *A Select Library of the Nicene and Post–Nicene Fathers of the Christian Church*, vol. IV (Grand Rapids: Eerdmans, 1980²)

– *Contra Gentes and De Incarnatione*, R.W. Thomson (ed., tr.), Oxford Early Christian Texts series (Oxford: Clarendon, 1971)

Augustine, *The City of God*, in P. Schaff (ed.) and M. Dods (tr.), *A Select Library of the Nicene and Post–Nicene Fathers of the Christian Church: St. Augustine: City of God and Christian Doctrine*, vol. II (Grand Rapids: Eerdmans, 1979²)

– *To Cledonius the Priest against Apollinarius*, ep. CI., in C. Browne and J.E. Swallow (trs.), *A Select Library of Nicene and Post–Nicene Fathers of the Christian Church*, vol. VII, (Grand Rapids: Eerdmans, 1983²)

– *Confessions*, in P. Schaff (ed.), *A Select Library of the Nicene and Post–Nicene Fathers of the Christian Church: The Confessions and Letters of St. Augustin*, vol. I (Grand Rapids: Eerdmans, 1979²)

– *The Free Choice of the Will*, in R.P. Russell (tr.), *The Fathers of the Church*, vol. 59, *Saint Augustine: The Teacher, The Free Choice of the Will, Grace and Free Will* (Washington, D.C.: Catholic University of America, 1968)

– *On the Grace of Christ and On Original Sin, On Nature and Grace, On the Soul and Its Origin,* and *On the Spirit and the Letter,* in P. Schaff (ed.), *A Select Library of the Nicene and Post–Nicene Fathers of the Christian Church: St. Augustine: Anti–Pelagian Writings*, vol. V, P. Holmes and R.E. Wallis (trs.), (Grand Rapids: Eerdmans, 1978²)

– *On the Trinity*, in P. Schaff (ed.), *A Select Library of the Nicene and Post–Nicene Fathers of the Christian Church: St. Augustine: On the Holy Trinity, Doctrinal Treatises, Moral Treatises*, vol. III, A.W. Haddan (tr.), (Grand Rapids: Eerdmans, 1980²)

– *Reply to Faustus the Manichaean*, in P. Schaff (ed.), *A Select Library of the Nicene and Post–Nicene Fathers: St. Augustine: The Writings Against the Manichaeans and Against the Donatists*, vol. IV (Grand Rapids: Eerdmans, 1983²)

Babacz, B., *St. Augustine's Theory of Knowledge: A Contemporary Analysis*, vol. 11, Texts and Studies in Religion series (Lewiston, N.Y.: Edwin Mellen, 1981)

Balthasar, H.U. von, *A Theological Anthropology* (New York: Sheed and Ward, 1967)

Barabas, S., *So Great Salvation: The History and Message of the Keswick Convention* (London: Marshall, Morgan and Scott, 1952)

Barclay, O., *Evangelicalism in Britain 1935–1995: A Personal Sketch* (Leicester: Inter–Varsity, 1997)

– *Whatever Happened to the Jesus Lane Lot?*, (Leicester: Inter–Varsity, 1977)

Barna, G., *What Americans Believe: An Annual Survey of Values and Religious Views in the United States* (Ventura, Calif.: Regal, 1991)

Barr, J., 'The Image of God in the Book of Genesis–A Study of Terminology', *Bulletin of the John Rylands Library* 51 (Autumn 1968), 11–26

– *Fundamentalism*, (Philadelphia: Westminster, 1978) Barth K., *Church Dogmatics*, I.1, G.T. Thomson (tr.), (Edinburgh: T & T Clark, 1936)

Barth, K. *Church Dogmatics*, I.2., III.2., IV.1, G.W. Bromiley and T.F. Torrance (eds.), G.W. Bromiley (tr.), (Edinburgh: T. & T. Clark, 1980)

– *The Word of God and the Word of Man*, D. Horton (tr.), (London: Hodder and Stoughton, 1928)

– 'No!', in *Natural Theology*, P. Fraenkel (tr.), (London: G. Bles, Centenary, 1946)

Barton, S.C., 'New Testament Interpretation as Performance', *Scottish Journal of Theology* 52, no. 2 (1999), 179–208

Basil, *An Ascetical Discourse and Exhortation on the Renunciation of the World and Spiritual Perfection*, in *The Fathers of the Church: A New Translation: St. Basil: Ascetical Works*, M.M. Wagner (tr.), vol. 9 (Washington, D. C.: Catholic University of America, 1950)

Bavinck, H., *The Doctrine of God*, W. Hendricksen (tr.), (Grand Rapids: Baker, 1951)

Baxter, R., *The Practical Works of Richard Baxter*, 4 vols. (London: George Virtue, 1838)

Bebbington, D.W., *Evangelicalism in Modern Britain: A History from the 1730s to the 1980s* (London: Unwin Hyman, 1989)

Beckwith, R.T., interview by D.J. Payne (12 January 1999) at Latimer House: Oxford

Belden, A.D., *George Whitefield–The Awakener* (London: Rockliff, 1953[2])

Berkhof, L., *Systematic Theology* (Grand Rapids: Eerdmans, 1941[4])

Berkouwer, G.C., *Faith and Sanctification*, J. Vriend (tr.), Studies in Dogmatics series (Grand Rapids: Eerdmans, 1952)

– *Holy Scripture*, J.B. Rogers (tr.), Studies in Dogmatics series (Grand Rapids: Eerdmans, 1975)

– *Man: the Image of God*, D.W. Jellema (tr.), Studies in Dogmatics series (Grand Rapids: Eerdmans, 1962)

– *The Person of Christ*, J. Vriend (tr.), Studies in Dogmatics series (Grand Rapids: Eerdmans, 1954)

– *The Work of Christ*, C. Lambregtse (tr.), Studies in Dogmatics series (Grand Rapids: Eerdmans, 1965)

Bettenson, H., (ed.), *The Early Christian Fathers: A Selection from the Writings of the Fathers from St. Clement of Rome to St. Athanasius*, H. Bettenson (tr.), (London: Oxford University Press, 1956)

Bicknell, E.J.A., *Theological Introduction to the Thirty–Nine Articles of the Church of England* (London: Longmans, Green and Co., 1955[3])

Bloesch, D.G., *Essentials of Evangelical Theology*, vol. 2 (San Francisco: Harper and Row, 1979)

Boa, K., *Conformed to His Image: Biblical and Practical Approaches to Spiritual Formation* (Grand Rapids: Zondervan, 2001)

Bonansea, B.M., *Man and His Approach to God in John Duns Scotus* (Lanham, Md.: University Press of America, 1983)

Bouwsma, W.J., 'The Spirituality of John Calvin', in J. Raitt (ed.), *Christian Spirituality II: High Middle Ages and Reformation*, World Spirituality: An Encyclopedic History of the Religious Quest series, vol. 17 (New York: Crossroad, 1987), 318–333

Bray, G., Review of A. McGrath, *To Know and Serve God: A Biography of James I. Packer*, *Churchman* 111, no. 4 (1997), 358–363

Brown, S.C., 'A Thematic Comparison of the Keswick, Chaferian, and Reformed Views of Sanctification', ThM thesis (Western Conservative Baptist Seminary, 1985)

Bruce, F.F., *The Epistles to the Colossians, to Philemon, and to the Ephesians*, New International Commentary on the New Testament series (Grand Rapids: Eerdmans, 1984)

Brunner, E., *The Christian Doctrine of Creation and Redemption: Dogmatics*, O. Wyon (tr.), (London: Lutterworth, 1952)

– *Man in Revolt: A Christian Anthropology*, O. Wyon (tr.), (Philadelphia: Westminster, 1947)

– 'Nature and Grace', in P. Fraenkel (tr.), *Natural Theology* (London: G. Bles, Centenary, 1946)

Bubacz, B., *St. Augustine's Theory of Knowledge: A Contemporary Analysis*, Texts and Studies in Religion series, vol. 11 (Lewiston, N.Y.: Edwin Mellen, 1981)

Burke, V.J., 'Augustine of Hippo: The Approach of the Soul to God', In E.R. Elder (ed.), *The Spirituality of Western Christendom* (Kalamazoo, Mich.: Cistercian, 1976), 1–12

Burns, J.P., (ed. and tr.), *Theological Anthropology*, Sources of Early Christian Thought series (Philadelphia: Fortress, 1981)

Cairns, D., *The Image of God in Man*, Fontana Library of Theology and Philosophy (London: SCM Press, 1973²)

Calvin, J., *Commentaries on the Catholic Epistles*, J. Owen (tr.), (Grand Rapids: Eerdmans, 1948²)

– *The Christian Life*, J.H. Leith (tr.), (San Francisco: Harper and Row, 1984)

– *Commentaries on the First Book of Moses Called Genesis*, J. King (tr.), *Calvin's Commentaries*, vol. I (Grand Rapids: Eerdmans, 1948)

– *Commentary on the Gospel According to John*, W. Pringle (tr.), vol. I (Grand Rapids: Eerdmans, 1956)

– *The Golden Book of the True Christian Life*, H.J.Van Andel (tr.), (Grand Rapids: Baker, 1970)

– *Institutes of the Christian Religion*, F.L. Battles (tr.), (Philadelphia: Westminster, 1960)

– *Instruction in Faith*, P.T. Fuhrman (tr.), (Philadelphia: Westminster, 1949)

– *John Calvin's Sermons on the Ten Commandments*, B.W. Farley (ed. and tr.), (Grand Rapids: Baker, 1980)

– *The Mystery of Godliness, and Other Selected Sermons* (Grand Rapids: Eerdmans, 1950)

– *The Piety of John Calvin: an Anthology Illustrative of the Spirituality of the Reformer of Geneva*, F.L. Battles (ed. and tr.), (Pittsburgh: Pittsburgh Theological Seminary, 1969)

– *Sermons on Deuteronomy*, 16ᵗʰ–17ᵗʰ Century Facsimile Editions (Reprint, Edinburgh: Banner of Truth, 1987²)

Campbell, J.M., *The Nature of the Atonement* (Edinburgh: Handsel, 1996²)

Canfield, J.M., *The Incredible Scofield and His Book* (Vallecito, Calif.: Ross House, 1988)

Carroll R., M.D., *Contexts for Amos: Prophetic Poetics in Latin American Perspective*, Journal for the Study of the Old Testament Supplement series, no. 132 (Sheffield: Sheffield Academic Press, 1992)

Catherwood, C., *Five Evangelical Leaders* (Wheaton: Harold Shaw, 1985)

Chadwick, H., *Augustine* (Oxford: Oxford University Press, 1986)

Chafer, L.S., *He That Is Spiritual: A Classic Study of the Biblical Doctrine of Spirituality* (n.p.: Our Hope Publisher, 1918)

– 'Ordination Doctrinal Statement', unpublished, typewritten manuscript (Dallas Theological Seminary archives, 1900)

– *Systematic Theology*, (Dallas: Dallas Seminary, 1947–48)

Chan, S., *Spiritual Theology*, (Downers Grove: InterVarsity Press, 1998)

Chang, C., *Engaging Unbelief: A Captivating Strategy from Augustine and Aquinas* (Downers Grove: InterVarsity, 2000)

Cho, B.G., 'A Critical Comparative Study of Pneumatology in U.K. (particularly England) Protestant Theology and the World Council of Churches Between 1965 and 1993', PhD thesis (The University of Wales, Lampeter, 1995)

Clement of Alexandria, *Exhortation to the Heathen* and *The Stromata, or Miscellanies*, in A. Roberts and J. Donaldson (eds.), *The Ante–Nicene Fathers: Translations of The Writings of the Fathers Down to A.D. 325: Fathers of the Second Century*, vol. II, (Grand Rapids: Eerdmans, 1979)

Clement of Rome, *The Epistles of Clement of Rome, Polycarp, and Ignatius; and of the Apologies of Justin Martyr and Tertullian*, T. Chevallier (tr.), (London: Francis and John Rivington, 1851²)

Clifford, A.C., *Atonement and Justification: English Evangelical Theology 1640–1790: An Evaluation* (Oxford: Clarendon, 1990)

Clines, D.J.A., 'The Image of God in Man', *Tyndale Bulletin* 19 (1968), 53–103.

Conn, H.M., *Eternal Word and Changing Worlds: Theology, Anthropology, and Mission in Trialogue* (Grand Rapids: Zondervan, 1984)

Copleston, F., *A History of Philosophy, Descartes to Leibniz*. The Bellarmine series, vol. IV (Paramus, N.J.: Newman, 1958)

Crutchfield, L.V., *The Origins of Dispensationalism: The Darby Factor*. (Lanham, Md.: University Press of America, 1992)

Dallimore, A., *The Life of Edward Irving: The Fore–runner of the Charismatic Movement* (Carlisle, Pa.: Banner of Truth, 1983)

Davies, H., *Worship and Theology in England: The Ecumenical Century: 1900–1965* (Princeton: Princeton University Press, 1965)

Dayton, D.W. and R.K. Johnston, (eds.), *The Variety of American Evangelicalism* (Downers Grove: InterVarsity, 1991)

Demarest, B.A., 'Analogy of Faith', in W.A. Elwell (ed.), *Evangelical Dictionary of Theology* (Grand Rapids: Baker, 1984), 43–44

– *Satisfy Your Soul*, (Colorado Springs: NavPress, 1999)

Dieter, M.E., *et al*, *Five Views on Sanctification* (Grand Rapids: Zondervan, 1987)

Dodd, C.H., *The Bible and the Greeks* (London: Hodder and Stoughton, 1935)

Douglas, J.D., (ed.), *The New Bible Dictionary* (London: Inter–Varsity, 1961)

Dowey, E.A., Jr., *The Knowledge of God in Calvin's Theology* (New York: Columbia University Press, 1952)

Dumbrell, W.J., 'Grace and Truth: The Progress of the Argument of the Prologue of John's Gospel', in D. Lewis and A. McGrath (eds.), *Doing Theology for the People of God: Studies in Honor of J.I. Packer* (Downers Grove: InterVarsity, 1996), 105–121

Dunning, H.R., *Grace, Faith, and Holiness: A Wesleyan Systematic Theology* (Kansas City: Beacon Hill, 1988)

– *Reflecting the Divine Image: Christian Ethics in Wesleyan Perspective* (Downers Grove: InterVarsity, 1998)

Elwell, W.A., (ed.), *Evangelical Dictionary of Theology* (Grand Rapids: Baker, 1984)

Engel, M.P., *John Calvin's Perspectival Anthropology* (Atlanta: Scholars Press, 1988)

Evans, C.S., 'Healing Old Wounds and Recovering Old Insights: Toward a Christian View of the Person for Today', in M.A. Noll and D.F. Wells (eds.), *Christian Faith and Practice* (Grand Rapids: Eerdmans, 1988), 68–86

Fackre, G., 'Evangelical, Evangelicalism', in A. Richardson and J. Bowden (eds.), *The Westminster Dictionary of Christian Theology* (Philadelphia: Westminster, 1983[3]), 191–192

Farley, I.D., 'Ryle, J(ohn) C(harles)', in D.M. Lewis (ed.), *The Blackwell Encyclopedia of Evangelical Biography 1730–1860* (Oxford: Blackwell, 1995), II.967

Fee, G.D., *The First Epistle to the Corinthians*, New International Commentary on the New Testament series (Grand Rapids: Eerdmans, 1987)

Ferguson, S.B., *John Owen on the Christian Life* (Edinburgh: Banner of Truth, 1987)

Ferguson, S.B., D.F. Wright, and J.I. Packer (eds.), *New Dictionary of Theology* (Downers Grove: InterVarsity, 1988)

Fernhout, H., 'Man: The Image and Glory of God', in A.H. DeGraaf and J.H. Olthuis (eds.), *Toward a Biblical View of Man* (Toronto: Association for the Advancement of Christian Scholarship, 1978), 5–34

Finney, C.G., *Lectures on Systematic Theology*, J.H. Fairchild (ed.) (Whittier, Calif.: Colporter Kemp, 1878)

– *Principles of Sanctification*, L.G. Parkhurst, Jr. (ed.), (Minneapolis: Bethany House, 1986)

The Fundamentals: A Testimony to the Truth, 4 vols. (Los Angeles: The Bible Institute of Los Angeles, 1917)

Gallup, G.H., Jr., *Religion in America: 1996* (Princeton: The Princeton Religion Research Center, 1996)

Gallup, G.H., Jr. and J. Castelli, *The People's Religion: American Faith in the 90's* (New York: MacMillan, 1989)

Gerrish, B.A., *Grace and Gratitude: The Eucharistic Theology of John Calvin* (Minneapolis: Fortress, 1993)

Giles, K., *The Trinity and Subordinationism: The Doctrine of God and the Contemporary Gender Debate* (Downers Grove: InterVarsity, 2002)

Gleason, R.C., 'B.B. Warfield and Lewis S. Chafer on Sanctification', *Journal of the Evangelical Theological Society* 40 (June 1997), 241–256

– *John Calvin and John Owen on Mortification: A Comparative Study in Reformed Spirituality*, Studies in Church History series, vol. III (New York: Peter Lang, 1995)

– Gonzalez, J.L., *Christian Thought Revisited: Three Types of Theology* (Nashville: Abingdon, 1989)

Gonzalez, J.L., *Christian Thought Revisited: Three Types of Theology* (Nashville: Abingdon, 1989)

Grave, S.A., 'Reid, Thomas', in P. Edwards (ed.), *The Encyclopedia of Philosophy*, vol. 7 (New York: Macmillan, 1967), 118–121

Greathouse, W.M. and H.R. Dunning, *An Introduction to Wesleyan Theology* (Kansas City: Beacon Hill, 1982)

Gregory Nazianzen, *Select Orations*, C.G. Browne and J.E. Swallow (trs.), in P. Schaff and H. Wace (eds.), *A Select Library of Nicene and Post–Nicene Fathers of the Christian Church* (Grand Rapids: Eerdmans, 1983²)

Grenz, S.J., *Renewing the Center: Evangelical Theology in a Post–Theological Era* (Grand Rapids: Baker, 2000)

– *The Social God and the Relational Self: A Trinitarian Theology of the Imago Dei* (Louisville, Ky.: Westminster John Knox, 2001)

– *Theology for the Community of God* (Nashville: Broadman and Holman, 1994)

Grenz, S.J. and J.R. Franke, *Beyond Foundationalism: Shaping Theology in a Postmodern Context* (Louisville, Ky.: Westminster John Knox, 2001)

Grundler, O., 'John Calvin: Ingrafting into Christ', in E.R. Elder (ed.), *The Spirituality of Western Christendom* (Kalamazoo, Mich.: Cistercian, 1976), 169–187

Gunton, C., *Christ and Creation* (Grand Rapids: Eerdmans, 1992)

Hall, C.A.M., *With the Spirit's Sword: The Drama of Spiritual Warfare in the Theology of John Calvin*, Basel Studies of Theology series, no. 3 (Richmond, Va.: John Knox, 1970)

Hart, T.A. and D. Thimell (eds.), *Christ in Our Place: The Humanity of God in Christ for the Reconciliation of the World: Essays Presented to James Torrance*, Princeton Theological Monographs (Exeter: Paternoster, 1989)

Hebert, G., *Fundamentalism and the Church of God* (London: SCM, 1957)

Henry, C.F.H., *Evangelicals in Search of Identity* (Waco, Tex.: Word, 1976)

– *God, Revelation and Authority*, 6 vols. (Waco, Tex.: Word, 1976–1983)

Heron, A.I.C., '*Homo Peccator* and the *Imago Dei*', in C.D. Kettler and T.H. Speidell (eds.), *Incarnational Ministry: The Presence of Christ in Church, Society, and Family: Essays in Honor of Ray S. Anderson* (Colorado Springs: Helmers and Howard, 1990), 32–57

Hodge, C., *Systematic Theology* (Grand Rapids: Eerdmans, 1982^2)

Hodges, Z.C., *Absolutely Free: A Biblical Reply to Lordship Salvation* (Grand Rapids: Zondervan, 1989)

Hoekema, A.E., *Created in God's Image* (Grand Rapids: Eerdmans, 1986)

Hoffecker, W.A., 'Schleiemacher, Friedrich Daniel Ernst', in W.A. Elwell (ed.), *Evangelical Dictionary of Theology* (Grand Rapids: Baker, 1984), 981–983

Hoitenga, D.J., Jr., *Faith and Reason from Plato to Plantinga: An Introduction to Reformed Epistemology* (Albany: State University of New York Press, 1991)

Hopkins, H.E., *Charles Simeon of Cambridge* (London: Hodder and Stoughton, 1977)

Houston, J.M., *The History and Distinctives of Evangelical Soul Care*, audio cassette (Denver: Denver Seminary, 5 April 2001)

– *Spiritual Direction in an Age of Confusion*, audio cassette (Vancouver: Regent College, n.d.)

Hughes, P.E., *The Second Epistle to the Corinthians*, New International Commentary on the New Testament series (Grand Rapids: Eerdmans, 1962)

– *The True Image: The Origin and Destiny of Man in Christ* (Grand Rapids: Eerdmans, 1989)

Hunter, J.D., *American Evangelicalism: Conservative Religion and the Quandry of Modernity* (New Brunswick, N.J.: Rutgers University Press, 1983)

Irenaeus. *Against Heresies*, in A. Roberts and J. Donaldson (eds.), *The Ante–Nicene Fathers: Translations of The Writings of the Fathers Down to A.D. 325: The Apostolic Fathers*, vol. I (New York: Charles Scribner's Sons, 1913^2)

Jennings, W.J., 'Conformed to His Image: The Imago Dei as a Christological Vision', in C.D. Kettler and T.H. Speidell (eds.), *Incarnational Ministry: Essays in Honor of Ray S. Anderson* (Colorado Springs: Helmers and Howard, 1990), 153–161

Jones, K.N., *Revelation and Reason in the Theology of Carl F. H. Henry, James I. Packer, and Ronald H. Nash* (Ann Arbor, Mich.: University Microfilms International, 1994)

Jones, S., *Calvin and the Rhetoric of Piety*, Columbia Series in Reformed Theology (Louisville, Ky.: Westminster/John Knox, 1995)

Johnson, D., *Contending for the Faith: A History of the Evangelical Movement in the Universities and Colleges* (Leicester: Inter–Varsity, 1979)

Kant, I., *Critique of Pure Reason*, N.K. Smith (tr.), (London: Macmillan, 1964)

Kantzer, K.S., 'Unity and Diversity in Evangelical Faith', in D.F. Wells and J.D. Woodbridge (eds.), *The Evangelicals: What They Believe, Who They Are, Where They Are Changing* (Nashville: Abingdon, 1975), 38–67

Kelly, D., H. McClure, and P.B. Rollinson (eds.), *The Westminister Confession of Faith* (Greenwood, S.C.: Attic, 1981²)

Kendall, R.T., *Calvin and English Calvinism to 1649* (Oxford: Oxford University Press, 1979)

Klein, W.W., C.L. Blomberg, and R.L. Hubbard, Jr., *Introduction to Biblical Interpretation* (Nashville: Thomas Nelson, 2003²)

Knight, H.H., III., *A Future for Truth: Evangelical Theology in a Postmodern World* (Nashville: Abingdon, 1997)

Komonchak, J.A., M. Collins, and D.A. Lane (eds.), *The New Dictionary of Theology* (Wilmington, Del.: Michael Glazier, 1987)

Koranteng–Pipim, S., 'The Role of the Holy Spirit in Biblical Interpretation: A Study in the Writings of James I. Packer', PhD thesis, (Seventh–day Adventist Theological Seminary/Andrews University, 1998)

Kraus, C.N., *Dispensationalism in America: Its Rise and Development* (Richmond, Va.: John Knox, 1958)

LaHaye, T., *The Spirit–Controlled Temperament* (Wheaton: Tyndale House, 1966)

Leith, J.H., *Assembly at Westminster: Reformed Theology in the Making* (Richmond, Va.: John Knox, 1973)

– *John Calvin's Doctrine of the Christian Life* (Louisville, Ky.: Westminster/John Knox, 1989)

Lewis, D. and A. McGrath (eds.), *Doing Theology for the People of God: Studies in Honor of J.I. Packer* (Downers Grove: InterVarsity, 1996)

Livingstone, E.A. (ed.), *The Oxford Dictionary of the Christian Church* (Oxford: Oxford University Press, 1997³)

Lonergan, B.J.F., *Method in Theology* (New York: Herder and Herder, 1972)

Lovelace, R.F., 'Puritan Spirituality: The Search for a Rightly Reformed Church', in L. Dupre and D.E. Saliers (eds.), *Christian Spirituality III: Post–Reformation and Modern*, World Spirituality: An Encyclopedic History of the Religious Quest series, vol. 18 (New York: Crossroad, 1989), 294–323

Luther, M., *The Bondage of the Will*, J.I. Packer and O.R. Johnston (trs.), (London: James Clarke, 1957)

– *Lectures on Genesis: Chapters 1–5*, in J. Pelikan (ed.), *Luther's Works*, vol. I (Saint Louis: Concordia, 1958)

Macauley, Ranald and Jerram Barrs, *Being Human: The Nature of Spiritual Experience* (Downers Grove: InterVarsity, 1978)

MacArthur, J.F., Jr., *The Gospel According to Jesus: What Does Jesus Mean When He Says "Follow Me"?* (Grand Rapids: Zondervan, 1988)

McDonald, H.D., 'Man, Doctrine of', in W.A. Elwell (ed.), *Evangelical Dictionary of Theology* (Grand Rapids: Baker, 1984), 676–680

Machen, J.G., *The Christian View of Man* (London: Banner of Truth, 1937)

McFarlane, G.W.P., *Christ and the Spirit: The Doctrine of the Incarnation according to Edward Irving* (Carlisle: Paternoster, 1996)

McGrath, A., *Christian Spirituality: An Introduction* (Oxford: Blackwell, 1999)

– *Historical Theology: An Introduction to the History of Christian Thought* Oxford: Blackwell, 1998)

– (ed.), *The J.I. Packer Collection* (Downers Grove: InterVarsity, 1999)

– *To Know and Serve God: A Biography of James I Packer* (London. Hodder Stoughton, 1997)

– *A Scientific Theology: Nature*, vol. I (Grand Rapids: Eerdmans, 2001)

Mackey, L., 'Slouching Toward Bethlehem: Deconstructive Strategies in Theology', *Anglican Theological Review* 65, no. 3 (1983), 255–272

McKim, D.K. (ed.), *Westminster Dictionary of Theological Terms* (Louisville, Ky.: Westminster/John Knox, 1996)

McNeill, J.T., *The History and Character of Calvinism* (New York: Oxford University Press, 1954)

Marsden, G.M., *Fundamentalism and American Culture: The Shaping of Twentieth–Century Evangelicalism: 1870–1925* (New York: Oxford University Press, 1980)

– *Reforming Fundamentalism: Fuller Seminary and the New Evangelicalism* (Grand Rapids: Eerdmans, 1987)

– *Understanding Fundamentalism and Evangelicalism* (Grand Rapids: Eerdmans, 1991)

Marshall, I.H., 'Sanctification in the Teaching of John Wesley and John Calvin', *Evangelical Quarterly* 34, no. 2 (1962), 75–82

Marty, M.E., *The Church: Mainline–Evangelical–Catholic* (New York: Crossroad, 1981)

Metzger, W., 'J. I. Packer: Surprised by Grace', in J. Woodbridge (ed.), *More Than Conquerors* (Chicago: Moody, 1992)

Mickelsen, A.B., *Interpreting the Bible* (Grand Rapids: Eerdmans, 1963)

Miles, M.R., *Desire and Delight: A New Reading of Augustine's Confessions* (New York: Crossroad, 1992)

– 'Theology, Anthropology, and the Human Body in Calvin's *Institutes of the Christian Religion*', *Harvard Theological Review* 74, no. 3 (1981), 303–323

Miethe, T.L., 'The Universal Power of the Atonement', in C.H. Pinnock (ed.), *The Grace of God, the Will of Man: A Case for Arminianism* (Grand Rapids: Zondervan, 1989), 71–95

Moberly, R.W.L., *The Bible, Theology, and Faith: A Study of Abraham and Jesus* (Cambridge: Cambridge University Press, 2000)

Moltmann, J., *God in Creation*, M. Kohl (tr.), (Minneapolis: Fortress, 1993)

– *Man: Christian Anthropology in the Conflicts of the Present*, J. Sturdy (tr.), (Philadelphia: Fortress, 1974)

Moreland, J.P., 'A Defense of a Substance Dualist View of the Soul', in J.P. Moreland and D.M. Ciocchi (eds.), *Christian Perspectives on Being Human: A Multidisciplinary Approach to Integration* (Grand Rapids: Baker, 1993), 55–85

– 'Spiritual Formation and the Nature of the Soul', *Christian Education Journal* 4, no. 2 (2000), 25–43

Morris, L., *The Atonement: Its Significance and Meaning* (Leicester: Inter-Varsity, 1983)

– *The First and Second Epistles to the Thessalonians*, New International Commentary on the New Testament series (Grand Rapids: Eerdmans, 1959)

Murray, I.H., *David Martyn Lloyd–Jones*, 2 vols. (Edinburgh: Banner of Truth, 1982, 1990)

Nash, R.H., *The Light of the Mind: St. Augustine's Theory of Knowledge* (Lexington, Ky.: University Press of Kentucky, 1969)

Neff, D., 'A Holy Nuisance', *Christianity Today* (January 2003), 5

Neill, S., Review of J.I. Packer, *Knowing God* in *Churchman* 88, no. 1 (1974), 77–78

Niebuhr, R., *The Nature and Destiny of Man: Human Nature*, vol. I (New York: Charles Scribner's Sons, 1964)

Nicole, R., 'J.I. Packer', in W. Elwell (ed.), *Handbook of Evangelical Theologians* (Grand Rapids: Baker, 1993), 379–387

Noble, T.A., 'Scripture and Experience', *Themelios* 23, no. 1 (1997), 30–39.

Noll, M.A., *Between Faith and Criticism: Evangelicals, Scholarship, and the Bible in America* (San Francisco: Harper and Row, 1986)

– 'The Last Puritan', *Christianity Today* (16 September 1996), 51–53

– (ed.), *The Princeton Theology, 1812–1921: Scripture, Science, and Theological Method from Archibald Alexander to Benjamin Breckinridge Warfield* (Grand Rapids: Baker, 2001)

– 'Warfield, Benjamin Breckinridge', in W.A. Elwell (ed.), *Evangelical Dictionary of Theology* (Grand Rapids: Baker, 1984), 1156

Noll, M.A., D.W. Bebbington, and G.A. Rawlyk (eds.), *Evangelicalism: Comparative Studies of Popular Protestantism in North America, the British Isles, and Beyond, 1700–1990* (New York: Oxford University Press, 1994)

Origen, *De Principiis*, in A. Roberts and J. Donaldson (ed.), *The Ante–Nicene Fathers: Translations of The Writings of the Fathers Down to A.D. 325*, vol. IV (Grand Rapids: Eerdmans, 1979[2])

Orr, J., *The Christian View of God and the World as Centring in the Incarnation: Being the Kerr Lectures for 1890–1891* (Grand Rapids: Eerdmans, 1948)

– *God's Image in Man and Its Defacement in the Light of Modern Denials* (Grand Rapids: Eerdmans, 1948)

– *The Progress of Dogma* (London: Hodder and Stoughton, 1901)

Osborn, G.R., *The Hermeneutical Spiral: A Comprehensive Guide toBiblical Interpretation* (Downers Grove: InterVarsity, 1991)

Osterhaven, M.E., 'American Theology in the Twentieth Century', in C.F.H. Henry (ed.), *Christian Faith and Modern Theology* (New York: Channel, 1964), 47–66

Owen, J., 'Corruption or Deprivation of the Mind by Sin', in W.H. Goold (ed.), *Works*, III.iii (London: Banner of Truth, 1965[2])

– *The Works of John Owen, D.D.*, W.H. Goold (ed.), (Edinburgh: T & T Clark, 1862)

Pannenberg, W., *Anthropology in Theological Perspective*, M.J. O'Connell (ed.), (Edinburgh: T & T Clark, 1985)

– *Christian Spirituality* (Philadelphia: Westminster, 1983)

Partee, C., 'The Soul in Plato, Platonism, and Calvin', *Scottish Journal of Theology* 22 (September 1969), 278–296

Percy, M., Review of D. Lewis and A. McGrath (eds.), *Doing Theology for the People of God: Studies in Honor of J.I. Packer*, *Reviews in Religion and Theology* 4, no. 2 (1997), 67–69

Pierard, R.V., 'Evangelicalism', in W. Elwell (ed.) *Evangelical Dictionary of Theology* (Grand Rapids: Baker, 1984), 379–382

Plantinga, C., Jr., 'Images of God', in M.A. Noll and D.F. Wells (eds.), *Christian Faith and Practice* (Grand Rapids: Eerdmans, 1988), 51–67

Plato., *The Dialogues of Plato: The Apology*, in M.J. Adler (ed.), B. Jowett (tr.), The Great Books of the Western World series, vol. 6 (Chicago: Encyclopaedia Britannica, 1993)

Poiret, P., *The Divine Economy: or, An Universal System of the Works and Purposes of God Towards Men Demonstrated*, vol. I. (London: 'Printed for R. Bonwicke in St. Paul's Church–Yard, M. Wotton in Fleet–Street, S. Manship and R. Parker in Cornhill'), 1713

Portalie, E., *A Guide to the Thought of Saint Augustine*, R.J. Bastian (tr.), Library of Living Catholic Thought (Chicago: Henry Regnery, 1960)

Porter, S.L., 'On the Renewal of Interest in the Doctrine of Sanctification: A Methodological Reminder', *Journal of the Evangelical Theological Society* 45, no. 3 (2002), 415–426

Quebedeaux, R., *The Worldly Evangelicals* (San Francisco: Harper and Row, 1978)

Ramm, B., *After Fundamentalism: The Future of Evangelical Theology* (San Francisco: Harper and Row, 1983)

– *Protestant Biblical Interpretation* (Grand Rapids: Baker, 1970^3)

Reid, T., *An Inquiry into the Human Mind: On the Principles of Common Sense* (University Park, Pa.: Pennsylvania State University Press, 1997)

Rice, H.L., *Reformed Spirituality: An Introduction for Believers* (Louisville, Ky.: Westminster/John Knox, 1991)

Richard, L.J., *The Spirituality of John Calvin* (Atlanta: John Knox, 1974)

Roennfeldt. R.C.W., *Clark H. Pinnock on Biblical Authority: An Evolving Position* (Berrien Springs, Mich.: Andrews University Press, 1993)

Ryle, J.C., *Holiness: Its Nature, Hindrances, Difficulties, and Roots*, in J.I. Packer, *Faithfulness and Holiness: The Witness of J.C. Ryle* (Wheaton: Crossway, 2002), 89–246

Ryrie, C.C., *Dispensationalism Today* (Chicago: Moody, 1965)

– *So Great Salvation: What It Means to Believe in Jesus Christ* (Wheaton: Victor, 1989)

Sandeen, E.R., *The Roots of Fundamentalism: British and American Millenarianism, 1800–1930* (Chicago: University of Chicago Press, 1970)

Sargent, T., *The Sacred Anointing: The Preaching of Dr. Martyn Lloyd–Jones* (Wheaton: Crossway, 1994)

Schleiermacher, F., *The Christian Faith*, H.R. Mackintosh and J.S. Stewart (eds.), (Edinburgh: T & T Clark, 1928)

Schwobel, C. and C.E. Gunton, (eds.), *Persons, Divine and Human: King's College Essays in Theological Anthropology* (Edinburgh: T & T Clark, 1991)

Scofield, C.I., *Rightly Dividing the Word of Truth* (New York: Loizeaux Brothers, 1896)

– (ed.), *The Scofield Reference Bible* (New York: Oxford University Press, 1909)

Scott, T., (tr.), *The Articles of the Synod of Dort* (Harrisonburg, Va.: Sprinkle, 1993)

Sherlock, C., *The Doctrine of Humanity*, Contours of Christian Theology series (Downers Grove: InterVarsity, 1996)

Shults, F. LeRon, *Reforming Theological Anthropology: After the Philosophical Turn to Relationality* (Grand Rapids: Eerdmans, 2003)

Smith, H.W., *The Christian's Secret of a Happy Life* (Chicago: Revell, 1883^2)

Smith, T.L., *Revivalism and Social Reform in Mid–Nineteenth–Century America* (New York: Abingdon, 1957)

Spangler, A. and C. Turner, *Heroes: Five Remarkable Christians Who Influenced Philip Yancey, Becky Pippert, J.I. Packer, Elisabeth Elliot and Charles Colson* (Leicester: Inter–Varsity, 1985)

Steer, R., *Guarding the Holy Fire: The Evangelicalism of John R.W. Stott, J.I. Packer, and Alister McGrath* (Grand Rapids: Baker, 1999)

Stendahl, K., 'The Apostle Paul and the Introspective Conscience of the West', *Journal for the Scientific Study of Religion* 1 (April 1962), 261–263

Stuermann, W.E. and K. Geocaris, 'The Image of Man: The Perspectives of Calvin and Freud', in H.N. Maloney (ed.), *Wholeness and Holiness* (Grand Rapids: Baker, 1983), 52–66

Sullivan, J.E., *The Image of God: The Doctrine of St. Augustine and Its Influence* (Dubuque, IA: Priory, 1963)

Tamburello, D.E., *Union with Christ: John Calvin and the Mysticism of St. Bernard*, Columbia Series in Reformed Theology (Louisville, Kentucky: Westminster/John Knox, 1994)

Tertullian, *On the Apparel of Women* and *On Exhortation to Chastity*, in A. Roberts and J. Donaldson (eds.), *The Ante–Nicene Fathers: Translations of The Writings of the Fathers Down to A.D. 325; Tertullian, Part Fourth, Minucius Felix; Commodian; Origen, Parts First And Second*, vol. IV (Grand Rapids: Eerdmans, 1979[2])

– *On Idolatry*, in A. Roberts and J. Donaldson (eds.), *The Ante–Nicene Fathers: Translations of The Writings of the Fathers Down to A.D. 325; Latin Christianity: Its Founder, Tertullian*, vol. III (Grand Rapids: Eerdmans, 1980[2])

– *On the Soul*, in *The Fathers of the Church: A New Translation*, vol. 10, R. Arbesmann, E.J. Daly, and E.A. Quain (trs.), (Washington, D. C.: Catholic University of America, 1950)

Thielicke, H., *Theological Ethics: Foundations*, W.H. Lazareth (ed.), vol. 1, J.W. Doberstein (tr.), (Grand Rapids: Eerdmans, 1979)

Thiselton, A.C., *New Horizons in Hermeneutics* (Grand Rapids: Zondervan, 1992)

Thomas, M.G., 'Calvin and English Calvinism: A Review Article', *Scottish Bulletin of Evangelical Theology* 16 (Autumn 1998), 111–127

Tickle, P.A., *Re–Discovering the Sacred: Spirituality in America* (New York: Crossroad, 1995)

Toon, P., *Puritans and Calvinism* (Swengel, PA: Reiner, 1973)

Toon, P. and M. Smout, *John Charles Ryle: Evangelical Bishop* (Cambridge: James Clarke, 1976)

Torrance, A.J., *Persons in Communion: An Essay on Trinitarian Description and Human Participation* (Edinburgh: T & T Clark, 1996)

Torrance, J.B., Introduction to J.M. Campbell, *The Nature of the Atonement* (Edinburgh: Handsel, 1996[2]), 1–16

Torrance, T.F., *Calvin's Doctrine of Man* (London: Butterworth Press, 1952)

– *The Christian Doctrine of God: One Being Three Persons* (Edinburgh: T & T Clark, 1996)

– *Divine Meaning: Studies in Patristic Hermeneutics* (Edinburgh: T & T Clark, 1995)
– *God and Rationality* (London: Oxford University Press, 1971)
– *The Ground and Grammar of Theology* (Belfast: Christian Journals, 1980)
– *The Hermeneutics of John Calvin*, Monograph Supplements to the Scottish Journal of Theology (Edinburgh: Scottish Academic Press, 1988)
– *Theological Science* (London: Oxford University Press, 1969)
– *Theology in Reconstruction* (Grand Rapids: Eerdmans, 1965)
Tracy, J., *The Great Awakening: A History of the Revival of Religion in the Time of Edwards and Whitefield* (Carlisle, Pa.: Banner of Truth, 1976)
Trumbull, C.G., *The Life Story of C. I. Scofield* (New York: Oxford University Press, 1920)
VanderMolen, R.J., 'Scholasticism, Protestant', in W.A. Elwell (ed.), *Evangelical Dictionary of Theology* (Grand Rapids: Baker, 1984), 984–985
Vander Stelt, J.C., *Philosophy and Scripture: A Study in Old Princeton and Westminster Theology* (Marlton, N.J.: Mack, 1978)
Vanhoozer, K.J., *First Theology: God, Scripture and Hermeneutics* (Downers Grove: InterVarsity, 2002)
– 'The Voice and the Actor: A Dramatic Proposal about the Ministry and Minstrelsy of Theology', in J.G. Stackhouse, Jr. (ed.), *Evangelical Futures: A Conversation on Theological Method* (Grand Rapids: Baker, 2000), 61–106
Wallace, R.S., *Calvin's Doctrine of the Christian Life* (Grand Rapids: Eerdmans, 1959)
Warfield, B.B., *The Works of Benjamin B. Warfield*, 10 vols. (Grand Rapids: Baker, 1981)
Watson, F., *Text, Church and World: Biblical Interpretation in Theological Perspective* (Grand Rapids: Eerdmans, 1994)
Watts, I., *Works* (Leeds: Edward Baines, 1800)
Weber, O., *Foundations of Dogmatics*, D.L. Guder (tr.), (Grand Rapids: Eerdmans, 1981)
Webster, J., 'Hermeneutics in Modern Theology: Some Doctrinal Reflections', *Scottish Journal of Theology* 51, no. 3 (1998), 307–341
Wells, D.F., (ed.), *The Princeton Theology*, Reformed Theology in America series, vol. 1 (Grand Rapids: Baker, 1989)
Wenham, G.J., *Genesis 1–15*, Word Biblical Commentary series, vol. I (Waco, Tex.: Word, 1987)
Wenham, J., *Facing Hell: The Story of a Nobody* (Carlisle: Paternoster, 1998)
Wesley, J., *The Works of John Wesley*, A.C. Outler (ed.), (Nashville: Abingdon, 1984)
Westermann, C., *Isaiah 40–66: A Commentary*, The Old Testament Library series (Philadelphia: Westminster, 1969)

The Westminster Confession of Faith: An Authentic Modern Version (Signal Mountain, Tenn.: Summertown, 1979²)

White, R.E.O., 'Sanctification', in W.A. Elwell (ed.), *Evangelical Dictionary of Theology* (Grand Rapids: Baker, 1984), 969–971

Wilson, R.W. and C.L. Blomberg, 'The Image of God in Humanity: A Biblical–Psychological Perspective', *Themelios* 18 (April 1993), 8–15

Wingren, G., *Man and the Incarnation: A Study in the Biblical Theology of Irenaeus*, R. Mackenzie (tr.), (Philadelphia: Muhlenberg, 1959)

Wolff, H.W., *Anthropology of the Old Testament*, Philadelphia: Fortress, 1974)

Wright, D.F., 'Whither Evangelical Theology in Scotland?', *Scottish Bulletin of Evangelical Theology* 16 (Autumn 1998), 93–96

Wright, N.T., *What Saint Paul Really Said: Was Paul of Tarsus the Real Founder of Christianity?* (Grand Rapids: Eerdmans, 1997)

Young, E.J., *The Book of Isaiah* (Grand Rapids: Eerdmans, 1972)

Zizioulas, J., *Being as Communion: Studies in Personhood and the Church* (New York: St. Vladimir's Seminary, 1993)

Zoba, W.M., 'Knowing Packer', *Christianity Today* (6 April 1998), 30–40

Index

Studies in Evangelical History and Thought
(All titles uniform with this volume)
Dates in bold are of projected publication

Andrew Atherstone
Oxford's Protestant Spy
The Controversial Career of Charles Golightly
Charles Golightly (1807–85) was a notorious Protestant polemicist. His life was
dedicated to resisting the spread of ritualism and liberalism within the Church of
England and the University of Oxford. For half a century he led many
memorable campaigns, such as building a martyr's memorial and attempting to
close a theological college. John Henry Newman, Samuel Wilberforce and
Benjamin Jowett were among his adversaries. This is the first study of
Golightly's controversial career.
2006 / 1-84227-364-7 / approx. 324pp

Clyde Binfield
Victorian Nonconformity in Eastern England
Studies of Victorian religion and society often concentrate on cities, suburbs,
and industrialisation. This study provides a contrast. Victorian Eastern
England—Essex, Suffolk, Norfolk, Cambridgeshire, and Huntingdonshire—was
rural, traditional, relatively unchanging. That is nonetheless a caricature which
discounts the industry in Norwich and Ipswich (as well as in Haverhill,
Stowmarket and Leiston) and ignores the impact of London on Essex, of
railways throughout the region, and of an ancient but changing university
(Cambridge) on the county town which housed it. It also entirely ignores the
political implications of such changes in a region noted for the variety of its
religious Dissent since the seventeenth century. This book explores Victorian
Eastern England and its Nonconformity. It brings to a wider readership a
pioneering thesis which has made a major contribution to a fresh evolution of
English religion and society.
2006 / 1-84227-216-0 / approx. 274pp

John Brencher
Martyn Lloyd-Jones (1899–1981) and Twentieth-Century Evangelicalism
This study critically demonstrates the significance of the life and ministry of
Martyn Lloyd-Jones for post-war British evangelicalism and demonstrates that
his preaching was his greatest influence on twentieth-century Christianity. The
factors which shaped his view of the church are examined, as is the way his
reformed evangelicalism led to a separatist ecclesiology which divided
evangelicals.
2002 / 1-84227-051-6 / xvi + 268pp

Jonathan D. Burnham
A Story of Conflict
*The Controversial Relationship between Benjamin Wills Newton and
John Nelson Darby*
Burnham explores the controversial relationship between the two principal
leaders of the early Brethren movement. In many ways Newton and Darby were
products of their times, and this study of their relationship provides insight not
only into the dynamics of early Brethrenism, but also into the progress of
nineteenth-century English and Irish evangelicalism.
2004 / 1-84227-191-1 / xxiv + 268pp

Grayson Carter
Anglican Evangelicals
Protestant Secessions from the Via Media, c.1800–1850
This study examines, within a chronological framework, the major themes and
personalities which influenced the outbreak of a number of Evangelical clerical
and lay secessions from the Church of England and Ireland during the first half
of the nineteenth century. Though the number of secessions was relatively
small—between a hundred and two hundred of the 'Gospel' clergy abandoned
the Church during this period—their influence was considerable, especially in
highlighting in embarrassing fashion the tensions between the evangelical
conversionist imperative and the principles of a national religious establishment.
Moreover, through much of this period there remained, just beneath the surface,
the potential threat of a large Evangelical disruption similar to that which
occurred in Scotland in 1843. Consequently, these secessions provoked great
consternation within the Church and within Evangelicalism itself, they
contributed to the outbreak of millennial speculation following the
'constitutional revolution' of 1828–32, they led to the formation of several new
denominations, and they sparked off a major Church–State crisis over the legal
right of a clergyman to secede and begin a new ministry within Protestant
Dissent.
2007 / 1-84227-401-5 / xvi + 470pp

J.N. Ian Dickson
Beyond Religious Discourse
Sermons, Preaching and Evangelical Protestants in Nineteenth-Century Irish Society
Drawing extensively on primary sources, this pioneer work in modern religious history explores the training of preachers, the construction of sermons and how Irish evangelicalism and the wider movement in Great Britain and the United States shaped the preaching event. Evangelical preaching and politics, sectarianism, denominations, education, class, social reform, gender, and revival are examined to advance the argument that evangelical sermons and preaching went significantly beyond religious discourse. The result is a book for those with interests in Irish history, culture and belief, popular religion and society, evangelicalism, preaching and communication.
2005 / 1-84227-217-9 / approx. 324pp

Neil T.R. Dickson
Brethren in Scotland 1838–2000
A Social Study of an Evangelical Movement
The Brethren were remarkably pervasive throughout Scottish society. This study of the Open Brethren in Scotland places them in their social context and examines their growth, development and relationship to society.
2003 / 1-84227-113-X / xxviii + 510pp

Crawford Gribben and Timothy C.F. Stunt (eds)
Prisoners of Hope?
Aspects of Evangelical Millennialism in Britain and Ireland, 1800–1880
This volume of essays offers a comprehensive account of the impact of evangelical millennialism in nineteenth-century Britain and Ireland.
2004 / 1-84227-224-1 / xiv + 208pp

Khim Harris
Evangelicals and Education
Evangelical Anglicans and Middle-Class Education in Nineteenth-Century England
This ground breaking study investigates the history of English public schools founded by nineteenth-century Evangelicals. It documents the rise of middle-class education and Evangelical societies such as the influential Church Association, and includes a useful biographical survey of prominent Evangelicals of the period.
2004 / 1-84227-250-0 / xviii + 422pp

Mark Hopkins
Nonconformity's Romantic Generation
Evangelical and Liberal Theologies in Victorian England
A study of the theological development of key leaders of the Baptist and
Congregational denominations at their period of greatest influence, including
C.H. Spurgeon and R.W. Dale, and of the controversies in which those among
them who embraced and rejected the liberal transformation of their evangelical
heritage opposed each other.
2004 / 1-84227-150-4 / xvi + 284pp

Don Horrocks
Laws of the Spiritual Order
*Innovation and Reconstruction in the Soteriology of Thomas Erskine
of Linlathen*
Don Horrocks argues that Thomas Erskine's unique historical and theological
significance as a soteriological innovator has been neglected. This timely
reassessment reveals Erskine as a creative, radical theologian of central and
enduring importance in Scottish nineteenth-century theology, perhaps equivalent
in significance to that of S.T. Coleridge in England.
2004 / 1-84227-192-X / xx + 362pp

Kenneth S. Jeffrey
When the Lord Walked the Land
The 1858–62 Revival in the North East of Scotland
Previous studies of revivals have tended to approach religious movements from
either a broad, national or a strictly local level. This study of the multifaceted
nature of the 1859 revival as it appeared in three distinct social contexts within a
single region reveals the heterogeneous nature of simultaneous religious
movements in the same vicinity.
2002 / 1-84227-057-5 / xxiv + 304pp

John Kenneth Lander
Itinerant Temples
Tent Methodism, 1814–1832
Tent preaching began in 1814 and the Tent Methodist sect resulted from
disputes with Bristol Wesleyan Methodists in 1820. The movement spread to
parts of Gloucestershire, Wiltshire, London and Liverpool, among other places.
Its demise started in 1826 after which one leader returned to the Wesleyans and
others became ministers in the Congregational and Baptist denominations.
2003 / 1-84227-151-2 / xx + 268pp

Donald M. Lewis
Lighten Their Darkness
The Evangelical Mission to Working-Class London, 1828–1860
This is a comprehensive and compelling study of the Church and the complexities of nineteenth-century London. Challenging our understanding of the culture in working London at this time, Lewis presents a well-structured and illustrated work that contributes substantially to the study of evangelicalism and mission in nineteenth-century Britain.

2001 / 1-84227-074-5 / xviii + 372pp

Herbert McGonigle
'Sufficient Saving Grace'
John Wesley's Evangelical Arminianism
A thorough investigation of the theological roots of John Wesley's evangelical Arminianism and how these convictions were hammered out in controversies on predestination, limited atonement and the perseverance of the saints.

2001 / 1-84227-045-1 / xvi + 350pp

Lisa S. Nolland
A Victorian Feminist Christian
Josephine Butler, the Prostitutes and God
Josephine Butler was an unlikely candidate for taking up the cause of prostitutes, as she did, with a fierce and self-disregarding passion. This book explores the particular mix of perspectives and experiences that came together to envision and empower her remarkable achievements. It highlights the vital role of her spirituality and the tragic loss of her daughter.

2004 / 1-84227-225-X / xxiv + 328pp

Don J. Payne
The Theology of the Christian Life in J.I. Packer's Thought
Theological Anthropology, Theological Method, and the Doctrine of Sanctification
J.I. Packer has wielded widespread influence on evangelicalism for more than three decades. This study pursues a nuanced understanding of Packer's theology of sanctification by tracing the development of his thought, showing how he reflects a particular version of Reformed theology, and examining the unique influence of theological anthropology and theological method on this area of his theology.

2005 / 1-84227-397-3 / approx. 374pp

Ian M. Randall
Evangelical Experiences
A Study in the Spirituality of English Evangelicalism 1918–1939
This book makes a detailed historical examination of evangelical spirituality between the First and Second World Wars. It shows how patterns of devotion led to tensions and divisions. In a wide-ranging study, Anglican, Wesleyan, Reformed and Pentecostal-charismatic spiritualities are analysed.
1999 / 0-85364-919-7 / xii + 310pp

Ian M. Randall
Spirituality and Social Change
The Contribution of F.B. Meyer (1847–1929)
This is a fresh appraisal of F.B. Meyer (1847–1929), a leading Free Church minister. Having been deeply affected by holiness spirituality, Meyer became the Keswick Convention's foremost international speaker. He combined spirituality with effective evangelism and socio-political activity. This study shows Meyer's significant contribution to spiritual renewal and social change.
2003 / 1-84227-195-4 / xx + 184pp

James Robinson
Pentecostal Origins
Early Pentecostalism in Ireland in the Context of the British Isles
Harvey Cox describes Pentecostalism as 'the fascinating spiritual child of our time' that has the potential, at the global scale, to contribute to the 'reshaping of religion in the twenty-first century'. This study grounds such sentiments by examining at the local scale the origin, development and nature of Pentecostalism in Ireland in its first twenty years. Illustrative, in a paradigmatic way, of how Pentecostalism became established within one region of the British Isles, it sets the story within the wider context of formative influences emanating from America, Europe and, in particular, other parts of the British Isles. As a synoptic regional study in Pentecostal history it is the first survey of its kind.
2005 / 1-84227-329-1 / xxviii + 378pp

Geoffrey Robson
Dark Satanic Mills?
Religion and Irreligion in Birmingham and the Black Country
This book analyses and interprets the nature and extent of popular Christian belief and practice in Birmingham and the Black Country during the first half of the nineteenth century, with particular reference to the impact of cholera epidemics and evangelism on church extension programmes.
2002 / 1-84227-102-4 / xiv + 294pp

Roger Shuff
Searching for the True Church
Brethren and Evangelicals in Mid-Twentieth-Century England
Roger Shuff holds that the influence of the Brethren movement on wider evangelical life in England in the twentieth century is often underrated. This book records and accounts for the fact that Brethren reached the peak of their strength at the time when evangelicalism was at it lowest ebb, immediately before World War II. However, the movement then moved into persistent decline as evangelicalism regained ground in the post war period. Accompanying this downward trend has been a sharp accentuation of the contrast between Brethren congregations who engage constructively with the non-Brethren scene and, at the other end of the spectrum, the isolationist group commonly referred to as 'Exclusive Brethren'.
2005 / 1-84227-254-3 / xviii+ 296pp

James H.S. Steven
Worship in the Spirit
Charismatic Worship in the Church of England
This book explores the nature and function of worship in six Church of England churches influenced by the Charismatic Movement, focusing on congregational singing and public prayer ministry. The theological adequacy of such ritual is discussed in relation to pneumatological and christological understandings in Christian worship.
2002 / 1-84227-103-2 / xvi + 238pp

Peter K. Stevenson
God in Our Nature
The Incarnational Theology of John McLeod Campbell
This radical reassessment of Campbell's thought arises from a comprehensive study of his preaching and theology. Previous accounts have overlooked both his sermons and his Christology. This study examines the distinctive Christology evident in his sermons and shows that it sheds new light on Campbell's much debated views about atonement.
2004 / 1-84227-218-7 / xxiv + 458pp

Kenneth J. Stewart
Restoring the Reformation
British Evangelicalism and the Réveil at Geneva 1816–1849
Restoring the Reformation traces British missionary initiative in post-Revolutionary Francophone Europe from the genesis of the London Missionary Society, the visits of Robert Haldane and Henry Drummond, and the founding of the Continental Society. While British Evangelicals aimed at the reviving of a foreign Protestant cause of momentous legend, they received unforeseen reciprocating emphases from the Continent which forced self-reflection on Evangelicalism's own relationship to the Reformation.
2006 / 1-84227-392-2 / approx. 190pp

Martin Wellings
Evangelicals Embattled
Responses of Evangelicals in the Church of England to Ritualism, Darwinism and Theological Liberalism 1890–1930
In the closing years of the nineteenth century and the first decades of the twentieth century Anglican Evangelicals faced a series of challenges. In responding to Anglo-Catholicism, liberal theology, Darwinism and biblical criticism, the unity and identity of the Evangelical school were severely tested.
2003 / 1-84227-049-4 / xviii + 352pp

James Whisenant
A Fragile Unity
Anti-Ritualism and the Division of Anglican Evangelicalism in the Nineteenth Century
This book deals with the ritualist controversy (approximately 1850–1900) from the perspective of its evangelical participants and considers the divisive effects it had on the party.
2003 / 1-84227-105-9 / xvi + 530pp

Haddon Willmer
Evangelicalism 1785–1835: An Essay (1962) and Reflections (2004)
Awarded the Hulsean Prize in the University of Cambridge in 1962, this interpretation of a classic period of English Evangelicalism, by a young church historian, is now supplemented by reflections on Evangelicalism from the vantage point of a retired Professor of Theology.
2006 / 1-84227-219-5 / approx. 350pp

Linda Wilson
Constrained by Zeal
Female Spirituality amongst Nonconformists 1825–1875

Constrained by Zeal investigates the neglected area of Nonconformist female spirituality. Against the background of separate spheres, it analyses the experience of women from four denominations, and argues that the churches provided a 'third sphere' in which they could find opportunities for participation.

2000 / 0-85364-972-3 / xvi + 294pp

Paternoster
9 Holdom Avenue,
Bletchley,
Milton Keynes MK1 1QR,
United Kingdom
Web: www.authenticmedia.co.uk/paternoster

ND - #0060 - 090625 - C0 - 229/152/19 - PB - 9781842273975 - Gloss Lamination